Microsoft® Official Academic Course

Microsoft PowerPoint 2010, Exam 77-883

WILEY

EDITOR	Bryan Gambrel
DIRECTOR OF SALES	Mitchell Beaton
EXECUTIVE MARKETING MANAGER	Chris Ruel
ASSISTANT MARKETING MANAGER	Debbie Martin
MICROSOFT STRATEGIC RELATIONSHIPS MANAGER	Merrick Van Dongen of Microsoft Learning
EDITORIAL PROGRAM ASSISTANT	Jennifer Lartz
CONTENT MANAGERS	Micheline Frederick, Kevin Holm
SENIOR PRODUCTION EDITOR	Kerry Weinstein
CREATIVE DIRECTOR	Harry Nolan
COVER DESIGNER	Jim O'Shea
INTERIOR DESIGNER	Amy Rosen
PHOTO EDITORS	Sheena Goldstein, Jennifer MacMillan
EXECUTIVE MEDIA EDITOR	Tom Kulesa
MEDIA EDITOR	Wendy Ashenberg

This book was set in Garamond by Aptara, Inc. and printed and bound by Courier Kendallville. The covers were printed by Lehigh Phoenix.

Founded in 1807, John Wiley & Sons, Inc. has been a valued source of knowledge and understanding for more than 200 years, helping people around the world meet their needs and fulfill their aspirations. Our company is built on a foundation of principles that include responsibility to the communities we serve and where we live and work. In 2008, we launched a Corporate Citizenship Initiative, a global effort to address the environmental, social, economic, and ethical challenges we face in our business. Among the issues we are addressing are carbon impact, paper specifications and procurement, ethical conduct within our business and among our vendors, and community and charitable support. For more information, please visit our website: www.wiley.com/go/citizenship.

ISBN 978-0-470-90852-5

Printed in the United States of America

10 9 8 7 6 5 4 3 2 1

Foreword from the Publisher

Wiley's publishing vision for the Microsoft Official Academic Course series is to provide students and instructors with the skills and knowledge they need to use Microsoft technology effectively in all aspects of their personal and professional lives. Quality instruction is required to help both educators and students get the most from Microsoft's software tools and to become more productive. Thus our mission is to make our instructional programs trusted educational companions for life.

To accomplish this mission, Wiley and Microsoft have partnered to develop the highest quality educational programs for information workers, IT professionals, and developers. Materials created by this partnership carry the brand name "Microsoft Official Academic Course," assuring instructors and students alike that the content of these textbooks is fully endorsed by Microsoft, and that they provide the highest quality information and instruction on Microsoft products. The Microsoft Official Academic Course textbooks are "Official" in still one more way—they are the officially sanctioned courseware for Microsoft IT Academy members.

The Microsoft Official Academic Course series focuses on *workforce development*. These programs are aimed at those students seeking to enter the workforce, change jobs, or embark on new careers as information workers, IT professionals, and developers. Microsoft Official Academic Course programs address their needs by emphasizing authentic workplace scenarios with an abundance of projects, exercises, cases, and assessments.

The Microsoft Official Academic Courses are mapped to Microsoft's extensive research and job-task analysis, the same research and analysis used to create the Microsoft Office Specialist (MOS) exams. The textbooks focus on real skills for real jobs. As students work through the projects and exercises in the textbooks, they enhance their level of knowledge and their ability to apply the latest Microsoft technology to everyday tasks. These students also gain resume-building credentials that can assist them in finding a job, in keeping their current job, or in furthering their education.

The concept of lifelong learning is today an utmost necessity. Job roles, and even whole job categories, are changing so quickly that none of us can stay competitive and productive without continuously updating our skills and capabilities. The Microsoft Official Academic Course offerings, and their focus on Microsoft certification exam preparation, provide a means for people to acquire and effectively update their skills and knowledge. Wiley supports students in this endeavor through the development and distribution of these courses as Microsoft's official academic publisher.

Today educational publishing requires attention to providing quality print and robust electronic content. By integrating Microsoft Official Academic Course products, *WileyPLUS*, and Microsoft certifications, we are better able to deliver efficient learning solutions for students and teachers alike.

Joseph Heider
General Manager and Senior Vice President

Preface

Welcome to the Microsoft Official Academic Course (MOAC) program for Microsoft Office 2010. MOAC is the collaboration between Microsoft Learning and John Wiley & Sons, Inc. publishing company. Microsoft and Wiley teamed up to produce a series of textbooks that deliver compelling and innovative teaching solutions to instructors and superior learning experiences for students. Infused and informed by in-depth knowledge from the creators of Microsoft Office and Windows, and crafted by a publisher known worldwide for the pedagogical quality of its products, these textbooks maximize skills transfer in minimum time. Students are challenged to reach their potential by using their new technical skills as highly productive members of the workforce.

Because this knowledge base comes directly from Microsoft, architect of the Office 2010 offering and creator of the Microsoft Office Specialist (MOS) exams (www.microsoft.com/learning/mcp/msbc), you are sure to receive the topical coverage that is most relevant to your personal and professional success. Microsoft's direct participation not only assures you that MOAC textbook content is accurate and current; it also means that students will receive the best instruction possible to enable their success on certification exams and in the workplace.

THE MICROSOFT OFFICIAL ACADEMIC COURSE PROGRAM

The Microsoft Official Academic Course series is a complete program for instructors and institutions to prepare and deliver great courses on Microsoft software technologies. With MOAC, we recognize that, because of the rapid pace of change in the technology and curriculum developed by Microsoft, there is an ongoing set of needs beyond classroom instruction tools for an instructor to be ready to teach the course. The MOAC program endeavors to provide solutions for all these needs in a systematic manner in order to ensure a successful and rewarding course experience for both instructor and student—technical and curriculum training for instructor readiness with new software releases; the software itself for student use at home for building hands-on skills, assessment, and validation of skill development; and a great set of tools for delivering instruction in the classroom and lab. All are important to the smooth delivery of an interesting course on Microsoft software, and all are provided with the MOAC program. We think about the model below as a gauge for ensuring that we completely support you in your goal of teaching a great course. As you evaluate your instructional materials options, you may wish to use the model for comparison purposes with available products.

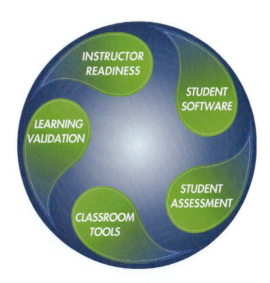

www.wiley.com/college/microsoft
or call the MOAC Toll-Free Number: 1+(888) 764-7001 (U.S. & Canada only)

PEDAGOGICAL FEATURES

The MOAC textbooks for Microsoft Office 2010 are designed to cover all the learning objectives for that MOS exam, which is referred to as its exam objective. The Microsoft Office Specialist (MOS) exam objectives are highlighted throughout the textbooks. Many pedagogical features have been developed specifically for Microsoft Official Academic Course programs. Unique features of our task-based approach include a Lesson Skill Matrix that correlates skills taught in each lesson to the MOS objectives; Certification, Workplace, and Internet Ready exercises; and three levels of increasingly rigorous lesson-ending activities, Competency, Proficiency, and Mastery Assessment.

Presenting the extensive procedural information and technical concepts woven throughout the textbook raises challenges for the student and instructor alike. The Illustrated Book Tour that follows provides a guide to the rich features contributing to Microsoft Official Academic Course program's pedagogical plan. Following is a list of key features in each lesson designed to prepare students for success on the certification exams and in the workplace:

- Each lesson begins with a **Lesson Skill Matrix**. More than a standard list of learning objectives, the skill matrix correlates each software skill covered in the lesson to the specific MOS exam objective domain.
- Each lesson features a real-world **Business case** scenario that places the software skills and knowledge to be acquired in a real-world setting.
- **Software Orientations** provide an overview of the software features students will be working with in the lesson. The orientation will detail the general properties of the software or specific features, such as a ribbon or dialog box; and it includes a large, labeled screen image.
- Concise and frequent **Step-by-Step** instructions teach students new features and provide an opportunity for hands-on practice. Numbered steps give detailed instructions to help students learn software skills. The steps also show results and screen images to match what students should see on their computer screens.
- **Illustrations** provide visual feedback as students work through the exercises. The images reinforce key concepts, provide visual clues about the steps, and allow students to check their progress.
- When the text instructs a student to click a particular button, **button images** are shown in the margin or in the text.
- Important technical vocabulary is listed in the **Key Terms** section at the beginning of the lesson. When these terms are used later in the lesson, they appear in bold italic type with yellow highlighter and are defined. The Glossary contains all of the key terms and their definitions.
- Engaging point-of-use **reader aids,** located throughout the lessons, tell students why this topic is relevant (*The Bottom Line*), provide students with helpful hints (*Take Note*), or show alternate ways to accomplish tasks (*Another Way*), or point out things to watch out for or avoid (*Troubleshooting*). Reader aids also provide additional relevant or background information that adds value to the lesson.
- **Certification Ready** features throughout the text signal students where a specific certification objective is covered. They provide students with a chance to check their understanding of that particular MOS exam objective and, if necessary, review the section of the lesson where it is covered. MOAC provides complete preparation for MOS certification.
- The **New Feature** icon appears near any software feature that is new to Office 2010.
- Each lesson ends with a **Skill Summary** recapping the MOS exam skills covered in the lesson.

- The **Knowledge Assessment** section provides a total of 20 questions from a mix of True/False, Fill in the Blank, Matching, or Multiple Choice, testing students on concepts learned in the lesson.
- **Competency, Proficiency, and Mastery Assessment** sections provide progressively more challenging lesson-ending activities.
- **Internet Ready** projects combine the knowledge that students acquire in a lesson with web-based task research.
- Integrated **Circling Back** projects provide students with an opportunity to renew and practice skills learned in previous lessons.
- **Workplace Ready** features preview how the Microsoft Office 2010 system applications are used in real-world situations.
- The student companion website contains the **online files** needed for each lesson. These data files are indicated by the @ icon in the margin of the textbook.

Illustrated Book Tour

LESSON FEATURES

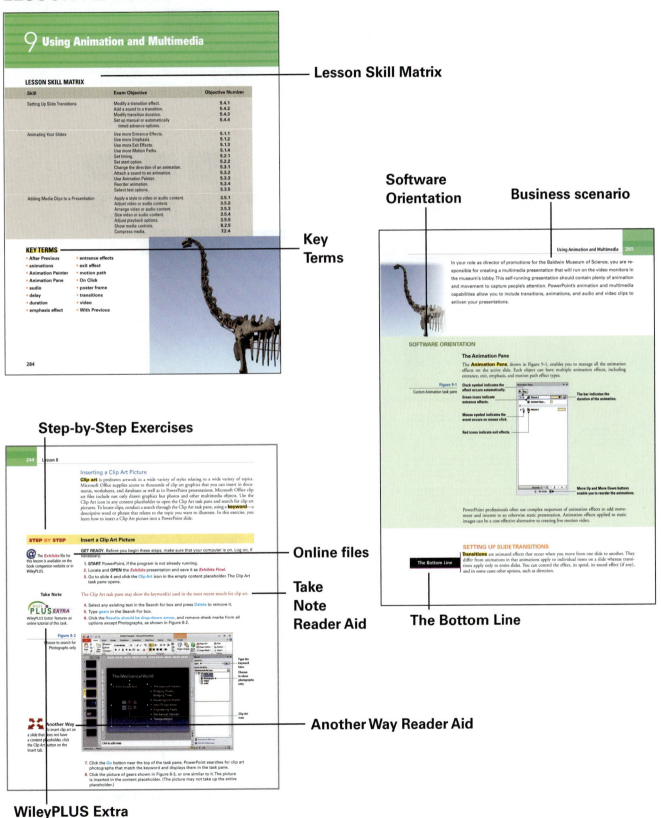

Lesson Skill Matrix

Key Terms

Software Orientation

Business scenario

Step-by-Step Exercises

Online files

Take Note Reader Aid

The Bottom Line

Another Way Reader Aid

WileyPLUS Extra

Screen Images with Callouts

Troubleshooting Reader Aid

**Microsoft Office Specialist
Certification Objective Alert**

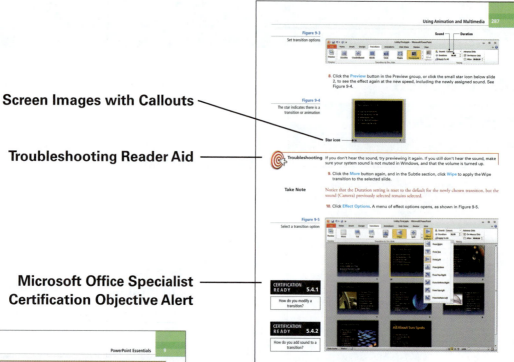

New Features

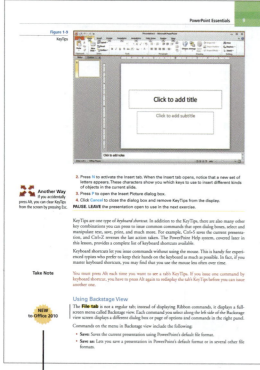

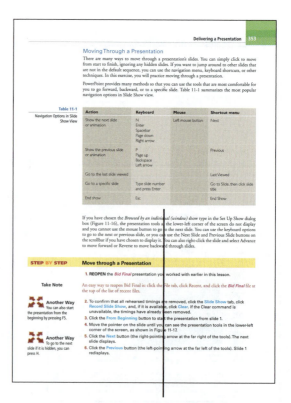

Easy-to-Read Tables

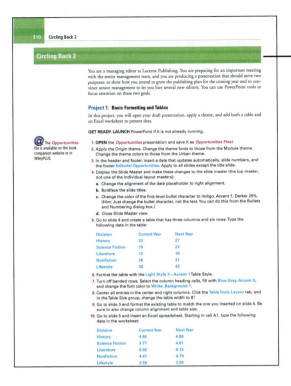

Circling Back Exercises

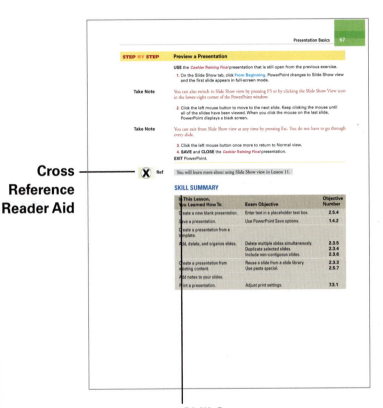

Cross Reference Reader Aid

Skill Summary

Knowledge Assessment Questions

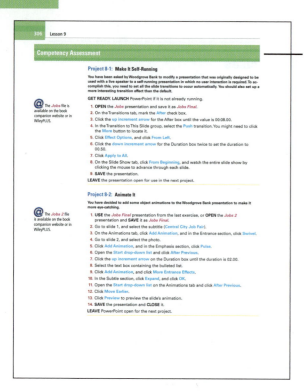

Competency Assessment Projects

Proficiency Assessment Projects

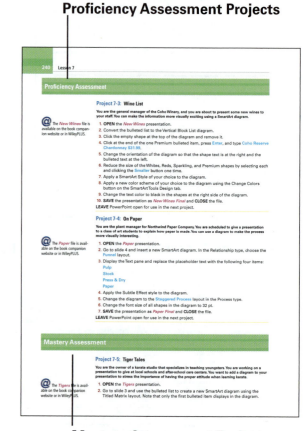

Internet Ready Project

Mastery Assessment Projects

Workplace Ready

Conventions and Features Used in This Book

This book uses particular fonts, symbols, and heading conventions to highlight important information or to call your attention to special steps. For more information about the features in each lesson, refer to the Illustrated Book Tour section.

NEW to Office 2010

This icon indicates a new or greatly improved Windows feature in this version of the software.

The Bottom Line

This feature provides a brief summary of the material to be covered in the section that follows.

CLOSE

Words in all capital letters indicate instructions for opening, saving, or closing files or programs. They also point out items you should check or actions you should take.

CERTIFICATION READY

This feature signals the point in the text where a specific certification objective is covered. It provides you with a chance to check your understanding of that particular MOS objective and, if necessary, review the section of the lesson where it is covered.

Take Note

Take Note reader aids, set in red text, provide helpful hints related to particular tasks or topics.

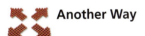 **Another Way**

Another Way provides an alternative procedure for accomplishing a particular task.

 Ref

These notes, set in gray shaded boxes, provide pointers to information discussed elsewhere in the textbook or describe interesting features that are not directly addressed in the current topic or exercise.

ALT + Tab

A plus sign (+) between two key names means that you must press both keys at the same time. Keys that you are instructed to press in an exercise will appear in the font shown here.

Key terms

Key terms appear in bold with yellow highlighting.

Key **My Name is**

Any text you are asked to key appears in **color.**

Click **OK**

Any button on the screen you are supposed to click on or select will also appear in **color.**

Budget Worksheet 1

The names of data files will appear in bold, italic and red for easy identification.

Instructor Support Program

The *Microsoft Official Academic Course* programs are accompanied by a rich array of resources that incorporate the extensive textbook visuals to form a pedagogically cohesive package. These resources provide all the materials instructors need to deploy and deliver their courses. The following resources are available online for download.

- The **Instructor's Guide** contains solutions to all the textbook exercises as well as chapter summaries and lecture notes. The Instructor's Guide and Syllabi for various term lengths are available from the Instructor's Book Companion Site (www.wiley.com/college/microsoft).

- The **Solution Files** for all the projects in the book are available online from our Instructor's Book Companion Site (www.wiley.com/college/microsoft).

- The **Test Bank** contains hundreds of questions organized by lesson in multiple-choice, true/false, short answer, and essay formats and is available to download from the Instructor's Book Companion Site (www.wiley.com/college/microsoft). A complete answer key is provided.

  This title's test bank is available for use in Respondus' easy-to-use software. You can download the test bank for free using your Respondus, Respondus LE, or StudyMate Author software.

  Respondus is a powerful tool for creating and managing exams that can be printed to paper or published directly to Blackboard, WebCT, Desire2Learn, eCollege, ANGEL, and other eLearning systems.

- A complete set of **PowerPoint Presentations** is available on the Instructor's Book Companion Site (www.wiley.com/college/microsoft) to enhance classroom presentations. Tailored to the text's topical coverage and Skills Matrix, these presentations are designed to convey key Microsoft Office 2010 concepts addressed in the text.

  All **images** from the text are on the Instructor's Book Companion Site (www.wiley.com/college/microsoft). You can incorporate them into your PowerPoint presentations, or create your own overhead transparencies and handouts.

  By using these visuals in class discussions, you can help focus students' attention on key elements of Office 2010 and help them understand how to use it effectively in the workplace.

- The **MSDN Academic Alliance** is designed to provide the easiest and most inexpensive developer tools, products, and technologies available to faculty and students in labs, classrooms, and on student PCs. A free three-year membership is available to qualified MOAC adopters.

- **Office Grader** automated grading system allows you to easily grade student data files in Word, Excel, PowerPoint, or Access format, against solution files. Save tens or hundreds of hours each semester with automated grading. More information on Office Grader is available from the Instructor's Book Companion Site (www.wiley.com/college/microsoft).

- The **Student Data Files** are available online on both the Instructor's Book Companion Site and for students on the Student Book Companion Site.

- Microsoft Official Academic Course books can be bundled with MOS exam vouchers from Certiport and MOS practice tests from GMetrix LLC or Certiport, available as a single bundle from Wiley, to create a **complete certification solution**. Instructors who use MOAC courseware in conjunction with a practice MOS exam find their students best-prepared for the MOS certification exam. Providing your students with the MOS exam voucher is the ultimate workforce preparation.

- When it comes to improving the classroom experience, there is no better source of ideas and inspiration than your fellow colleagues. The **Wiley Faculty Network** connects teachers with technology, facilitates the exchange of best practices, and helps to enhance instructional efficiency and effectiveness. Faculty Network activities include technology training and tutorials, virtual seminars, peer-to-peer exchanges of experiences and ideas, personal consulting, and sharing of resources. For details, visit www.WhereFacultyConnect.com.

WILEYPLUS

Broad developments in education over the past decade have influenced the instructional approach taken in the Microsoft Official Academic Course programs. The way that students learn, especially about new technologies, has changed dramatically in the Internet era. Electronic learning materials and Internet-based instruction is now as much a part of classroom instruction as printed textbooks. WileyPLUS provides the technology to create an environment where students reach their full potential and experience academic success that will last a lifetime.

WileyPLUS is a powerful and highly integrated suite of teaching and learning resources designed to bridge the gap between what happens in the classroom and what happens at home and on the job. WileyPLUS provides instructors with the resources to teach their students new technologies and guide them to reach their goals of getting ahead in the job market by having the skills to become certified and advance in the workforce. For students, WileyPLUS provides the tools for study and practice that are available to them 24/7, wherever and whenever they want to study. WileyPLUS includes a complete online version of the student textbook; PowerPoint presentations; homework and practice assignments and quizzes; image galleries; test bank questions; grade book; and all the instructor resources in one easy-to-use website.

The following features are new to WileyPLUS for Office 2010:

- In addition to the hundreds of questions included in the WileyPLUS courses that are not included in the test bank or textbook, we've added over a dozen additional projects that can be assigned to students.
- Many more animated tutorials, videos, and audio clips to support students as they learn the latest Office 2010 features.

MSDN ACADEMIC ALLIANCE

Free Three-Year Membership Available to Qualified Adopters!

The Microsoft Developer Network Academic Alliance (MSDN AA) is designed to provide the easiest and most inexpensive way for universities to make the latest Microsoft developer tools, products, and technologies available in labs, classrooms, and on student PCs. MSDN AA is an annual membership program for departments teaching Science, Technology, Engineering, and Mathematics (STEM) courses. The membership provides a complete solution to keep academic labs, faculty, and students on the leading edge of technology.

Software available in the MSDN AA program is provided at no charge to adopting departments through the Wiley and Microsoft publishing partnership.

As a bonus to this free offer, faculty will be introduced to Microsoft's Faculty Connection and Academic Resource Center. It takes time and preparation to keep students engaged while giving them a fundamental understanding of theory, and the Microsoft Faculty Connection is designed to help STEM professors with this preparation by providing articles, curriculum, and tools that professors can use to engage and inspire today's technology students.

Contact your Wiley rep for details.

For more information about the MSDN Academic Alliance program, go to **msdn.microsoft.com/academic/**.

IMPORTANT WEB ADDRESSES AND PHONE NUMBERS

To locate the Wiley Higher Education Rep in your area, go to www.wiley.com/college, select Instructors under Resources, and click on the Who's My Rep link, or call the MOAC toll-free number: 1 + (888) 764-7001 (U.S. and Canada only).

To learn more about becoming a Microsoft Certified Professional and exam availability, visit www.microsoft.com/learning/mcp.

WHY MOS CERTIFICATION?

Microsoft Office Specialist (MOS) 2010 is a valuable credential that recognizes the desktop computing skills needed to use the full features and functionality of the Microsoft Office 2010 suite.

In the worldwide job market, Microsoft Office Specialist is the primary tool companies use to validate the proficiency of their employees in the latest productivity tools and technology, helping them select job candidates based on globally recognized standards for verifying skills. The results of an independent research study show that businesses with certified employees are more productive compared to non-certified employees and that certified employees bring immediate value to their jobs.

In academia, as in the business world, institutions upgrading to Office 2010 may seek ways to protect and maximize their technology investment. By offering certification, they validate that decision—because powerful Office 2010 applications such as Word, Excel, and PowerPoint can be effectively used to demonstrate increases in academic preparedness and workforce readiness.

Individuals seek certification to increase their own personal sense of accomplishment and to create advancement opportunities by establishing a leadership position in their school or department, thereby differentiating their skill sets in a competitive college admissions and job market.

BOOK COMPANION WEBSITE

The students' book companion site for the MOAC series, www.wiley.com/college/microsoft, includes any resources, exercise files, and web links that will be used in conjunction with this course.

WILEY DESKTOP EDITIONS

Wiley MOAC Desktop Editions are innovative, electronic versions of printed textbooks. Students buy the desktop version for 50% off the U.S. price of the printed text and get the added value of permanence and portability. Wiley Desktop Editions provide students with numerous additional benefits that are not available with other e-text solutions.

Wiley Desktop Editions are NOT subscriptions; students download the Wiley Desktop Edition to their computer desktops. Students own the content they buy and keep it for as long as they want. Once a Wiley Desktop Edition is downloaded to the computer desktop, students have instant access to all of the content without being online. Students can also print the sections they prefer to read in hard copy. Students also have access to fully integrated resources within their Wiley Desktop Edition. From highlighting their e-text to taking and sharing notes, students can easily personalize their Wiley Desktop Edition as they are reading or following along in class.

COURSESMART

CourseSmart goes beyond traditional expectations providing instant, online access to the textbooks and course materials you need at a lower cost option. You can save time and hassle with a digital eTextbook that allows you to search for the most relevant content at the very moment you need it. To learn more go to: www.coursesmart.com.

PREPARING TO TAKE THE MICROSOFT OFFICE SPECIALIST (MOS) EXAM

The Microsoft Office Specialist credential has been upgraded to validate skills with the Microsoft Office 2010 system. The MOS certifications target information workers and cover the most popular business applications such as Word 2010, PowerPoint 2010, Excel 2010, Access 2010, and Outlook 2010.

By becoming certified, you demonstrate to employers that you have achieved a predictable level of skill in the use of a particular Office application. Employers often require certification either as a condition of employment or as a condition of advancement within the company or other organization. The certification examinations are sponsored by Microsoft but administered through exam delivery partners like Certiport.

To learn more about becoming a Microsoft Certified Application Specialist and exam availability, visit www.microsoft.com/learning/msbc.

Preparing to Take an Exam

Unless you are a very experienced user, you will need to use a test preparation course to prepare for the test to complete it correctly and within the time allowed. The Microsoft Official Academic Course series is designed to prepare you with a strong knowledge of all exam topics. With some additional review and practice on your own, you should feel confident in your ability to pass the appropriate exam.

After you decide which exam to take, review the list of objectives for the exam. This list can be found in Appendix A at the back of this book. You can also easily identify tasks that are included in the objective list by locating the Lesson Skill Matrix at the start of each lesson and the Certification Ready sidebars in the margin of the lessons in this book.

To take the MOS test, visit www.microsoft.com/learning/msbc to locate your nearest testing center. Then call the testing center directly to schedule your test. The amount of advance notice you should provide will vary for different testing centers, and it typically depends on the number of computers available at the testing center, the number of other testers who have already been scheduled for the day on which you want to take the test, and the number of times per week that the testing center offers MOS testing. In general, you should call to schedule your test at least two weeks prior to the date on which you want to take the test.

When you arrive at the testing center, you might be asked for proof of identity. A driver's license or passport is an acceptable form of identification. If you do not have either of these items of documentation, call your testing center and ask what alternative forms of identification will be accepted. If you are retaking a test, bring your MOS identification number, which will have been given to you when you previously took the test. If you have not prepaid or if your organization has not already arranged to make payment for you, you will need to pay the test-taking fee when you arrive.

Test Format

All MOS certification tests are live, performance-based tests. There are no multiple-choice, true/false, or short-answer questions. Instructions are general: you are told the basic tasks to perform on the computer, but you aren't given any help in figuring out how to perform them. You are not permitted to use reference material other than the application's Help system.

As you complete the tasks stated in a particular test question, the testing software monitors your actions. Following is an example question.

> Open the file named *Wiley Guests* and select the word *Welcome* in the first paragraph. Change the font to 12 point, and apply bold formatting. Select the words *at your convenience* in the second paragraph, move them to the end of the first paragraph using drag and drop, and then center the first paragraph.

When the test administrator seats you at a computer, you will see an online form that you use to enter information about yourself (name, address, and other information required to process your exam results). While you complete the form, the software will generate the test from a master test bank and then prompt you to continue. The first test question will appear in a window. Read the question carefully, and then perform all the tasks stated in the test question. When you have finished completing all tasks for a question, click the Next Question button.

You have 45 to 60 minutes to complete all questions, depending on the test that you are taking. The testing software assesses your results as soon as you complete the test, and the test administrator can print the results of the test so that you will have a record of any tasks that you performed incorrectly. A passing grade is 75 percent or higher. If you pass, you will receive a certificate in the mail within two to four weeks. If you do not pass, you can study and practice the skills that you missed and then schedule to retake the test at a later date.

Tips for Successfully Completing the Test

The following tips and suggestions are the result of feedback received from many individuals who have taken one or more MOS tests.

- **Make sure that you are thoroughly prepared.** If you have extensively used the application for which you are being tested, you might feel confident that you are prepared for the test. However, the test might include questions that involve tasks that you rarely or never perform when you use the application at your place of business, at school, or at home. You must be knowledgeable in all the MOS objectives for the test that you will take.

- **Read each exam question carefully.** An exam question might include several tasks that you are to perform. A partially correct response to a test question is counted as an incorrect response. In the example question on the previous page, you might apply bold formatting and move the words *at your convenience* to the correct location, but forget to center the first paragraph. This would count as an incorrect response and would result in a lower test score.

- **Use the Help system only when necessary.** You are allowed to use the application's Help system, but relying on the Help system too much will slow you down and possibly prevent you from completing the test within the allotted time. Use the Help system only when necessary.

- **Keep track of your time.** The test does not display the amount of time that you have left, so you need to keep track of the time yourself by monitoring your start time and the required end time on your watch or a clock in the testing center (if there is one). The test program displays the number of items that you have completed along with the total number of test items (for example, "35 of 40 items have been completed"). Use this information to gauge your pace.

- **You cannot return to a question once you've skipped it.** If you skip a question, you cannot return to it later. You should skip a question only if you are certain that you cannot complete the tasks correctly.

• **Make sure you understand the instructions for each question.** As soon as you are finished reading a question and you click in the application window, a condensed version of the instruction is displayed in a corner of the screen. If you are unsure whether you have completed all tasks stated in the test question, click the Instructions button on the test information bar at the bottom of the screen and then reread the question. Close the instruction window when you are finished. Do this as often as necessary to ensure you have read the question correctly and that you have completed all the tasks stated in the question.

If You Do Not Pass the Test

If you do not pass, you can use the assessment printout as a guide to practice the items that you missed. There is no limit to the number of times that you can retake a test; however, you must pay the fee each time that you take the test. When you retake the test, expect to see some of the same test items on the subsequent test; the test software randomly generates the test items from a master test bank before you begin the test. Also expect to see several questions that did not appear on the previous test.

Office 2010 Professional Six-Month Trial Software

Some editions of the textbooks in the MOAC Office 2010 series come with six-month trial editions of Office 2010 Professional. If your book includes a trial, there is a CD adhered to the inside cover of your book. This section pertains only to the editions that are packaged with an Office 2010 Professional trial.

STEP BY STEP   **Installing the Microsoft Office System 2010 Six-Month Trial**

1. Insert the trial software CD-ROM into the CD drive on your computer. The CD will be detected, and the Setup.exe file should automatically begin to run on your computer.
2. When prompted for the Office Product Key, enter the Product Key provided with the software, and then click **Next**.
3. Enter [your name] and [organization user name], and then click **Next**.
4. Read the End-User License Agreement, select the **I Accept the Terms in the License Agreement** check box, and then click **Next**.
5. Select the install option, verify the installation location or click **Browse** to change the installation location, and then click **Next**.
6. Verify the program installation preferences, and then click **Next**.

Click **Finish** to complete the setup.

UPGRADING MICROSOFT OFFICE PROFESSIONAL 2010 SIX-MONTH TRIAL SOFTWARE TO THE FULL PRODUCT

You can convert the software into full use without removing or reinstalling software on your computer. When you complete your trial, you can purchase a product license from any Microsoft reseller and enter a valid Product Key when prompted during setup.

UNINSTALLING THE TRIAL SOFTWARE AND RETURNING TO YOUR PREVIOUS OFFICE VERSION

If you want to return to your previous version of Office, you need to uninstall the trial software. This should be done through the Add or Remove Programs icon in Control Panel (or Uninstall a program in the Control Panel of Windows Vista).

STEP BY STEP   **Uninstall Trial Software**

1. Quit any programs that are running.
2. In Control Panel, click **Programs and Features** (**Add or Remove Programs** in Windows XP).
3. Click **Microsoft Office Professional 2010**, and then click **Uninstall** (**Remove** in Windows XP).

Take Note

If you selected the option to remove a previous version of Office during installation of the trial software, you need to reinstall your previous version of Office. If you did not remove your previous version of Office, you can start each of your Office programs either through the Start menu or by opening files for each program. In some cases, you may have to re-create some of your shortcuts and default settings.

STUDENT DATA FILES

All of the practice files that you will use as you perform the exercises in the book are available for download on our student companion site. By using the practice files, you will not waste time creating the samples used in the lessons, and you can concentrate on learning how to use Microsoft Office 2010. With the files and the step-by-step instructions in the lessons, you will learn by doing, which is an easy and effective way to acquire and remember new skills.

Copying the Practice Files

Your instructor might already have copied the practice files before you arrive in class. However, your instructor might ask you to copy the practice files on your own at the start of class. Also, if you want to work through any of the exercises in this book on your own at home or at your place of business after class, you may want to copy the practice files.

STEP BY STEP   **Copy the Practice Files**

OPEN Internet Explorer.

1. In Internet Explorer, go to the student companion site: www.wiley.com
2. Search for your book title in the upper-right corner.
3. On the Search Results page, locate your book and click on the **Visit the Companion Sites** link.
4. Select **Student Companion Site** from the pop-up box.
5. In the left-hand column, under "Browse by Resource" select **Student Data Files**.
6. Now select **Student Data Files** from the center of the screen.
7. On the File Download dialog box, select **Save** to save the data files to your external drive (often called a ZIP drive or a USB drive or a thumb drive) or a local drive.
8. In the Save As dialog box, select a local drive in the left-hand panel that you'd like to save your files to; again, this should be an external drive or a local drive. Remember the drive name that you saved it to.

Acknowledgments

We'd like to thank the many reviewers who pored over the manuscript and provided invaluable feedback in the service of quality instructional materials.

Access 2010

Tammie Bolling, *Tennessee Technology Center—Jacksboro*
Mary Corcoran, *Bellevue College*
Trish Culp, *triOS College—Business Technology Healthcare*
Jana Hambruch, *Lee County School District*
Aditi Mukherjee, *University of Florida—Gainesville*

Excel 2010

Tammie Bolling, *Tennessee Technology Center—Jacksboro*
Mary Corcoran, *Bellevue College*
Trish Culp, *triOS College—Business Technology Healthcare*
Dee Hobson, *Richland College*
Christie Hovey, *Lincoln Land Community College*
Ralph Phillips, *Central Oregon Community College*
Rajeev Sachdev, *triOS College—Business Technology Healthcare*

Outlook 2010

Mary Harnishfeger, *Ivy Tech State College—Bloomington*
Sandra Miller, *Wenatchee Valley College*
Bob Reeves, *Vincennes University*
Lourdes Sevilla, *Southwestern College—Chula Vista*
Phyllis E. Traylor, *St. Philips College*

PowerPoint 2010

Natasha Carter, *SUNY—ATTAIN*
Dr. Susan Evans Jennings, *Stephen F. Austin State University*
Sue Van Lanen, *Gwinnett Technical College*
Carol J. McPeek, *SUNY—ATTAIN*
Michelle Poertner, *Northwestern Michigan College*
Tim Sylvester, *Glendale Community College (AZ)*

Project 2010

Tatyana Pashnyak, *Bainbridge College*
Debi Griggs, *Bellevue College*

Word 2010

Portia Hatfield, *Tennessee Technology Center—Jacksboro*
Terri Holly, *Indian River State College*
Pat McMahon, *South Suburban College*
Barb Purvis, *Centura College*
Janet Sebesy, *Cuyahoga Community College*

We would also like to thank Lutz Ziob, Jason Bunge, Ben Watson, David Bramble, Merrick Van Dongen, Don Field, Pablo Bernal, and Wendy Johnson at Microsoft for their encouragement and support in making the Microsoft Official Academic Course program the finest instructional materials for mastering the newest Microsoft technologies for both students and instructors. Finally, we would like to thank Lorna Gentry of Content LLC for developmental editing and Jeff Riley and his team at Box Twelve Communications for technical editing.

About the Author

FAITHE WEMPEN

Faithe Wempen, MA, is a Microsoft Office Master Instructor and an A+ Certified PC technician and has authored over 100 books on Microsoft applications and operating systems. Her first book was *Abort, Retry, Fail: 101 MS-DOS Error Messages.* More recent titles include *Microsoft Office 2010 for Seniors for Dummies* and *The PowerPoint 2010 Bible.*

Faithe's online courses in Office applications have educated over a quarter of a million students for clients including CNET, Hewlett Packard, and Sony. Her articles on maximizing Office productivity have appeared in *Microsoft Office PRO* and *Microsoft Office Power User* magazines, as well as on TechRepublic.com and CertCities.com. She also spent eight years as an adjunct instructor of Computer Technology at Indiana University/Purdue University at Indianapolis (IUPUI), specializing in teaching PC hardware, operating systems, and Office applications.

Brief Contents

Contents

1 PowerPoint Essentials 1

2 Presentation Basics 35

3 Working with Text 73

4   Designing a Presentation   124

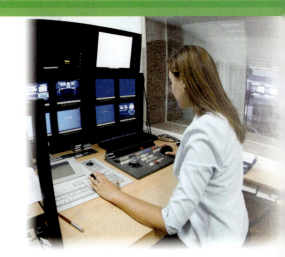

5 Adding Tables to Slides   159

6 Using Charts in a Presentation   190

7 Creating SmartArt Graphics 217

8 Adding Graphics to a Presentation   242

9 Using Animation and Multimedia 284

10 Securing and Sharing a Presentation 315

11 Delivering a Presentation 337

LESSON SKILL MATRIX

Skills	Exam Objective	Objective Number
Working in the PowerPoint Window	Work with multiple presentation windows simultaneously.	1.2.1
	Show the Quick Access Toolbar (QAT) below the ribbon.	1.3.1
Working with an Existing Presentation	Adjust views by using the ribbon.	1.1.1
	Adjust views by status bar commands.	1.1.2
	Enter text in a placeholder text box.	2.5.4
	Copy and paste text.	2.5.6

KEY TERMS

- Backstage view
- command
- current slide
- dialog box launcher
- dialog box
- drop-down arrow
- drop-down list
- File tab
- group
- I-beam pointer
- KeyTip
- Mini toolbar
- Normal view
- Notes Page view
- placeholder
- Quick Access Toolbar
- Reading View
- Ribbon
- ScreenTip
- shortcut menu
- Slide Show view
- Slide Sorter view
- tab
- text box
- views
- zoom

Blue Yonder Airlines is a small but rapidly growing company that offers charter flights to adventurous or exotic locations. The service is designed for small groups, such as corporate management teams or directors who want to mix business and pleasure in a packaged getaway. As an enterprise account manager, your job is to introduce Blue Yonder Airlines to executives in mid-sized and large companies. Your goal is to convince these managers to use your charter service when arranging off-site gatherings that require group travel. Microsoft PowerPoint 2010 provides the perfect set of tools for presenting this information to your potential customers. In this lesson, you will start PowerPoint and open an introductory presentation about Blue Yonder Airlines. You will learn to navigate, edit, save, print, and close a presentation.

SOFTWARE ORIENTATION

Microsoft PowerPoint's Opening Screen

Before you begin working in Microsoft PowerPoint, you should be familiar with the primary user interface. When you first start Microsoft PowerPoint, you will see a screen similar to the one shown in Figure 1-1. However, if your copy of PowerPoint has been customized, what you see may be slightly different from what is shown. You can use this figure as a reference throughout this lesson and the rest of this book.

Figure 1-1

The PowerPoint window

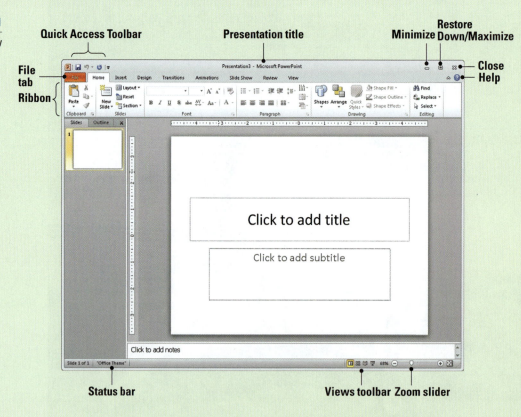

The Ribbon across the top of the window contains a set of tabs; each tab has a different collection of buttons and tools on it. Additional tabs appear when you select certain types of content, such as graphics or tables.

WORKING IN THE POWERPOINT WINDOW

The Bottom Line

To use PowerPoint 2010 efficiently, you need to learn how to navigate in the PowerPoint application window.

Starting PowerPoint

Before you can use PowerPoint, you need to start the program. In this exercise, you learn to start PowerPoint using the Start button and the Microsoft Office menu.

STEP BY STEP | **Start PowerPoint**

GET READY. Before you begin these steps, make sure that your computer is on. Log on, if necessary.

WileyPLUS Extra! features an online tutorial on this task.

1. On the Windows taskbar at the bottom of your screen, click the **Start** button, and then click **All Programs**. A menu of installed programs appears.
2. Click **Microsoft Office**. A submenu opens, listing the available programs in your installation of Microsoft Office.
3. Click **Microsoft PowerPoint 2010**, as shown in Figure 1-2. PowerPoint starts and a new, blank presentation appears in the PowerPoint window.

Figure 1-2

Starting PowerPoint

Desktop

Microsoft Office folder

Microsoft PowerPoint 2010

Start button

Taskbar

Another Way
If PowerPoint has recently been used on your computer, it may appear on the top level of the Start menu, when you first click the Start button. If it appears there, you can click that shortcut to start the program, rather than clicking All Programs and Microsoft Office to find it.

Another Way
You can also click the Start button and then begin typing PowerPoint; after you have typed the first few letters, PowerPoint should appear above the Start button; click on it there to start the program.

PAUSE. LEAVE the blank presentation open to use in the next exercise.

Selecting Tools and Commands

A **command** is a tool (such as an icon, a button, or a list) that tells PowerPoint to perform a specific task. Each tab provides commands that are relevant to the kind of task you are performing—whether you are formatting a slide, adding animations to a presentation, or setting up a slide show for display. Most of the tools and commands for working with PowerPoint are accessible through PowerPoint's Ribbon. In addition to the Ribbon, PowerPoint also offers tools and commands on the File menu (also known as **Backstage view**), a Quick Access toolbar, a floating mini-toolbar, and a status bar.

Using the Ribbon

In this exercise, you learn how to select commands from the **Ribbon**, which is the tabbed tool-bar at the top of the window. The Ribbon is divided into **tabs**, and each tab contains several **groups** of related commands.

On the Ribbon, some command groups feature a tool called a **dialog box launcher**—a small arrow in the group's lower-right corner. You can click the arrow to open a **dialog box**, which provides tools and options related to a specific task. To close a dialog box without accepting any changes you may have made to it, click the Cancel button.

Some of the Ribbon's tools have small, downward-pointing arrows next to them. These arrows are called **drop-down arrows**; when you click one, a **drop-down list** opens, displaying options you can choose (such as a list of fonts). You can choose the option you want by clicking it.

If you need more space on your screen, you can minimize (hide) the Ribbon by double-clicking the active tab. To restore the Ribbon, double-click the active tab again.

STEP BY STEP   Use the Ribbon

USE the new, blank presentation that is still open from the previous exercise.

1. Look at the Ribbon, which appears in Figure 1-3. Note that each tab contains several groups of related commands. By default, the Home tab is active.

Figure 1-3

The Ribbon

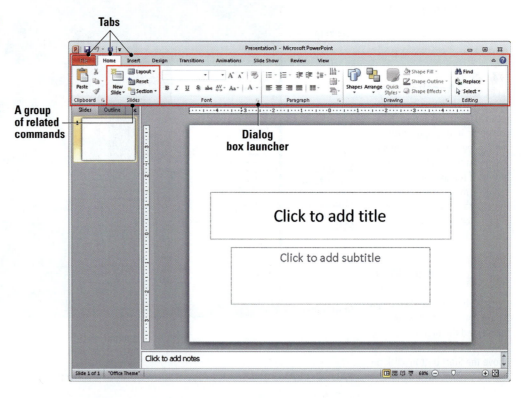

Another Way
You can also open the Font dialog box by pressing Ctrl+Shift+F. Many common commands have keyboard shortcuts; the PowerPoint Help system (covered later in this lesson) can help you identify them.

2. Click the **Design** tab to make it active. The groups of commands change.
3. Click the **Home** tab.
4. On the slide, click anywhere in the text **Click to add title**. The text disappears and a blinking insertion point appears.

 Ref   You will learn about adding and editing text later in this lesson.

5. In the lower-right corner of the Font group, click the **dialog box launcher** (the small box with a diagonal, downward-pointing arrow, as shown in Figure 1-3). Clicking this button opens PowerPoint's Font dialog box. Click **Cancel** to close the dialog box.

6. In the Font group, click the **Font list drop-down arrow**. A drop-down list appears, as shown in Figure 1-4. This list shows all the fonts that are currently available for use. The default font for titles is Calibri.

Figure 1-4

The Font list

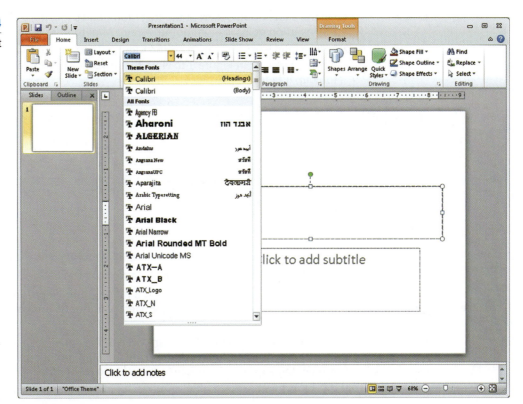

Another Way
You can also minimize the Ribbon by right-clicking one of its tabs and clicking Minimize the Ribbon. Repeat that procedure to redisplay the Ribbon. You can also use the arrow to the left of the Help button that appears as a question mark in a blue circle in the upper-right corner of the PowerPoint window to minimize or restore the Ribbon.

7. Click the **drop-down arrow** again to close the list.
8. Double-click the **Home** tab. This action minimizes the Ribbon, hiding the groups of commands but leaving the tabs' names visible on the screen.
9. Double-click the **Home** tab again to redisplay the groups.

PAUSE. LEAVE the presentation open to use in the next exercise.

Take Note

If you aren't sure what a command does, just point to it. When the mouse pointer rests on a tool, a ScreenTip appears. A basic **ScreenTip** displays the tool's name and shortcut key (if a shortcut exists for that tool). Some of the Ribbon's tools have enhanced ScreenTips that also provide a brief description of the tool.

Using the Mini Toolbar

In this exercise, you practice using the **Mini toolbar**, a small toolbar that appears when you point to text that has been selected (highlighted). The Mini toolbar displays tools for formatting text appearance and alignment. The Mini toolbar is faint and semi-transparent until you point to it; then it becomes bright and opaque, indicating that the toolbar is active. If you right-click selected text, PowerPoint displays both the Mini toolbar and a **shortcut menu**, which displays additional commands.

Use the Mini Toolbar

USE the presentation that is still on the screen from the preceding exercise.

1. On the slide, double-click at the insertion point's location. Because you double-clicked, the insertion point is highlighted. A faint Mini toolbar appears.

2. Point to the Font command on the Mini toolbar; the toolbar becomes brighter and easier to see, as in Figure 1-5. Note that if you move the mouse pointer away from the toolbar, it fades.

Figure 1-5

The Mini toolbar appears by the highlighted insertion point

Mini toolbar

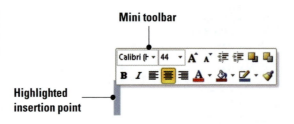

Highlighted insertion point

3. Click the **Font drop-down** arrow in the Mini toolbar. The list of available fonts opens.

Another Way
You can also press Esc to close an open drop-down list.

4. Click the **Font drop-down** arrow again to close the list.

5. Move the mouse pointer back to the highlighted insertion point, then right-click. A shortcut menu with commonly used commands appears along with the Mini toolbar.

6. Move the mouse pointer to a blank area of the slide (such as the upper-left corner), then click twice. The first click removes the Mini toolbar and shortcut menu from the screen; the second click restores the slide to its original state.

PAUSE. LEAVE the presentation open to use in the next exercise.

Using the Quick Access Toolbar

The **Quick Access Toolbar** displays commands that you use frequently. By default, the Save, Undo, and Redo commands appear on the toolbar. You can add any commands to the Quick Access Toolbar for easy access to the commands you use most frequently. You can also choose where the Quick Access Toolbar appears via the Customize Quick Access Toolbar button's menu. In this exercise, you learn to use and customize the Quick Access Toolbar.

The Save command quickly saves an existing presentation while you are working on it or when you are done with it. If you have not yet given the presentation a file name, PowerPoint will prompt you for a name by launching the Save As dialog box, as happened in the preceding exercise. If you have previously saved the file, the dialog box does not reopen.

The Undo command lets you reverse ("undo") the action of your last command. The Redo button lets you reverse an undo action. If either the Undo or Redo command is gray, then you cannot undo or redo.

Use the Quick Access Toolbar

USE the presentation that is still open from the previous exercise.

1. Look for the Quick Access Toolbar in the upper-left corner of the PowerPoint window. The Quick Access Toolbar appears in Figure 1-6, with its tools labeled. Yours may look different if it has been customized.

Figure 1-6

The Quick Access Toolbar

Undo   Redo

Customize Quick Access Toolbar

Save —

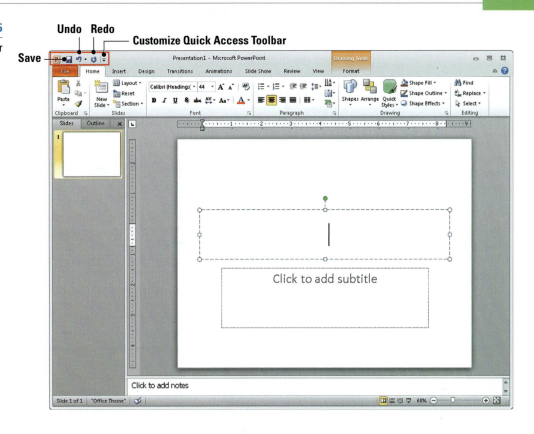

2. Click the **Save** button on the Quick Access Toolbar. The Save As dialog box appears.

3. Click **Cancel** to close the dialog box.

4. Click the **Customize Quick Access Toolbar** button. A menu appears, as shown in Figure 1-7. This menu lets you choose the tools you want to appear on the Quick Access Toolbar.

Another Way
You can also press Esc to close a dialog box.

Figure 1-7

Customizing the Quick Access Toolbar

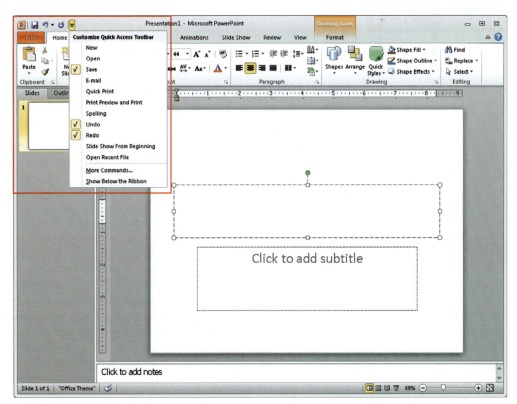

5. Click **Show Below the Ribbon**. The toolbar moves down and appears directly beneath the Ribbon.

6. Click the **Customize Quick Access Toolbar** button again. Click **Show Above the Ribbon**. The toolbar moves back to its original location.

7. On the Home tab, right-click the **Bold** button. A shortcut menu appears, as in Figure 1-8.

Figure 1-8

Adding a button to the Quick Access Toolbar

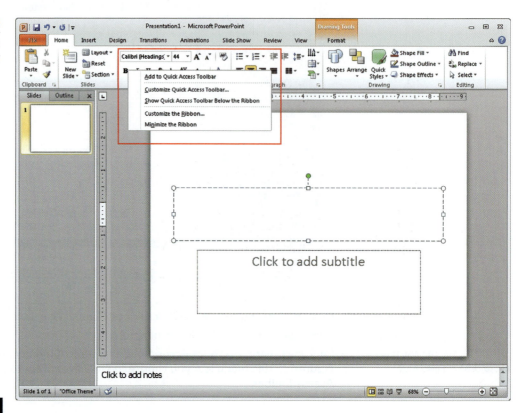

CERTIFICATION READY   1.3.1

How do you show the Quick Access Toolbar below the ribbon?

8. Click **Add to Quick Access Toolbar**. A copy of the Bold button appears on the toolbar.

9. On the Quick Access Toolbar, right-click the **Bold** button. A shortcut menu appears.

10. Click **Remove from Quick Access Toolbar**. The copy of the Bold button is removed.

PAUSE. LEAVE the presentation open to use in the next exercise.

Using KeyTips

When you press the Alt key, small letters and numbers—called **KeyTips**—appear on the Ribbon. To issue a command by using its KeyTip, press the Alt key, and then press the key or keys that correspond to the command you want to use. Every command on the Ribbon has a KeyTip.

STEP BY STEP   Use KeyTips

USE the presentation that is still open from the previous exercise.

1. Press **Alt**. Letters and numbers appear on the Ribbon and the Quick Access Toolbar, as shown in Figure 1-9. These characters show you which keyboard keys you can press to access the tabs or the items on the Quick Access Toolbar.

Figure 1-9

KeyTips

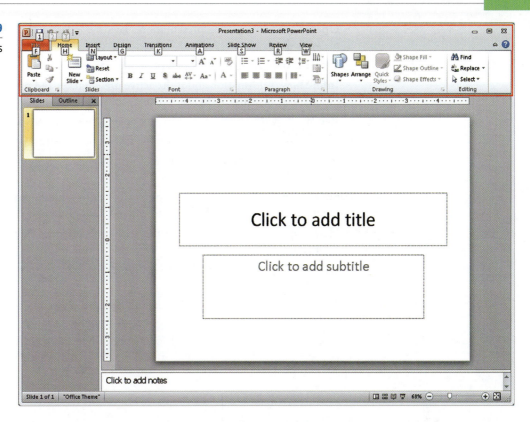

2. Press **N** to activate the Insert tab. When the Insert tab opens, notice that a new set of letters appears. These characters show you which keys to use to insert different kinds of objects in the current slide.

3. Press **P** to open the Insert Picture dialog box.

4. Click **Cancel** to close the dialog box and remove KeyTips from the display.

PAUSE. LEAVE the presentation open to use in the next exercise.

Another Way
If you accidentally press Alt, you can clear KeyTips from the screen by pressing Esc.

KeyTips are one type of *keyboard shortcut*. In addition to the KeyTips, there are also many other key combinations you can press to issue common commands that open dialog boxes, select and manipulate text, save, print, and much more. For example, Ctrl+S saves the current presentation, and Ctrl+Z reverses the last action taken. The PowerPoint Help system, covered later in this lesson, provides a complete list of keyboard shortcuts available.

Keyboard shortcuts let you issue commands without using the mouse. This is handy for experienced typists who prefer to keep their hands on the keyboard as much as possible. In fact, if you master keyboard shortcuts, you may find that you use the mouse less often over time.

Take Note   You must press Alt each time you want to see a tab's KeyTips. If you issue one command by keyboard shortcut, you have to press Alt again to redisplay the tab's KeyTips before you can issue another one.

Using Backstage View

NEW to Office 2010

The **File tab** is not a regular tab; instead of displaying Ribbon commands, it displays a full-screen menu called Backstage view. Each command you select along the left side of the Backstage view screen displays a different dialog box or page of options and commands in the right panel.

Commands on the menu in Backstage view include the following:

• **Save:** Saves the current presentation using PowerPoint's default file format.

• **Save as:** Lets you save a presentation in PowerPoint's default format or in several other file formats.

- **Open:** Opens an existing presentation stored on a disk, either on your computer's disk or a network drive.
- **Close:** Closes the currently open presentation.
- **Info:** Shows information about the active presentation and provides commands that control permissions, sharing, and version management.
- **Recent:** Provides shortcuts to recently opened presentations and file locations.
- **New:** Lists available templates from which you can create a new presentation.
- **Print:** Provides settings and options for printing a presentation in any of a variety of formats.
- **Save & Send:** Offers a variety of options for saving a presentation in different formats, sending it to others, and publishing it to video, CD, or other media.
- **Help:** Opens the PowerPoint Help system, and provides links for other help and support resources.
- **Options:** Opens the PowerPoint Options dialog box, from which you can configure many aspects of program operation.
- **Exit:** Closes the PowerPoint application, and also closes any open files.

Take Note   In PowerPoint 2007, instead of a File command, there was a File tab in the upper-left corner of the PowerPoint window. Clicking that button opened a menu that was similar to the menu and commands in Backstage view.

Use Backstage View

USE the presentation you used in the previous exercise.

1. Click the **File** tab on the Ribbon. Backstage view opens, as shown in Figure 1-10.

Figure 1-10

Backstage view

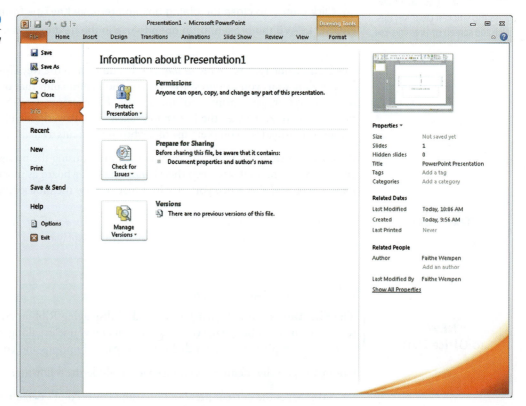

2. Click **Save & Send**. A page of commands and subcommands appears, as in Figure 1-11. Send Using E-mail is selected by default, and the right side of the window lists commands for sending your work to others.

Figure 1-11

The Save & Send commands in Backstage view

3. Click **Create a Video**. Options and commands for doing that activity appear at the right.
4. Click **Recent**. A list of recently opened files appears.
5. Click **New**. A list of templates appears.
6. Click **Open**. The Open dialog box appears.
7. Click **Cancel** to close the dialog box without making a selection.
8. Click the **File** tab again to redisplay Backstage view.
9. Click the **Home** tab to leave Backstage view.

PAUSE. LEAVE the presentation open to use in the next exercise.

Another Way
You can also press Esc to close Backstage view.

Another Way
To open the File menu by using KeyTips, press Alt, and then press F.

Working with PowerPoint's Help System

PowerPoint's Help system is rich in information, illustrations, and tips that can help you complete any task as you create a presentation. Some of PowerPoint's help information is stored on your computer, and much more is available via the Internet. Finding the right information is easy: you can pick a topic from the Help system's table of contents, browse a directory of help topics, or perform keyword searches by entering terms that best describe the task you want to complete. In this exercise, you learn to access and use PowerPoint's Help system.

Use the Help System

USE the presentation that is open from the previous exercise.

Another Way
You can also open the Help window by pressing F1.

1. Click the **Microsoft Office PowerPoint Help** button ❓ at the right end of the Ribbon. The PowerPoint Help window appears. If the Help system is connected to the Internet, it appears as shown in Figure 1-12, and a Connected to Office.com indicator appears in the lower-right corner if your computer is connected.

Figure 1-12

The PowerPoint Help window when connected to the Internet

Use this Search box to search for information within the PowerPoint help system.

When connected to Internet, online Help search is also available.

Indicator shows connection status.

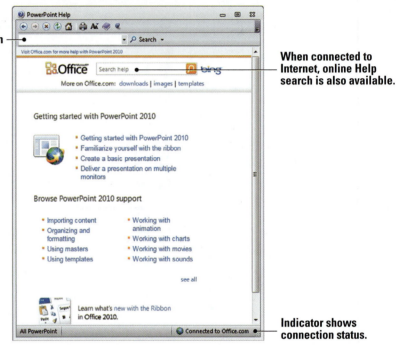

2. Click the **Connected to Office.com** button. The Connection Status menu appears.

3. Click **Show content only from this computer**. Notice that the Connected to Office.com button now appears as Offline, and the Help window changes as in Figure 1-13.

Figure 1-13

The PowerPoint Help window when offline

When not connected to Internet, only local search is available.

Connection indicator shows Offline.

Take Note

Even if Office is set to work offline, you can still search for help online. Instead of clicking the Search button, click the drop-down arrow button to its right. When the menu opens, click Content from Office Online. The choice will affect only the current search.

4. Click the **Search** box, type **Ribbon**, and then click the **Search** button or press **Enter**. A list of help topics appears, as shown in Figure 1-14.

Figure 1-14

Searching for help articles about the Ribbon

Change Font Size button

Type search word here.

Read this article.

Show Table of Contents button

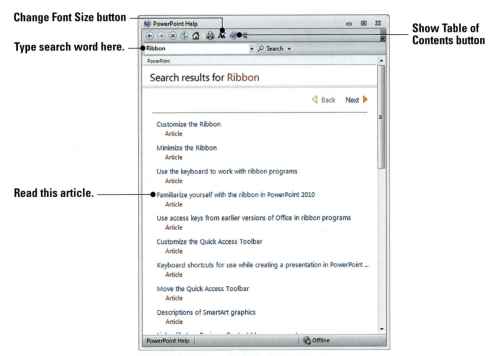

5. Click the **Familiarize yourself with the Ribbon in PowerPoint 2010** hyperlink. The corresponding article appears. Read the article if you wish.

6. Click the **Show Table of Contents** button. The Table of Contents opens in a pane on the left side of the Help window. The article about the Ribbon continues to appear at the right side.

7. Scroll up to the top of the Table of Contents pane and click the **What's New?** link.

8. Click **What's New in PowerPoint 2010?**. The help topic appears in the window, as shown in Figure 1-15.

Home button

Figure 1-15

Article explaining the new features in PowerPoint 2010

9. Click the **Home** button. The top-level topic list appears in the right pane. The left pane continues to show the Table of Contents.

10. Click the **Close** button to close the Help window.

PAUSE. LEAVE the presentation open to use in the next exercise.

PowerPoint's Help window gives you access to many different help topics. A help topic is an article about a specific PowerPoint feature. Help topics can assist you with virtually any task or problem you encounter while working with PowerPoint.

The Help window is set up like a browser window and features some of the same tools you will find in your Web browser, including:

- **Back:** Jumps to the previously opened Help topic.
- **Forward:** Jumps to the next opened Help topic.
- **Stop:** Stops any action in progress.
- **Refresh:** Reloads the current Help topic.
- **Home:** Returns to the initial Help window.
- **Print:** Prints the currently open Help topic.

Take Note

Many PowerPoint dialog boxes contain a Help button. When you click it, a Help window opens with information about the dialog box.

You can find help in several ways. For example, you can open the Table of Contents and scan the list for help on a specific topic. You can also type a word or phrase into the Search box, and then click the Search button. A list of related help topics appears in the Help window.

The Search button gives you more options when looking for help. If you click the drop-down arrow next to the Search button, you can search for help online or offline, look for PowerPoint templates, find information for developers, and more.

The Connection Status menu lets you decide whether to access the help topics that are available online, or just those topics that are installed on your computer (called "offline help"). If your computer has an "always on" connection to the Internet—such as a cable modem or a LAN connection—you will probably want to access online content. If your computer has a dial-up connection, or if you simply do not want to download help topics every time you click the Help button, you can choose *Show content only from this computer* to work with only locally stored help topics.

Closing a Presentation

When you close a presentation, PowerPoint removes it from the screen. PowerPoint continues running so you can work with other files. You should always save and close any open presentations before you exit PowerPoint or shut down your computer. In this exercise, you will practice closing an open presentation.

STEP BY STEP   **Close a Presentation**

USE the presentation that is open from the previous exercise.

1. Click the **File** tab; Backstage view appears.
2. Click **Close**. PowerPoint clears the presentation from the screen.

PAUSE. LEAVE PowerPoint open to use in the next exercise.

WORKING WITH AN EXISTING PRESENTATION

The Bottom Line

If you want to work with an existing presentation, you need to open it. After opening a presentation, you can use PowerPoint's View commands to change the way the presentation is displayed onscreen; different views are suitable for different types of presentation editing and management tasks. You can also use PowerPoint's Zoom tools to make slides look larger or smaller on the screen. The following exercises show you how to view your slides in different ways, and how to add, edit, and delete text on your slides. You will then learn how to print a presentation and to save it to a disk.

Opening an Existing Presentation

PowerPoint makes it easy to work on a presentation over time. If you can't finish a slide show today, you can reopen it later and resume working on it. The Open dialog box lets you open a presentation that has already been saved on a disk. Presentations can be stored on any disk on your PC or network or on removable media (such as a CD). You can use the Look In box to navigate to the file's location, and then click the file to select it. This exercise shows you how to use the Open button to open an existing presentation—one that has already been created and saved as a file on a disk.

STEP BY STEP   **Open an Existing Presentation**

WileyPLUS Extra! features an online tutorial of this task.

GET READY. To open an existing presentation, do the following.

1. Click the **File** tab to open Backstage view.
2. Click **Open**. The Open dialog box appears, as shown in Figure 1-16.

Figure 1-16

The Open dialog box

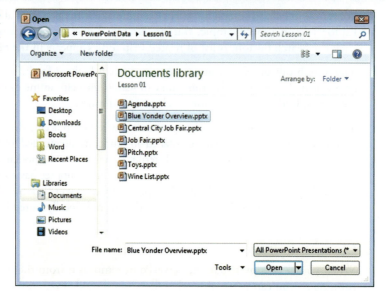

 **Another Way**
You can also open the Open dialog box by pressing Ctrl+O.

 The *Blue Yonder Overview* file is available on the book companion website or in WileyPLUS.

 **Another Way**
Instead of clicking the file's name in the Open dialog box and then clicking the Open button, you can double-click the file's name to open the presentation.

3. Locate and select *Blue Yonder Overview*, then click Open. The presentation appears on your screen, as shown in Figure 1-17.

Figure 1-17

The *Blue Yonder Overview* presentation

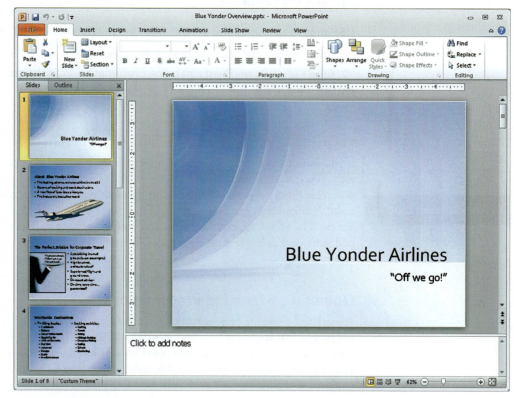

 **Another Way**
If a presentation has been opened recently, its name should appear on the Recent Documents list. After opening Backstage view, click Recent, and then click the presentation's name to open it.

PAUSE. LEAVE the presentation open to use in the next exercise.

Viewing a Presentation in Different Ways

PowerPoint's various **views** enable you to see your presentation in a variety of ways. For example, in Normal view, you can work with just one slide at a time, which is helpful when you are adding text or graphics to a slide. Alternately, in Slide Sorter view, you can view all the slides in a presentation at the same time, which makes it easy to rearrange the slides. The following exercise shows you how to change PowerPoint's views.

STEP BY STEP   **Change PowerPoint's Views**

USE the presentation that you opened during the previous exercise.

1. Click the **View** tab, as shown in Figure 1-18. Notice that the Normal button is highlighted on both the Ribbon and the Views toolbar in the bottom-right corner of the PowerPoint window.

Figure 1-18

Normal view, with the View tab selected

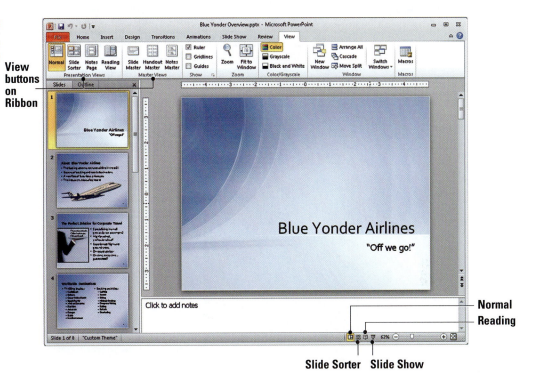

2. Click the **Slide Sorter View** button to change to Slide Sorter view, as shown in Figure 1-19.

Figure 1-19

Slide Sorter view

Another Way

Instead of using the Ribbon to change views, you can use the View toolbar in the lower-right corner of the PowerPoint window.

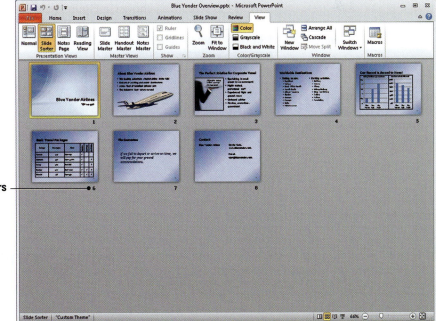

Take Note
If formatted slides are hard to read in Slide Sorter view, press Alt and click a slide to see its heading clearly.

3. Click **slide 2**, and then click the **Notes Page View** button. PowerPoint switches to Notes Page view, as shown in Figure 1-20.

Figure 1-20

Notes Page view

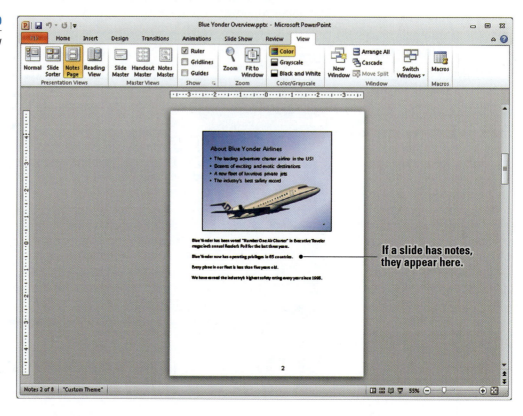

Take Note
There is no button for Notes Page view on the Views toolbar at the bottom of the PowerPoint window; you must access it via the Ribbon.

4. Click the **Slide Show** tab, and click **From Beginning**. The first slide of the presentation fills the screen, as shown in Figure 1-21.

Figure 1-21

Slide Show view

 **Another Way**
You can also switch to Slide Show view by pressing F5.

5. Press **Esc** to exit Slide Show view and return to Notes Page view.

6. Click the **View** tab, and click the **Reading View** button. The first slide appears in a reading window. It looks just like Figure 1-21 except it does not fill the screen.

7. Close the reading window by pressing Esc.

8. On the View toolbar, click the **Normal View** button. PowerPoint switches back to Normal view.

PAUSE. LEAVE the presentation open to use in the next exercise.

PowerPoint provides these views:

- **Normal view** is the default view that lets you focus on an individual slide. The slide you are currently editing is called the **current slide**. The current slide appears in the Slide pane, which is the largest of the view's three panes. Below the Slide pane is the Notes pane, where you can add and edit notes you want to associate with the current slide. In the left pane—called the Slides/Outline pane—you can use the Slides tab to jump from one slide to another, as you will see later in this lesson. On the Outline tab, you can add text to a slide or copy or move text from one slide to another.

- **Slide Sorter view** displays all the slides in a presentation on a single screen. (If there are more slides than can fit in one screen, you can use scroll bars to move slides in and out of view.) In Slide Show view, you can reorganize a slide show by dragging slides to different positions. You can also duplicate and delete slides in this view.

- **Notes Page view** shows one slide at a time, along with any notes that are associated with the slide. This view lets you create and edit notes. You may find it easier to work with notes in this view than in Normal view. You can also print notes pages for your presentation; they are printed as they appear in Notes Page view.

- **Slide Show view** lets you preview your presentation on the screen, so you can see it the way your audience will see it.

- **Reading view** is like Slide Show view except it's in a window rather than filling the entire screen. Displaying the presentation in a window enables you to also work in other windows at the same time.

 Ref

You will work with PowerPoint's printing options and practice previewing a presentation later in this lesson.

Using Zoom

PowerPoint's **zoom** tools let you change the magnification of slides on the screen. By zooming out, you can see an entire slide; by zooming in, you can inspect one area of the slide. Both views have advantages: higher magnifications make it easier to position objects on the slide, and lower magnifications enable you to see how all the parts of a slide look as a whole. In this exercise, you practice using the zoom tool.

STEP BY STEP | **Use Zoom**

USE the presentation that is open from the previous exercise.

1. Click the **slide** in the Slide pane, to ensure that the Slide pane is active. As a reminder, the Slide pane is the large pane on the right side of Normal view, in which one slide appears at a time.

2. On the View tab, click the **Zoom** button. The Zoom dialog box appears, as shown in Figure 1-22.

CERTIFICATION READY **1.1.1**

How do you change views using the Ribbon?

CERTIFICATION READY **1.1.2**

How do you change views using the status bar buttons?

Another Way
You can click the Zoom level indicator at the far left of the Zoom control (located on the right end of the Status Bar) to display the Zoom dialog box.

Figure 1-22

The Zoom dialog box

 **Another Way**
You can drag the Zoom control's slider bar to the right or left to change the zoom level. However, in Normal view, the slider controls only the Slides pane, regardless of what pane is selected. If you want to change the zoom for the Slides/Outline pane, you must use the dialog box.

3. Click the **200%** option button, then click **OK**. In the Slide pane, the slide is magnified by 200%. Notice that you can no longer see the entire slide.

4. Click the **Zoom Out** button at the left end of the Zoom control, at the lower-right of the screen, as shown in Figure 1-23. Continue clicking the button until the zoom level drops to 100%. Notice that, even at 100% magnification, the slide is too large for the Slide pane.

Figure 1-23

Using the Zoom controls

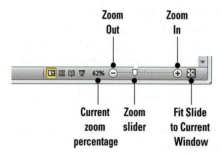

Take Note   You can resize the Slide pane by dragging its bottom border up or down, or by dragging its left-hand border to the right or left. The Slides/Outline pane and Notes pane also change size when you drag the borders.

5. Click the **Fit slide to current window** button at the far right end of the Zoom control. PowerPoint zooms out to fit the entire slide in the Slide pane.

PAUSE. LEAVE the presentation open to use in the next exercise.

You can use either the Zoom dialog box or the Zoom control to change magnification levels. In the Zoom dialog box, you can zoom in or out by choosing one of seven preset magnification levels, or you can use the Percent spin control to set the zoom level precisely. All zoom options are available in Normal view. In Slide Sorter view, some zoom options are available, but the Fit slide to current window tool is not.

Viewing Multiple Presentations at Once

You can have multiple presentations open at the same time in PowerPoint, and you can arrange their windows so that they are all visible at once. This makes it easy to drag-and-drop content between windows, and also to compare different versions of a presentation. In the following exercise you will open two presentations and arrange them.

STEP BY STEP   **Arrange Multiple Presentation Windows**

@ The *Job Fair 1* file is available on the book companion website or in WileyPLUS.

USE the presentation that is open from the previous exercise.

1. Click the **File** tab.

2. Click **Open**. The Open dialog box appears.

CERTIFICATION READY   **1.2.1**

How do you work with multiple presentation windows simultaneously?

3. Locate and open *Job Fair 1*. The presentation appears on your screen.

4. Click the **View** tab.

5. Click **Arrange All** in the Window command group. The presentations appear side-by-side, as in Figure 1-24.

Figure 1-24

Two presentations open side-by-side

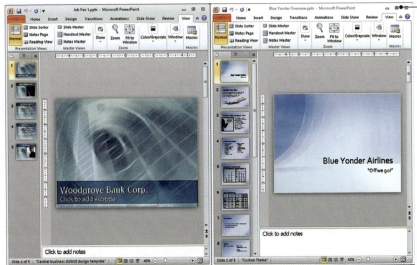

Maximize button

6. Use the Close button to close the Job Fair presentation, as you learned in "Closing a Presentation" earlier in this lesson.

7. In the Blue Yonder Overview window, click the **Maximize** button 🔲 in the upper-right corner. The PowerPoint window once again fills the screen.

PAUSE. LEAVE the presentation open for the next exercise.

Moving Between Slides

PowerPoint provides a number of methods for moving through a presentation in different views. You can move from one slide to another with either the mouse or the keyboard. You can specify that a certain slide should be displayed, or you can browse the available slides to identify the one you want based on its content.

Using the Mouse to Scroll Through a Presentation

PowerPoint's scroll bars let you move up and down through your presentation. When you drag the scroll box in the Slide pane, PowerPoint displays a ScreenTip with the slide number and slide title to show which slide will appear on screen when you release the mouse button. Click the scroll buttons to move up or down one line or one slide at a time, depending on the current zoom level. Click and hold a scroll button to move more quickly or drag a scroll box to move even more quickly. In this exercise, you use the mouse to scroll through a PowerPoint presentation.

STEP BY STEP   **Scroll Through a Presentation Using the Mouse**

USE the presentation that is open and maximized from the previous exercise.

1. Click the **scroll down** button on the right side of the Slide pane, as shown in Figure 1-25. Because the zoom level is set at Fit Slide to Current Window, slide 2 appears on the screen.

Figure 1-25

Scroll tools

Separate scroll bar for
Slides/Outline pane

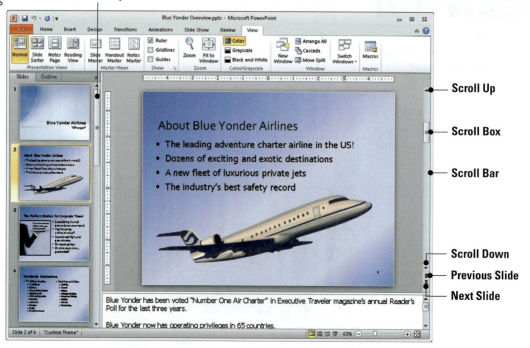

Scroll Up

Scroll Box

Scroll Bar

Scroll Down

Previous Slide

Next Slide

2. Use the zoom control to change the zoom level to 100%, then click the **scroll down** button twice. Because the slide is now larger than the Slide pane, the scroll button scrolls the slide down in small increments instead of jumping to the next slide.

3. Click the **Fit to Window** button in the Zoom command group on the View tab Ribbon.

4. At the bottom of the scroll bar, click the **Next Slide** button twice. Slide 3 appears, and then slide 4 appears.

5. In the Slides tab of the Slides/Outline pane, scroll down to locate slide 5, and click it. The selected slide appears in the Slide pane, as shown in Figure 1-26.

Figure 1-26

Click a slide's thumbnail image
on the Slides tab to jump
to that slide

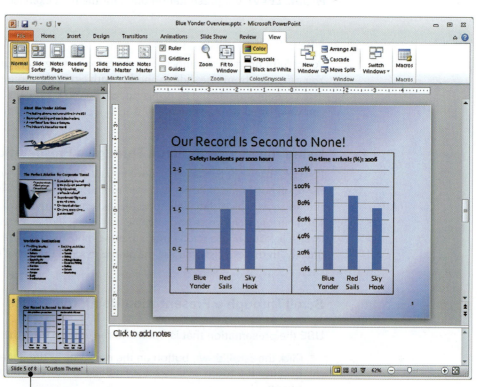

The current slide's number
appears on the status bar

Take Note The current slide's number always appears in the lower-left corner of the status bar.

6. Point to the scroll box that appears to the right of the Slides/Outline pane, and then drag the scroll box all the way down to the bottom of the scroll bar. The last slide (slide 8) appears on the Slides tab, but slide 5 remains visible in the Slide pane.

7. Click the **Previous Slide** button (at the bottom right of the Slide pane, as shown earlier in Figure 1-25). Slide 4 appears in the Slide pane; notice that the slide also appears highlighted on the Slides tab.

8. Click the scroll box that appears to the right of the Slide pane, and then drag the scroll box all the way up to the top of the scroll bar. You return to the beginning of the presentation.

PAUSE. LEAVE the presentation open for the next exercise.

In Normal view, both the Slide pane and the Slides/Outline pane have scroll bars, buttons, and boxes. If there is text in the Notes pane, scroll tools will appear there to let you move up and down through the text, if necessary. In Slide Sorter view and Notes Page view, scroll tools will appear on the right side of the window if they are needed.

In Normal view, you can click the Previous Slide button to move up to the previous slide and click the Next Slide button to move to the following slide.

Using the Keyboard to Move Through a Presentation

Your keyboard's cursor control keys let you jump from one slide to another, as long as no text or object is selected on a slide. If text is selected, the arrow keys move the insertion point within the text; however, the Page Up, Page Down, Home, and End keys will still let you move from slide to slide. In this exercise, you practice using the keyboard to navigate through presentations.

STEP BY STEP **Move Through a Presentation Using the Keyboard**

USE the presentation that is open from the previous exercise.

1. With slide 1 visible in Normal view in the Slide pane, press **Page Down** on your keyboard. Slide 2 appears.

2. Press **Page Down** to jump to slide 3.

3. Press **Page Down** to jump to slide 4.

4. Press **Page Up** to go back to slide 3.

5. Press **Page Up** to move up to slide 2.

6. Press **Page Up** to view slide 1.

7. Press **End** to jump to slide 8, the last slide in the presentation.

8. Press **Home** to return to slide 1.

PAUSE. LEAVE the presentation open to use in the next exercise.

Working with Text

Text is not typed directly onto a slide in PowerPoint, but instead is placed in **text boxes**. A text box is, as the name implies, a box that holds text that you type into it. Most of the available slide layouts have one or more placeholders that become text boxes when you type text into them, and you can also add more text boxes manually to slides, as you will learn in Lesson 3. Text can be placed on a slide either by typing it directly into a text box or placeholder, or by typing in the Outline pane in Normal view. In the following exercises, you will practice adding text to a placeholder; adding text to the Outline tab; selecting, replacing, and deleting text on a slide; and copying and moving text from one slide to another.

CERTIFICATION
READY 2.5.4

How do you add text to a placeholder box?

Adding Text to a Placeholder

In this exercise, you practice entering text in **a placeholder**, which is a box that can hold either text or a graphic object. The placeholders available depend on the slide layout. In the Blue Yonder presentation, slide 1 is an example of a Title Slide layout; it contains two placeholders—one for the title and one for the subtitle. Placeholders make it easy to add text—just click in the placeholder, and then type the text.

STEP BY STEP   Add Text to a Text Placeholder

USE the presentation that is open from the previous exercise.

1. Click the **Home** tab. On slide 1, click at the beginning of the slide's title (Blue Yonder Airlines). The borders of the title's placeholder appear, as shown in Figure 1-27, and a blinking insertion point appears before the word *Blue*.

Figure 1-27

The title placeholder and insertion point

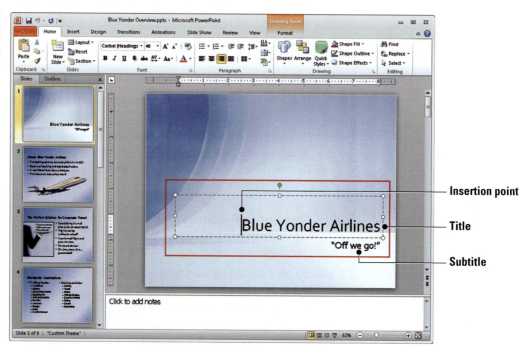

2. Click the slide's **subtitle**, which is the second line of text. The subtitle's placeholder appears, as does the insertion point.

3. Go to slide 4 by clicking the slide in the Slides/Outline pane, or by pressing Page Down until it appears.

4. Click after the word *Snorkeling* in the second column. The insertion point appears.

5. Press **Enter** to start a new line, and type **Scuba**.

6. Press **Enter**, and then type **Sightseeing**. Your slide should look like the one shown in Figure 1-28.

Figure 1-28

Slide 4 with added text

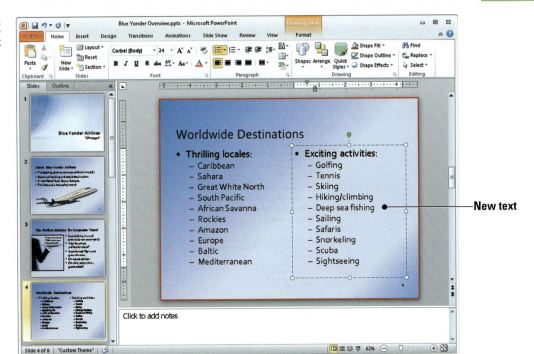

New text

PAUSE. LEAVE the presentation open for the next exercise.

Adding Text on the Outline Tab

Working on the Outline tab is like working in a word processor. PowerPoint displays the text from each slide on the Outline tab, without any backgrounds, placeholders, or anything else that might distract you from your writing. You can navigate a presentation on the Outline tab the same way you use the Slides tab—scroll to the desired slide's outline, and then click it. Here, you practice adding text on the Outline tab.

Add Text on the Outline Tab

USE the presentation that is open from the previous exercise.

1. Go to slide 8. This slide is supposed to contain contact information, but the mailing address and telephone number are missing.
2. In the Slides/Outline pane, click the **Outline** tab. Because slide 8 is the current slide, its text is highlighted on the tab.

Take Note   Remember that you can adjust the Zoom level for the Outline tab, or any other pane, as needed if the content is not shown at a convenient size for working with it.

3. On the Outline tab, click after the word *Airlines* to place the insertion point there.
4. Press **Enter** to start a new line.
5. On the new line, type **12 Ferris St.**, and then press **Enter**. As you type the new text on the Outline tab, notice that it appears on the slide.
6. Type **Diehard, TN 34567**, and then press **Enter**.
7. Type **(707) 555-AWAY**. Your slide should look like the one shown in Figure 1-29.

Figure 1-29

Text added to the Outline tab
appears on the slide

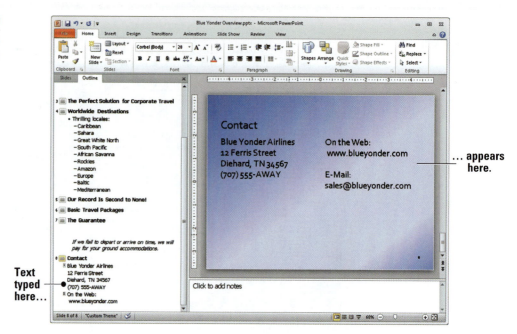

Figure 1-29

Text added to the Outline tab
appears on the slide

8. In the Slides/Outline pane, click the **Slides** tab.

PAUSE. LEAVE the presentation open for the next exercise.

Selecting, Replacing, and Deleting Text

You can edit, replace, and delete text directly on a slide. First, you must select the text to let PowerPoint know you want to edit it. You can select any amount of text by dragging the mouse pointer across it. When you move the mouse pointer over text, it changes to an **I-beam pointer**, a vertically oriented pointer that resembles the letter I. This pointer makes it easy to select text precisely. In this exercise, you practice editing text in PowerPoint.

STEP BY STEP
Select, Replace, and Delete Text

USE the presentation that is open from the previous exercise.

1. Go to slide 3, and in the fourth item of the bulleted list on the right, double-click the word **advisor** to select it, as shown in Figure 1-30.

Figure 1-30

Selected text

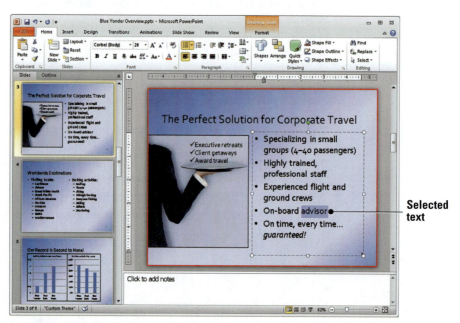

2. While the text is selected, type **concierge**. The new text replaces the selected text.

3. Go to slide 7, and select the word **ground** by dragging the mouse pointer over it. (The mouse pointer changes from an arrow to an I-beam whenever it is in a text placeholder, as shown in Figure 1-31.)

Figure 1-31

Selecting text and the I-beam pointer

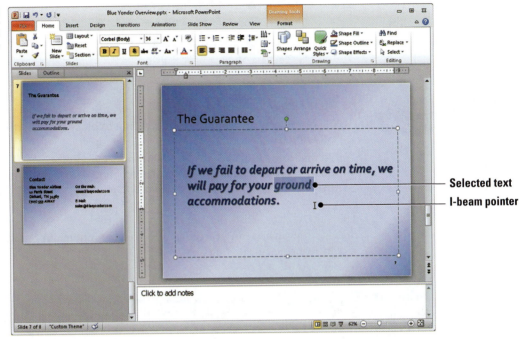

Figure 1-31

Selecting text and the I-beam pointer

4. Press **Delete** to delete the word from the slide.

PAUSE. LEAVE the presentation open for the next exercise.

Whenever you select text in PowerPoint—whether it is a single character or all the text on a slide—it is highlighted with a colored background. Once the text is selected, you can type new text in its place or delete it.

Take Note   Only text from text-based placeholders appears in the Outline pane; text from manually created text boxes (see Lesson 2) and from graphics and charts does not appear.

Copying and Moving Text from One Slide to Another

In this exercise, you practice copying and moving text from one slide to another, using the Copy, Cut, and Paste commands. You can use these commands on many kinds of objects in PowerPoint, including pictures, charts, and placeholders. Don't be surprised if these commands become your most frequently used tools, because they can save you a great deal of typing.

STEP BY STEP   **Copy and Move Text from One Slide to Another**

USE the presentation that is open from the previous exercise.

1. Go to slide 2, and in the slide's title placeholder, select **Blue Yonder Airlines** by dragging the mouse pointer across the text.

2. On the Home tab, click the **Copy** button, as shown in Figure 1-32.

Figure 1-32

Clipboard tools

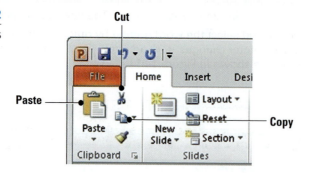

Another Way

You can issue the Copy command by pressing Ctrl+C.

3. Go to slide 7.

4. Click **between the two words of the title** to place the insertion point before the word *Guarantee*.

5. On the Home tab, click the **Paste** button. PowerPoint inserts the copied text at the insertion point's position, as shown in Figure 1-33. Press the **Spacebar** if necessary to insert a space before the word *Guarantee*.

Take Note

The Paste Options icon that appears near the pasted text in Figure 1-33 opens a menu when clicked; from that menu you can choose pasting options. In this case you will ignore the icon, accepting the default pasting options.

Figure 1-33

Selected text has been copied to slide 7

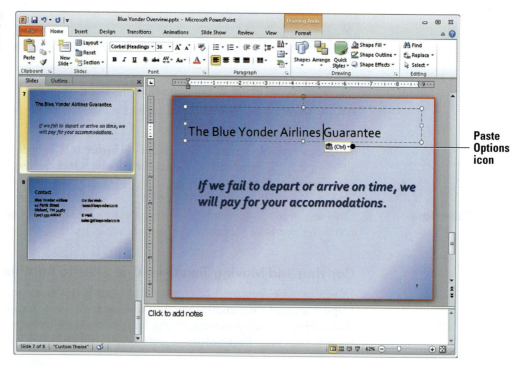

Paste Options icon

Another Way

You can issue the Paste command by pressing Ctrl+V.

Another Way

You can issue the Cut command by pressing Ctrl+X.

6. Go to slide 3.

7. Select the last item of the bulleted list on the right side of the slide.

8. On the Home tab, click the **Cut** button. The selected item is removed from the list.

9. Go to slide 2.

10. Click below the last item of the bulleted list, just above the airplane's tail.

11. On the Home tab, click the **Paste** button. The item appears at the bottom of the list.

12. Click anywhere in the blank area around the slide to clear the placeholder's border from the screen. Your slide should look like the one shown in Figure 1-34.

Figure 1-34

Selected text has been
moved to slide 2

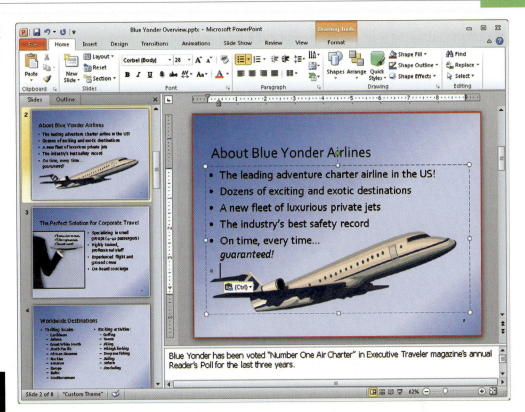

CERTIFICATION
R E A D Y   **2.5.6**

How do you copy and paste
text?

PAUSE. LEAVE the presentation open for the next exercise.

Printing a Presentation

PowerPoint's Print command sends the currently open presentation to the printer. The default settings produce a printout of the entire presentation, one slide per page, on whatever printer is set up in Windows as the default.

STEP BY STEP   **Print a Presentation with the Default Settings**

USE the presentation that is open from the previous exercise.

Another Way
You can press
Ctrl+P instead of steps 1 and 2.

1. Click the **File** tab.
2. Click **Print**. Print options appear. You will learn about them in Lesson 2; leave the defaults set for now.
3. Click the **Print** button. PowerPoint prints the entire presentation, using the default print settings, assuming your PC has at least one printer set up.

 Ref   Printing options are discussed in Lesson 2.

PAUSE. LEAVE the document open to use in the next exercise.

Saving an Edited Presentation

Whenever you work on a presentation, you should save it to a disk—especially if you have made changes that you want to keep. In this exercise, you will practice saving a presentation with a different file name, in native PowerPoint 2010 format.

Ref   In Lesson 10, you will learn how to save a presentation in other formats for sharing with people who might not have PowerPoint 2010 installed.

Save an Edited Presentation

USE the presentation that is open from the previous exercise.

1. Click the **File** tab to open Backstage view.
2. Click **Save As**. The Save As dialog box appears, as shown in Figure 1-35. The file location defaults to whatever location was most recently accessed.

Figure 1-35

Save As dialog box

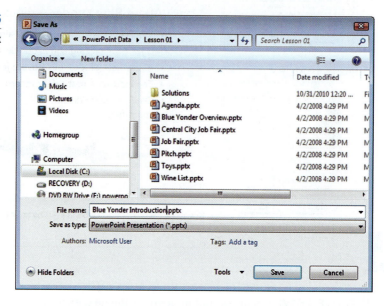

3. Select the location where you want to save your files (ask your instructor for guidance), and then type *Blue Yonder Introduction* in the File name box.

Take Note   Ask your instructor if you should append your initials to the end of each file name for the exercises in this book, to keep your files separate from those of other students.

4. Click **Save**.
5. Click the **Close** button to close the presentation.

PAUSE. LEAVE PowerPoint open to use in the next exercise.

   Ref

Presentations created in PowerPoint 2007 and 2010 are incompatible with earlier versions of PowerPoint. However, you can save in an earlier format for backward compatibility; that skill is covered in Lesson 2.

When you need to save an existing presentation in a new location or with a different file name, use the Save As command. In the Save As dialog box, you can specify a different disk drive and folder to store the file; you can also give the file a different name in the File name box. After the presentation is saved in the new location and with its new file name, you can click the Save button on the Quick Access Toolbar when you need to resave the file.

Take Note   You can also download a free conversion utility for earlier versions of PowerPoint that will allow them to open files in PowerPoint 2007/2010 format. See http://office.microsoft.com/en-us/office-2003-resource-kit/office-converter-pack-HA001151358.aspx?redir=0 for details.

Exiting PowerPoint

When you exit PowerPoint, the program closes and is removed from your computer's memory. In this exercise, you will practice exiting PowerPoint.

Exit PowerPoint

GET READY. In order to exit PowerPoint, do the following.

1. Click the **File** tab.
2. Click **Exit**. PowerPoint closes.

SKILL SUMMARY

In This Lesson You Learned How To:	Exam Objective	Objective Number
Work in the PowerPoint window.	Work with multiple presentation windows simultaneously.	1.2.1
	Show the Quick Access Toolbar (QAT) below the ribbon.	1.3.1
Work with an existing presentation.	Adjust views by using the ribbon.	1.1.1
	Adjust views by status bar commands.	1.1.2
	Enter text in a placeholder text box.	2.5.4
	Copy and paste text.	2.5.6

Knowledge Assessment

Matching

Match the term in Column 1 to its description in Column 2.

Column 1		Column 2	
1.	Tab	a.	Includes the Slide, Notes, and Slide/Outline panes
2.	Ribbon	b.	A small toolbar that appears when you point to selected text
3.	Normal view	c.	Shows the keyboard key that will issue a command
4.	Current slide	d.	To highlight text for editing
5.	Backstage view	e.	A set of related tools on the Ribbon
6.	Mini toolbar	f.	Displays commands for managing files
7.	Placeholder	g.	The slide you are editing
8.	KeyTip	h.	A Ribbon tool that opens a dialog box
9.	Dialog box launcher	i.	A large toolbar that presents tools in related groups
10.	Select	j.	A box, built into many slides, that holds text or an object

True/False

Circle T if the statement is true or F if the statement is false.

T   F   1. If you need more room on the screen, you can hide the Ribbon.

T   F   2. When you start PowerPoint, the last presentation you worked on appears on the screen.

T   F   3. When you save a presentation that has been previously saved, clicking the Save button on the Quick Access Toolbar reopens the Save As dialog box.

T   F   4. The Quick Access Toolbar appears faint, but turns brighter as the mouse pointer gets closer.

T   F   5. To close a dialog box without accepting any changes you may have made to it, click the Cancel button.

T   F   **6.** You can use the Undo command to reverse the last action you took.

T   F   **7.** To print a presentation, open Backstage view and click Print.

T   F   **8.** Backstage view gives you access to all of PowerPoint's design tools.

T   F   **9.** You can use the Cut and Paste commands to move text from one slide to another slide.

T   F   **10.** In Normal view, PowerPoint displays five different panes for viewing different aspects of your slides.

Competency Assessment

Project 1-1: The Central City Job Fair

As personnel manager for Woodgrove Bank, you have accepted an invitation to give a presentation at a local job fair. Your goal is to recruit applicants for positions as bank tellers. You have created the presentation but need to finish it.

GET READY. LAUNCH PowerPoint if it is not already running.

@ The *Job Fair 1* file is available on the companion website or in WileyPLUS.

1. Click the **File** tab and open the presentation named *Job Fair 1* from the data files for this lesson.

2. Save the presentation as *Central City Job Fair*.

3. On slide 1, click in the subtitle box to place the insertion point there, and then type **Central City Job Fair**. Go to slide 2.

4. In the title of slide 2, select the words **Woodgrove Bank** by dragging the mouse pointer over them, and then replace the selected text by typing **Us**.

5. In the bulleted list, click after the word *assets* to place the insertion point there.

6. Press **Enter** to move the insertion point down to a new, blank line.

7. Type **Voted "Best Local Bank" by City Magazine, 2010**. The new text will wrap to fit in the box.

8. Click the **Next Slide** button to go to slide 3. In the slide's outline, select the words *Help Wanted* (do not select the colon), and then press **Delete** to delete the text.

9. Type **Now Hiring**.

10. Click at the end of the first item in the bulleted list, and then press **Enter** to create a new line in the list.

11. Type **Responsible for cash drawer and station bookkeeping**.

12. Click the **Slides** tab, and then press **Page Down** to go to slide 4.

13. Select the last item in the bulleted list by dragging the mouse pointer across it.

14. On the Ribbon, click the **Home** tab, if necessary, and then click the **Cut** button. On the Slides tab, click **slide 5**.

15. Click at the end of the last item in the bulleted list to place the insertion point there, and then press **Enter**.

16. On the Ribbon, click the **Paste** button. The item you cut from slide 4 is pasted into slide 5.

17. **SAVE** the presentation and **CLOSE** the file.

LEAVE PowerPoint open for the next project.

Project 1-2: Messenger Service

Consolidated Messenger is a new company offering in-town courier service to corporate and private customers. As the company's owner, you want to tell as many people as possible about your new service, and a presentation can help you do it. You need to review your presentation, make some minor changes, and print it.

GET READY. LAUNCH PowerPoint if it is not already running.

The *Pitch* file is available on the companion website or in WileyPLUS.

1. Click the **File** tab and open the presentation named *Pitch* from the data files for this lesson, and save it as *Messenger Pitch*.
2. Read slide 1. On the Slides tab, click **slide 2** and read it.
3. Click the **scroll down** box to go to slide 3, and then read it.
4. Click the **Next Slide** button to go to slide 4, and then read it.
5. Press **Page Down** to go to slide 5, and then read it.
6. Press **Enter** to go to slide 6, and then read it.
7. Press **Home** to return to the beginning of the presentation.
8. On slide 1, select the words **and Delivery** by dragging the mouse pointer over them.
9. Press **Delete** to delete the selected text from the subtitle. Go to slide 2.
10. On slide 2, select the word **delayed** and type **scheduled** in its place.
11. Select the third item in the bulleted list (**24-hour emergency service**) by dragging the mouse pointer over it.
12. On the Home tab of the Ribbon, click the **Copy** button. Go to slide 5.
13. On slide 5, click at the end of the last item in the bulleted list to place the insertion point there.
14. Press **Enter** to move the insertion point down to a new, blank line. On the Ribbon, click the **Paste** button.
15. Click at the end of the newly pasted line to move the insertion point there, and then type **$250**. Go to slide 6.
16. On slide 6, click at the end of the last line of text in the left-hand column, and then press **Enter**.
17. Type **555-1087 (daytime)**, and then press **Enter**.
18. Type **555-1088 (emergency)**, and then press **Enter**.
19. Type **555-1089 (fax)**.
20. Go to slide 1. Click the **File** tab.
21. When Backstage view opens, click **Print**. Then click the **Print** button to print with the default settings.
22. **SAVE** the presentation and **CLOSE** the file.

LEAVE PowerPoint open for the next project.

Proficiency Assessment

Project 1-3: The Big Meeting

You are the director of documentation at Litware, Inc., which develops software for use in elementary schools. You have scheduled a conference with the writing staff and are working on an agenda for the meeting. Because the agenda is a single PowerPoint slide, you can display it on a projection screen for reference during the meeting.

The *Agenda* file is available on the companion website or in WileyPLUS.

1. **OPEN** the *Agenda* file from the data files for this lesson and save it as *Final Agenda*.
2. Copy the second line of the bulleted list and paste the copy below the original as a new bullet point.
3. In the newly pasted line, replace the word *Upcoming* with **Revised**.
4. On the Outline tab, add a new line to the end of the agenda. On the new line, type **Adjourn**.

5. Print the presentation.
6. **SAVE** the presentation, then **CLOSE** the file.
LEAVE PowerPoint open for the next project.

Project 1-4: Job Fair, Part 2

You have decided to make some last-minute changes to your presentation before going to the job fair.

@ The *Job Fair 2* file is available on the companion website or in WileyPLUS.

1. **OPEN** *Job Fair 2* from the data files for this lesson and save it as *Final Job Fair*.
2. Copy the word *Woodgrove* on slide 1. In the title of slide 2, delete the word *Us* and paste the copied word in its place.
3. On slide 2, change the word *owned* to managed.
4. On slide 4, add the line References a must to the bottom of the bulleted list.
5. Print the presentation.
6. **SAVE** the presentation, then **CLOSE** the file.
LEAVE PowerPoint open for the next project.

Mastery Assessment

Project 1-5: Price Fixing

You are the general manager of the restaurant at Coho Winery. It's time to update the staff on the restaurant's new wine selections and prices, and a slide show is a good way to give everyone the details. An easy way to handle this job is to open last season's presentation and update it with new wines and prices.

@ The *Wine List* file is available on the companion website or in WileyPLUS.

1. **OPEN** *Wine List* from the data files for this lesson and save it as *New Wine List*.
2. Move *Coho Premium Chardonnay—$29.99* from slide 2 to the bottom of slide 4.
3. On slide 3, increase the price of every wine by one dollar.
4. Print the presentation.
5. **SAVE** the presentation, then **CLOSE** the file.
LEAVE PowerPoint open for the next project.

Project 1-6: A Trip to Toyland

As a product manager for Tailspin Toys, you introduce new products to many other people in the company, such as the marketing and sales staff. You need to finalize a presentation about several new toys.

@ The *Toys* file is available on the companion website or in WileyPLUS.

1. **OPEN** *Toys* from the data files for this lesson and save it as *New Toys*.
2. Copy *List Price: $14.99* on slide 2 and paste it at the bottom of the bulleted lists on slides 3 and 4.
3. Change the teddy bear's name from *Rory* to George.
4. Change the top's speed from *800* to 1,200.
5. Print the presentation.
6. **SAVE** the presentation and **CLOSE** the file.
EXIT PowerPoint.

INTERNET READY

Use PowerPoint Help to access online information about the new features in PowerPoint 2010. *Up to* *Speed with PowerPoint 2010* provides a short online course or demo explaining the new features. Browse these or other topics in PowerPoint's Help online.

LESSON SKILL MATRIX

Skill	Exam Objective	Objective Number
Creating a New Blank Presentation	Enter text in a Placeholder text box.	2.5.4
Saving a Presentation	Use PowerPoint Save options.	1.4.2
Creating a Presentation from a Template		
Adding, Deleting, and Organizing Slides	Delete multiple slides simultaneously. Duplicate selected slides. Include non-contiguous slides.	2.3.5 2.3.4 2.3.6
Creating a Presentation from Existing Content	Reuse a slide from a slide library. Use paste special.	2.3.3 2.5.7
Adding Notes to Your Slides		
Printing a Presentation	Adjust print settings.	7.3.1

KEY TERMS

- contiguous
- handout
- indent level
- layout
- non-contiguous
- note
- Presenter view
- slide library
- template
- themes
- thumbnails

Northwind Traders is a retailer of high-quality outdoor apparel and accessories for men, women, and children. The company has six stores in the Minneapolis–St. Paul area and a thriving online presence. As an assistant general manager, you help oversee the company's daily operations, hire and train new employees, and develop strategic plans. You also perform day-to-day functions assigned by the general manager. Your job frequently requires you to present information to an audience—for example, when training new workers on company policies or when providing executives with information about revenue or expenses. These duties often require you to create presentations from scratch, and PowerPoint 2007 lets you do that in several ways. In this lesson, you will learn different methods for creating presentations. You will also learn how to organize the slides in a presentation, add notes to your slides, select printing options, preview a slide show, and save a presentation for the first time.

SOFTWARE ORIENTATION

Microsoft PowerPoint's New Presentation Dialog Box

PowerPoint's New Presentation window gives you many choices for creating a new presentation. Figure 2-1 shows the New Presentation window. It is accessed by clicking the File tab to enter Backstage view, then clicking New.

Figure 2-1

New Presentation window

Click here to start with a blank presentation.

Select one of these categories.

The templates or themes in the chosen category appear here.

The Preview pane shows what your selected theme or template looks like.

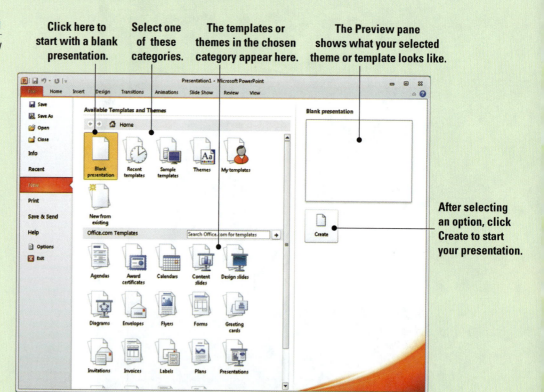

After selecting an option, click Create to start your presentation.

This window enables you to create a new, blank presentation; work from a template or theme stored on your computer; search for templates online; or create a new presentation from an existing one.

CREATING A NEW BLANK PRESENTATION

The Bottom Line

When you start PowerPoint, a new, blank presentation appears, containing a single slide. The fastest and simplest way to create a new presentation is to start with a blank presentation. You can add text to the presentation, and then format the slides later.

Creating a Blank Presentation

You can use the single slide that opens with a new, blank presentation to begin creating your new presentation. In this exercise, you will learn how to open a blank presentation.

STEP BY STEP   **Create a Blank Presentation**

GET READY. Before you begin these steps, make sure that your computer is on. Log on, if necessary.

1. **START** PowerPoint, if the program is not already running.
2. Click the **File** tab. Backstage view opens.
3. Click **New**. The New Presentation window opens, as shown previously in Figure 2-1.

Take Note   You need to use the New Presentation window only when another presentation is open, when no presentation is open, or when you want to create a new presentation based on a template or theme.

4. In the Available Templates and Themes pane, click the **Blank Presentation** icon, then click the **Create** button in the lower-right corner of the New Presentation window. A new, blank presentation appears in Normal view, as shown in Figure 2-2.

Figure 2-2

A blank presentation begins with a title slide

The thumbnail of the slide appears blank because the empty text placeholders do not appear on it.

The default slide uses the Title Slide layout.

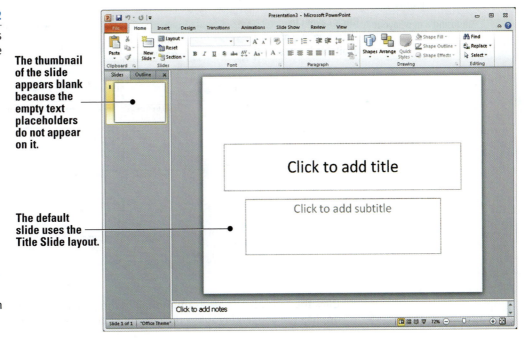

Another Way
Press Ctrl+N to open a new, blank presentation without using the New Presentation window. If another presentation is already open, the blank presentation opens in a separate window.

PAUSE. LEAVE the blank presentation open to use in the next exercise.

There are two advantages to using a blank presentation to start a slide show. First, PowerPoint displays a blank presentation every time the program starts, so you always have immediate access to the first slide of a new presentation. Second, because the presentation is not formatted (meaning there are no backgrounds, colors, or pictures), you can focus on writing your text. Many experienced PowerPoint users prefer to start with a blank presentation because they know they can format their slides after the text is finished.

Changing a Slide's Layout

Most slides have a **layout**—a predefined arrangement of placeholders for text or objects (such as charts or pictures). PowerPoint has a variety of built-in layouts that you can use at any time. Layouts are shown in the Layout gallery as **thumbnails**—small pictures showing each available layout. Choose the layout that is best suited to display the text or objects you want to place on the slide. You can change a slide's layout at any time to arrange text or objects on the slide exactly the way you want. The following exercise shows you how to apply a different layout to the current slide.

STEP BY STEP	Choose a Different Layout

USE the new, blank presentation that is still open from the previous exercise.

WileyPLUS Extra! features an online tutorial of this task.

1. Click the **Home** tab to make it active, if necessary, then click **Layout**. A drop-down menu (called a *gallery*) appears, displaying PowerPoint's default layouts, as shown in Figure 2-3. The title of the gallery is Office Theme, indicating that all these layouts come from the default theme (named Office).

Figure 2-3

Choosing a new layout

Click Layout to open a gallery of available layouts.

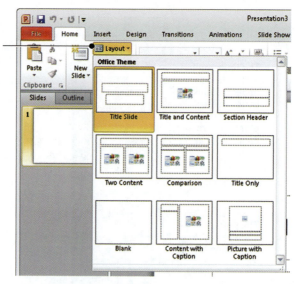

2. Click the **Title and Content** thumbnail in the gallery. The gallery closes and PowerPoint applies the chosen layout to the current slide, as shown in Figure 2-4.

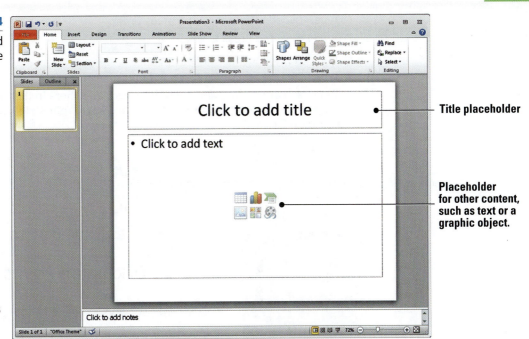

Figure 2-4

The new layout applied to the current slide

Title placeholder

Placeholder for other content, such as text or a graphic object.

Another Way
To change a slide's layout, right-click a blank area of the slide outside a placeholder. When the shortcut menu opens, point to Layout, and then click a layout.

PAUSE. LEAVE the presentation open to use in the next exercise.

In this exercise, you chose the Title and Content layout, which contains a placeholder for the slide's title and a second placeholder that can display text, a picture, a table, or some other kind of object.

Ref   You will work with other slide layouts in Lesson 4.

You can change a slide's layout whether the slide is blank or contains text. If the slide already has text, PowerPoint will fit the text into the new layout's placeholders. If the new layout does not have an appropriate placeholder for the existing content, the existing content remains on the slide, but is not part of the layout.

Adding Text to a Blank Slide

If a blank slide has one or more text placeholders, you can easily add text to the slide. To enter text, just click the sample text in the placeholder, and then type your text. In this exercise, you will enter text into a blank slide's placeholders to create a set of discussion points for a meeting of store managers. The slide you work with in this exercise has a title placeholder and a content placeholder that can hold text and other types of content.

STEP BY STEP   **Add Text to a Blank Slide**

USE the slide that is still on the screen from the preceding exercise.

1. Click the title placeholder at the top of the slide. The text *Click to add title* disappears and a blinking insertion point appears in the placeholder.
2. Type **Discussion Points**.
3. Click the text at the top of the lower placeholder. The words *Click to add text* disappear and the insertion point appears.
4. Type **Customer surveys**, then press **Enter** to move the insertion point down to a new line.
5. Type **Inventory tracking** and press **Enter**.

6. Type **Absenteeism policy** and press **Enter**.

7. Type **Break** and press **Enter**.

8. Type **Store security** and press **Enter**.

9. Type **Store closing procedures** and press **Enter**.

10. Type **Cash drawer management**, then click anywhere in the blank area outside the placeholder to clear its borders from the screen. Your slide should look like the one shown in Figure 2-5.

Figure 2-5

The completed slide

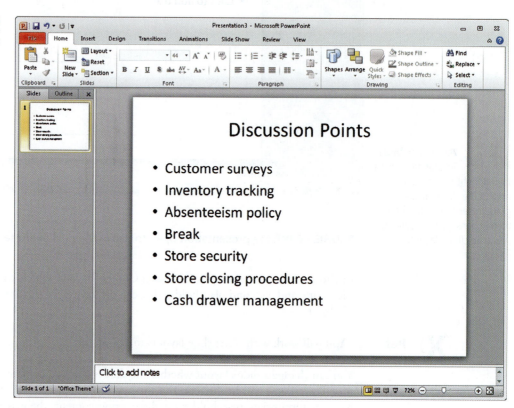

PAUSE. LEAVE the presentation open to use in the next exercise.

Take Note   If you click any of the icons in the lower placeholder, PowerPoint will display tools for adding non-text content, such as a table or chart. These types of content are covered in later lessons.

Even when a multiple-slide presentation is not needed at a meeting, displaying an agenda, a list of discussion points, or a list of breakout rooms can be helpful for the group.

SAVING A PRESENTATION

The Bottom Line   When you create a new presentation, it exists only in your computer's memory. If you want to keep the presentation, you must save it on a disk or to a network location or flash drive. After you save a file, you can close it, then reopen it again later and resume working on it. The following exercises show you how to save a new presentation to a disk, how to save the presentation in a different file format, and how to work with PowerPoint's Save options.

Saving a New Presentation for the First Time

When you save a presentation for the first time, PowerPoint displays the Save As dialog box so you can give the presentation a name before saving it. In this exercise, you will name and save the presentation you created earlier.

Save a New Presentation

USE the presentation that is still on the screen from the preceding exercise.

Another Way
When saving a presentation for the first time, you can open the Save As dialog box by pressing Ctrl+S.

1. On the Quick Access Toolbar, click **Save**. The Save As dialog box appears.
2. Navigate to the folder where you want to save your files.
3. Select the text in the File name box by dragging the mouse pointer over it, and then press **Delete** to delete it.
4. Type **Managers Meeting**, as shown in Figure 2-6.

Figure 2-6

Saving the presentation for the first time

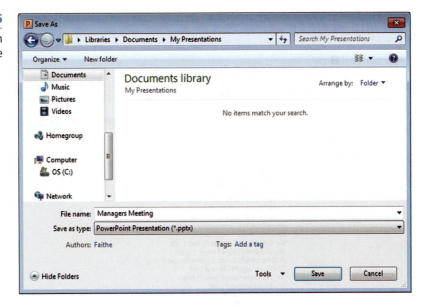

5. Click **Save**. PowerPoint saves the presentation in the folder you chose, under the name you have given it.

PAUSE. LEAVE the presentation open to use in the next exercise.

When you save a presentation (or any type of document), be sure to give it a name that describes its contents. This will help you identify your presentations more easily when you are trying to find the right one.

Choosing a Different File Format

PowerPoint can save presentations in several different file formats. In this exercise, you will save your presentation in a format that is compatible with earlier versions of PowerPoint.

Choose a Different File Format

USE the *Managers Meeting* presentation that is still open from the previous exercise.

1. Click the **File** tab, then click the **Save As** command. The Save As dialog box reappears.
2. Next to Save as Type, click the current type: **PowerPoint Presentation**. A menu of file types opens.

3. Click **PowerPoint 97-2003 Presentation**. The file type changes. See Figure 2-7.

Figure 2-7

Saving with a different file format

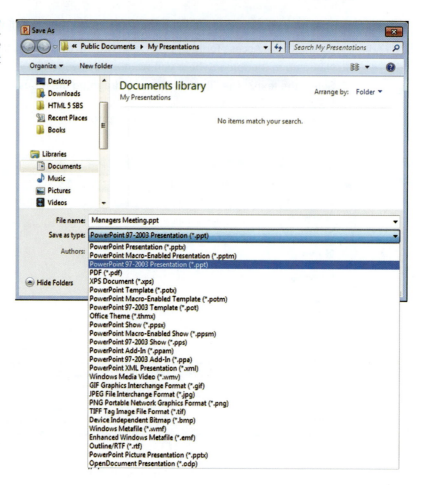

4. Navigate to the folder where you want to save your files. (This step is not necessary if you want to save the file in the same folder you used in the previous exercise.)

Take Note

Because you are saving the presentation in a different file format, it is not necessary to give it a new name. Files of different formats can have the same file name. This exercise renames it anyway.

5. Select the file's name in the File name box, delete the name, and then type **Old Format Discussion Points**.

6. Click **Save**, and then close the presentation.

PAUSE. LEAVE PowerPoint open to use in the next exercise.

By default, PowerPoint 2010 saves presentations in a type of XML format, which is not compatible with earlier versions of PowerPoint. If you want to be able to use a presentation with an older version of PowerPoint, you can save it by using the PowerPoint 97-2003 Presentation file format. (PowerPoint 2007 uses the same XML-based format as PowerPoint 2010, so no special version is necessary to share with users of PowerPoint 2007.)

You can save a presentation in other formats as well. For example, if you select the PowerPoint Show format, the presentation will always open in Slide Show view, rather than in Normal view. You can also save a presentation as a template, or as a series of graphics, or in a macro-enabled format.

 Ref

Lesson 10 covers the details of saving in many different formats, including saving slides as pictures and saving presentations in PDF or XPS format.

Working with Save Options

PowerPoint has settings that control the default file location, the default file format, and more. If you find yourself frequently changing the file location or file type when you save a presentation, it may be worth your time to change the settings in PowerPoint that specify the defaults. In the following exercise, you learn how to modify the application's save settings.

STEP BY STEP   **Set the Save Options**

Take Note   No presentation is open as you begin this exercise, but that's not important. These steps can be completed without having a presentation open.

GET READY. To set the save options, do the following:

1. Click the **File** tab and then click **Options**. The PowerPoint Options dialog box opens.

2. Click the **Save** category in the left panel of the dialog box. The Save Options appear in the right panel.

3. Click on the **Save Files In This Format drop-down list** and examine the available file types. See Figure 2-8. Do not change the current setting (PowerPoint Presentation).

Figure 2-8

Choices available for the default file format in which to save

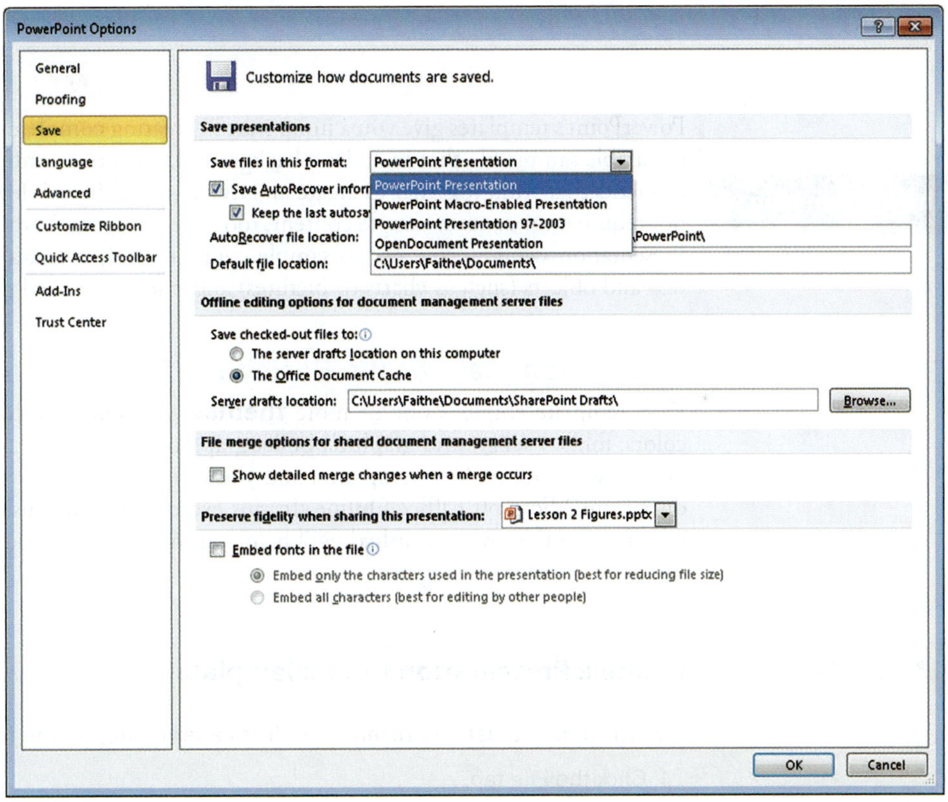

4. In the Default file location text box, take note of the location referenced.

Take Note   By default, files are stored in the Documents (or My Documents) folder for the current user. In Windows Vista and Windows 7, this is the C:\Users*username*\Documents folder, where username is the current user. That's what appears as the default in Figure 2-8, for example.

5. (Optional) Change the location in the Default file location text box to the location where you are storing your completed work for this course. If you do this, you will not have to change the location for saving and opening files every time you want to save or open files for class exercises and projects.

6. Click **OK** to close the dialog box.

7. Click **Save**, then close the presentation.

PAUSE. LEAVE PowerPoint open to use in the next exercise.

You can choose to create regular PowerPoint 2010 presentations, PowerPoint 97-2003 presentations, macro-enabled presentations, or OpenDocument presentations by default. OpenDocument is a widely accepted generic format for presentation files, useful for sharing files with people who use OpenOffice and other freeware office suites.

You can set a default save location of any accessible drive, including not only folders on your hard disk, but also network locations and removable drives. (It is not usually a good idea to set the default location to a drive that is not always available, however.) The location you specify will appear in both the Save As and Open dialog boxes by default.

Also in the save options, you can set an interval at which PowerPoint autosaves your work. Autosaving helps PowerPoint recover any work that would otherwise be lost if your PC shuts off or crashes while there are unsaved changes to a presentation. The default interval is 10 minutes.

CERTIFICATION
READY   **1.4.2**

How do you set save options in PowerPoint?

CREATING A PRESENTATION FROM A TEMPLATE

The Bottom Line

PowerPoint's templates give you a jump start in creating complete presentations. A **template** is a reusable sample file that includes a background, layouts, coordinating fonts, and other design elements that work together to create an attractive, finished slide show. Templates may (but are not required to) contain sample content, too. The templates in the Themes category in the New Presentation window contain no sample content—only formatting. You can insert your own text and objects (such as charts or pictures) and build a finished presentation very quickly.

Using a Template as the Basis for a Presentation

Each template employs one or more **themes**. A theme is a collection of settings including colors, fonts, background graphics, bullet graphics, and margin and placement settings. Power-Point has several built-in templates, and you can create your own templates or download new ones from Microsoft Office Online. In this exercise, you will use a built-in template to start a presentation that, when finished, will help you show pictures and descriptions of new products to a group of store managers.

STEP BY STEP   **Create a Presentation from a Template**

GET READY. To create a presentation from a template, do the following:

1. Click the **File** tab.

2. Click **New** in the left panel of Backstage view to open the New Presentation window.

3. Under Available Templates and Themes, click **Sample Templates**. Thumbnail images of the templates stored on your PC appear, as shown in Figure 2-9. A preview of the selected template appears in the Preview pane on the right side of the New Presentation window.

Figure 2-9

Selecting a sample template

Sample of template appears here.

Click Back to return to previous screen.

Select a template.

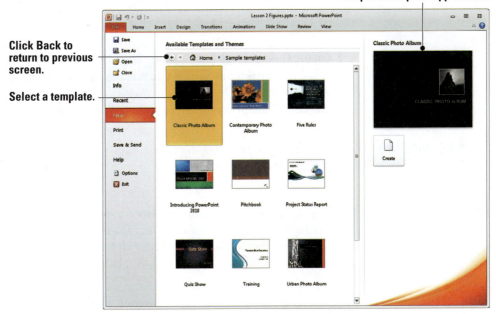

4. Click the **Classic Photo Album** thumbnail, then click **Create** in the Preview pane. PowerPoint opens a new presentation based on the selected template. It contains several sample slides with text and graphics.

5. On slide 1, select **CLASSIC PHOTO ALBUM** and type **NORTHWIND TRADERS** to replace it.

6. Click the text in the subtitle placeholder to place the insertion point there, and then type **New Product Preview**. See Figure 2-10.

Figure 2-10

Customizing the text on the first slide

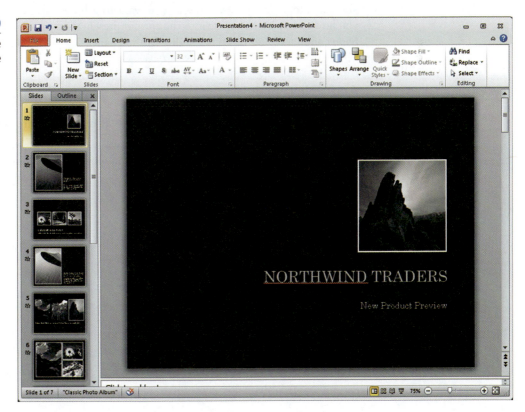

Take Note   In Figure 2-10, and perhaps on your screen too, NORTHWIND has a wavy red underline, indicating that the word is not in PowerPoint's dictionary. You can ignore that for now. Lesson 3 covers using the spell-check feature.

> 7. On the Quick Access Toolbar, click **Save**. The Save As dialog box appears.
> 8. Navigate to the folder where you want to save your files, then save the presentation with the file name **New Product Preview**.
>
> **PAUSE. LEAVE** the presentation open to use in the next exercise.

Take Note   You can change a presentation's theme from the Design tab; you don't have to create a new presentation based on a template just to get a new look. You will learn how to change themes in Lesson 4.

It is important to choose a template that is appropriate for your audience and your message. If you need to deliver business information to a group of managers, for example, choose a template that looks professional and does not have elements that will distract the audience from getting your message. Conversely, a whimsical template might work better for a group of young people.

A basic assortment of templates is available via Sample Templates, as you saw in the preceding exercise. These templates are stored on your hard disk, along with PowerPoint itself, and are always available. You can also access other templates online by selecting from the Office.com Templates section of the New Presentation window.

ADDING, DELETING, AND ORGANIZING SLIDES

The Bottom Line   A template's sample slides can provide a basic structure as a starting point, but you will probably want to make some changes. In PowerPoint it is easy to add, delete, and reorder the slides in a presentation to suit your unique needs.

Adding a New Slide to a Presentation

You can add as many new slides as you want to a presentation. The following exercise shows you how to insert a new slide into the current presentation in two different ways: using the New Slide command, and using the Slides/Outline pane.

STEP BY STEP   **Add a New Slide**

USE the **New Product Preview** presentation that is still open from the previous exercise.

> 1. On the Home tab, click the **New Slide button drop-down arrow**. A gallery opens, showing thumbnail images of the slide layouts that are available for this template, as shown in Figure 2-11.

Figure 2-11

New Slide gallery

Click the desired layout.

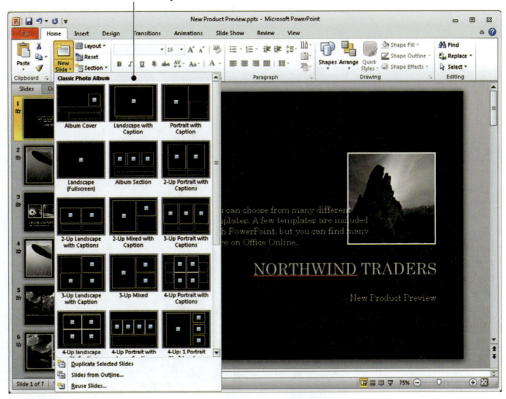

Figure 2-11

New Slide gallery

2. Scroll down to the bottom of the gallery, then click **Title and Content**.

Take Note   To view the New Slide gallery, you must click the New Slide button's drop-down arrow. If you click the face of the New Slide button, PowerPoint will insert the default new slide for the current template.

3. On the new slide, click the **title placeholder** and type **THIS YEAR'S NEW PRODUCTS**.

4. Click the sample text at the top of the second placeholder, and then type the following items, placing each item on its own line:

Women's jackets

Men's jackets

Boots

Backpacks

Flannel shirts

Fleece

Turtlenecks

Underwear

Socks

5. Click in the area surrounding the slide to clear the placeholder's border. When you are done, your slide should look like the one shown in Figure 2-12.

Figure 2-12

The inserted slide

6. On the View tab, click the **Normal** button to switch to Normal view, and in the Slides/Outline pane, click the **Outline** tab.

Take Note   Some of the slides in the Outline tab show no text in their Title placeholder; that's because this presentation is based on a photo album template.

7. Click to place the text insertion point after the word *Socks* in slide 2 and press **Enter**, creating a new paragraph. At this point the new paragraph is a bullet on slide 2.

8. Press **Shift+Tab**. The new paragraph is promoted into a new slide title.

9. Type **Clearance Items** and press **Enter**. A new paragraph appears. Because the previous paragraph was a slide title, the new one is too.

10. Press **Tab**. The new paragraph is indented so that it is a bullet on the Clearance Items slide.

11. Type the following items, pressing **Enter** after each one to place it in its own paragraph:

    Biking accessories

    Camping supplies

    Spelunking gear

12. After all the text is typed in for the new slide, it appears in the Outline as shown in Figure 2-13.

Figure 2-13

A slide added via the Outline

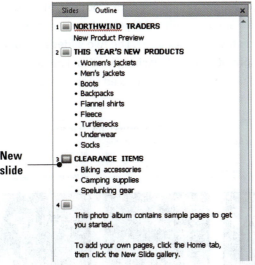

New slide

Another Way
With the Slides tab selected in the Slides/Outline pane, you can click to place a flashing horizontal line after an existing slide, and then press Enter to create a new blank slide that uses the same layout as the one before it.

PAUSE. LEAVE the presentation open to use in the next exercise.

Duplicating Selected Slides

If you want several similar slides in a presentation, you may be able to save some time by duplicating some of the slides and then modifying the copies. The following exercise shows how to select the slides you want to duplicate, even when they are non-contiguous, and make copies of them. You will also learn how to use the Duplicate Selected Slides command to make duplicates of slides.

STEP BY STEP   **Duplicate Non-Contiguous Slides**

USE the *New Product Preview* presentation that is still open from the previous exercise.

1. Click the **Slide Sorter** button on the View tab to switch to Slide Sorter view. The presentation's slides appear together in a single pane.

2. Change the Zoom level to 90% for the Slide Sorter pane by clicking the **minus sign** button at the left end of the Zoom slider. See Figure 2-14.

Figure 2-14

Slide Sorter view at 90% Zoom

Choose Slide Sorter view.

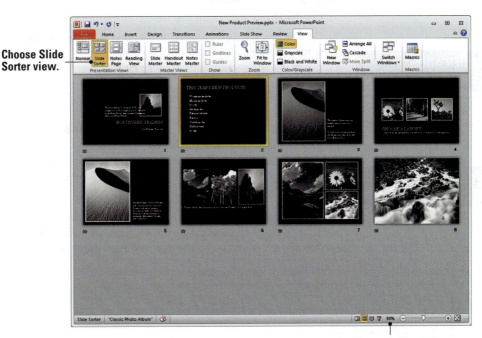

Set Zoom level to 90%.

Another Way
You can also press Ctrl+C to copy, and Ctrl+V to paste.

3. Click **slide 4**. A yellow outline appears around it, indicating that it is selected.
4. Hold down **Ctrl** and click **slide 7**. A yellow outline appears around it too.
5. Click the **Home** tab and click **Copy**. The two slides are copied to the Clipboard.
6. Click to the right of slide 9. A flashing vertical line appears there.
7. On the Home tab, click **Paste**. The copied slides are pasted after slide 9, as in Figure 2-15.

Figure 2-15

Copied slides are pasted

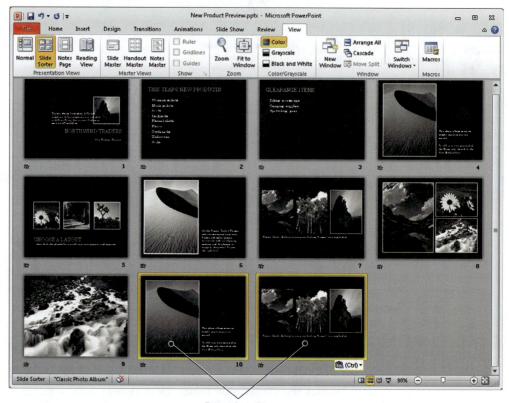

Pasted copies

8. Click **slide 2** to select it.
9. On the Home tab, open the **New Slide button's drop-down list**.
10. Click **Duplicate Selected Slides**. A copy of slide 2 is pasted directly following the original slide 2.
11. **SAVE** the presentation file and **CLOSE** it.

PAUSE. LEAVE PowerPoint open for the next exercise.

CERTIFICATION READY **2.3.4**

How do you select non-contiguous slides?

CERTIFICATION READY **2.3.6**

How do you duplicate selected slides?

Contiguous means "together." **Non-contiguous** slides are not adjacent to one another in the presentation. As you just learned, to select non-contiguous slides, hold down Ctrl as you click each one you want. To select contiguous slides, you can use the Shift type. Click the first slide in the group, and then hold down Shift as you click the last slide in the group. All the intervening slides are selected also.

You can also select slides from the Slides/Outline pane. On the Slides tab, select slide thumbnails just as in Slide Sorter view. On the Outline tab, click the small rounded rectangle (the Slide icon) to the left of the slide title to select everything on that slide. See Figure 2-16.

Figure 2-16

To select a slide on the Outline
tab, click its Slide icon

Figure 2-16

To select a slide on the Outline
tab, click its Slide icon

Slide icon

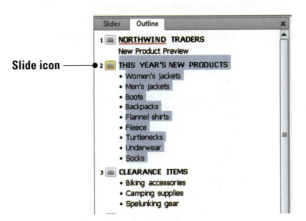

Rearranging the Slides in a Presentation

It is important to organize your slides so they best support your message. In PowerPoint, reorganizing slides is a simple drag-and-drop procedure. In Slide Sorter view (or on the Slides tab in Normal view), you can click a slide and drag it to a new location in the presentation. A line shows you where the slide will be placed when you drop it. Moving a slide is a simple procedure, as you will learn in the following exercise.

Rearrange the Slides in a Presentation

@ The *Management Values* file is available on the book companion website or in WileyPLUS.

GET READY. To rearrange the slides in a presentation, do the following:

1. **OPEN** the *Management Values* presentation and save it as *Management Values Final*.
2. Click the **View** tab, then click the **Slide Sorter** button to switch to Slide Sorter view. The presentation's slides appear together in a single window.
3. Use the Zoom control in the Status Bar to set the Zoom to 70%.
4. Click **slide 5** and begin dragging it toward the space between slides 3 and 4. When a vertical line appears between slides 3 and 4 (as shown in Figure 2-17), release the mouse button. The moved slide is now slide 4.

Figure 2-17

Moving a slide in Slide
Sorter view

Drag the slide from here...

...to here.

5. Switch to Normal view, and display the Outline tab in the Slides/Outline pane.
6. On the Outline tab, click the icon to the left of slide 7's title. All the text from slide 7 is selected.

7. Drag slide 7's icon downward. When a vertical line appears between slides 8 and 9, release the mouse button. The moved slide is now slide 8. See Figure 2-18.

Figure 2-18

Moving a slide on the Outline tab of the Slides/Outline pane

Drag a slide up or down by its icon.

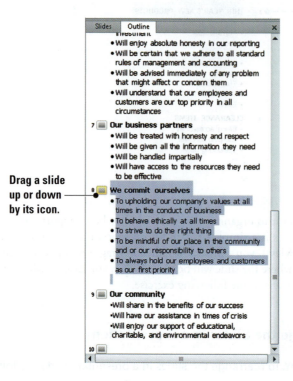

8. In the Slides/Outline pane, display the Slides tab, and select **slide 8**.

9. Drag slide 8 downward. When a vertical line appears between slides 9 and 10, as in Figure 2-19, release the mouse button. The moved slide is now slide 9.

Figure 2-19

Moving a slide on the Outline tab of the Slides/Outline pane

Another Way
You can also use the Clipboard to move slides: select a slide and use the Cut command (Ctrl+X) to move it to the Clipboard, and then position the insertion point and use the Paste command (Ctrl+V) to paste it from the Clipboard.

Horizontal line indicates where the slide is being moved.

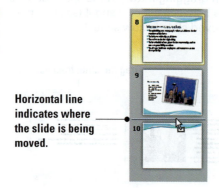

10. SAVE the presentation.

PAUSE. LEAVE the presentation open to use in the next exercise.

Deleting a Slide

When you don't want to keep a slide in a presentation, you can delete it. The following exercise shows you how.

Delete a Slide

Another Way
You can also delete
a selected slide by clicking the
Delete button on the Home tab.

USE the *Management Values Final* presentation that is still open from the previous exercise.

1. In Slide Sorter view, click **slide 10**.
2. Press the **Delete** key. The slide is removed from the presentation.
3. **SAVE** the presentation.

CLOSE the presentation file. **LEAVE** PowerPoint open for the next exercise.

**CERTIFICATION
READY   2.3.5**

How do you delete multiple
slides simultaneously?

To select more than one slide at a time for deletion, hold down the Ctrl key and click each slide you want to delete. (If you change your mind, you can deselect the selected slides by clicking in a blank area of the PowerPoint window.) You can then delete all the selected slides at the same time.

PowerPoint does not ask whether you are sure if you want to delete a slide, so it's important to be careful before deleting. If you accidentally delete a slide, click the Undo button on the Quick Access Toolbar right away to bring the slide back. See Figure 2-20.

Figure 2-20

Undo an accidental deletion

Undo button

CREATING A PRESENTATION FROM EXISTING CONTENT

The Bottom Line

If the content you want to present already exists in another form, it makes sense to reuse it rather than starting from scratch. PowerPoint imports content easily from a variety of formats, including Word outlines, other PowerPoint presentations, and slide libraries.

Using Content from Word

Microsoft Word's Outline view enables you to create a well-structured hierarchical outline consisting of multiple heading levels. You can then open such outlines in PowerPoint, where each of the major headings becomes a slide title and each of the minor headings becomes a bullet of body text.

Start a Presentation from a Word Outline

GET READY. To start a presentation from a Word outline, do the following:

1. Click the **File** tab.
2. Click **Open** to display the Open dialog box.
3. If needed, navigate to the folder that contains the data files for this lesson. The Open dialog box might have opened to that location automatically.
4. Open the File type drop-down list by clicking the **All PowerPoint Presentations** button.
5. In the File type list, click **All Outlines**. The file listing in the dialog box changes to show outlines (including Word documents). The file location is the same; the only thing that's changed is the filter that determines which file types are displayed. See Figure 2-21.

**CERTIFICATION
READY   2.3.1**

How do you insert an outline
in PowerPoint?

Figure 2-21

Open a Word outline file

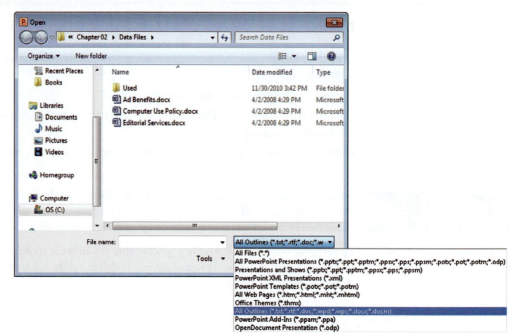

The *Computer Use Policy* file is available on the book companion website or in WileyPLUS.

6. Click *Computer Use Policy.docx*.

7. Click the **Open** button. The outline opens as a new presentation.

8. **SAVE** the new presentation as *Computer Use Policy Final.pptx*.

Take Note

Even though you used the Open command and not the New command, PowerPoint still started a new presentation. Look at the file name in the title bar of the application; it is a generic name such as Presentation5, not the name of the original Word document. That's why you have to save it in step 8.

PAUSE. LEAVE the presentation open to use in the next exercise.

If you create an outline in Microsoft Word, you can import it into PowerPoint and generate slides from it. Before you can create slides from a Word outline, the outline must be formatted correctly. Paragraphs formatted with Word's Heading 1 style become slide titles. Paragraphs formatted with subheading styles (such as Heading 2 or Heading 3) are converted into bulleted lists in the slides' subtitle placeholders. Any Word document may be opened in PowerPoint and converted to a presentation, but documents that are not structured as outlines may require quite a bit of cleanup in PowerPoint after importing.

Promoting or Demoting Outline Content

After importing data from a Word outline or other external source, you may find that the outline levels are not set as you would like them for some text. You can promote a paragraph to make it a higher level in the outline, or demote it to make it a lower level.

STEP BY STEP   **Promote and Demote Content**

USE the *Computer Use Policy Final* presentation that is still open from the previous exercise.

1. Select **slide 2**, and click at the beginning of the second line of the bulleted list (*Desktops, laptops and handheld systems*).

2. Press **Tab**. The second bulleted list item is demoted, making it subordinate to the preceding item in the list (*Computers:*).

3. Click at the beginning of the third line of the bulleted list (*Network servers and hardware*) and press **Tab**. The item is demoted.

4. Select the last two bullets on the slide and press **Tab**. They are both demoted to a lower outline level. Figure 2-22 shows the completed slide.

Figure 2-22

Several paragraphs have been demoted, creating a multilevel list

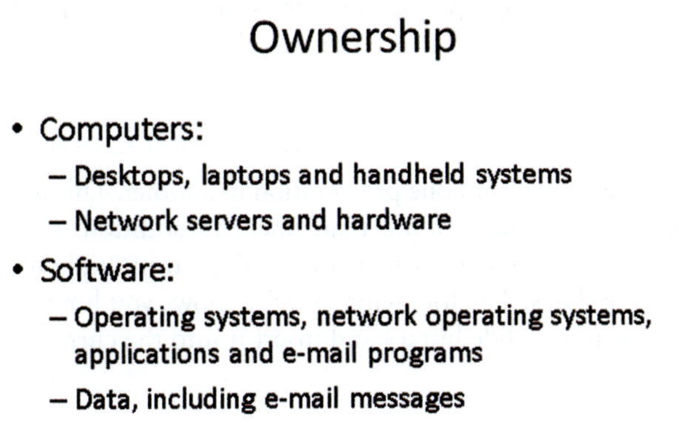

Ownership

- Computers:
  - Desktops, laptops and handheld systems
  - Network servers and hardware
- Software:
  - Operating systems, network operating systems, applications and e-mail programs
  - Data, including e-mail messages

5. In the Slides/Outline pane, click the **Outline** tab.

6. On the Outline tab, select the last three paragraphs on slide 2 (The *Software* heading and both of its subordinate bullet points).

7. Press **Shift+Tab**. The Software heading is promoted to its own slide, and the two bullet points beneath it are promoted to first-level bullet points.

8. Delete the colon (:) following *Software* on the slide title. See Figure 2-23.

Figure 2-23

Software has been moved to its own slide by promotion

Software

- Operating systems, network operating systems, applications and e-mail programs
- Data, including e-mail messages

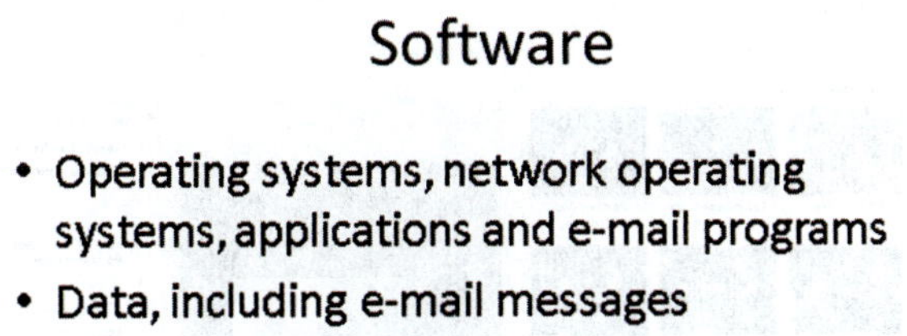

9. Select the slide 2 title (Ownership) and press **Delete** to remove it. The bullets that were subordinate to it move to slide 1.

10. On slide 1, select the bullets that were previously subordinate to Ownership (Computers: and the two bullet points subordinate to it) and press **Shift+Tab**. The selected text is promoted to its own slide.

11. Select the **Computers:** title on the slide layout and type **Hardware** to replace it. Figure 2-24 shows the completed slide.

Figure 2-24

Hardware (previously Computers) has been moved to its own slide by promotion

Hardware

- Desktops, laptops and handheld systems
- Network servers and hardware

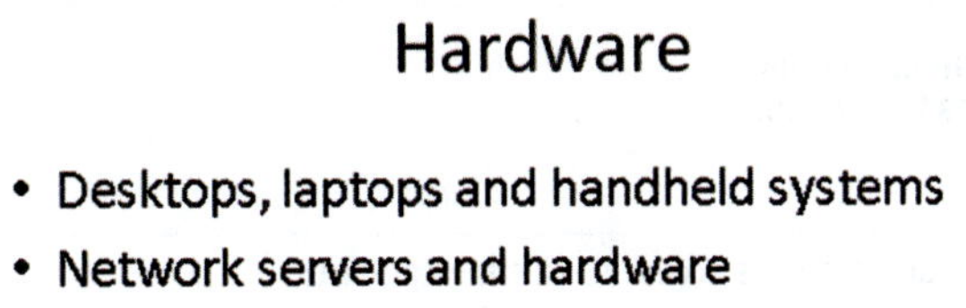

12. **SAVE** the presentation and then close the file.

PAUSE. LEAVE PowerPoint open to use in the next exercise.

Just like the headings in a book's outline, some of the items in a list are superior while others are subordinate. In a PowerPoint slide, the relationship between items in a list is shown by indent level. An item's **indent level** is the distance it is indented from the placeholder's left border. Superior items are indented less than subordinate ones. You can change the indent level of an item in a list by using the Decrease List Level and Increase List Level buttons on the Home tab of the Ribbon. Promoting a paragraph to the top level makes it into the title of its own slide, and everything subordinate to it becomes the slide's content.

Reusing Slides from Presentations and Libraries

It is easy to reuse a slide from one presentation in another. This technique frees you from creating the same slide from scratch more than once. In addition, some companies store frequently used slides in Slide Libraries on their file servers, so multiple users can draw from a common pool of premade slides. The following exercise shows you how to locate a slide from a different presentation or from a slide library and insert it into the current presentation.

STEP BY STEP   **Reuse a Slide from a Presentation**

REOPEN the *New Product Preview* presentation that you created earlier in this lesson.

1. On the Home tab, click the **New Slide button drop-down arrow**. At the bottom of the gallery that appears, click **Reuse Slides**. The Reuse Slides task pane opens on the right side of the PowerPoint window, as shown in Figure 2-25.

CERTIFICATION READY   2.3.2

How do you reuse slides from a saved presentation?

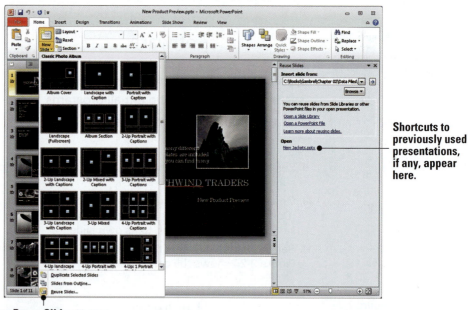

Shortcuts to previously used presentations, if any, appear here.

Choose Reuse Slides to open the Reuse Slides task pane.

Figure 2-25

Reuse Slides task pane provides access to existing content

@ The *New Jackets* file is available on the book companion website or in WileyPLUS.

2. In the task pane, click the **Browse** button. A drop-down list opens. Click **Browse File**. The Browse dialog box opens.

3. Locate and open *New Jackets*. The presentation's slides appear in the task pane, as shown in Figure 2-26.

Figure 2-26

New Jackets presentation
open in the Reuse Slides
task pane

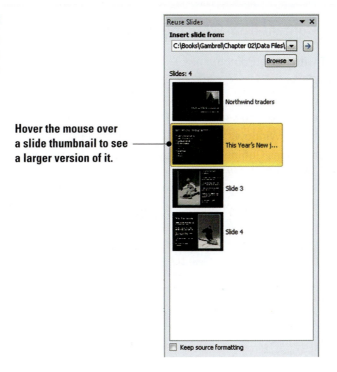

Hover the mouse over
a slide thumbnail to see ——
a larger version of it.

4. In the task pane, hover the mouse over slide 2. A larger version of the slide appears.

5. In the Slides/Outline pane, on the Slides tab, click **slide 2** to select it.

6. In the task pane, click **slide 2** of the *New Jackets* presentation. The slide is inserted into the *New Product Preview* presentation as the new slide 3.

7. Click the **Close** button in the upper-right corner of the task pane.

8. **SAVE** and **CLOSE** the *New Product Preview* presentation.

PAUSE. LEAVE PowerPoint open to use in the next exercise.

Over time, you will probably create many presentations, and some of them may share common information. The Reuse Slide command lets you copy slides from one presentation to another. By copying finished slides in this manner, you can avoid recreating similar slides over and over again.

You can import slides from other presentations, as you just practiced, or you can import them from slide libraries. A **slide library** is a feature on a SharePoint server that enables people to publish presentations with each slide saved as an individual file, so that others can reuse slides on an individual basis without having to think about which presentation they originally came from. Because using a slide library requires access to a SharePoint server that has special software installed on it for slide libraries, this book does not practice using one. However, the steps for selecting a slide from a slide library are very similar to those for selecting from a presentation. Follow the preceding steps, but in step 2, instead of choosing Browse File, choose Browse Slide Library.

**CERTIFICATION
READY   2.3.3**

How do you reuse a slide
from a slide library?

Pasting Content from Other Sources

PowerPoint readily accepts content from almost any Windows application. One way to import content is to use the Clipboard, because nearly all Windows applications support Clipboard use. You can use the Paste Options icon after pasting content to choose how it will be pasted, or use Paste Special to select special pasting methods. In this exercise, you learn how to paste content from a Word document into PowerPoint, and you practice using the Paste Special command to maintain the content's original formatting.

| STEP BY STEP | **Paste Content from Word into PowerPoint** |

START with PowerPoint open.

@ The *Cashier Training* and *Other Resources* files are available on the book companion website or in WileyPLUS.

1. **OPEN** the *Cashier Training* presentation and **SAVE** it as *Cashier Training Final*.
2. **START** Microsoft Word, and open *Other Resources.docx* in it. The procedure for opening files in Word is the same as in PowerPoint.
3. Using the Windows taskbar, switch back to the *Cashier Training Final* file in PowerPoint.
4. In the Slides/Outline pane in PowerPoint, display the Outline tab, and scroll down to the bottom of the presentation.
5. Click after the last bullet point on the last slide and press **Enter**, creating a new paragraph.
6. Press **Shift**+**Tab** to promote the new paragraph to a new slide. See Figure 2-27.

Figure 2-27

Create a new slide at the end of the presentation to hold the imported content

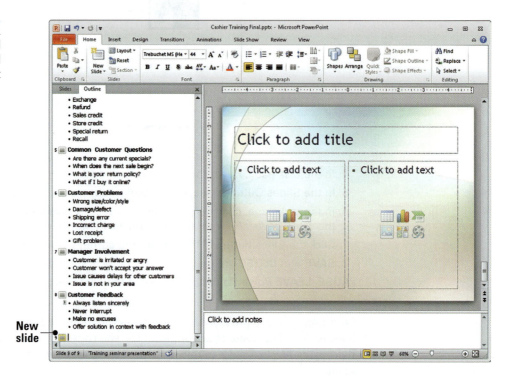

7. Using the Windows taskbar, switch to the *Other Resources* file in Word. Select the heading (Other Resources) and press **Ctrl**+**C** to copy it to the Clipboard.
8. Switch back to PowerPoint. If the insertion point is not already on the Outline tab next to the slide 9 icon, click to place it there.
9. Press **Ctrl**+**V** to paste the text. The text appears as the slide's title, and a Paste Options icon 📋 (Ctrl) ▾ appears below the text. If you don't see the icon, move the mouse pointer over slide 9's icon to the left of the pasted text.
10. Click the **Paste Options** icon to open its menu. Its menu contains three icons, shown in Figure 2-28.

Figure 2-28

Use the icons on the Paste options menu to specify how pasted content should be pasted

Keep Source Formatting

Use Destination Theme

Keep Text Only

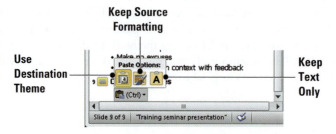

11. Click **Keep Source Formatting** (the middle icon). The pasted text's font changes to the original font it had in the Word document.

12. Switch to the *Other Resources* file in Word, and select the bulleted list. Press **Ctrl+C** to copy it to the Clipboard.

13. Switch to PowerPoint, and click the **Click To Add Text placeholder** on the left side of the slide (in the Slide pane) to move the insertion point into that text box.

14. On the Home tab, click the **Paste button drop-down arrow**. A menu opens, containing the same types of icons as found on the Paste Options icon's menu (step 6), and also containing a Paste Special command. See Figure 2-29.

Figure 2-29

Use the Paste button's menu to select special types of pasting

Clicking the top part of the icon would activate the default Paste command.

Click the bottom part of the icon to access the menu.

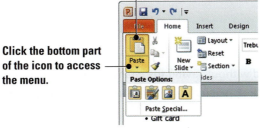

15. Click **Paste Special**. The Paste Special dialog box opens.

16. Verify that the Paste option button is selected.

17. On the As list, click **Formatted Text (RTF)**. See Figure 2-30.

Figure 2-30

Paste Special dialog box

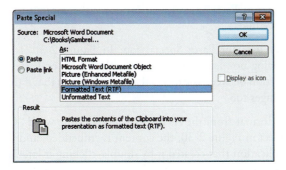

18. Click **OK**. The text is pasted into the slide keeping the text's original formatting. The text overflows the placeholder's borders. That is normal at this point.

19. Triple-click the last bullet on the slide (Special training) to select it, and press **Ctrl+X** to cut it to the Clipboard.

20. Click in the **Click To Add Text placeholder** on the right side of the slide, and press **Ctrl+V** to paste the bullet into that placeholder box. The finished slide should resemble Figure 2-31.

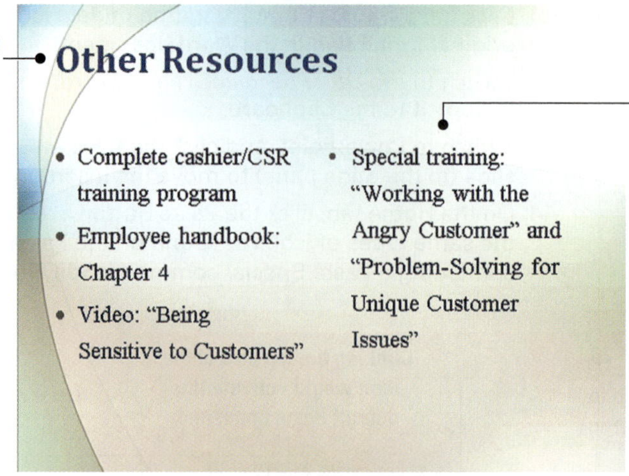

Figure 2-31

The completed imported content

Formatting retained from original data source →

This bullet point was cut-and-pasted from the left text placeholder.

> ● **Other Resources**
>
> ● Complete cashier/CSR training program
> ● Employee handbook: Chapter 4
> ● Video: "Being Sensitive to Customers"
>
> ● Special training: "Working with the Angry Customer" and "Problem-Solving for Unique Customer Issues"

21. **SAVE** the *Cashier Training Final* presentation.
22. **CLOSE** Word without saving the changes to *Other Resources.docx*.

PAUSE. LEAVE the presentation open to use in the next exercise.

Pasting from one application to another using the Clipboard works for almost all Windows-based applications, because they support the Clipboard. You can also drag-and-drop content from the other application's window into PowerPoint, but that works only if the source application supports drag-and-drop (not all applications do).

When you paste content into PowerPoint from other applications via the Clipboard, by default the pasted content takes on the formatting of the PowerPoint slide on which you place it. Using the Paste Options, or Paste Special, you can force the content to keep the formatting it had in its original source file.

There are other uses for Paste Special too. In Figure 2-30, for example, you saw that the Paste Special dialog box lets you choose to either Paste or Paste Link. Pasting a link creates a dynamic connection between the original and the copy, so that if the original changes, the copy in PowerPoint changes too.

If you choose a format from the As list that includes the word "Object," as in Microsoft Word Document Object in Figure 2-30, the content is embedded, and you will be able to reopen it in the original application that created it by double-clicking it later. In the preceding exercise, you neither pasted nor embedded; you simply pasted using non-default formatting.

ADDING NOTES TO YOUR SLIDES

The Bottom Line

A **note** is a piece of additional information you associate with a slide. Notes might not fit on a slide, but might contain information which the presenter wants to tell the audience as they view the slide. Suppose, for example, you are using a chart to show financial data to the audience but do not have room on the slide for a lot of details. You can add those details as notes, and they will remind you to share the details with your audience during your presentation. Notes do not appear on the screen when you show your presentation to an audience, but you can view notes in a couple of ways. The following exercises show you how to add notes to your slides.

Adding Notes in the Notes Pane

When you have just a few lines of notes to type, you may find it easier to work in the Notes pane in Normal view than to switch to Notes Page view. Just click in the Notes pane and start typing. Notes you enter here will not be displayed to the audience during the slide show; they are for your own reference only.

Add Notes in the Notes Pane

USE the *Cashier Training Final* presentation that is still open from the previous exercise.

1. Display slide 2 in Normal view.
2. Click in the Notes pane (below the Slide pane) to place the insertion point there.
3. In the Notes pane, type **Emphasize the importance of building customer goodwill as a cashier**. Your screen should look like the one shown in Figure 2-32.

Figure 2-32

Type notes in the Notes pane below the slide in Normal view

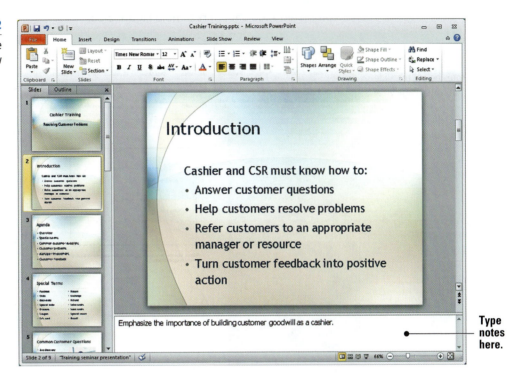

Type notes here.

4. **SAVE** the presentation.

PAUSE. LEAVE the presentation open to use in the next exercise.

Take Note   You can edit and delete text in the Notes pane just as you can in the Slide pane or on the Outline tab. Select text with the mouse pointer; use the Delete and Backspace keys to delete text.

Notes do not appear on the screen in Slide Show view, so the audience does not see them. You can see your notes by printing them or by using PowerPoint's **Presenter view**. Presenter view lets you use two monitors when delivering your presentation to an audience. One monitor displays your slides in Slide Show view. You can use the second monitor to view your notes, among other things.

 Ref   You will learn more about Presenter View in Lesson 11.

Adding Notes in Notes Pages View

Notes Page view is a special view that displays each slide along with its associated notes. Each slide and its notes appear on a white background; the content is sized as it would be when printed on a standard sheet of paper. You can view and edit notes directly in the note placeholder, which is located below the slide. In this exercise, you learn how to add notes in Notes Pages View.

Add Notes in Notes Page View

USE the *Cashier Training Final* presentation that is still open from the previous exercise.

1. Display slide 2 if it is not already displayed.
2. On the View tab, click the **Notes Pages** button to switch to Notes Page view.
3. On the vertical scroll bar, click below the scroll box once to move to slide 3.
4. Click in the **Click To Add Text box** below the slide, and type **Welcome employees to the training session and introduce yourself. Briefly go through the agenda points.** The completed slide should resemble Figure 2-33.

Figure 2-33

Type notes below the slide in Notes Page view

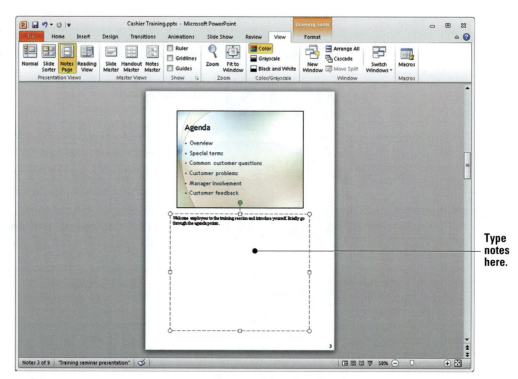

5. **SAVE** the presentation.

PAUSE. LEAVE the presentation open to use in the next exercise.

Take Note   If you have difficulty seeing what you are typing, use the Zoom control to zoom in.

PRINTING A PRESENTATION

The Bottom Line   PowerPoint gives you many options for printing your slides. In the following exercises, you learn how to preview a presentation before printing it, how to choose a printer, how to set print options, and how to print a presentation in both color and grayscale mode.

Using Print Preview and Changing the Print Layout

PowerPoint's Print Preview feature shows you how your slides will look on paper before you print them. When you change to a different print layout, Print Preview reflects the change, so you can try out different potential layouts for your presentation printouts before committing one to paper. This exercise shows you how to use Print Preview.

Use Print Preview and Change the Print Layout

USE the *Cashier Training Final* presentation that is still open from the previous exercise.

1. Switch to Normal view, and display slide 1.
2. Click the **File** tab, and click **Print**. A preview of the print job appears on the right side of the window. The default print layout is Full Page Slides, as in Figure 2-34.

Figure 2-34

Print Preview appears to the right of the print options in Backstage view.

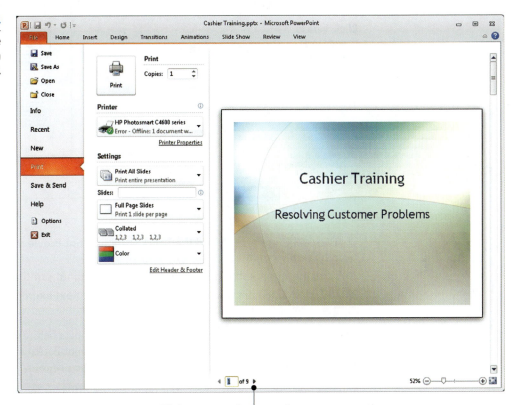

Click arrow to advance to the next page.

Take Note   If the printer selected under the Printer heading prints only in black and white, Print Preview will display your slides in grayscale. The default printer is set within Windows, not within PowerPoint; open the Printers folder in the Control Panel in Windows to change the default printer.

3. Click the right-pointing arrow at the bottom of the window. A preview of slide 2 appears.
4. To the left of the preview, under the Settings heading, click **Full Page Slides** to open a menu of layouts.
5. Click **6 Slides Vertical** on the menu of layouts. Print Preview changes to show a page containing six small slides, as in Figure 2-35.

Figure 2-35

Print Preview shows how the
page will print with the
chosen layout

Click here to
change to a
different layout.

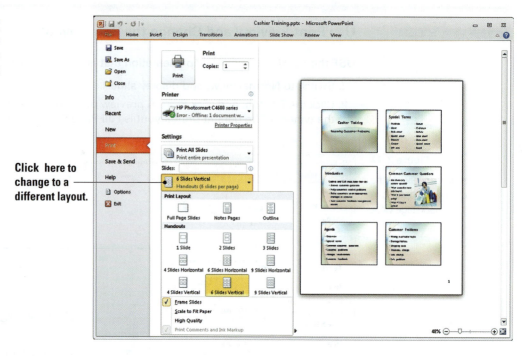

6. Click **6 Slides Vertical**, and then click **Outline**. Print Preview shows the presentation as a text-only outline.

7. Click the **Home** tab to leave Backstage view without printing anything.

PAUSE. LEAVE the presentation open to use in the next exercise.

Print Preview allows you to see how your slides will appear before you print them. In PowerPoint 2010, Print Preview is integrated into the Print section of Backstage view, so you can see how the changes you make to the print settings will change the printout.

You can preview and print a presentation in several different formats:

- **Full Page Slides:** One slide prints per page as large as possible.
- **Notes Pages:** One slide prints per page with any notes below it.
- **Outline:** The text of the presentation prints in outline form; graphics do not print.
- **Handouts:** Multiple slides print per page, designed for distribution to an audience. The exact number depends on the setting you choose (between two and nine).

Setting Print Options

In addition to choosing a layout, PowerPoint lets you set a number of other attributes before printing a presentation. The following exercise shows you how to set some of these printing options. One of these options is grayscale mode, in which there are no colors; each color appears as a shade of gray. Grayscale mode is often used for draft copies because it minimizes the use of expensive colored ink or toner.

USE the *Cashier Training Final* presentation that is still open from the previous exercise.

Another Way
You can also press Ctrl+P to open the Print section of Backstage view.

1. Click the **File** tab, and click **Print**. The printing options and Print Preview appear in Backstage view.

2. In the Copies box at the top of the window, type **2** to print two copies.

3. Click the name of the printer under the Printer heading. A menu appears of other available printers (if any). See Figure 2-36.

Figure 2-36

Other available printers appear on the Printer list

4. Click away from the open menu to close it without making a change.

5. In the Slides text box (under Print All Slides), type **1-3**. This sets only the first three slides to be printed, and Print All Slides changes to Custom Range.

6. Click the **Custom Range** button, and note the command at the bottom of its menu: Print Hidden Slides. That option is not currently available because there are no hidden slides in this presentation.

7. Click away from the menu to close it without making a change.

8. Click the **Collated** button to open a menu of collation options. When you are printing multiple copies, you can choose to have the copies collated or not.

9. Click away from the Collated button's menu to close it without making a change.

10. Click the **Color** button to open a menu of color options.

Take Note   If a black and white printer is selected, the Color button will appear as a Grayscale button instead.

11. Click **Pure Black and White** from the Color button's menu. Print Preview changes to show how the setting will affect the printouts.

Take Note   In some presentations, there is a difference between Grayscale and Pure Black and White modes. In this particular presentation, there is not, because there are no non-background graphics to convert to grayscale images. Figure 2-37 shows the preview of slide 1 in Pure Black and White mode.

Figure 2-37

A preview of slide 1 in Pure
Black and White mode

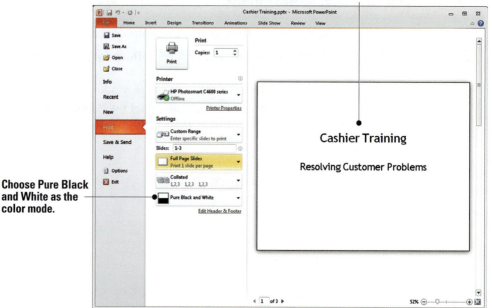

Printout will omit background and will show text in black.

**Choose Pure Black
and White as the
color mode.**

Cashier Training

Resolving Customer Problems

12. Click the **Full Page Slides** button to open its menu.

13. At the bottom of the menu, click **Frame Slides**. A border is added to each slide.

14. If you want to print now, click the **Print** button. Otherwise click the **Home** tab or press **Esc** to leave Backstage view without printing.

PAUSE. LEAVE the presentation open to use in the next exercise.

The Print section of Backstage view provides an array of options that help you print your presentations exactly the way you want. You can select a printer and enter a number of copies, a page range, and a color mode, as you saw in the preceding exercise. You can also choose a print layout, and specify whether a multi-copy print job should be collated or not.

At the bottom of the Full Page Slides button's menu are some extra commands. One of these, Frame Slides, you saw in the preceding exercise. Here's a complete list of the commands:

- **Frame slides:** This option prints a fine black border around each slide.
- **Scale to fit paper:** If your printer uses unusual-size sheets, this option tells PowerPoint to scale the slides to fit on the paper.
- **High quality:** If your slides are formatted with shadows under text or graphics, choose this option to print the shadows.
- **Print comments and ink markup:** This option lets you print any comments and hand-written notes that have been added to the presentation. The option is not available if the presentation does not include comments or markups.

 Ref

Comments are covered in Lesson 9.

Previewing a Presentation on the Screen

**CERTIFICATION
READY   7.3.1**

How do you adjust print
settings before printing a
presentation?

Before you show your presentation to an audience, you should preview it in Slide Show view. In Slide Show view, PowerPoint displays every slide in the presentation, in order from beginning to end. To advance to the next slide, you can click the left mouse button. To move to other slides besides the next one, you can right-click and select other options from the menu that appears. This exercise shows you how to use PowerPoint's tools for running a slide show on your own computer's screen.

Preview a Presentation

USE the *Cashier Training Final* presentation that is still open from the previous exercise.

1. On the Slide Show tab, click **From Beginning**. PowerPoint changes to Slide Show view and the first slide appears in full-screen mode.

Take Note   You can also switch to Slide Show view by pressing F5 or by clicking the Slide Show View icon in the lower-right corner of the PowerPoint window.

2. Click the left mouse button to move to the next slide. Keep clicking the mouse until all of the slides have been viewed. When you click the mouse on the last slide, PowerPoint displays a black screen.

Take Note   You can exit from Slide Show view at any time by pressing Esc. You do not have to go through every slide.

3. Click the left mouse button once more to return to Normal view.
4. **SAVE** and **CLOSE** the *Cashier Training Final* presentation.

EXIT PowerPoint.

 Ref   You will learn more about using Slide Show view in Lesson 11.

SKILL SUMMARY

In This Lesson You Learned How To:	Exam Objective	Objective Number
Create a new blank presentation.	Enter text in a placeholder text box.	2.5.4
Save a presentation.	Use PowerPoint Save options.	1.4.2
Create a presentation from a template.		
Add, delete, and organize slides.	Delete multiple slides simultaneously. Duplicate selected slides. Include non-contiguous slides.	2.3.5 2.3.4 2.3.6
Create a presentation from existing content.	Reuse a slide from a slide library. Use paste special.	2.3.3 2.5.7
Add notes to your slides.		
Print a presentation.	Adjust print settings.	7.3.1

Knowledge Assessment

Matching

Match the term in Column 1 to its description in Column 2.

Column 1

1. Note
2. Template
3. Handout
4. Print Preview
5. Presenter view
6. Demote
7. Layout
8. Thumbnail
9. Grayscale
10. Indent level

Column 2

a. Shows how a presentation will appear on paper
b. A black-and-white printing mode that saves colored ink or toner
c. Additional information associated with a slide that the audience will not see
d. A predefined arrangement of placeholders
e. To decrease the outline level of a paragraph on a slide
f. A small picture of a slide
g. The distance from a placeholder's left border
h. A predesigned presentation
i. A printed copy of a presentation for audience use
j. Lets you see notes on one screen while the audience sees slides on another

True/False

Circle T if the statement is true or F if the statement is false.

T F 1. A new, blank presentation appears on your screen when you launch PowerPoint.

T F 2. Once a layout has been applied to a slide, it cannot be changed.

T F 3. When you save a presentation for the first time, the Save As dialog box appears.

T F 4. If you want to be able to use a presentation with an older version of PowerPoint, you can save it by using the PowerPoint 97-2003 Presentation file format.

T F 5. Many PowerPoint templates feature a set of complementing colors, fonts, and effects called a layout.

T F 6. You can copy and paste content from most Windows applications into PowerPoint.

T F 7. One way to copy a slide is to right-click its thumbnail and then click Copy.

T F 8. Notes appear on the screen with the slides in Slide Show view.

T F 9. PowerPoint can print just the text of your slide without printing any graphics via an Outline layout.

T F 10. If you use a printer that does not print in color, your slides will appear in grayscale when viewed in Print Preview.

Competency Assessment

Project 2-1: Tonight's Guest Speaker

As director of the Citywide Business Alliance, one of your jobs is to introduce the guest speaker at the organization's monthly meeting. To do this, you will create a new presentation from a theme template, and then reuse a slide with information about the speaker from a different presentation.

GET READY. LAUNCH PowerPoint if it is not already running.

1. Click the **File** tab, and then click **New** to open the New Presentation window.
2. Click **Themes**. Click **Apex** and then click **Create**.

3. In the Click to Add Title placeholder box, type **Citywide Business Alliance**.

4. In the Click to Add Subtitle placeholder box, type **Guest Speaker: Stephanie Bourne**.

5. On the Home tab, click the arrow below the New Slide button to open its menu, and then click **Reuse Slides**.

6. In the Reuse Slides task pane, click the **Browse** button, and then click **Browse File**.

7. Navigate to the location where the sample files for this lesson are stored and open the *Bourne.pptx* presentation file.

8. In the Reuse Slides task pane, click **slide 1**. The slide is added to your new presentation. Close the task pane.

9. Click the **File**, and then click **Print**. The Print controls appear in Backstage view.

10. Click the Color button, and on the menu that appears, click **Grayscale**.

11. Click the **Full Page Slides** button, and on the menu that appears, click **2 Slides**.

12. Click **Print** to print the handout in grayscale mode.

13. Click the **File** tab and click **Save As**.

14. Open the Save as type drop-down list and click **PowerPoint 97-2003 Presentation**.

15. Navigate to the folder where you want to save the presentation.

16. Select the text in the File name box, press **Delete**, and then type **Speaker**.

17. Click **Save**. If the Compatibility Checker task pane appears, click **Continue**.

18. **CLOSE** the file.

LEAVE PowerPoint open for use in the next project.

@ The *Bourne* file is available on the book companion website or in WileyPLUS.

Project 2-2: Advertise with Us

As an account manager for The Phone Company, you are always trying to convince potential customers of the benefits of advertising in the local phone directory. A PowerPoint presentation can help you make your case. You need to create a presentation from a Word document that lists some reasons why businesses should purchase ad space in your directory.

GET READY. LAUNCH PowerPoint if it is not already running.

1. If you start PowerPoint, a new blank presentation appears automatically. If PowerPoint was already running and there is not a new blank presentation open, press **Ctrl+N** to start a new blank presentation.

2. Click in the slide's title placeholder, and then type **Why Advertise with Us?**.

3. Click in the subtitle placeholder, and then type **The Phone Company**.

4. Click outside the text placeholder to clear its border.

5. On the Ribbon's Home tab, click the **New Slide drop-down arrow**. At the bottom of the gallery of slide layouts, click **Slides from Outline**.

6. In the Insert Outline dialog box, locate and select the Microsoft Word document named *Ad Benefits*. Click **Insert**. PowerPoint inserts five new slides using content from the outline.

7. Switch to Slide Sorter view. Drag slide 5 to a new position between slides 1 and 2.

8. Click **slide 6**, and then press **Delete** to remove the slide from the presentation.

9. Switch to Notes Page view, and then go to slide 1.

10. Click in the text box below the slide, and then type **Give the client a copy of the directory**.

11. Switch to Normal view.

12. On the Quick Access Toolbar, click **Save**. The Save As dialog box opens.

13. Navigate to the folder where you want to save the presentation.

14. Replace the default name in the File name box with **Benefits**.

15. Click **Save**. **CLOSE** the file.

LEAVE PowerPoint open for use in the next project.

@ The *Ad Benefits* file is available on the book companion website or in WileyPLUS.

Project 2-3: Send People to Their Rooms

You are an assistant marketing manager at Shelbourne, Ltd., which develops process control software for use in manufacturing. You are coordinating a set of panel discussions at the company's annual sales and marketing meeting. At the start of the afternoon session, you must tell the groups which conference rooms to use for their discussions. To help deliver your message, you need to create a single-slide presentation that lists the panels' room assignments. You can display the slide on a projection screen for reference while you announce the room assignments.

1. **CREATE** a new, blank presentation.
2. Change the blank slide's layout to Title and Content. In the slide's title placeholder, type **Panel Discussions**.
3. In the second placeholder, type the following items, placing each item on its own line:

   Aligning with Partners, Room 104

   Building Incentives, Room 101

   Creating New Value, Room 102

   Managing Expenses, Room 108

   Opening New Markets, Room 112

   Recapturing Lost Accounts, Room 107

   Strengthening Client Relationships, Room 110
4. In the Notes pane, type **Refreshments will be delivered to each room during the 3:00 pm break**.
5. Print one copy of the presentation.
6. **SAVE** the presentation as *Room Assignments*, then **CLOSE** the file.

LEAVE PowerPoint open for use in the next project.

Project 2-4: Editorial Services

You are the editorial director for Lucerne Publishing, a small publishing house that provides editorial services to other businesses. Your sales manager has asked you to prepare a simple presentation that lists the services offered by your editorial staff. You can create this presentation from an outline that was created earlier.

1. **CREATE** a new, blank presentation.
2. Type **Lucerne Publishing** in the title placeholder.
3. Type **Editorial Services** in the subtitle placeholder, and then click outside the placeholder.
4. Use the Slides from Outline command to locate the Microsoft Word document named *Editorial Services*, and then click **Insert**.
5. In the Slides/Outline pane, click **slide 6**.
6. Use the Reuse Slides command to locate and open the *About Lucerne* presentation, and then add slide 3 from that presentation to the end of your new presentation as the final slide.
7. Print one copy of the presentation in a layout that shows nine slides per page.
8. **SAVE** the presentation as *Lucerne Editorial Services*, and then **CLOSE** the file.

LEAVE PowerPoint open for use in the next project.

@ The *Editorial Services* file is available on the book companion website or in WileyPLUS.

@ The *About Lucerne* file is available on the book companion website or in WileyPLUS.

Mastery Assessment

Project 2-5: The Final Gallery Crawl

As director of the Graphic Design Institute, you have volunteered to coordinate your city's last-ever gallery crawl—an annual charity event that enables the public to visit several art galleries for one price. Fortunately, this year's crawl is almost identical to last year's event, so when you create a presentation for the local arts council, you can use last year's presentation as the basis for a new one.

 The *Gallery Crawl* file is available on the book companion website or in WileyPLUS.

1. **OPEN** the New Presentation window, and start a new presentation using the existing file *Gallery Crawl*.
2. In Slide Sorter view, switch the positions of slides 6 and 7.
3. In Normal view, reword the subtitle of slide 1 to read Our last ever!
4. Print the presentation in grayscale.
5. View the presentation from beginning to end in Slide Show view.
6. **SAVE** the presentation as *Final Gallery Crawl*, and then **CLOSE** the file.

LEAVE PowerPoint open for use in the next project.

Project 2-6: The Final, Final Gallery Crawl

Having just finished your presentation for the last-ever gallery crawl, you realize that one of the museum curators uses an older version of PowerPoint. You need to save a copy of the presentation so he can use it on his computer.

The *Final Gallery Crawl* file is available on the book companion website or in WileyPLUS.

1. **OPEN** *Final Gallery Crawl* from the data files for this lesson, or open the version you created in Project 2-5.
2. **SAVE** the presentation with the file name *Compatible Gallery Crawl* in PowerPoint 97-2003 format. **CLOSE** the file without making any other changes.

EXIT PowerPoint.

INTERNET READY

Use PowerPoint Help to access online information about presentation templates. Learn how to download new templates from Office Online, and then download at least one new template to your computer.

Workplace*Ready*

PRESENTING WITH A PURPOSE

Many professionals have experienced "death by PowerPoint." They can tell you what it's like to sit through a presentation that is boring or too long and will usually tell you that the presenter did not understand how to use slides effectively. But an ineffective presentation can be worse than dull; it can actually prevent your audience from getting your message.

The following guidelines will help you (and your audience) get the most from a slide show:

- **Be brief:** Make only one major point per slide, using only a few bullets to support that point. A presentation should include only enough slides to support its major points.
- **Write concisely:** Keep your text short; sentence fragments work well on slides.
- **Focus on content:** Formatting is nice, but too much formatting can overwhelm the text and obscure your message.
- **Keep graphics relevant:** A nice picture can enhance a slide's meaning; a chart or table may support your point better than words alone. But use graphics only where they are needed.
- **Be consistent:** Use the same fonts, background, and colors throughout the presentation. If you use different design elements on each slide, your audience will become distracted (and maybe irritated).
- **Make sure slides are readable:** Ask someone else to review your slides before you show them to your audience. Make sure the reviewer can read all the text and see the graphics clearly.
- **Practice, practice, practice:** Never deliver a presentation "cold." Practice running the slide show and delivering your comments along with it. Practice your spoken parts out loud. Be sure to work on your timing, so you know just how long to keep each slide on the screen before going to the next one. Ask someone to watch you practice and offer feedback.

LESSON SKILL MATRIX

Skill	Exam Objective	Objective Number
Formatting Characters	Use text effects.	2.5.1
	Use Format Painter.	2.5.8
	Use AutoFit.	2.6.10
Formatting Paragraphs	Change text format.	2.5.2
Working with Lists	Changing the formatting of bulleted and numbered lists.	2.5.3
Inserting and Formatting WordArt	Change WordArt.	3.3.3
	Change the fill color or texture (of WordArt).	3.3.2
Creating and Formatting Text Boxes	Apply formatting to a text box.	2.6.1
	Change the outline of a text box.	2.6.2
	Change the shape of the text box.	2.6.3
	Apply effects.	2.6.4
	Set the current text box formatting as the default for new text boxes.	2.6.8
	Change text format.	2.5.2
	Adjust text in a text box.	2.6.9
	Set internal margins.	2.6.7
	Create columns in a text box.	2.6.6
	Set the alignment.	2.6.5
Use Proofing Tools	Use PowerPoint proofing.	1.4.1
	Use spelling and thesaurus features.	6.2.1

KEY TERMS

- bulleted list
- fonts
- Format Painter
- formatting
- line spacing
- numbered list
- Quick Style
- text boxes
- texture
- WordArt

Fourth Coffee is a "boutique" company devoted to producing and distributing fine coffees and teas. As the sales manager for Fourth Coffee, you often produce and deliver presentations to your staff and managers on topics such as realizing the full profit potential of your delivery systems. Whenever you create a presentation, consider how the information appears to your viewers. If the text in your slides is difficult to read or haphazardly formatted, or if you cram too much text into your slides, your presentations will not be professional looking. In this lesson, you learn some basics of text formatting, including formatting characters and paragraphs, creating and formatting lists, using WordArt to "jazz up" your text, and creating and modifying text boxes.

SOFTWARE ORIENTATION

Microsoft PowerPoint's Basic Text Formatting Tools

Most of PowerPoint's basic text formatting tools are found on the Home tab of the Ribbon, as shown in Figure 3-1. These are the tools you will use most often when working with text.

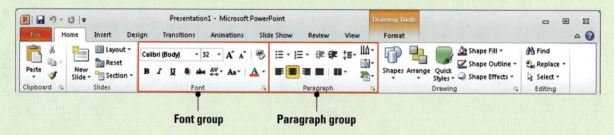

Font group   **Paragraph group**

Figure 3-1

Basic text formatting tools

There are two groups of text formatting tools on the Ribbon: the Font group and the Paragraph group. They allow you to fine-tune the text on your slides, right down to an individual character. These groups also provide access to the Font and Paragraph dialog boxes, which give you even more control over your text's appearance.

FORMATTING CHARACTERS

The Bottom Line

The term **formatting** refers to the appearance of text or objects on a slide. Most of Power-Point's tools are devoted to formatting the various parts of your slides. All PowerPoint presentations are formatted with specific fonts, font sizes, and font attributes such as style and color. You can change the way characters look on a slide by using commands in the Font group on the Home tab or the Mini toolbar. The Format Painter can save you time by allowing you to copy formats from selected text to other text items.

Choosing Fonts and Font Sizes

Fonts (sometimes called typefaces) are sets of characters, numbers, and symbols in a specific style or design. You can change the font and font size at any time on your slides. The following exercise shows you how to do this both with the Mini toolbar and with the Ribbon.

@ The *Sales* Pipeline file is available on the book companion website or in WileyPLUS.

WileyPLUS Extra! features an online tutorial of this task.

GET READY. Before you begin these steps, make sure that your computer is on. Log on, if necessary.

1. Start PowerPoint, if the program is not already running.
2. Locate and open **Sales Pipeline** and save it as **Sales Pipeline Formats**.
3. Go to slide 2. In the first row of the table, double-click **Timing**. The Mini toolbar appears above the selected text (Figure 3-2). It appears semi-transparent until you point at it, and then it appears more brightly.

Figure 3-2

The Mini toolbar

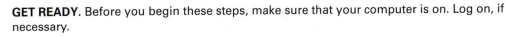

4. Click the **Font drop-down arrow**. A list of fonts appears.
5. Click **Berlin Sans FB Demi**. PowerPoint applies the chosen font to the selected text.
6. Click the **Font Size drop-down arrow**. A list of font sizes appears. See Figure 3-3.

Figure 3-3

Choosing a new font size from the Mini toolbar

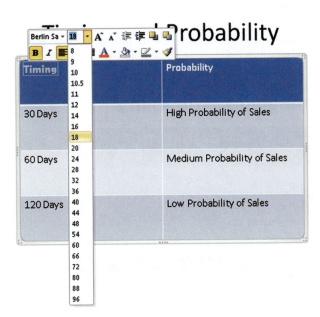

7. Click **32**. PowerPoint applies the chosen font size to the selected text.
8. Double-click **Probability** in the top right cell of the table.

9. On the Home tab of the Ribbon, click the **Font drop-down arrow**. A list of fonts appears. See Figure 3-4.

Figure 3-4

Choosing a new font from the Ribbon

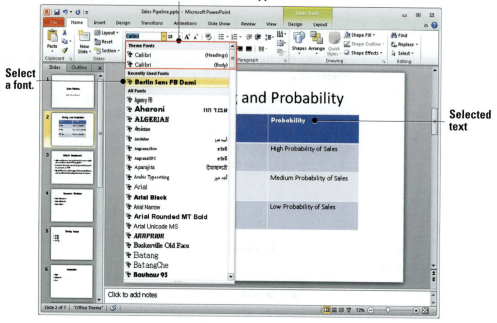

Theme fonts are the default fonts, used for any text that does not have some other font applied.

Select a font.

Selected text

10. Select the **Berlin Sans FB Demi** font.
11. On the Home tab of the Ribbon, click the **Font Size drop-down arrow**. A list of font sizes appears.
12. Click **32**.
13. Click away from the selected text to deselect it. Your slide should look like the one shown in Figure 3-5.

Figure 3-5

The new font and font size applied to the table headings

Timing and Probability

Timing	Probability
30 Days	High Probability of Sales
60 Days	Medium Probability of Sales
120 Days	Low Probability of Sales

14. **SAVE** the presentation.

PAUSE. LEAVE the presentation open to use in the next exercise.

Take Note   To maintain formatting consistency between slides in a presentation, you might prefer to change the font and font size on the Slide Master, which flows down the change to all slides automatically. Lesson 4 covers Slide Masters.

By default, PowerPoint presentations have two fonts: one font for the headings and one for the body text. (The same font can be used for both.) These font choices are a result of the theme. A theme is a set of formatting specifications, including the colors, fonts, graphic effects, and slide layouts available. All presentations have a theme, even blank ones.

To return to the default fonts provided by the theme, select a font from the Theme Fonts section of the Font drop-down list, as shown in Figure 3-4. If you choose anything other than a theme font, as in the preceding exercise, applying a different theme will have no effect on that text, because manually applied fonts take precedence over theme fonts.

Using AutoFit to Change Text Size

By default, text in the placeholder boxes on a slide layout are set to AutoFit, so that if you type more text into them than will fit, the text automatically gets smaller so that it will fit into the placeholder box. If you then delete some of the text so that there is more room available, the text once again enlarges, up to its default size. You can change the AutoFit setting for a text box or placeholder as needed.

STEP BY STEP   **Change AutoFit Behavior**

USE the *Sales Pipeline Formats* presentation that is still open from the preceding exercise.

1. On slide 3, type the following additional bullet points at the bottom of the slide:

   • **Helps Engineering staff do long-range planning for future product enhancements**
   • **Provides Marketing staff with critical data about customer needs and preferences**

   As you begin to type the second bullet point, AutoFit engages, and makes the text in the text box smaller so that it will all continue to fit.

2. Click the **AutoFit** icon in the lower-left corner of the text box. A menu appears. See Figure 3-6.

Figure 3-6

Set AutoFit behavior

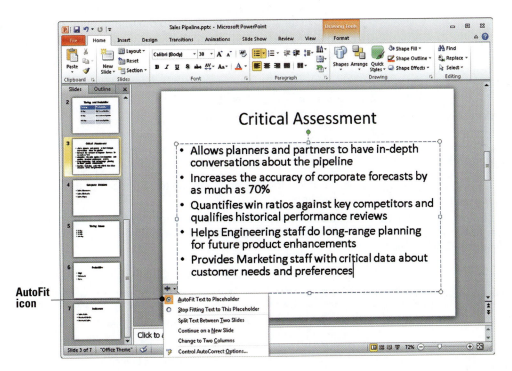

AutoFit icon

3. Click **Stop Fitting Text to This Placeholder**. The text returns to its default size and overflows the bottom of the text box.

Take Note   Notice the other choices in Figure 3-6. You can choose to split text between two slides, continue on a new slide, or change to a two-column layout.

4. Click the **AutoFit** icon again, and click **AutoFit Text to Placeholder**.
5. **SAVE** the presentation.

PAUSE. LEAVE the presentation open to use in the next exercise.

CERTIFICATION READY   2.6.10

How do you use Autofit?

AutoFit is enabled by default because it is a useful feature that most users appreciate in most situations. Rather than finding the maximum font size by trial and error that will allow the text to fit in the allotted space, you can rely on AutoFit to figure that out for you. There are some situations, though, where AutoFit may not be appropriate. For example, you might want the slide titles to always appear in the same size font.

Take Note   In manually created text boxes (covered later in this lesson), AutoFit is not enabled by default; instead, the text box itself resizes as needed to hold the text.

Applying Font Styles and Effects

Text on a PowerPoint slide can be boldfaced or italicized (called *font styles*), underlined, or formatted with other attributes such as strikethrough or shadow (called *effects*). In the following exercise, you will apply a font style and an effect to text on a slide, as well as adjust character spacing.

STEP BY STEP   **Apply Font Styles and Effects**

USE the *Sales Pipeline Formats* presentation that is still open from the previous exercise.

1. On slide 2, double-click **Timing** in the top left cell of the table. The Mini toolbar appears above the selected text. Point to the Mini toolbar so you can see it better.
2. Click the **Italic** button on the Mini toolbar, shown in Figure 3-7. PowerPoint formats the selected text in italic.

Figure 3-7

Italicize selected text from the Mini toolbar

Italics button

 Another Way
To apply italic formatting to a selection, you can also press Ctrl+I or click the Italic button in the Font group of the Ribbon. You can also right-click and choose Font.

3. Double-click **Probability** in the top right cell of the table and italicize it using any method.
4. Double-click **Timing** in the top left cell of the table, and then click the **Font dialog box launcher** on the Ribbon, shown in Figure 3-8, to produce the Font dialog box.

Figure 3-8

Click the dialog box launcher in the Font group

Dialog box launcher

5. In the Font dialog box, on the Font tab, click to mark the **Small Caps** check box.

6. Click the **Character Spacing** tab.

7. Click the **Spacing drop-down arrow**, then click **Expanded** in the list, as shown in Figure 3-9.

Figure 3-9

Character Spacing tab of the Font dialog box

Expand character spacing.

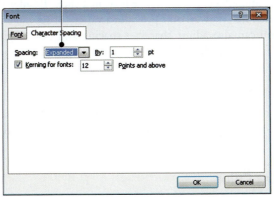

8. Click **OK**. PowerPoint places 1 point of spacing between the letters and applies the Small Caps effect.

9. Double-click **Probability** in the top right cell of the table.

10. On the Quick Access Toolbar, click the **Repeat** button. PowerPoint repeats the last command you issued, applying the new character spacing to the selected text. Your slide should look like the one shown in Figure 3-10.

Figure 3-10

Completed text formatting

Repeat button

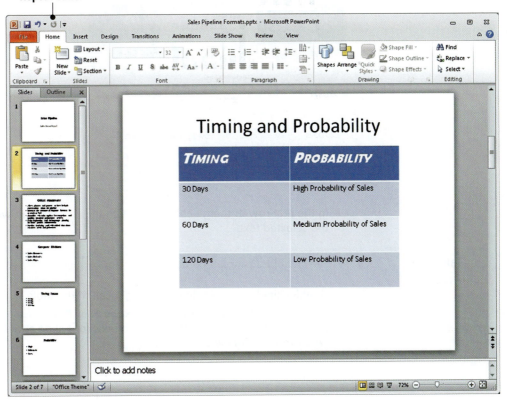

11. **SAVE** the presentation.

PAUSE. LEAVE the presentation open to use in the next exercise.

 Ref

WordArt styles can also be used to format text and apply effects. They are covered later in this lesson.

CERTIFICATION READY   **2.5.1**

How do you apply text effects?

Use font styles and effects to emphasize text on a slide. Besides the standard font styles—bold, italic, and underline—PowerPoint provides a variety of special effects such as strikethrough and small caps. You can also adjust character spacing and case to give your text a special look. To access more font effects, click the Font group's dialog box launcher to open the Font dialog box.

Changing Font Color

An easy way to change text appearance is to modify its color. Use the Font Color button in the Font group to access a palette of colors you can apply to selected text.

STEP BY STEP   **Change Font Color**

USE the *Sales Pipeline Formats* presentation that is still open from the previous exercise.

1. On slide 2, double-click **Timing** in the top left cell of the table. The Mini toolbar appears above the selected text.
2. Click the **Font Color drop-down arrow** on the Mini toolbar. A palette of colors appears, as shown in Figure 3-11.

Figure 3-11

Choosing a different font color from the Mini toolbar

Click the arrow to open the Font Color button's palette.

3. In the first row of theme colors, click **Orange, Accent 6**. PowerPoint applies the color to the selected text.

Take Note   When you hold the mouse pointer over a color box, the color's name appears in a ScreenTip.

4. Double-click **Probability** in the top right cell of the table.
5. On the Home tab on the Ribbon, click the **Font Color drop-down arrow** and apply the color **Orange, Accent 6** to the selected text. Your slide should resemble Figure 3-12 when you are finished.

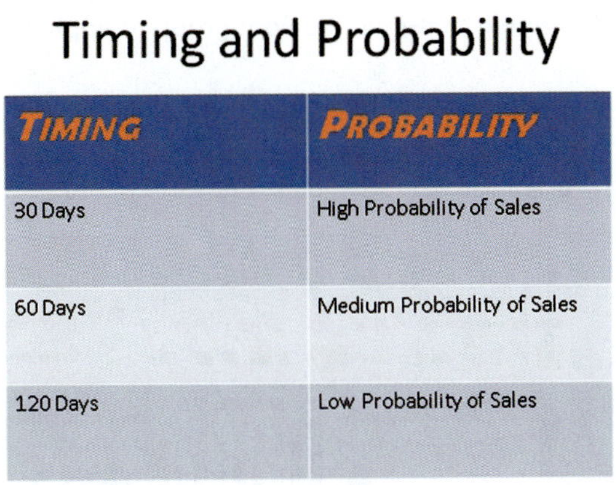

Figure 3-12

Color has been applied to the
table headings

Timing and Probability

TIMING	PROBABILITY
30 Days	High Probability of Sales
60 Days	Medium Probability of Sales
120 Days	Low Probability of Sales

6. SAVE the presentation.

PAUSE. LEAVE the presentation open to use in the next exercise.

PowerPoint provides an almost limitless selection of colors that can be applied to fonts. You can select any color for your text, but it is usually best to use one of the colors provided by the presentation's theme, as you did in the preceding exercise. Each PowerPoint theme includes a set of coordinating colors, which appear in the color palette when you click the Font Color button. By selecting one of the theme's colors, you can be sure that all the font colors in your slides will look well together on the screen, making them easier to read.

If you want to use a color that is not included in the theme, select one of the Standard Colors at the bottom of the color palette (see Figure 3-11) or click More Colors to open the Colors dialog box. In the Colors dialog box, you can choose from dozens of standard colors or create a custom color.

The difference between a theme color and a standard color is apparent when you switch to a different theme or color scheme, as you will learn to do in Lesson 4. A theme color will change to match the new colors for the presentation, but a standard color will remain fixed.

Copying Character Formats with the Format Painter

As you format text in your presentations, you will want to keep similar types of text formatted the same way. **Format Painter** is a tool that copies formatting from one block of text to another. In this exercise you will use Format Painter to copy some formatting.

STEP BY STEP **Copy Character Formats with the Format Painter**

USE the *Sales Pipeline Formats* presentation that is still open from the previous exercise.

1. On slide 2, select the text in the title placeholder.

2. Change the font color to **Blue, Accent 1, Darker 25%**.

Take Note   To find that color, point to the Blue Accent 1 color in the palette (fifth from the left) and then slide the mouse down over the various tints and shades of that color until you find the one for which the ScreenTip shows *Darker 25%*.

3. Click the **Bold** button in the Ribbon's Font group to apply the bold font style.

4. Click the **Text Shadow** button in the Font group to apply the shadow font style. See Figure 3-13.

Figure 3-13

Format the title text

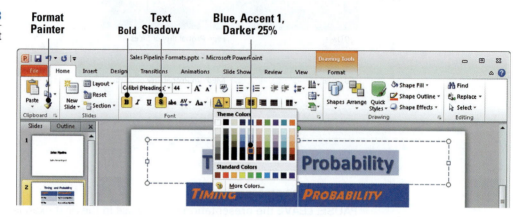

5. With the text still selected, click the **Format Painter** button in the Clipboard group.

6. Go to slide 3 and click the word **Assessment**. The formatting is painted onto that word.

7. Click the **Format Painter** button again to copy the formatting that is now applied to Assessment.

8. Drag across the word *Critical*, releasing the mouse button when the word is selected. The formatting is painted onto that word.

9. Double-click the **Format Painter** button. Double-clicking it makes the feature stay on until you turn it off.

10. Go to each of the remaining slides in the presentation and drag across all the text in the title of each slide, then use Format Painter to apply the new formatting to the text.

11. If you accidentally click anywhere that does not contain editable text, the Format Painter feature turns off. If that happens, select some of the already formatted text and then click the Format Painter button to turn the feature back on.

12. When you are finished painting formatting, press **Esc** or click the **Format Painter** button again to turn the feature off.

13. **SAVE** the presentation.

PAUSE. LEAVE the presentation open to use in the next exercise.

Format Painter makes it easy to apply the same formatting to multiple blocks of text, no matter where they are in the presentation. If you want to copy a format only once, simply click the button. To copy a format multiple times, double-click the button, and the feature will stay on until you turn it off. Not only does this tool reduce your workload, but it also ensures consistency throughout a presentation. (Another way to achieve consistency is to make changes to the Slide Master rather than to individual slides; you'll learn about that in Lesson 4.)

The Format Painter can copy not only character formats but paragraph formats such as alignments and line spacing. You learn about paragraph formats in the next section.

> **CERTIFICATION READY   2.5.8**
>
> How do you copy character formatting with the Format Painter?

FORMATTING PARAGRAPHS

The Bottom Line

You can change the look of paragraph text by modifying alignment or line spacing. When you apply formatting to a paragraph, all the text within that paragraph receives the same formatting.

Aligning Paragraphs

By default, PowerPoint aligns text along the left margin. In this exercise, you change the alignment of items in a bulleted list to customize a slide's appearance.

Align Paragraphs

USE the *Sales Pipeline Format* presentation that is still open from the previous exercise.

1. On slide 4, click in the second bulleted item (*Sales Districts*).
2. On the Home tab, click the **Center** button in the Ribbon's Paragraph group. PowerPoint aligns the paragraph in the center of the text box.
3. Click in the third bulleted item (*Sales Reps*).
4. Click the **Align Text Right** button in the Paragraph group. PowerPoint aligns the paragraph to the right side of the text placeholder. Your slide should look like the one shown in Figure 3-14.

Figure 3-14

Aligning paragraphs to the left, center, and right

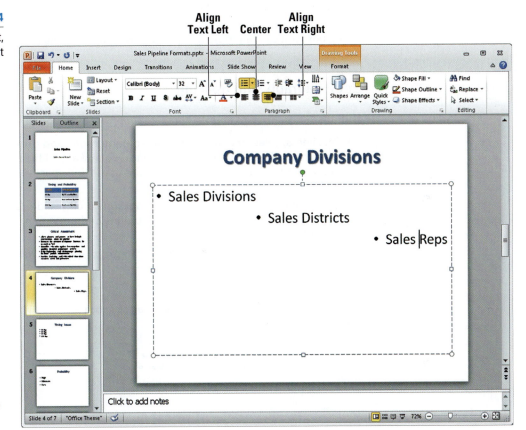

Another Way
The paragraph alignment tools also appear on the Mini toolbar when you right-click within a paragraph.

5. **SAVE** the presentation.

PAUSE. LEAVE the presentation open to use in the next exercise.

When you apply paragraph formats such as alignment, you do not have to select the entire paragraph of text. Just click anywhere in the paragraph and apply the format. The formatting applies to the entire paragraph, even if the paragraph is several lines or sentences long.

When you begin a new paragraph by pressing Enter after an existing paragraph, the new paragraph keeps the same alignment and formatting as the paragraph above it. For example, if you start a new paragraph after a paragraph aligned to the right, the new paragraph aligns to the right as well.

Another Way
To left-align text, press Ctrl+L. To center text, press Ctrl+E. To right-align text, press Ctrl+R. You can also right-click and choose Paragraph and set alignment in the Paragraph dialog box.

PowerPoint provides four paragraph alignment options:

- **Align Text Left** aligns the paragraph at the left edge of the object in which the text resides, whether the object containing the text is a placeholder, a table cell, or a text box.
- **Center** aligns the paragraph in the center of the object.

CERTIFICATION
READY   2.5.2

How do you format text
alignment?

- **Align Text Right:** Aligns the paragraph at the right edge of the object.
- **Justify:** Aligns text to both the left and right margins to distribute the paragraph of text evenly across the width of the object, if possible. PowerPoint justifies text by adding spaces between words and characters. The final line of a justified paragraph is left-aligned, so if the paragraph occupies only one line, it will appear left-aligned.

Setting Line Spacing

In this exercise, you learn how to adjust **line spacing** to allow more or less room between lines of a paragraph, and also between paragraphs. Line spacing changes can help you display text more attractively or fit more text on a slide. By default, PowerPoint formats your paragraphs so that one line of blank space lies between each paragraph and between the lines within a paragraph. Use the Line Spacing button to adjust the spacing to 1.0, 1.5, 2.0, 2.5, or 3.0. You also can use the Line Spacing Options command to display the Paragraph dialog box. With this dialog box, you can fine-tune the spacing between each paragraph.

STEP BY STEP   **Set Paragraph Line Spacing**

USE the *Sales Pipeline Formats* presentation that is still open from the previous exercise.

1. On slide 3, select the last two bulleted paragraphs and press **Delete**. You are doing this so that AutoFit no longer resizes the text to make it all fit, and so there is enough room in the text box to clearly see the results of the line spacing change you are going to be making.

2. Select all the remaining bulleted paragraphs on the slide. One way to do this is to click inside the text box that contains the bullets and press **Ctrl+A**. You can also drag across the bullets to select them.

3. Click the **Line Spacing** button in the Paragraph group. A list of line spacing options appears, as shown in Figure 3-15.

Figure 3-15

Set an amount of spacing between lines

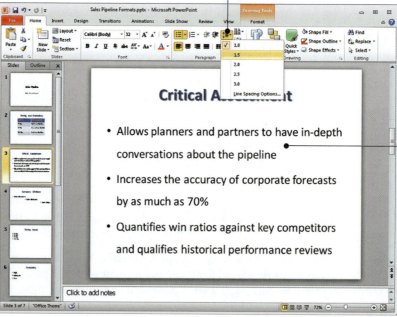

1.5 lines of space between each line of each paragraph

Another Way
You can also open the Paragraph dialog box by clicking the dialog box launcher in the Paragraph group.

4. Select **1.5.** PowerPoint formats the paragraphs so each line is separated by 1.5 lines of blank space.

5. Click the **Line Spacing** button again, and click **Line Spacing Options** at the bottom of the menu. The Paragraph dialog box opens.

6. In the Spacing section of the dialog box, set the following values:

   Before: **0 pt**

   After: **9 pt**

7. Open the Line Spacing drop-down list and click **Exactly.** Then in the text box to its right, type **38.** The dialog box settings should look like Figure 3-16.

Figure 3-16

In the Paragraph dialog box, you can set spacing both between lines within a paragraph and before/after each paragraph

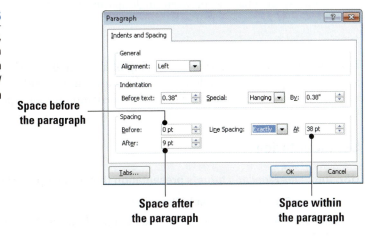

Space before the paragraph

Space after the paragraph

Space within the paragraph

8. Click **OK.** The settings are applied to all the bullets on the slide.

9. Click away from the bullets to deselect them. The slide should resemble Figure 3-17.

Figure 3-17

The slide with line spacing applied

Critical Assessment

- Allows planners and partners to have in-depth conversations about the pipeline

- Increases the accuracy of corporate forecasts by as much as 70%

- Quantifies win ratios against key competitors and qualifies historical performance reviews

10. **SAVE** the presentation.

PAUSE. LEAVE the presentation open to use in the next exercise.

The Line Spacing drop-down list in the Paragraph dialog box enables you to select from these settings:

- **Single:** Sets the spacing to what single spacing would be for the font size in use. The actual amount changes depending on the largest font size used in that paragraph.
- **1.5 Lines:** Sets the spacing halfway between single spacing and double spacing.
- **Double:** Sets the spacing to what double spacing would be for the font size in use.
- **Exactly:** Sets the spacing to a precise number of points. If you change the font size(s) in use, this value does not change automatically.
- **Multiple:** Enables you to specify a multiplier for spacing. For example, you might enter 1.25 for spacing halfway between single-spacing and 1.5 Lines spacing.

CERTIFICATION
READY   2.5.2

How do you format text by adjusting line spacing?

Setting Indentation

Indentation controls the horizontal spacing of a paragraph, much as line spacing controls its vertical spacing. Indentation determines how far from the text box's left and right margins the text appears. In this exercise you will set the indentation for some paragraphs.

STEP BY STEP   **Set Indentation**

USE the *Sales Pipeline Formats* presentation that is still open from the previous exercise.

1. On slide 3, click in the first bulleted paragraph.

Another Way
Instead of clicking the dialog box launcher, you can right-click and choose Paragraph.

2. Click the **dialog box launcher** for the Paragraph group. The Paragraph dialog box opens.

3. In the Indentation section of the dialog box, set the **Before Text** value to **0.7"**. See Figure 3-18.

Figure 3-18

Change the indentation in the Paragraph dialog box

The Before Text indent applies to all lines of the paragraph.

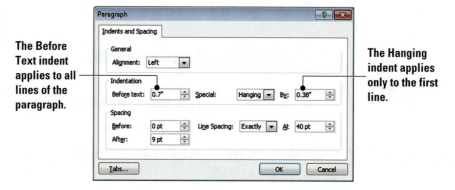

The Hanging indent applies only to the first line.

Take Note   The Before Text setting refers to the paragraph as a whole. A hanging indent is a reverse indent, and applies only to the first line.

4. Click **OK**. The new setting is applied. Both lines of the first bullet are indented more than the other bullets, as in Figure 3-19. The placement of the bullet in relation to the rest of the text has not changed.

Additional
indentation

• • Allows planners and partners to have in-
depth conversations about the pipeline

• Increases the accuracy of corporate forecasts
by as much as 70%

• Quantifies win ratios against key competitors
and qualifies historical performance reviews

5. Use **Format Painter** to copy the first paragraph's formatting to the other two paragraphs, or select those paragraphs and repeat steps 3-4.

6. Click in the first paragraph again.

7. Click the **dialog box launcher** for the Paragraph group. The Paragraph dialog box opens.

8. Set the Hanging indent to **0.6"** and click **OK** to apply the new setting.

Take Note   The bullet character has moved to the left in relation to the paragraph; the paragraph text has not moved.

9. Use **Format Painter** to copy the first paragraph's formatting to the other two paragraphs, or select those paragraphs and repeat steps 6-7 for them.

10. **SAVE** the *Sales Pipeline Formats* presentation and close it.

PAUSE. LEAVE PowerPoint open to use in the next exercise.

By promoting and demoting bulleted paragraphs in the outline level, as you learned to do in Lesson 2, you can indirectly control their indentation. However, you can also directly change paragraphs' indentations via the Paragraph dialog box without altering their outline level. This is useful when you want to change how a paragraph is formatted without changing its meaning or importance in the presentation's message.

There are two indentation settings. The first one, Before Text, applies to all lines in the paragraph. The second one is a specialty setting that varies according to the paragraph type:

• **Hanging:** A reverse indent. The first line (which usually contains a bullet character when Hanging is used) is reverse-indented by the specified amount. In other words, the first line has a lesser indent than the other lines, so it hangs off into the left margin. In the preceding steps, the hanging indent was 0.6".

• **First Line:** A standard first-line indent. The first line is indented an extra amount on top of what is specified for the Before Text indentation setting.

• **(None):** This setting removes any special indents for the first line.

**CERTIFICATION
READY   2.5.2**

How do you format text with
indentation?

Indents can be set for any paragraph, but are often the most useful for bulleted and numbered lists. You will learn more about creating and formatting lists in the next section.

WORKING WITH LISTS

The Bottom Line

Lists make the information on slides easy to read and remember. PowerPoint provides for several levels of bulleted lists that you can modify for special effects. You can also create numbered lists when your slide text implies a specific order.

Creating Numbered Lists

PowerPoint enables you to create **numbered lists** to place a list of itemized information in numeric order. Numbered lists are used for procedural steps, action items, and other information where the order in which the items appear is significant. In the following exercise, you create a numbered list from a list of items on a slide.

STEP BY STEP   **Create Numbered Lists**

 The *Leveraging Corporate Cash* file is available on the book companion website or in WileyPLUS.

 **EXTRA**

WileyPLUS Extra! features an online tutorial of this task.

GET READY. To create a numbered list, perform the following steps:

1. **OPEN** the *Leveraging Corporate Cash* presentation and save it as *Leveraging Corporate Cash Lists*.
2. On slide 2, click in the first line of the text in the text placeholder (*Determine inventory turnover*).
3. Click the **Numbering** button in the Paragraph group. PowerPoint formats the sentence with a number 1.
4. Select the last three lines in the text placeholder.
5. Click the **Numbering** button. PowerPoint applies numbers 2 through 4.
6. Click outside the text placeholder to clear any text selection. Your slide should look like the one shown in Figure 3-20.

Figure 3-20

A numbered list

Numbering button

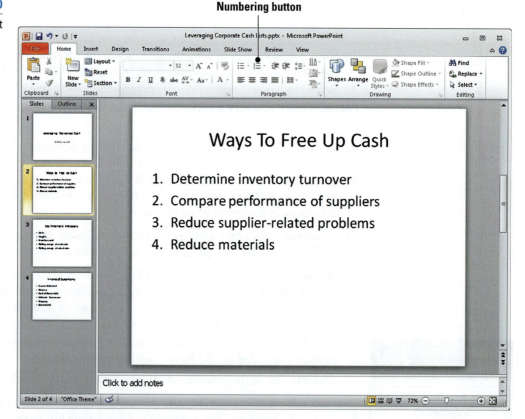

 **Another Way**
To number a paragraph, right-click the paragraph, and then click Numbering on the shortcut menu.

Another Way
You can also drag across the list to select it.

7. Click in the text box containing the numbered list and press **Ctrl+A** to select the entire list.
8. Click the **down arrow** to the right of the Numbering button, opening a gallery of numbering styles.
9. Click the uppercase Roman numeral style as in Figure 3-21.

Figure 3-21

Changing the numbered list's numbering style

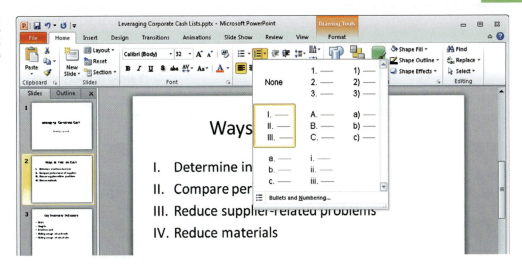

10. **SAVE** the presentation.

PAUSE. LEAVE the presentation open to use in the next exercise.

When you create a numbered list on a slide, you can continue it automatically after the last item by pressing Enter. PowerPoint automatically numbers the new paragraph with the next number in the sequence of numbers so you can continue the list uninterrupted. To turn off numbering, press Enter twice or click the Numbering button on the Home tab.

By default, PowerPoint numbers items using numerals followed by periods. You can, however, change the numbering format to numerals followed by parentheses, upper- or lowercase Roman numerals, or upper- or lowercase letters. To change the numbering format, click the Numbering button's drop-down arrow and select a new format from the gallery.

For even more control over the numbering format, click Bullets and Numbering on the gallery to display the Bullets and Numbering dialog box. You can use this dialog box to choose what number to start the list with, change the size of the numbers, or change their color. You will work with that dialog box in the next exercise.

Working with Bulleted Lists

Bullets are small dots, arrows, circles, diamonds, or other graphics that appear before a short phrase or word. A **bulleted list** is a set of paragraphs (two or more) that each start with a bullet symbol. Bulleted lists are the most popular way to present items on PowerPoint presentations. In fact, most of PowerPoint's text placeholders automatically format text as a bulleted list. In the following exercise, you will change the formats of a bulleted list.

STEP BY STEP   **Work with Bulleted Lists**

USE the *Leveraging Corporate Cash Lists* presentation that is still open from the previous exercise.

1. On slide 3, select all of the bulleted list items in the text box. To do this, you can either drag across them or press **Ctrl+A**.

2. Click the **drop-down arrow** to the right of the Bullets button in the Paragraph group. PowerPoint displays a gallery of bullet styles.

Take Note   If a series of paragraphs does not have bullets, you can add them by selecting the paragraphs, and then clicking the Bullets button in the Paragraph group.

3. Click **Check mark bullet**, as shown in Figure 3-22. PowerPoint applies the bullet style to the selected paragraphs.

Figure 3-22

Select a different bullet character

Click arrow to open gallery.

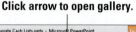

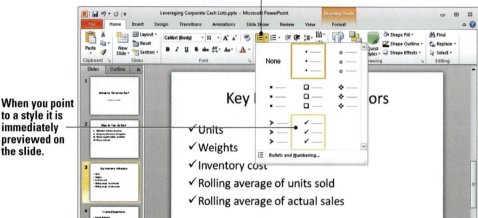

When you point to a style it is immediately previewed on the slide.

4. With the text still selected, click the **Bullets drop-down arrow** again, and then click **Bullets and Numbering**. The Bullets and Numbering dialog box appears, as shown in Figure 3-23.

Figure 3-23

The Bullets and Numbering dialog box

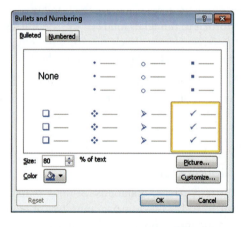

5. In the Size box, type **80**. This reduces the bullets' size to 80% of the text's size.

6. Click the **Color drop-down arrow**, and then click **Blue, Accent 1**. (It's the fifth color from the right on the first line.) This changes the color of the bullets.

7. Click **OK**. PowerPoint applies the selections.

8. **SAVE** the *Leveraging Corporate Cash Lists* presentation and close it.

PAUSE. LEAVE PowerPoint open to use in the next exercise.

CERTIFICATION READY   2.5.3

How do you change the formatting of a bulleted or numbered list?

Each PowerPoint theme supplies bullet characters for up to nine levels of bullets, and these characters differ according to theme. When you create a bulleted list on your slide, you can continue it automatically after the last item by pressing Enter. PowerPoint automatically adds the new paragraph with a bullet.

INSERTING AND FORMATTING WORDART

The Bottom Line

The **WordArt** feature allows you to use text to create a graphic object. PowerPoint's WordArt feature can change standard text into flashy, eye-catching graphics. Use WordArt's formatting options to change the WordArt fill or outline color or apply special effects. You can also apply WordArt styles to any slide text to give it special emphasis.

Inserting a WordArt Graphic

In this exercise, you enhance the appearance of slide titles by converting them to WordArt.

Insert a WordArt Graphic

@ The *Full Profit Potential* file is available on the book companion website or in WileyPLUS.

GET READY. To insert a WordArt graphic, perform the following steps:

1. **OPEN** the *Full Profit Potential* presentation, and save it as *Full Profit*. Notice that the first slide has a subtitle, but no title placeholder.

2. Click the **Insert** tab on the Ribbon, and click the **WordArt** button to display a gallery of WordArt styles, as shown in Figure 3-24.

Figure 3-24

Gallery of WordArt styles

Slect this WordArt style

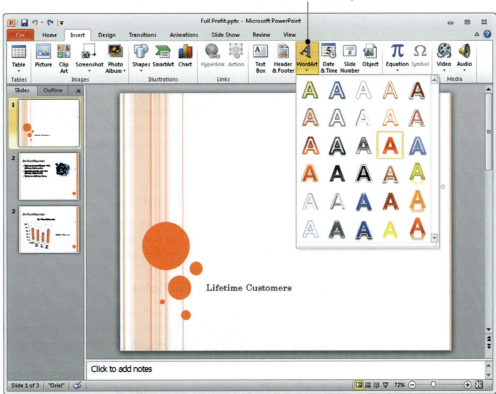

3. Click the **Gradient Fill – Orange Accent 1** WordArt style. PowerPoint displays the WordArt graphic with the sample text *Your Text Here*.

4. Type **Full Profit** to replace the sample text. Your slide should resemble Figure 3-25.

Figure 3-25

A new WordArt graphic
on a slide

5. SAVE the presentation.

PAUSE. LEAVE the presentation open to use in the next exercise.

After you have inserted the WordArt graphic, you can format it in a number of ways. You can change the style from the WordArt gallery, you can modify the fill or the outline, or you can apply a number of interesting special effects. You can also modify the text of the graphic at any time. Click the graphic to open the placeholder, just as when editing a slide's title or body text, and then edit the text as desired.

Formatting a WordArt Graphic

To format a WordArt graphic, you use the tools on one of PowerPoint's contextual tabs, the Drawing Tools Format tab. In the next several exercises, you will use these tools to modify the WordArt's fill and outline and apply an effect.

Changing the WordArt Fill Color

The WordArt *fill color* is the color you see inside the WordArt characters. You can change the fill color by using the color palette for the current theme or any other available color. You can also apply a special effect fill to WordArt such as a texture, gradient, or pattern.

STEP BY STEP   **Apply a Solid Fill Color to WordArt**

USE the *Full Profit* presentation that is still open from the previous exercise.

1. Select the **WordArt graphic** on slide 1. Note that the Drawing Tools Format tab becomes active on the Ribbon.

2. Click the **Drawing Tools Format** tab and locate the WordArt Styles group.

3. Click the **Text Fill drop-down arrow**. PowerPoint displays the Theme Colors palette.

4. Click the **Blue, Accent 2, Darker 25%** theme color as the fill color, as shown in Figure 3-26. PowerPoint changes the fill of the graphic.

Figure 3-26

Filling a WordArt object with a solid color

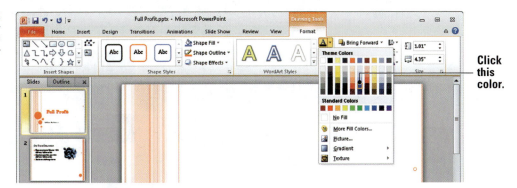

5. **SAVE** the presentation.

PAUSE. LEAVE the presentation open to use in the next exercise.

One way to fine-tune the graphic you have inserted is to change the fill color of the WordArt object. You can use any of the colors on the Theme Colors palette to make sure the object coordinates with other items in the presentation.

You can also choose from the Standard Colors palette or select another color from the Colors dialog box. To access these colors, click More Fill Colors on the palette (Figure 3-26) to open the Colors dialog box. You can "mix" your own colors on the Custom tab or click the Standard tab to choose from a palette of premixed colors.

Applying a Texture Fill to WordArt

Textures are graphics that repeat to fill an object with a surface that resembles a familiar material, such as straw, marble, paper, or wood. The texture graphics are specially designed so that the left edge blends in with the right edge (and the top edge with the bottom edge), so that when you place copies side by side, it looks like one seamless surface. In this exercise, you practice applying a texture fill to WordArt.

STEP BY STEP   **Apply a Texture Fill to WordArt**

USE the *Full Profit* presentation that is still open from the previous exercise.

1. Select the WordArt graphic on slide 1 if it is not already selected.

2. On the Drawing Tools Format tab, click the **Text Fill drop-down arrow**. PowerPoint displays the Theme Colors palette.

3. Point to Texture, and then click the **Green Marble** texture. See Figure 3-27. PowerPoint changes the fill of the graphic.

Figure 3-27

Filling a WordArt object with a texture

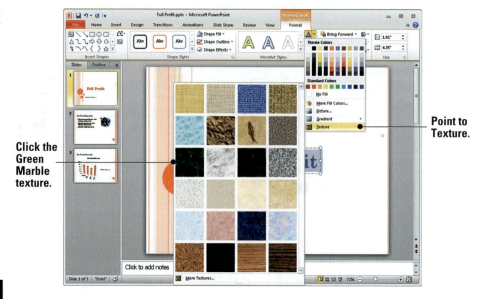

Click the Green Marble texture.

Point to Texture.

4. **SAVE** the presentation.

PAUSE. LEAVE the presentation open to use in the next exercise.

Changing the WordArt Outline Color

Most WordArt styles include a colored outline around the edges of the WordArt characters. Just as with a WordArt object's fill color, you can fine-tune the outline color of the object. You have the same color options as for changing a fill color. The Text Outline Theme Colors palette also allows you to remove the outline, change its weight, or apply a dash style to the outline. In this exercise, you learn how to change the outline color to fine-tune a WordArt graphic.

STEP BY STEP   **Change the WordArt Outline Color**

USE the *Full Profit* presentation that is still open from the previous exercise.

1. Select the WordArt graphic on slide 1 if necessary.

2. Click the **Text Outline drop-down arrow**. PowerPoint displays the Theme Colors palette. See Figure 3-28.

Figure 3-28

Changing the border color of a WordArt object

Text Outline button

Click More Outline Colors.

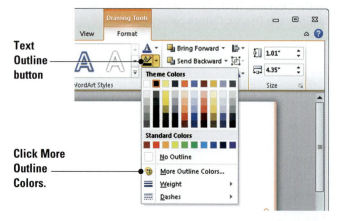

3. Click **More Outline Colors**. The Colors dialog box opens.

4. On the standard tab, click a **dark green hexagon**. See Figure 3-29.

Figure 3-29

Choose a color from the Colors dialog box

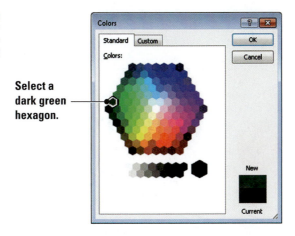

Select a dark green hexagon.

5. Click **OK**. The dark green background blends in with the green texture fill, so it is not obvious to see.

6. Zoom in on the object to 200% to see it more clearly. Zoom out to 100% when you are finished looking at the border.

7. With the WordArt still selected, click the **Text Outline drop-down arrow** again, point to Weight, and click **3 pt**. The outline becomes more dramatic and easier to see.

8. Click the **Text Outline drop-down arrow** again, and click **No Outline**. The outline disappears.

PAUSE. LEAVE the presentation open to use in the next exercise.

CERTIFICATION READY   3.3.3

How do you modify a WordArt graphic?

Applying Special Effects to WordArt

You can apply special effects to your WordArt objects, such as shadows, reflections, glows, transformations, and more. These effects can also be applied to the other object types that you will learn about in later lessons, such as drawn lines and shapes.

STEP BY STEP   Apply Special Effects to WordArt

USE the *Full Profit* presentation that is still open from the previous exercise.

1. Select the WordArt graphic on slide 1, if necessary.

2. Click the **Text Effects drop-down arrow**. PowerPoint displays the Text Effects menu.

3. Click **Reflection**. PowerPoint displays the reflection special effects, as shown in Figure 3-30.

Figure 3-30

A reflection special effect added to the WordArt object

Point to Reflection.

Click this Reflection type.

4. Click **Tight Reflection, touching**. PowerPoint adds the reflection special effect to the WordArt object.

5. Click the WordArt graphic and drag it close to the subtitle, as shown in Figure 3-31.

Figure 3-31

The WordArt text repositioned above the subtitle

6. **SAVE** the presentation.

PAUSE. LEAVE the presentation open to use in the next exercise.

CERTIFICATION READY   3.3.3

How do you format WordArt?

WordArt special effects provide a way to spice up an ordinary slide. Although you should not use WordArt special effects on all your slides, you may want to look for spots in your presentations where a little artistic punch will liven up your slide show. Always consider your audience and your topic when adding special effects. For example, a presentation discussing plant closings and layoffs would not be an appropriate place for a cheerful-looking WordArt graphic.

Formatting Text with WordArt Styles

You do not have to insert a WordArt graphic to use the WordArt styles. You can apply WordArt styles to any text in a slide. Applying WordArt styles to regular text in a presentation is an additional way to format the text to customize the presentation. You can use the same features you used to format the WordArt graphic to format a title or bulleted text: Text Fill, Text Outline, and Text Effects. In this exercise, you practice applying WordArt styles to text.

STEP BY STEP   **Format Text with WordArt Styles**

USE the *Full Profit* presentation that is still open from the previous exercise.

1. Go to slide 2.
2. Select the slide title, On-Time Delivery.
3. On the Drawing Tools Format tab, click the More button, as shown in Figure 3-32, to produce the WordArt Styles gallery.

Figure 3-32

The More button opens the WordArt Styles gallery

More buttons

4. Click the Fill – Accent 2, Warm Matte Bevel WordArt style. See Figure 3-33. The style is applied to the selected text.

Figure 3-33

Select a WordArt style

Select this style.

5. Click outside the text placeholder to clear its border. The title should look like the one shown in Figure 3-34.

Figure 3-34

The title with WordArt applied

On-Time Delivery

6. **SAVE** and close the *Full Profit* presentation.

PAUSE. LEAVE PowerPoint open to use in the next exercise.

CREATING AND FORMATTING TEXT BOXES

The Bottom Line

Although PowerPoint layouts are very flexible and provide a number of ways to insert text, you may occasionally need to insert text in a location for which there is no default placeholder. **Text boxes** are the answer in this circumstance. A text box is a free-floating box into which you can type text. You can use text boxes as containers for extra text that is not part of a placeholder. A text box can hold a few words, an entire paragraph of text, or even several paragraphs of text. Text boxes make it easy to position content anywhere on a slide.

Adding a Text Box to a Slide

Text boxes can be used to place text on a slide anyplace you want it. In this exercise, you add a text box to a slide and then insert text into the text box.

STEP BY STEP   **Add a Text Box to a Slide**

@ The *Profit Analysis* file is available on the book companion website or in WileyPLUS.

1. **OPEN** the *Profit An ysis* presentation and save it as *Profit Analysis Boxes*.
2. Go to slide 1.
3. On the Insert tab, click **Text Box** in the Text group. The cursor changes to a text insertion pointer.
4. Move the pointer to the right side of the slide about two-thirds of the way up.
5. Click and hold down the mouse button. Drag the mouse down and to the right to create a rectangle.
6. Release the mouse button. The rectangle changes to a text box, as shown in Figure 3-35.

Figure 3-35

Inserting a text box

Fourth Coffee — Text box

Profit Analysis

WAYS TO MAXIMIZE OUR PROFITS

Take Note

When you release the mouse button after creating a text box, the Ribbon automatically displays the Home tab.

7. Type **Fourth Coffee** in the text box.
8. Click outside the text box to clear its border. Your slide should look like the one shown in Figure 3-35.
9. **SAVE** the presentation.

PAUSE. LEAVE the presentation open to use in the next exercise.

You have two options when creating a text box. If you simply click the slide with the text box pointer, you create a text box in which text will not wrap. As you enter text, the text box expands horizontally to accommodate the text. If you want to create a text box that will contain the text in a specific area, with text wrapping from line to line, you draw a desired width with the text box pointer, as you did in the preceding steps. When text reaches that border, it wraps to the next line.

Take Note   You can change a text box's wrap setting. Right-click its border and click Format Shape. On the Text Box tab of the Format Shape dialog box, mark or clear the Wrap Text in Shape check box.

Resizing a Text Box

Text boxes can be resized to make room for the addition of other text boxes or objects or to rearrange a text box's contents. In this exercise, you practice resizing text boxes on a PowerPoint slide.

STEP BY STEP   **Resize a Text Box**

USE the *Profit Analysis Boxes* presentation that is still open from the previous exercise.

1. On the View tab, click to mark the **Ruler** check box so that rulers appear around the slide.
2. Display slide 2.
3. On the Insert tab, click **Text Box** in the Text group.
4. Drag to draw a text box under the Divisional Breakdown title. Make the text box approximately 4" wide.

Take Note   The height you draw the text box does not matter because the height automatically fits the content. When blank, the text box is one line high. It expands as you type more lines.

5. Type the following items into the text box, pressing **Enter** after each item to start a new paragraph, as shown in Figure 3-36.

   Sales

   Marketing

   Purchasing

   Production

   Distribution

   Customer Service

   Human Resources

   Product Development

   Information Technology

   Administration

Figure 3-36

Type text into the text box

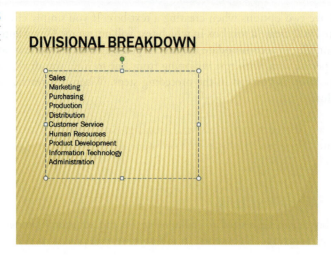

6. Move the mouse pointer to the white square in the middle of the text box's right border. This is a resizing handle, or selection handle. The pointer changes to a double-headed arrow, as shown in Figure 3-37.

Figure 3-37

Position the mouse pointer over the right-side handle on the text box frame

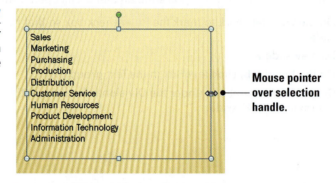

7. Click and hold down the mouse button.

Take Note   A text box has eight resizing handles: one in each corner and one in the middle of each side.

8. Drag the mouse pointer to the left until the text box's right border is close to the text (all entries should still be on a single line).

9. Release the mouse button. The text box resizes to a smaller size. Your slide should look like the one in Figure 3-38.

Figure 3-38

The resized text box

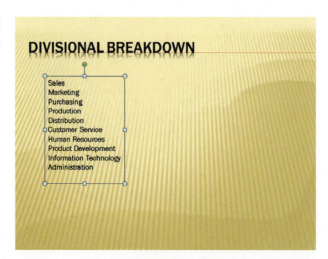

10. Click outside the text box to clear its border.

11. **SAVE** the presentation.

PAUSE. LEAVE the presentation open to use in the next exercise.

Formatting a Text Box

You can apply many different types of formatting to text boxes to make them more eye-catching and graphical. You can apply a Quick Style, add a border, or apply a solid, gradient, texture, or pattern fill to its background.

Applying a Quick Style to a Text Box

PowerPoint's **Quick Styles** allow you to quickly format any text box or placeholder with a combination of fill, border, and effect formats to make the object stand out on the slide. In this exercise, you apply a Quick Style to a text box, but PowerPoint also provides Quick Styles for other features such as tables, SmartArt graphics, charts, and pictures.

STEP BY STEP   **Apply a Quick Style to a Text Box**

USE the *Profit Analysis Boxes* presentation that is still open from the previous exercise.

1. Go to slide 1.

2. Click the Fourth Coffee text box to select it.

3. On the Home tab, click the **Quick Styles** button to display a gallery of Quick Styles.

4. Select the **Intense Effect—Accent 6** Quick Style, the last thumbnail in the last row. See Figure 3-39. The Quick Style formatting is applied to the text box.

Figure 3-39

A Quick Style applied to a text box

Select this Quick Style.

5. **SAVE** the presentation.

PAUSE. LEAVE the presentation open to use in the next exercise.

There are several advantages to using Quick Styles to format an object. Each Quick Style provides a number of formatting options that would take more time to apply separately. Quick Styles give a professional appearance to slides. Using Quick Styles can also make it easy to format consistently throughout a presentation.

Applying Fill and Border Formatting to a Text Box

If you want more control over formatting applied to a text box, you can use the Shape Fill and Shape Outline tools to set the formatting for a text box on your own. In this exercise, you apply fill and border formatting to a text box.

STEP BY STEP **Apply Fill and Border Formatting to a Text Box**

USE the *Profit Analysis Boxes* presentation that is still open from the previous exercise.

1. Go to slide 2.
2. Click inside the text box list. PowerPoint displays the text box border and sizing handles.
3. On the Drawing Tools Format tab, click the **Shape Fill drop-down arrow** in the Drawing group. The Theme Colors palette for the text box fill color appears.
4. Click the **Light Yellow, Background 2, Darker 25%** theme color. PowerPoint formats the text box fill with this color. See Figure 3-40.

Figure 3-40

Select a shape fill

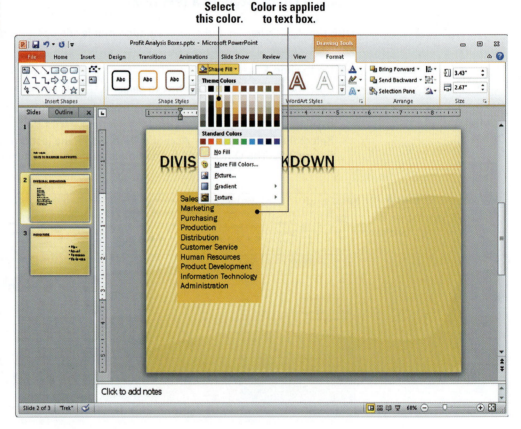

5. Click the **Shape Outline drop-down arrow**. The Theme Colors palette for the text box border color appears.
6. Click the **Orange, Accent 1, Darker 25%** theme color. PowerPoint formats the text box border with this color.
7. Click the **Shape Outline drop-down arrow** again.
8. Click **Weight**. A menu with line weights appears.
9. Click **3 pt**. PowerPoint resizes the text box border to a 3-point border size. See Figure 3-41.

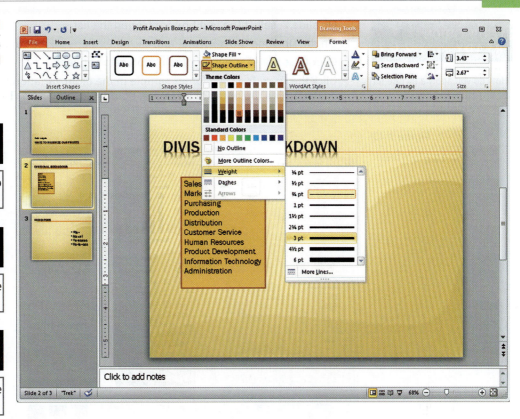

Figure 3-41

A 3-pt shape outline
has been applied

CERTIFICATION
READY   **2.6.1**

How do you apply a fill color to
a text box?

CERTIFICATION
READY   **2.6.2**

How do you change the outline
color of a text box?

CERTIFICATION
READY   **2.6.2**

How do you change the outline
weight of a text box?

Take Note

You can change the style of a text box's outline from solid to dashed or dotted by selecting the
Dashes option from the Shape Outline drop-down menu.

CERTIFICATION
READY   **2.6.2**

How do you change the outline
style of a text box?

10. **SAVE** the presentation.

PAUSE. LEAVE the presentation open to use in the next exercise.

Applying Special Fills to a Text Box

You are not limited to plain solid colors for text box fills. You can fill using gradients, patterns,
textures, and pictures to create interesting special effects. In this exercise, you insert a picture and
apply a gradient color to a text box.

STEP BY STEP   **Apply Picture and Gradient Fills to a Text Box**

USE the *Profit Analysis Boxes* presentation that is still open from the previous exercise.

1. On slide 1, select the Fourth Coffee text box.
2. On the Drawing Tools Format tab, click the **Shape Fill** button. A menu opens.
3. In the menu, click **Picture**. The Insert Picture dialog box opens.
4. Navigate to the location of the data files for this lesson and click **Coffee.jpg**.
5. Click **Insert**. The Insert Picture dialog box closes and the picture is inserted as a
   background in the text box, as in Figure 3-42.

Figure 3-42

A picture applied as a text box
background

CERTIFICATION
R E A D Y   **2.6.1**

How do you apply a picture fill
to a text box?

6. On slide 2, select the text box containing the list.

7. On the Drawing Tools Format tab, click the **Shape Fill** button. A menu appears.

8. Click **Gradient**. A menu of gradient presets appears.

9. Click the **From Top Left Corner** sample in the Light Variations section. See Figure 3-43. To determine the name of a sample, point at it so a ScreenTip appears with its name.

Figure 3-43

Select a gradient preset

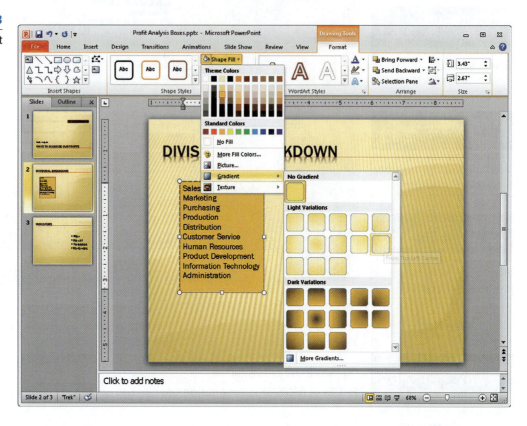

10. On the Drawing Tools Format tab, click **Shape Fill**, click **Gradient**, and click **More Gradients**. The Format Shape dialog box opens.

11. Click the **Color** button, and click **Orange, Accent 2** (see Figure 3-44). The new gradient color is immediately applied to the text box.

Figure 3-44

Select a different color for the gradient

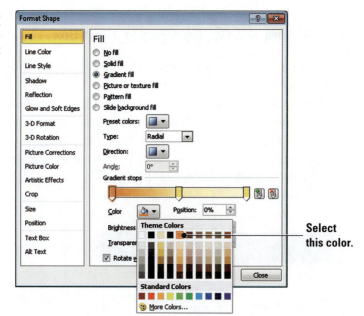

CERTIFICATION
READY   2.6.1

How do you apply a gradient
fill to a text box?

12. Click **Close** to close the dialog box.

13. **SAVE** the presentation.

PAUSE. LEAVE the presentation open to use in the next exercise.

Gradient fills can be much more complex than the simple ones you applied in the preceding exercise. You can choose from several preset color combinations in the Format Shape dialog box (Figure 3-44), or create your own color combinations. The slider in the dialog box can be adjusted to create multipoint gradient effects in which you choose exactly which colors appear and in what proportions. You can also adjust the brightness and transparency of the gradient at various points in the fill.

Applying Texture and Pattern Fills

Texture and pattern fills are alternatives to plain colored fills. As you learned earlier in the lesson, a texture fill repeats a small graphic to fill the area; texture graphics are specially designed so that the edges blend together and it looks like a single graphic. Texture graphics usually simulate some type of textured material like wood, marble, or fabric. A pattern fill is a repeating pattern that consists of a background color and a foreground color, like the pattern on a checked table cloth or a pinstripe suit. In the following exercise you apply texture and pattern fills to a text box.

STEP BY STEP   **Apply Texture and Pattern Fills to a Text Box**

USE the *Profit Analysis Boxes* presentation that is still open from the previous exercise.

1. On slide 2, click and drag to draw a new text box to the right of the existing one, approximately 4.5" in width.

2. In the new text box, type the following: **Each division makes a unique and valuable contribution to the organization**.

3. Select the new text box, and on the Drawing Tools Format tab, click **Shape Fill**, and point to Texture in the menu that appears.

4. Click the **Papyrus** texture (see Figure 3-45). It is applied to the text box.

Figure 3-45

Apply a texture fill to a text box

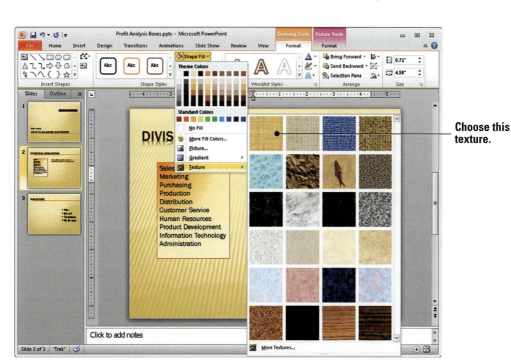

5. On slide 3, select the text box containing the bulleted list.

6. Right-click the text box's border and click **Format Shape**. The Format Shape dialog box opens.

7. Click **Fill**, and then click **Pattern Fill**. A selection of patterns appears.

8. Click the **Light Downward Diagonal** pattern (third pattern in first row).

9. Click the **Foreground Color** button to browse for a color.

10. Click **Light Yellow Background 2, Darker 25%**. See Figure 3-46.

Figure 3-46

Apply a pattern fill to a
text box

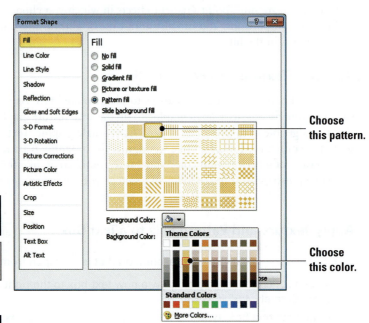

Choose
this pattern.

Choose
this color.

11. Click **Close** to close the dialog box. The new background appears in the text box.

12. **SAVE** the presentation.

PAUSE. LEAVE the presentation open to use in the next exercise.

Changing Text Box Shape and Applying Effects

You can apply the same special effects to text boxes as you can to WordArt, drawn shapes, and other objects. These special effects include reflection, glow, 3-D effects, shadows, soft edges, and beveling. You can also modify the shape of a text box, using any of the dozens of preset shapes that PowerPoint offers. In this exercise, you learn how to change the shape of a text box and apply shape effects.

STEP BY STEP   **Change Text Box Shape and Apply Effects**

USE the *Profit Analysis Boxes* presentation that is still open from the previous exercise.

1. On slide 1, select the Fourth Coffee text box.

2. On the Drawing Tools Format tab, in the Insert Shapes group, click the **Edit Shape** button. A menu opens.

3. Click **Change Shape**. A fly-out menu of shapes appears (see Figur 3-47).

Figure 3-47

Choose a different shape for the text box

Edit Shape button   Rounded Rectangle

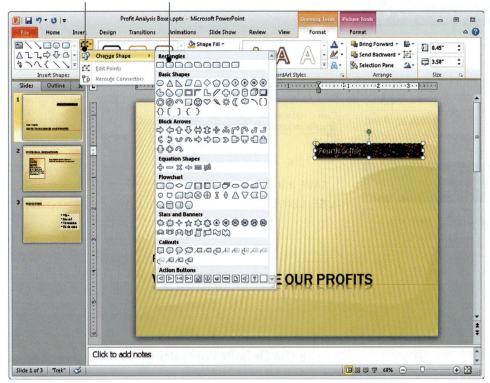

4. In the first row, click the **Rounded Rectangle**; the new shape is applied to the text box.

5. Click away from the shape so that you can see it better. The corners of the text box are now rounded.

6. On slide 2, select the Each Division text box on the right.

7. On the Drawing Tools Format tab, click the **Shape Effects** button. A menu of effects appears.

8. Point to Bevel to produce the Bevel options menu.

9. Click the **Circle bevel** effect (first effect in the first row of the Bevel section), as shown in Figure 3-48. The bevel effect is applied to the text box.

Figure 3-48

Select a bevel effect

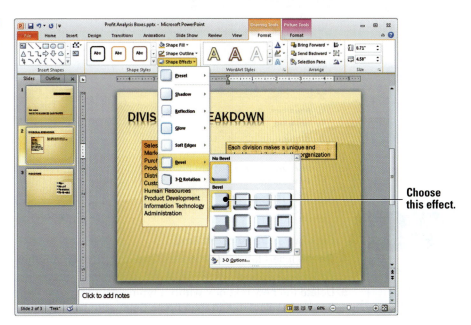

Choose this effect.

10. Click the **Shape Effects** button again, and point to Shadow to produce the shadow options menu.
11. Click the **Offset Diagonal Bottom Right** shadow (the first shadow in the Outer section).
12. Click away from the text box to see the changes better. It should resemble Figure 3-49.

Figure 3-49

The text box with bevel and
shadow effects applied

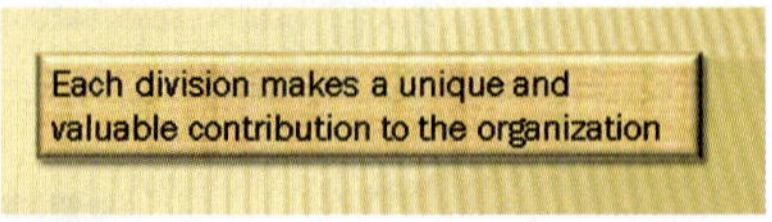

Each division makes a unique and
valuable contribution to the organization

13. **SAVE** the presentation.

PAUSE. LEAVE the presentation open to use in the next exercise.

Changing the Default Formatting for New Text Boxes

If you are going to create lots of text boxes in a presentation, there are ways you can save time in formatting them. One way is to redefine the default for new text boxes to match your desired settings, as you learn to do in this exercise.

STEP BY STEP   **Change the Default Formatting for New Text Boxes**

USE the *Profit Analysis Boxes* presentation that is still open from the previous exercise.

1. On slide 2, select the text box on the right.

Take Note   Make sure you select its outer border rather than clicking inside it. (For this activity, it makes a difference.) The outer border should appear solid, not dashed, when selected.

2. Right-click the text box's outer border. A menu appears, as shown in Figure 3-50.

Figure 3-50

Make the current text box's
formatting the default for new
text boxes

3. Click **Set as Default Text Box**.
4. On the Insert tab, click **Text Box**, and drag to draw another text box on slide 2. Notice that it is formatted the same as the other one.
5. Delete the new text box without typing anything in it. To delete a text box, click its border to select it, and then press **Delete** on the keyboard.

6. SAVE the presentation.

PAUSE. LEAVE the presentation open to use in the next exercise.

Working with Text in a Text Box

You can format the text within a text box in a number of ways: adjust alignment, change text orientation, set text margins, modify the text wrap settings, and even set the text in multiple columns.

Aligning Text in a Text Box

You use the same alignment options in a text box that are available for a text placeholder: left, center, right, and justify. By default, PowerPoint aligns text in new text boxes to the left. If you align text to a different position, such as right, and then add a new paragraph by pressing Enter from that text, the new paragraph keeps the right-aligned formatting. In the following exercise, you align text to the center of the text box.

STEP BY STEP   **Align Text in a Text Box**

USE the *Profit Analysis Boxes* presentation that is still open from the previous exercise.

1. On slide 1, click anywhere in the first line in the Profit Analysis text box.
2. Click the **Center** button. PowerPoint aligns the text so that it is centered between the left and right border of the text box.
3. Repeat this process for the Ways to Maximize Our Profits text box.
4. Click outside the text box to clear its border. Your slide should look like the one in Figure 3-51.

Figure 3-51

Center the text in the title and subtitle boxes on the first slide

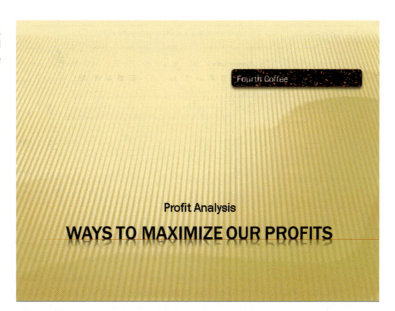

5. SAVE the presentation.

PAUSE. LEAVE the presentation open to use in the next exercise.

Take Note   If you resize a text box that has centered text, the text re-centers automatically based on the final size of the text box.

CERTIFICATION
READY   2.5.2

How do you align text within
text boxes?

The Justify alignment option keeps long passages of text even on the left and right margins of a text box, similar to the way newspapers and many books align text. PowerPoint adds extra space between words if necessary to stretch a line to meet the right margin. This can result in a very "gappy" look that you can improve by adjusting font size and/or the width of the text box. The last line of each paragraph is not affected, since Justify does not work on single-line paragraphs.

Orienting Text in a Text Box

You can change the text direction in a text box so that text runs from bottom to top or stacks one letter atop the other. This can make text in the text box more visually interesting. You can also change orientation by rotating the text box itself. The following exercise shows how to rotate the text in a text box in two different ways.

STEP BY STEP   **Orient Text in a Text Box**

USE the *Profit Analysis Boxes* presentation that is still open from the previous exercise.

1. Go to slide 1.
2. Select the Fourth Coffee text box.
3. On the Home tab, click the **Text Alignment drop-down arrow** in the Paragraph group. Ensure that the text is formatted to appear at the top of the text box.
4. On the Home tab, click the **Text Direction drop-down arrow** in the Paragraph group. A menu of text direction choices displays.
5. Click **Rotate all text 270°**, as shown in Figure 3-52. PowerPoint changes the orientation of the text in the text box to run from the bottom of the text box to the top.

Figure 3-52

Rotate the text 270 degrees

Text Direction

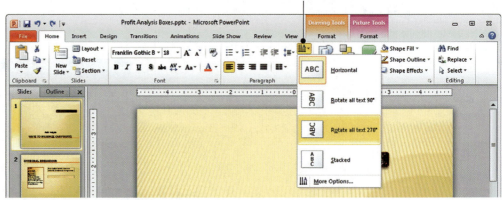

6. Drag the bottom selection handle downward on the text box, increasing the height of the text box so the text appears in a single vertical column.
7. Using the **Font Size drop-down list** on the Home tab, increase the text size to **32** points. Resize the text box again if necessary so the text is on a single line.
8. Click on the text box and drag it to the left side of the slide.

9. Click outside the text box to clear its border. Your slide should look like the one in Figure 3-53.

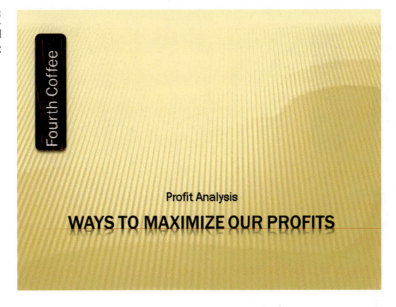

Take Note   The coffee bean graphic in the text box was distorted when the text box was resized. It is still usable, though, because now it looks like a stylized texture. If you wanted to maintain the coffee bean graphic while rotating the text, you could use the method shown in the following steps instead to rotate the entire text box.

10. Draw another text box on slide 1 and type **Sales Department** in the text box.
11. Move the mouse to the round, green rotation handle at the top center of the text box. The mouse pointer changes to an open-ended circle with an arrow point.
12. Click and hold down the mouse button.
13. Move the mouse to the right so that the outline of the text box starts to rotate around its center, as shown in Figure 3-54.

14. Rotate the text box to about a 30-degree angle, and then release the mouse button.
15. Move the rotated text box into the upper-right corner of the slide.

16. Click outside the text box to clear its sizing handles. Your slide should look like the one in Figure 3-55.

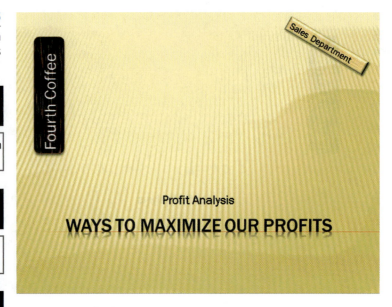

17. SAVE the presentation.

PAUSE. LEAVE the presentation open to use in the next exercise.

Orienting text boxes can be a design enhancement for your slides. For example, you might create a text box that includes your company name in it. Instead of drawing the text box horizontally on the slide, draw it so it is taller than wide and then choose one of the Text Direction button options to change text orientation. You can also rotate a text box or any placeholder for a special effect.

Setting the Margins in a Text Box

PowerPoint enables you to set the margins in a text box. Margins control the distance between the text and the outer border of the text box. In this exercise you will change the right and left margins on a text box.

STEP BY STEP   **Set the Margins in a Text Box**

USE the *Profit Analysis Boxes* presentation that is still open from the previous exercise.

1. Go to slide 3.
2. Select the text box on the right side of the slide, and drag it to the left side of the slide, under the Indicators title.
3. Right-click inside the text box and click **Format Shape** on the shortcut menu. The Format Shape dialog box opens.
4. Click **Text Box** in the left pane of the Format Shape dialog box. Text box layout options appear, as shown in Figure 3-56.

Figure 3-56

Set the margins in the Format Shape dialog box

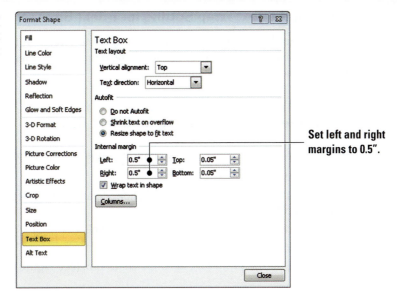

Set left and right margins to 0.5".

5. Click the **Left spin button** (up arrow) to set the left margin at **0.5"**.

6. Click the **Right spin button** to set the right margin at **0.5"**. Figure 3-56 shows the correct settings.

7. Click **Close**. PowerPoint applies the margin changes to the text box.

8. Widen the text box to 4" so that each bullet point appears on a single line. Your slide should look like the one shown in Figure 3-57.

Figure 3-57

Text box with new margins

How do you set internal margins in text boxes?

9. **SAVE** the presentation.

PAUSE. LEAVE the presentation open to use in the next exercise.

Resizing text box margins enables you to fine-tune text placement within a text box. For example, if you want text to appear 1 inch away from the left side of the text box, change the Left box to 1.0. You might want to do this if your slide design needs to have text align with other items placed on the slide. If you have chosen to format a text box or placeholder with a fill, increasing margins can also prevent the text from appearing to crowd the edges of the text box.

Changing the Text Wrap Setting for a Text Box

Depending on the type of text box and the way it was created, it may or may not be set to wrap the text automatically to the next line when the right margin is reached. In the next exercise you will learn how to view and change this setting.

Change the Text Wrap Setting for a Text Box

USE the *Profit Analysis Boxes* presentation that is still open from the previous exercise.

1. Go to slide 2.
2. If there is an empty text box on the slide, delete it. To delete a text box, select its outer border and press the **Delete** key.
3. Right-click the Each division... text box and click **Format Shape**.
4. Click **Text Box** on the left.
5. Click to clear the **Wrap text in shape** check box (see Figure 3-58).

Figure 3-58

The Wrap Text in Shape check box controls text wrap

Wrap text in shape text box

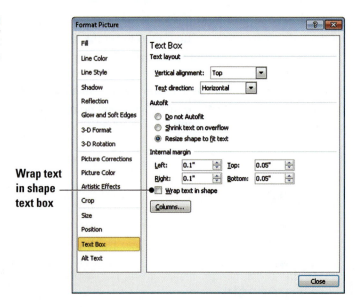

6. Click **Close** to close the dialog box. The text now overruns the slide because it is on a single line.
7. Click in the text box, and click after the word *and* to place the insertion point there.
8. Press **Shift**+**Enter** to manually insert a line break.

PAUSE. LEAVE the presentation open to use in the next exercise.

Setting Up Columns in a Text Box

PowerPoint enables you to create columns in text boxes to present information you want to set up in lists across the slide but do not want to place in PowerPoint tables. As you enter text or other items into a column, PowerPoint fills up the first column and then wraps text to the next column. Viewers of your presentation may have an easier time reading and remembering lists formatted into multiple columns. You can create columns in any text box, placeholder, or shape. In the following exercise you will change a text box so that it uses two columns.

STEP BY STEP   **Set Up Columns in a Text Box**

USE the *Profit Analysis Boxes* presentation that is still open from the previous exercise.

1. On slide 2, drag the *Each division…* text box to the bottom of the slide.
2. Click in the text box that contains the list of divisions.
3. On the Home tab, click the **Columns** button. A menu appears, as shown in Figure 3-59.

Figure 3-59

Set the text box in two columns

4. Click **Two Columns**. PowerPoint formats the list of items into two columns. The columns are truncated at this point because the text box is not wide enough.
5. Drag the right border of the text box to the right to widen it enough that two columns can appear side by side with neither one truncated.
6. On the Drawing Tools Format tab, click the **Shape Height button's down-pointing spin arrow**, decreasing the shape height, until each column contains five lines of text, as shown in Figure 3-60.

Figure 3-60

Decrease the shape height and increase its width to accommodate the multicolumn list

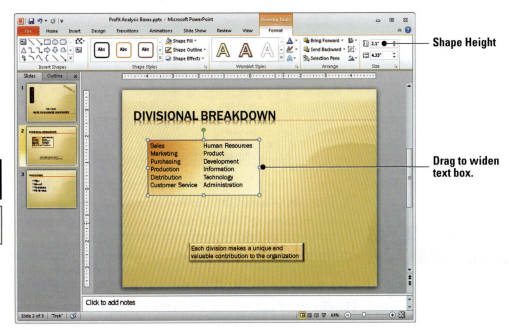

CERTIFICATION READY   2.6.6

How do you create columns in a text box?

   **Another Way**
If you need two lists on a slide but do not want to use columns, create two text boxes and position them side by side, or switch to a slide layout that contains two side-by-side placeholder boxes.

7. **SAVE** the *Profit Analysis Boxes* presentation.

PAUSE. LEAVE the presentation open to use in the next exercise.

Take Note   If the column choices in the Column drop-down menu do not meet your needs, click the More Columns option to display the Columns dialog box. Here you can set any number of columns and adjust the spacing between columns.

Aligning Text Boxes on a Slide

In addition to aligning the text within a text box, you can align the text box itself with other objects on the slide, including other text boxes. Doing so ensures that the items on a slide align precisely and neatly with one another when it is appropriate for them to do so. For example, you might have two text boxes side by side, and top-aligning them with one another ensures that the slide's overall appearance is balanced.

STEP BY STEP   **Align Text Boxes**

USE the *Profit Analysis Boxes* presentation that is still open from the previous exercise.

1. On slide 2, click the text box that contains the bulleted list, to select the text box. Click the border, not inside the box.
2. Hold down the Shift key and click the text box at the bottom of the slide. It is also selected.
3. On the Drawing Tools Format tab, click the **Align** button. A menu appears, as shown in Figure 3-61.

Figure 3-61

Choose how text boxes should align

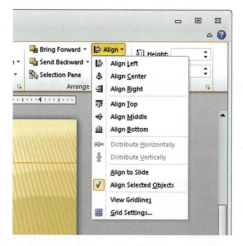

4. Click **Align Center**. The two text boxes are centered in relation to one another.
5. On the Drawing Tools Format tab, click the **Align** button again, and click **Align to Slide**. Nothing changes in the text box placement yet.

CERTIFICATION READY   2.6.5

How do you set alignment of text boxes?

6. On the Drawing Tools Format tab, click the **Align** button again, and click **Align Center**. Both text boxes become center-aligned in relation to the slide itself.
7. **SAVE** and close the *Profit Analysis Boxes* presentation.

LEAVE PowerPoint open to use in the next exercise.

Take Note   The Left, Right, and Center commands on the Align menu refer to horizontal alignment, either in relation to the slide or to other selected content. The Top, Middle, and Bottom commands refer to vertical alignment.

USING PROOFING TOOLS

The Bottom Line   The Spelling and Thesaurus features in PowerPoint help you ensure your presentation's text is professionally written and edited, free from spelling errors.

Checking Spelling

The Spelling feature in PowerPoint compares each word in the presentation to its built-in and custom dictionaries, and flags any words that it does not find, plus any instances of repeated words, such as *the the*. You can then evaluate the found words and decide how to proceed with each one. Misspelled words appear with a wavy red underline in the presentation, and you can deal with each one individually by right-clicking it. Alternately you can open the Spelling dialog box and work through all the possible misspellings at once. In this exercise, you practice using PowerPoint's Spelling feature using both of those methods.

STEP BY STEP	Check Spelling

@ The *TV Options* file is available on the book companion website or in WileyPLUS.

GET READY. To check spelling, perform the following tasks:

1. **OPEN** the *TV Options* presentation and save it as *TV Options Corrected*.
2. On slide 1, notice that the word *Satelite* is misspelled, and that it has a wavy red underline.
3. Right-click the word *Satelite*. A list of possible spelling corrections appears.
4. In the list, click **Satellite**. The correction is made (See Figure 3-62).

Figure 3-62

Correct a single misspelled word from the shortcut menu

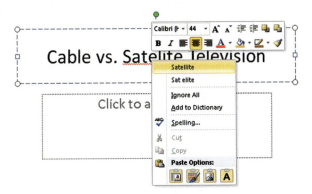

5. On the Review tab, click **Spelling** in the Proofing group. The Spelling dialog box opens, and the Spelling feature finds and flags the next misspelled word, as shown in Figure 3-63. The Change to Suggestions list contains only one possible correction.

Figure 3-63

Correct multiple spelling errors quickly with the Spelling dialog box

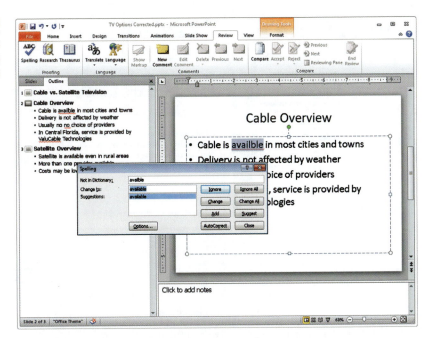

6. Click **Change** to change to the correct spelling of *available*. The next problem identified is a repeated word, *no*.

7. Click **Delete** to delete one of the words *no*. The next problem that appears is a proper name, *ValuCable*, which is actually a correct spelling.

8. Click **Ignore** to ignore the potential misspelling. You could have also clicked Add to add it to the dictionary, but because it is a made-up word for this exercise, Ignore is more appropriate.

9. Click **Change** to change to the correct spelling of *cable*. A message appears that the spelling check is complete.

10. Click **OK** to close the dialog box.

11. **SAVE** the presentation.

PAUSE. LEAVE the presentation open for the next exercise.

Use caution with the Change All button, because it may make changes you do not intend. For example, if you correct all instances at once where you have typed *pian* instead of *pain*, it will also change all instances of *piano* to *paino*.

Using the Thesaurus

A thesaurus is a reference book or utility that offers suggestions for words that are similar in meaning to the word you are looking up (synonyms) or that are opposite in meaning (antonyms). PowerPoint includes a built-in thesaurus. In the following exercise you will use it to find an alternate word.

STEP BY STEP **Change a Word with the Thesaurus**

USE the *TV Options Corrected* presentation that is still open from the previous exercise.

1. On slide 3, select the word **Costs**.

2. On the Review tab, click **Thesaurus**. The Research task pane opens with the Thesaurus controls displayed, along with a list of terms related to the word you have selected.

3. In the Research task pane, hover the mouse pointer over the word Charges. Click the **down arrow** that appears to the right of Charges, then click **Insert** from the menu that appears, as shown in Figure 3-64. The word *Costs* changes to *Charges* on the slide.

Figure 3-64

Find word alternatives with Thesaurus

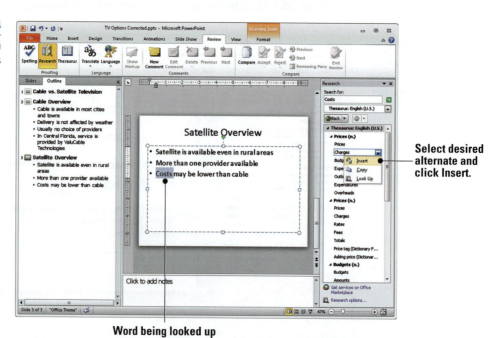

Select desired alternate and click Insert.

Word being looked up

CERTIFICATION
READY   6.2.1

How do you use the Spelling and Thesaurus features?

4. In the task pane, click the word **Prices**. The display changes to show synonyms of that word.

5. Click the **Back** button in the task pane to return to the list of synonyms for Costs.

SAVE the presentation and **EXIT** PowerPoint.

SKILL SUMMARY

In This Lesson You Learned How To:	Exam Objective	Objective Number
Format characters.	Change text format.	2.5.2
	Use text effects.	2.5.1
	Use Format Painter.	2.5.8
	Use AutoFit.	2.6.10
Format paragraphs.	Change text format.	2.5.2
Work with lists.	Changing the formatting of bulleted and numbered lists.	2.5.3
Insert and format WordArt.	Change WordArt.	3.3.3
	Change the fill color or texture (of WordArt).	3.3.2
Create and format text boxes.	Apply formatting to a text box.	2.6.1
	Change the outline of a text box.	2.6.2
	Change the shape of the text box.	2.6.3
	Apply effects.	2.6.4
	Set the current text box formatting as the default for new text boxes.	2.6.8
	Change text format.	2.5.2
	Adjust text in a text box.	2.6.9
	Set internal margins.	2.6.7
	Create columns in a text box.	2.6.6
	Set the alignment.	2.6.5
Use proofing tools.	Use PowerPoint proofing.	1.4.1
	Use spelling and thesaurus features.	6.2.1

Knowledge Assessment

Fill in the Blank

Fill in each blank with the term or phrase that best completes the statement.

1. A(n) _____ is a container for text on a slide.

2. A(n) _____ is a set of characters, numbers, and symbols in a specific style or design.

3. The _____ feature, when needed, shrinks the size of the text in a text box in order to fit it in the box.

4. A(n) _____ is a symbol that appears to the left of each paragraph in a list.

5. The _____ feature enables you to copy formatting from one block of text to another.

6. _____ text is aligned to both the left and right margins of a text box.

7. A(n) _____ indent is a reverse indent for the first line of a paragraph, where the first line is indented less than the other lines.

8. A(n) _____ object is text in the form of a graphic.

9. The _____ in PowerPoint can be used to look up synonyms.

10. To _____ a text box, drag one of its selection handles.

Multiple Choice

Circle the correct answer.

1. You can select a different font from the _____ tab on the Ribbon.

   a. Home

   b. Font

   c. Layout

   d. Review

2. You can select fonts and font sizes either from the Ribbon or the _____.

   a. Status bar

   b. Scroll bar

   c. Mini toolbar

   d. File menu

3. Which of the following is not a paragraph alignment type?

   a. All

   b. Center

   c. Justify

   d. Right

4. When selecting a color, such as from the Font Color button's palette, the colors on the top row are:

   a. standard colors

   b. tints

   c. shades

   d. theme colors

5. Most of PowerPoint's text placeholders automatically format text as a(n) _____ list.

   a. numbered

   b. bulleted

   c. sorted

   d. itemized

6. Reflection is one type of _____ you can apply to WordArt.

   a. effect

   b. font

   c. alignment

   d. spacing

7. A text box's _____ determine(s) how close the text comes to the sides, top, and bottom border of the box.

   a. orientation

   b. margins

   c. padding

   d. alignment

8. To apply a WordArt style to existing text on a slide, you must first:

   a. format the text with a Quick Style

   b. insert a text box

   c. select the text

   d. change the text's alignment

9. What does it mean when a word has a wavy red underline?

    a. The word is inconsistently formatted compared to the surrounding text.

    b. There is a grammar error.

    c. The word is not in the dictionary.

    d. The capitalization does not match that of the surrounding text.

10. A thesaurus enables you to look up synonyms and _____.

    a. alternate spellings

    b. antonyms

    c. translations

    d. pronunciations

Competency Assessment

Project 3-1: Blended Coffees

As director of marketing for Fourth Coffee, you have prepared a product brochure for new company employees. This year's brochure includes a new page of refreshments that you need to format. You will use Quick Styles to format the title and text placeholders. You will also correct a spelling error.

GET READY. LAUNCH PowerPoint if it is not already running.

The *Coffee Products* file is available on the book companion website or in WileyPLUS.

1. **OPEN** the *Coffee Products* presentation and save it as *Coffee Products Brochure*.

2. Go to slide 2 and click anywhere in the slide title.

3. Click the **Quick Styles** button to display the Quick Styles gallery.

4. Click the **Moderate Effect – Orange, Accent 1** style.

5. Click in any of the bulleted product items.

6. Click the **Quick Styles** button.

7. Click the **Subtle Effect – Orange, Accent 1** style.

8. Right-click the red-underlined word and select *caffeine* as the correct spelling.

9. **SAVE** the presentation and **CLOSE** the file.

LEAVE PowerPoint open for the next project.

Project 3-2: Typecasting with Typefaces

As an account representative for the Graphic Design Institute, you are responsible for securing sales leads for your company's print and poster division. One way to do this is to send out a promotional flyer using a slide from a company PowerPoint presentation. As you select the slide, you notice that the fonts are not appropriate for your flyer. You need to modify both the font and size of the slide's text.

The *Graphic Designs* file is available on the book companion website or in WileyPLUS.

1. **OPEN** the *Graphic Designs* presentation.

2. On slide 1, select all the text under the three photographs.

3. Click the **Font drop-down arrow**.

4. Click **Brush Script MT**.

5. Click the **Font Size drop-down arrow**.

6. Click **32**.

7. Click anywhere in the second paragraph (*Graphic Design Institute*).

8. Click the **Center** button in the Paragraph group.

9. Select the first paragraph of text, and then click the **Format Painter** in the Clipboard group.

10. Go to slide 2, and then drag the Format Painter pointer over the text on the right side of the slide.

11. **SAVE** the presentation as *Graphic Designs Final* and **CLOSE** the file.

LEAVE PowerPoint open for the next project.

Project 3-3: Destinations

As the owner and operator of Margie's Travel, you are involved with many aspects of sales, marketing, customer service, and new products and services. Today you want to format the text in a slide presentation that includes new European destinations.

@ The *New Destinations* file is available on the book companion website or in WileyPLUS.

1. **OPEN** the *New Destinations* presentation.
2. Go to slide 2 and select the slide's title text. Click the **Bold** button to make the title boldface.
3. Select all the text in the bulleted list. Click the **Align Text Left** button to align the list along the left side of the text placeholder.
4. With the list still selected, open the Bullets and Numbering dialog box. Change the bullets' color to **Orange, Accent 2**, and then resize the bullets so they are 90% of the text's size.
5. Click the **Font Color drop-down arrow**, and then change the list's font color to **Dark Green, Background 2, Lighter 80%**.
6. Click **Text Box** on the Insert tab, and then click below the picture on the slide to create a nonwrapping text box.
7. In the text box, type **Companion Flies Free until Jan. 1!**.
8. On the Home tab, click the **Quick Styles** button and apply the **Colored Outline – Olive Green, Accent 1** Quick Style to the text box.
9. **SAVE** the presentation as *New Destinations Final* and **CLOSE** the file.

LEAVE PowerPoint open for the next project.

Project 3-4: Business To Business Imports

You are the lone marketing research person in your company, World Wide Importers. You often find exciting and potentially highly profitable new products that go overlooked by some of the senior staff. You need to draw attention to these products, and PowerPoint can help. Create a short presentation that uses WordArt to jazz up your presentation. This presentation will focus on precision equipment your company can start importing.

@ The *World Wide Importers* file is available on the book companion website or in WileyPLUS.

1. **OPEN** the *World Wide Importers* presentation.
2. With slide 1 on the screen, on the Home tab, open the WordArt gallery and select **Gradient Fill – Aqua Accent 1, Outline – White, Glow – Accent 2**. (It's the first style in the fourth row.)
3. In the WordArt text box that appears, type **World Wide Importers**. Reposition the text box so it is just above the subtitle and centered between the left and right edges of the slide.
4. On the Drawing Tools Format tab, in the WordArt Styles group, open the Text Fill color palette and click **Aqua, Accent 1, Darker 25%**.
5. Open the Text Effects menu and select the **Cool Slant** bevel effect. (It's the rightmost style in the first row of the Bevel section.)
6. Go to slide 2 and select all the text in the bulleted list.
7. Change the font size to **24**, and then change the line spacing to **1.5**.
8. Click the **Numbering** button to convert the list into a numbered list.
9. Go to slide 3. Insert a text box under the slide's title. Type the following items into the text box, putting each item on its own line:

   Digital controls

   Heat sensors

   Laser guides

   Light sensors

   Motion detectors

   Pressure monitors

   Regulators

   Timing systems

10. Select all the text in the text box and change the font size to **24**.

11. On the Home tab, open the Quick Styles gallery and click **Colored Fill – Gray 50%, Accent 4**.

12. Click the **Columns** button, and then click **Two Columns**.

13. Resize the text box as needed, so that four items appear in each column within the text box.

14. **SAVE** the presentation as *World Wide Importers Final* and **CLOSE** the file.

LEAVE PowerPoint open for the next project.

Mastery Assessment

Project 3-5: Pop Quiz

As an instructor at the School of Fine Art, you decide to use a slide show to give beginning students the first pop quiz on art history. You need to finish the presentation by formatting the text and removing some unneeded text boxes.

@ The *Art History* file is available on the book companion website or in WileyPLUS.

1. **OPEN** the *Art History* presentation.

2. On slides 2, 3, and 4, do each of the following:

    a. Format the slide's title with the **Intense Effect – Dark Blue, Dark 1** Quick Style.

    b. Convert the bulleted list of answers into a numbered list.

    c. Delete the text box (containing the correct answer) at the bottom of the slide.

3. **SAVE** the presentation as *Art History Final* and **CLOSE** the file.

LEAVE PowerPoint open for the next project.

Project 3-6: Graphic Design Drafts

As the manager of the account representative that prepared the Graphic Designs slide, you want to put a few finishing touches on the slide before it is published. To protect against someone inadvertently printing the slide, you need to add a text box across the entire slide that labels the slide as a "Draft."

1. **OPEN** the *Graphic Designs Final* presentation you completed in Project 3-2.

2. **SAVE** the presentation as *Graphic Designs Draft*.

3. Add a text box at the top of slide 1, and type **DRAFT** into the text box.

4. Rotate the text box at a 45-degree angle across the center photo on the slide.

5. Enlarge the text to **88** points. Resize the text box as needed by dragging its sizing handles so the text fits properly inside the box.

6. Using Text Effects on the Drawing Tools Format tab, apply the **Aqua, 18 point glow, Accent Color 1** glow effect to the text.

7. **SAVE** and **CLOSE** the presentation.

CLOSE PowerPoint.

INTERNET READY

Launch your browser and visit the Microsoft website at http://www.microsoft.com. On the Microsoft home page, click in the Search box, type the word *fonts*, and then click the Search button. Look for pages on the Microsoft site that offer information about fonts; read the information to learn about how fonts are created and to find tips for using fonts wisely in your documents and presentations.

4 Designing a Presentation

LESSON SKILL MATRIX

Skill	Exam Objective	Objective Number
Formatting Presentations with Themes	Modify themes.	2.4.2
Changing Slide Backgrounds	Apply formatting to a slide.	2.4.4
Working with Different Layouts	Switch to a different slide layout.	2.4.3
Inserting a Date, Footer, and Slide Numbers	Set up slide footers.	2.4.5
Linking to Web Pages and Other Programs	Add hyperlinks to graphical elements.	3.1.7
Working with Sections	Format sections.	2.4.1
Customizing Slide Masters		

KEY TERMS

- action
- action button
- font theme
- footer
- header
- hyperlink
- layout
- layout master
- section
- slide master
- theme

124

Southridge Video is a small company that offers video services to the community, such as videography for special events, video editing services, and duplication and conversion services. As a sales representative for Southridge Video, you often present information on the company to those who are considering the use of professional-level video services. In this lesson, you will add design elements to a simple presentation to polish and improve its appearance. You will also learn how to break down a presentation into sections and to customize slide masters to make global changes to a presentation.

SOFTWARE ORIENTATION

Microsoft PowerPoint's Themes Gallery

PowerPoint's Themes gallery offers 40 unique designs you can apply to presentations to format the slides with colors, fonts, effects, and backgrounds. Figure 4-1 shows the Themes gallery.

Figure 4-1

The Themes gallery

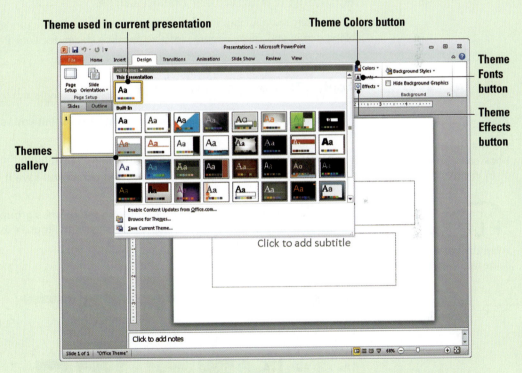

Use PowerPoint's built-in themes to give your presentation a polished, professional look without a lot of trial and error. You can preview a theme by pointing at it in the Themes gallery, and then apply it to the presentation by clicking it.

FORMATTING PRESENTATIONS WITH THEMES

A PowerPoint **theme** includes a set of colors designed to work well together, a set of fonts (one for headings and one for body text), special effects that can be applied to objects such as pictures or shapes, and often a graphic background. The theme also controls the layout of placeholders on each slide. Use a theme to quickly apply a unified look to one or more slides in a presentation (or to the entire presentation). You can also modify a theme and save your changes as a new custom theme.

PowerPoint makes it easy to see how a theme will look on your slides by offering a *live preview*: As you move the mouse pointer over each theme in the gallery, that theme's formats display on the current slide. This formatting feature takes a great deal of guesswork out of the design process—if you don't like a theme's appearance, just move the pointer to a different theme or click outside the gallery to restore the previous appearance.

Clicking a theme applies it to all slides in a presentation. You can also apply a theme to a single slide or a selection of slides by making the selection, right-clicking the theme, and choosing Apply to Selected Slides.

A theme differs from a template in that it contains no sample content—only formatting specifications.

Applying a Theme to a Presentation

In this exercise, you learn how to select a theme from the Themes gallery to replace the default blank design and create a more visually appealing design for your PowerPoint presentations.

Apply a Theme to a Presentation

The *Special Events* file is available on the book companion website or in WileyPLUS.

WileyPLUS Extra! features an online tutorial of this task.

GET READY. Before you begin these steps, make sure that your computer is on. Log on, if necessary.

1. **START** PowerPoint, if the program is not already running.
2. Locate and open the *Special Events* presentation and save it as *Special Events Final*.
3. Make sure slide 1 is selected.
4. On the **Design** tab, click the **More** button in the Themes group. PowerPoint's available themes display in the Themes gallery, as shown in Figure 4-2.

Figure 4-2

The Themes gallery

5. Point to any of the themes in the gallery. Notice that a ScreenTip displays the theme's name and the theme formats are instantly applied to the slide behind the gallery.

6. Right-click the **Clarity** theme (second theme in the second row); a pop-up menu appears. In the menu, click **Apply to Selected Slides**. The Clarity theme is applied only to slide 1.

Take Note The theme names are in alphabetical order in the gallery.

7. Click the **More** button again in the Themes group to reopen the Themes gallery.

8. Right-click the **Origin** theme, and click **Apply to Selected Slides** to apply it to all slides.

9. Scroll through the slides to see how the theme has supplied new colors, fonts, bullet symbols, and layouts. Slide 1 should resemble Figure 4-3.

Figure 4-3

Origin theme applied to all slides in the presentation

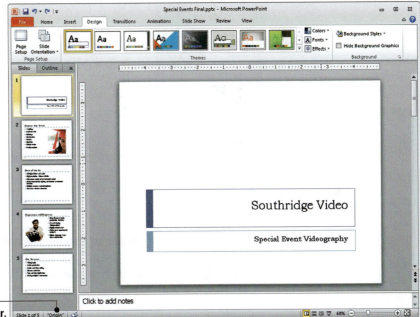

Current theme name appears on the status bar.

10. SAVE the presentation.

PAUSE. LEAVE the presentation open to use in the next exercise.

Take Note The name of the current theme is displayed on the status bar to the right of the slide number information.

Changing Theme Colors

If you don't like the colors used in the theme you've chosen, you can change them. You can select the colors from some other theme, or you can create your own color theme. When you apply the colors from another theme, your current theme fonts, background graphics, and effects remain the same—only the colors change. In this exercise, you choose a different color theme for a presentation.

STEP BY STEP **Change Theme Colors**

USE the *Special Events Final* presentation that is still open from the previous exercise.

1. Click the **Colors** button in the Themes group. A gallery displays showing color palettes for all available themes.

2. Move the pointer over some of the color palettes to see the live preview of those colors on the current slide (see Figure 4-4).

Figure 4-4

Apply a different color theme to the presentation

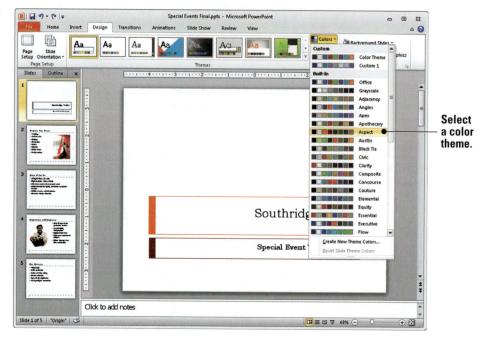

Select a color theme.

3. Click the **Aspect** theme color palette. The new colors are applied to the presentation.

4. Click the **Colors** button again, and then click **Create New Theme Colors** at the bottom of the gallery. The dialog box opens to allow you to replace colors in the current color palette.

Take Note   Color palettes and font combinations are identified by theme name to make it easy to select them.

5. Click the drop-down arrow next to the light green color designated for Hyperlinks.

6. Click **Gray 80% Background 2, Lighter 25%** on the Theme Colors palette to change the color for hyperlinks to a medium gray (see Figure 4-5).

Figure 4-5

The Create New Theme Colors dialog box

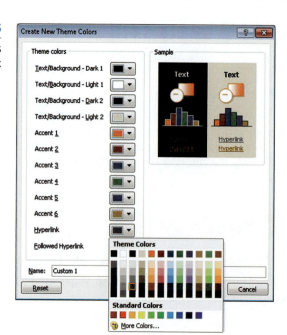

CERTIFICATION
READY 2.4.2

How do you modify
themes?

7. Select the text in the Name box and type **Southridge** in its place.
8. Click **Save** to save the new color palette.
9. **SAVE** the presentation.

PAUSE. LEAVE the presentation open to use in the next exercise.

To create a unique appearance, you can choose new colors for theme elements in the Create New Theme Colors dialog box. This dialog box displays the theme's color palette and shows you what element each color applies to. A preview area shows the colors in use; as you change colors, the preview changes to show how the new colors work together. If you don't like the choices you have made, use the Reset button to restore the default colors.

You can save a new color theme to make it available for use with any theme. Saved color themes display at the top of the Theme Colors gallery in the Custom section. To save a color theme, on the Design tab, click Colors, and click Create New Theme Colors.

Changing Theme Fonts

Each theme supplies a combination of two fonts to be applied to headings and text. Collectively these two fonts are called a **font theme**. Each font theme's name is the same as the theme from which it came. For example, there is an overall theme called Origin, and also a font theme called Origin that consists of its fonts. That's useful because you can pick and choose elements of different themes to use in your presentation—the layouts of one theme, the colors of another, and the fonts of yet another. In the following exercise, you choose a different font theme for a presentation.

STEP BY STEP | **Change Theme Fonts**

USE the *Special Events Final* presentation that is still open from the previous exercise.

1. Click the **Fonts** button in the Themes group. A gallery displays showing font combinations for all available themes.
2. Move the pointer over some of the font combinations to see the live preview of those fonts on the current slide.
3. Click the **Trek** font combination, as shown in Figure 4-6. The new fonts are applied to the presentation.

Figure 4-6

Choose a new theme font

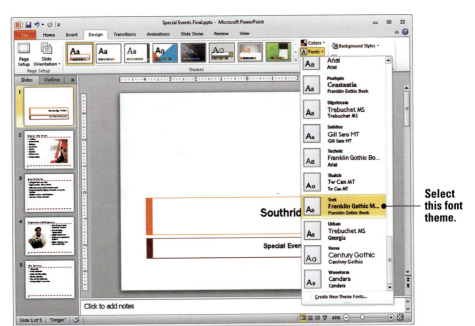

Select
this font
theme.

4. **SAVE** the presentation.

PAUSE. LEAVE the presentation open to use in the next exercise.

PowerPoint supplies a wide variety of font combinations to allow you to choose among traditional *serif fonts* and contemporary *sans serif* fonts. A serif is a "tail" or flourish on the edges of each letter, such as the tiny vertical lines hanging off the top edges of a capital T. The body text in this book uses a serif font; the headings use a sans-serif font. The choice you make depends a great deal on the subject of your presentation and the impression you are trying to convey with your slides.

As with theme colors, you can select your own theme fonts and save them to be available to apply to any theme. Click Create New Theme Fonts at the bottom of the Theme Fonts gallery, select a heading font and body font, and then save the combination with a new name.

CHANGING SLIDE BACKGROUNDS

The Bottom Line

Themes provide a default background for all slides formatted with that theme. To customize a theme or draw attention to one or more slides, you can apply a different background.

Selecting a Theme Background

The Background Styles gallery allows you to choose from plain, light, or dark backgrounds and gradient backgrounds that gradually change from light to dark. Background colors are determined by the theme. Some background styles include graphic effects such as fine lines or textures over the entire background. Use the Background Styles gallery to quickly apply a different solid-color or gradient background based on theme colors. You can apply a background to one or more selected slides or to all slides in the presentation. In this exercise, you will select a background style from the preset backgrounds provided by the theme.

STEP BY STEP   **Select a Theme Background**

USE the *Special Events Final* presentation that is still open from the previous exercise.

1. Go to slide 1.
2. On the Design tab, click the **Background Styles** button in the Background group. A gallery displays as shown in Figure 4-7, showing some background styles created using the theme's designated background colors.

Figure 4-7

Background Styles gallery

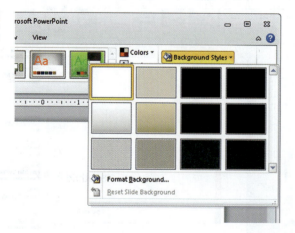

Take Note   Hover the pointer on a background style to see its name and preview it on the current slide.

3. Right-click **Style 6**, then click **Apply to Selected Slides**. The background style is applied to slide 1 only.

4. **SAVE** the presentation.

PAUSE. LEAVE the presentation open to use in the next exercise.

The area of the slide that is considered to be "background" can change depending on the theme. For example, some themes have graphics overlaid on a colored background, so that your choice of background color peeks through in only a few spots.

Applying a Custom Background

The same background options that you learned about in Lesson 3 for text boxes also apply to slide backgrounds. Use the Format Background dialog box to create and modify any background, even a default theme background. You can apply a solid color or gradient fill, or select a picture or texture for the background. Options for each of these fill types allow you to modify the fill to suit your needs. In this exercise, you will create your own custom background.

STEP BY STEP　　　**Apply a Custom Background**

USE the *Special Events Final* presentation that is still open from the previous exercise.

1. With slide 1 still active, click the **Background Styles** button, then click **Format Background** at the bottom of the gallery. The Format Background dialog box opens. It shows a gradient because the style you selected in the previous exercise was a gradient.

Take Note　If you wished to apply a solid color background to the slide, you would select the Solid Fill option from the Format Background dialog box.

Another Way
Display the Format Background dialog box by right-clicking any blank area of the slide background and then clicking Format Background from the shortcut menu. Or, click the Background group's dialog box launcher.

2. Click the **Preset Colors drop-down arrow** and in the drop-down list, click the **Gold** preset. The slide background changes behind the dialog box.

3. Click the **Type drop-down arrow** and click **Rectangular** in the drop-down list (see Figure 4-8). The pattern of the gradient changes.

Figure 4-8

Format Background dialog box with gradient controls

Select Gradient fill if it is not already selected.

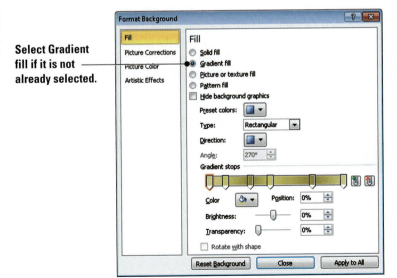

4. Click the **Solid Fill** option button. The controls change to those for solid colors.

5. Click the **Color drop-down arrow** and in the gallery that appears, click **Tan, Accent 6** (the last color in the color theme gallery).

6. Drag the Transparency slider to **35%**. The fill lightens because it is now partly transparent. See Figure 4-9.

Figure 4-9

Options for solid-color
background fills

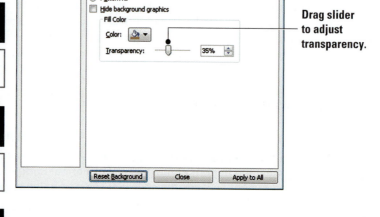

7. Click **Picture or texture fill**. The controls change to those for pictures and textures.

8. Click the **Texture** button, and then click the **Sand** texture (third texture in second row).

9. Click **Pattern**. The controls change to those for patterns.

10. Click the **10%** pattern (first pattern in second row).

11. Open the **Foreground Color drop-down list** and click **Orange, Accent 1**.

12. Click **Close**. The pattern background is applied to only the current slide (slide 1).

13. **SAVE** the presentation.

PAUSE. LEAVE the presentation open to use in the next exercise.

 Another Way
If you had wanted
to apply the new background
to all the slides, you could have
clicked Apply to All before
clicking Close in step 12.

For any background choice, you can increase transparency to "wash out" the background so it doesn't overwhelm your text. For a solid color, you might increase its transparency. For a gradient fill background, you can adjust the gradient by adding or removing colors. By default, a new slide background created in this dialog box applies only to the current slide. Click the Apply to All button to apply the background to the entire presentation.

WORKING WITH DIFFERENT LAYOUTS

The Bottom Line

Slide **layouts** control the position of text and objects on a slide. Select a layout according to the content you need to add to it. If your current layout does not present information as you want it, you can change the layout.

Working with a Different Slide Layout

If you have applied a theme, the slide layout gallery shows available layouts with theme formatting. If more than one theme is in use in the presentation (for example, if you applied a different theme to only selected slides), the slide layout gallery shows available layouts from all themes so you can pick and choose among a greater variety of layout options. In this exercise, you learn to apply a different slide layout to a PowerPoint slide. In this exercise, you will choose a different layout for a slide.

STEP BY STEP   **Work with a Different Slide Layout**

USE the *Special Events Final* presentation that is still open from the previous exercise.

1. Click the **Home** tab on the Ribbon.
2. Go to slide 5 and click **New Slide** in the Slides group. PowerPoint adds a new slide with the same layout as slide 5, Title and Content.
3. Type the title **Contact Information**.
4. Type the following information as the first bullet point in the text placeholder:

   457 Gray Road
   North Hills, OH 45678

Take Note   Use **Shift+Enter** after typing *Road* to start a new line without starting a new paragraph.

5. Type these additional bullet points:

   Phone: (513) 555-6543
   Fax: (513) 555-5432

6. Select the entire bulleted list and click the **Bullets** button on the Home tab to turn off the bullets. Your slide should look like Figure 4-10.

Figure 4-10

Add contact information to the slide

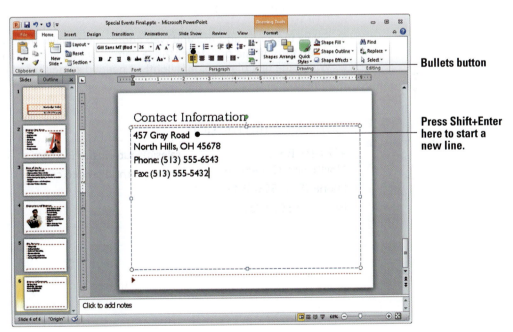

7. On the Home tab, click the **Layout** button to display the slide layout gallery shown in Figure 4-11.

Figure 4-11

Slide layout gallery

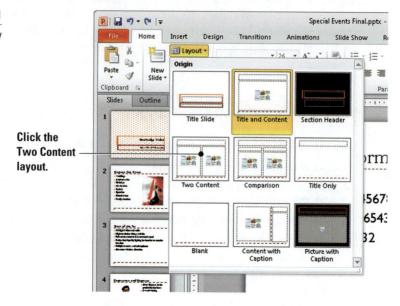

Click the Two Content layout.

8. Click **Two Content** to change the layout to two side-by-side content placeholders.

9. In the second placeholder, type the following bullet points:

sales@southridgevideo.com

www.southridgevideo.com

Take Note   If you press the spacebar after typing an email or Web address, PowerPoint automatically formats the text as a hyperlink.

10. Select the email address and Web address, then click the **Bullets** button on the Home tab to turn off the bullets for those items. Your slide should look similar to Figure 4-12. Widen the text placeholder slightly if needed so neither of the addresses wrap to two lines.

Figure 4-12

The completed slide

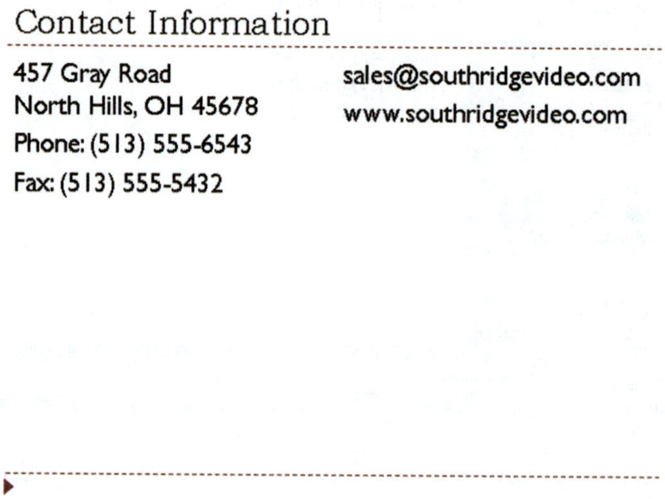

Contact Information

457 Gray Road
North Hills, OH 45678
Phone: (513) 555-6543
Fax: (513) 555-5432

sales@southridgevideo.com
www.southridgevideo.com

**CERTIFICATION
R E A D Y** **2.4.3**

How do you change
a slide's layout?

11. SAVE the presentation.

PAUSE. LEAVE the presentation open to use in the next exercise.

The layouts that appear in the slide layout gallery depend on the layouts stored in the Slide Master, which you will learn about later in this lesson.

INSERTING A DATE, FOOTER, AND SLIDE NUMBERS

The Bottom Line

Adding a date, footer, and slide numbers to a presentation can help you identify and organize slides. In this exercise, you learn how to apply these useful elements to one or more slides.

Inserting a Date, Footer, and Slide Numbers

A **footer** is text that repeats at the bottom of each slide in a presentation. Use a footer to record the slide title, company name, or other important information that you want the audience to keep in mind as they view the slides. In this exercise, you apply a footer, a date, and slide numbers to a PowerPoint presentation.

STEP BY STEP **Insert a Date, Footer, and Slide Numbers**

USE the *Special Events Final* presentation that is still open from the previous exercise.

1. Click the **Insert** tab, and then click the **Header & Footer** button. The Header and Footer dialog box opens.
2. Click the **Date and time** check box, and then click **Update automatically** if it isn't already selected.
3. Click to select the **Slide number** check box.
4. Click the **Footer** check box and then type **Special Events** in the text box below the check box.
5. Click the **Don't show on title slide** check box. The dialog box should resemble Figure 4-13 at this point. The date will be today's date rather than the date shown in Figure 4-13.

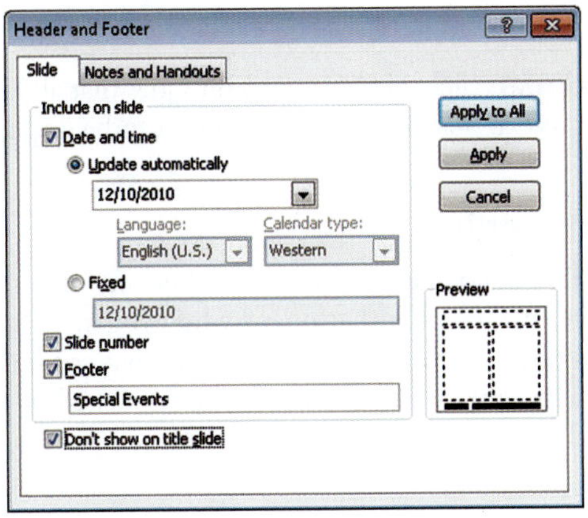

Figure 4-13

Header and Footer dialog box

6. Click **Apply to All** to apply the date, footer, and slide number to all slides except the title slide. Slide 6 should look similar to Figure 4-14.

Figure 4-14

A slide number, footer, and date on a slide

Contact Information

457 Gray Road
North Hills, OH 45678
Phone: (513) 555-6543
Fax: (513) 555-5432

sales@southridgevideo.com
www.southridgevideo.com

Slide number ────── **Footer**

▶ 6   Special Events   12/10/2010 ●─── **Date**

 Another Way
You can also open the Header & Footer dialog box by clicking the Date & Time button or the Slide Number button.

7. **SAVE** the presentation.

PAUSE. LEAVE the presentation open to use in the next exercise.

You have two choices when inserting a date: a date that automatically updates by changing to the current date each time the presentation is opened or a fixed date, which stays the same until you decide to change it. If it is important to indicate when slides were created or presented, use a fixed date.

CERTIFICATION READY   **2.4.5**

How do you set up slide footers?

You may have noticed that the Header and Footer dialog box has another tab, the Header tab. When you create notes pages and handouts, you can specify a **header** to appear at the top of every page. A header is repeated text, much like a footer, except it appears at the top of each page. Headers do not appear onscreen in Slide Show view—only on printouts. You can also create footers for notes pages and handouts.

 Ref

You will work with handouts in Lesson 10.

LINKING TO WEB PAGES AND OTHER PROGRAMS

The Bottom Line

You can set up **hyperlinks** (clickable shortcuts) on slides that allow you to jump to a specific slide in the presentation or to external content. Hyperlinks can be displayed as either text or a graphic.

Adding a Text Hyperlink

Use the Insert Hyperlink dialog box to set up links between slides or from slides to other targets. (The *target* is the page, file, or slide that opens when you click a link.) If you select text before inserting the hyperlink, that text will become the link that can be clicked. If you select a graphic before inserting the hyperlink, the hyperlink will be attached to the graphic, so that clicking it activates the hyperlink. In this exercise, you will create a text hyperlink.

STEP BY STEP   **Add a Text Hyperlink**

USE the *Special Events Final* presentation that is still open from the previous exercise.

1. Go to slide 6, and select the website address (**www.southridgevideo.com**).

2. Click the **Hyperlink** button on the Insert tab. The Insert Hyperlink dialog box opens.

Take Note   Depending on how you typed the address in the previous exercise, PowerPoint may have already turned www.southridgevideo.com into a hyperlink. If so, the Edit Hyperlink dialog box opens instead.

 3. Click in the **Address** box and type **http://www.southridgevideo.com** as the target of the link text (see Figure 4-15).

Figure 4-15

The Insert Hyperlink dialog box

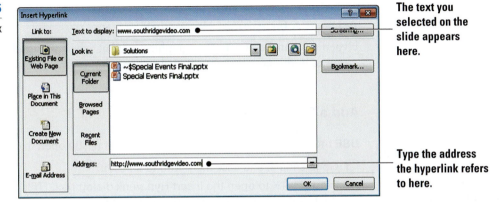

The text you selected on the slide appears here.

Type the address the hyperlink refers to here.

 4. Click **OK**. The website address is formatted with the theme's hyperlink color and an underline.
 5. Go to slide 1, and select **Southridge Video**.
 6. Click the **Hyperlink** button on the Insert tab. The Insert Hyperlink dialog box opens.
 7. In the Link To list on the left side of the dialog box click **Place in This Document**. A list of slides from the current presentation appears.
 8. Click **6. Contact Information**, as shown in Figure 4-16.

Figure 4-16

Creating a hyperlink to another slide

Click here to see a list of slides.

Select the desired slide.

It is common for slide previews to appear blurry.

 9. Click **OK**; PowerPoint identifies slide 6 as the target for this hyperlink.
 10. **SAVE** the presentation.

PAUSE. LEAVE the presentation open to use in the next exercise.

You can create links to a number of different types of targets using the Insert Hyperlink dialog box.

 • Choose **Existing File or Web Page** to link to any web page or any file on your system or network. Use the Look in box, the Browse the Web button, or the Browse File button to locate the desired page or file, or type the URL or path in the Address box.

 • Choose **Place in This Document** to display a list of the current presentation's slides and custom shows. Click the slide or custom show that you want to display when the link is clicked.

- Choose **Create New Document** to create a link to a new document. You supply the path and the name for the new document and then choose whether to add content to the document now or later.
- Choose **E-mail Address** to type an email address to which you want to link.

You can add hyperlinks to a slide in Normal view, but the links will work only in Slide Show view.

Adding a Graphical Hyperlink

Hyperlinks can be attached to graphics, so that when you click the graphic, the hyperlink executes. In this exercise, you will make an existing graphic into a hyperlink.

STEP BY STEP   **Add a Graphical Hyperlink**

Another Way
You can also right-click and choose Hyperlink to open the Insert Hyperlink dialog box.

CERTIFICATION
R E A D Y   3.1.7

How do you add hyperlinks to graphical elements?

USE the *Special Events Final* presentation that is still open from the previous exercise.

1. Go to slide 4, and click the photo to select it.
2. Press **Ctrl+K** to open the Insert Hyperlink dialog box. (This is a keyboard shortcut for the Insert Hyperlink command you used previously.)
3. Click **Place in This Document**. A list of slides from the current presentation appears.
4. Click **6. Contact Information**.
5. Click **OK**.
6. **SAVE** the presentation.

PAUSE. LEAVE the presentation open to use in the next exercise.

If you need to change a link's target, click anywhere in the link and then click the Hyperlink button, or right-click it and click Edit Hyperlink. The Edit Hyperlink dialog box opens, offering the same functionality as the Insert Hyperlink dialog box. You can remove a link by right-clicking the link and selecting Remove Hyperlink from the shortcut menu.

Adding an Action to a Slide

Use **actions** to perform tasks such as jumping to a new slide or starting a different program. Actions can be applied to text or shapes such as **action buttons**. An action button is a shape from the Shapes gallery to which you can assign a hyperlink or some other action. (You can assign actions to any object, not just an action button. However, action buttons are specifically designed for that purpose.)

Besides allowing you to set up links to specific slides or files, you can use action settings to run a particular program, run a macro, or perform an action with an object such as an embedded Excel worksheet. You can also play a sound from a list of default sounds or any sound file on your system.

STEP BY STEP   **Add an Action to a Slide**

USE the *Special Events Final* presentation that is still open from the previous exercise.

1. Go to slide 5.
2. Click the **Shapes** button on the Insert tab to display a gallery of drawing shapes.
3. Click the **Action Button: Information** shape in the middle of the last row of shapes, as shown in Figure 4-17.

Figure 4-17

Create an information
action button

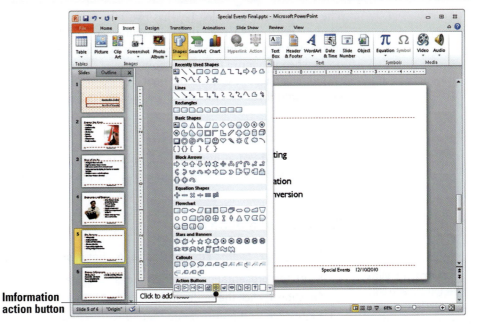

Another Way
The Shapes button
is also available on the
Home tab.

**Imformation
action button**

Another Way
If you drag to draw
the button instead of clicking,
you can make it any size
you like.

4. The pointer changes to a crosshair. Click near the bottom of the slide to draw the button there at its default size. As soon as you release the mouse button, the Action Settings dialog box opens.

5. Click **Hyperlink to** and then click the **drop-down arrow** of the text box below it.

6. Scroll to the bottom of the list of possible link targets and click **Other File**, as shown in Figure 4-18. The Hyperlink to Other File dialog box opens.

Figure 4-18

Choose to hyperlink
to another file

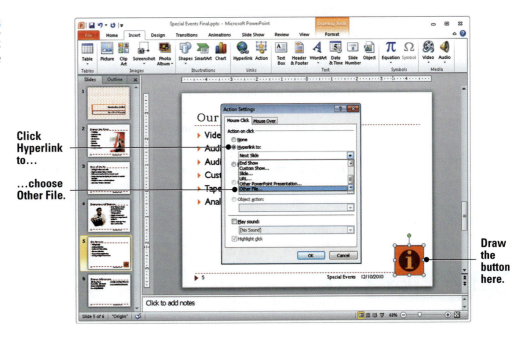

**Click
Hyperlink
to…**

**…choose
Other File.**

**Draw
the
button
here.**

The *Service Fees*
file is available on the
book companion website
or in WileyPLUS.

7. Navigate to the data files for this lesson, click the *Service Fees* file, and then click **OK** to apply your selection and return to the Action Settings dialog box.

8. Click **OK** again to close the Action Settings dialog box.

9. **SAVE** the presentation.

PAUSE. LEAVE the presentation open to use in the next exercise.

The Action Settings dialog box has two tabs that contain identical options. The default tab, Mouse Click, offers actions that will occur when you click the mouse pointer on the action item, such as the action button you drew in this exercise. The Mouse Over tab offers actions that will occur when you move the mouse pointer over the action item. It is therefore possible to attach two different actions to the same item. For example, you can specify that an action button will play a sound if you rest the mouse pointer on it and display a new slide if you click it.

Testing Links in a Slide Show

Hyperlinks and action buttons work only in Slide Show view, so you must enter Slide Show view in order to test them. In this exercise, you will enter Slide Show view and test hyperlinks.

STEP BY STEP	Test Links in a Slide Show

USE the *Special Events Final* presentation that is still open from the previous exercise.

Another Way
You can also enter Slide Show view by clicking the Slide Show tab and clicking From Beginning.

1. **SAVE** the presentation and then press **F5** to start the slide show from slide 1.
2. On slide 1, click the underlined **Southridge Video** text. The show jumps to slide 6.
3. Right-click, and on the menu that appears, choose **Last Viewed** to return to slide 1.
4. Click the mouse button three times to advance to slide 4, and then click the photo. The show jumps to slide 6.
5. Right-click, and on the menu that appears, choose **Last Viewed** to return to slide 4.
6. Click the mouse button to advance to slide 5, and then click the **Information** button. A spreadsheet opens in Excel.
7. Close Excel without making or saving any changes.
8. On the Windows taskbar, switch back to the running presentation show.
9. Click the mouse button to advance to slide 6.
10. Click the underlined **hyperlink**.

Take Note   The website address you entered is a dummy address supported by Microsoft to allow you to practice creating links. It redirects you to a Microsoft site.

11. Close the web browser and end the slide show.
12. Close the presentation, saving your changes to it.

PAUSE. LEAVE PowerPoint open to use in the next exercise.

When you activate links or actions during a slide show, the target of the link or action is displayed in the full screen, like the slides in the slide show. After working with the external content, you can return to the slide show by selecting it from the taskbar in Windows.

WORKING WITH SECTIONS

The Bottom Line

To organize a long presentation, you can create **sections**, which are dividers that group slides into logical clusters, as folders organize groups of related papers. You can then work with the sections rather than with individual slides, moving or deleting an entire section as a group.

Creating Sections

You can create sections that organize the slides for easier management. This is especially useful in a lengthy presentation that covers multiple topics; each topic can be a section. In this exercise, you create some sections and then use them to manipulate content.

Create Sections

USE the *Blue Yonder Introduction* presentation.

@ The *Blue Yonder Introduction* file is available on the book companion website or in WileyPLUS.

1. Locate and open the *Blue Yonder Introduction* presentation and save it as *Blue Yonder Sections*.

2. Go to slide 2. In the Slides tab of the Slides/Outline pane on the left of the PowerPoint screen, right-click **slide 2** and click **Add Section** from the menu that appears (see Figure 4-19). A new section bar labeled Untitled Section appears in the Slides/Outline pane above slide 2, indicating that the new section begins with that slide.

Figure 4-19

Add a section

Right-click the slide the section should begin with.

Click Add Section.

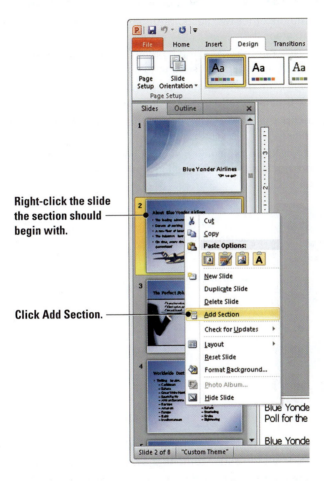

3. Go to slide 5. In the Slides/Outline pane, right-click **slide 5** and click **Add Section**. Another new section (also labeled Untitled) appears above slide 5 in the Slides/Outline pane. Repeat these actions to create another new section above slide 7.

4. Click the **Untitled Section** bar above slide 2. Slides 2, 3, and 4 become selected.

5. Right-click the Untitled Section bar you just clicked and choose **Rename Section** from the menu that appears. The Rename Section dialog box opens, as shown in Figure 4-20.

Figure 4-20

Rename a section

6. Type **Introduction** in the Section Name box and click **OK**.

7. Rename the other two sections **Detail** and **Conclusion**, using the same actions you used in steps 4-6.

8. Right-click the **Detail section** heading in the Slides/Outline pane and click **Move Section Up** to move that section to appear before the Introduction section.

9. Right-click the **Detail section** heading again and click **Move Section Down**. The Detail section moves back to its original location.

10. Right-click the **Introduction** section heading in the Slides/Outline pane and click **Collapse All**. All the sections collapse in the Slides/Outline pane.

11. Double-click the **Conclusion** section heading. That section is expanded so you can see the individual slides in it. See Figure 4-21.

Figure 4-21

Collapse and expand sections

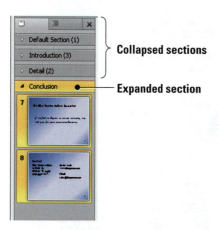

12. Right-click the **Conclusion** section and click **Remove Section**. The section heading is removed, but the slides remain; they are added to the Detail section.

13. Click the **Introduction** section heading to select it, and then on the Design tab, click **Background Styles**. On the background styles palette that appears, right-click **Style 1** (the white background) and click **Apply to Selected Styles**. Only the slides in the selected section change their background color.

14. **SAVE** the presentation and **CLOSE** it.

PAUSE. LEAVE PowerPoint open to use in the next exercise.

Sections offer an easy way of selecting groups of slides together, so you can move them, format them, or even delete them. To delete an entire section, right-click the section header and click Remove Section & Slides. In the preceding exercise, you removed a section but kept the slides. Sections also enable you to rearrange groups of slides easily, by moving a section up or down in order.

CERTIFICATION READY 2.4.1

How do you format sections?

Sections are invisible to the audience when you present a slide show. If you want to make it more obvious that you have organized the presentation into sections, you may wish to insert summary slides at the beginning or end of each section.

SOFTWARE ORIENTATION

PowerPoint's Slide Master View

Slide Master view, shown in Figure 4-22, provides tools for modifying the master slides on which all of the current presentation's layouts and formats are based. You can modify the slide master itself, or any of the individual layout masters subordinate to it.

Figure 4-22

Slide Master view

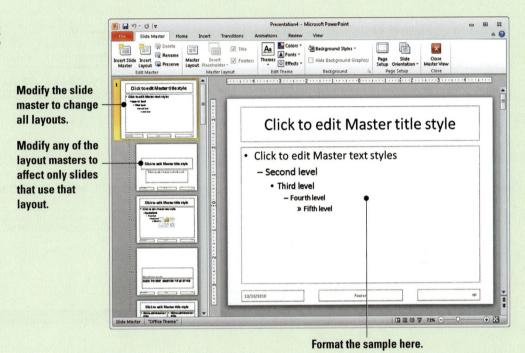

Modify the slide master to change all layouts.

Modify any of the layout masters to affect only slides that use that layout.

Format the sample here.

Use the tools on the Slide Master tab and the slide in the Slide pane to customize formats that will apply to all slides in a presentation. If you make changes to the topmost slide in the left pane, the changes apply to all layouts. If you click a specific layout below it to change, the changes apply to all slides that use that layout.

CUSTOMIZING SLIDE MASTERS

The Bottom Line

The **slide master** for a presentation stores information on the current theme, layout of place-holders, bullet characters, and other formats that affect all slides in a presentation. If you want to make design changes that will apply to many or all slides in a presentation, you can save a great deal of time by modifying the slide master rather than applying changes on each slide. Slide Master view makes it easy to change formats globally for a presentation by displaying the slide master and all layouts available in the current presentation. Customizing a slide master makes it easy to apply changes consistently throughout a presentation.

Applying a Theme to a Slide Master

To customize a slide master, you use Slide Master view. Slide Master view has its own tab on the Ribbon to provide tools you can use to change the masters. In this exercise, you apply a theme to a slide master to change its look.

Apply a Theme to a Slide Master

The *Rates* file is available on the book companion website or in WileyPLUS.

GET READY. To apply a theme to a slide master, perform the following steps:

1. Locate and open the *Rates* presentation and save it as *Rates Masters*.
2. With slide 1 active, click the **View** tab.
3. Click the **Slide Master** button in the Presentation Views group. Slide Master view opens with the Title Slide Layout selected in the left pane, as shown in Figure 4-23.

Figure 4-23

Slide Master view with the Title Slide layout selected

WileyPLUS Extra! features an online tutorial of this task.

Title Slide layout selected

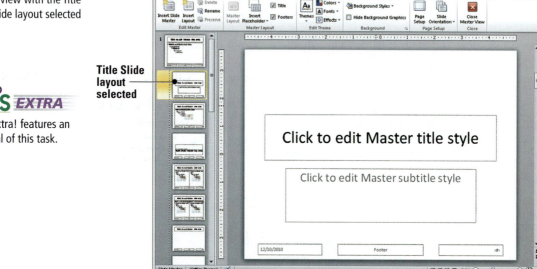

4. Click the first slide in the left pane, the slide master for the current theme. (It's the top slide in the left pane, the one that is slightly larger than the others.)
5. Click the **Themes** button in the Slide Master tab to produce the Themes gallery; click the **Solstice** theme in the gallery. The theme is applied to the slide master as well as all slide layouts in the left pane, as shown in Figure 4-24

Figure 4-24

A new theme applied to the slide master and its layouts

Applying a theme to the Slide Master...

...also applies it to each of the layouts.

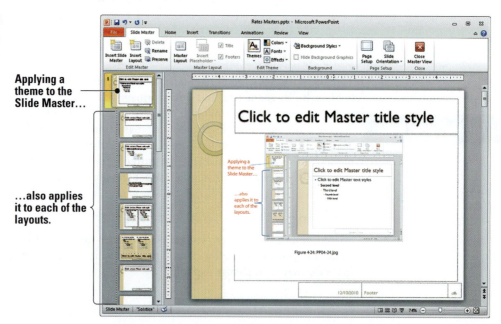

Take Note Remember, you can find a theme's name by hovering the mouse over it. The themes appear in alphabetical order.

     6. **SAVE** the presentation.

PAUSE. LEAVE the presentation open in Slide Master view to use in the next exercise.

The slide master, displayed at the top of the left pane, looks like a blank Title and Content slide. To make a change to the master, edit it just the way you would edit any slide using tools on any of the Ribbon's tabs. For example, to change the font of the slide title, click the title, display the Home tab, and use the Font list to select a new font. Change bullet characters by clicking in any of the nine levels of bullets and then selecting a new bullet character from the Bullets and Numbering dialog box.

Some changes you make to the slide master display on the masters for other slide layouts. You can also click any of these layouts to display it in the Slide pane so you can make changes to that layout. Any changes you make to these layouts will display on slides that use those layouts. Your changed masters display in the slide layout gallery to be available when you create new slides.

Moving and Resizing Placeholders on a Slide Master

You may have noticed that some designs place slide content in different locations from others. This is because the placeholders on the slide master are positioned differently. You can move and resize the placeholders on the slide master to create different effects yourself. Each slide master has a set of **layout masters** that determine the number, type, and position of the placeholders on a particular type of slide. In Slide Master view, the layout masters are beneath the Slide Master, and slightly indented in the left pane to show that they are subordinate to it. Any changes you make to the placeholders on the Slide Master itself flow down to the layout masters. In this exercise, you change the layout for a particular layout master.

STEP BY STEP   **Move and Resize Placeholders**

USE the *Rates Masters* presentation that is still open from the previous exercise.

1. In Slide Master view, click to select the layout master for the Title Slide Layout in the left pane (hover your cursor over the slide to see a KeyTip indicating the layout master's name). The Title Slide layout master appears in the right pane.

2. In the Title Slide layout master, click the outer border of the subtitle placeholder (click to edit Master subtitle style) to select that text box.

3. Drag the bottom selection handle upward to decrease the height of the subtitle placeholder to 1″ (see Figure 4-25).

Figure 4-25

Resizing a placeholder

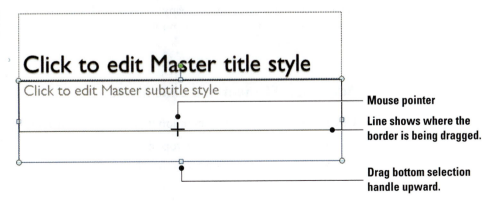

Click to edit Master title style

Click to edit Master subtitle style

Mouse pointer

Line shows where the border is being dragged.

Drag bottom selection handle upward.

4. Position the mouse pointer over the border of the subtitle placeholder, but not over a selection handle, so that the mouse pointer becomes a four-headed arrow (see Figure 4-26). Click and drag the box to the bottom of the slide.

Figure 4-26

Moving a placeholder

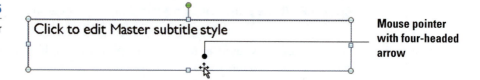

Mouse pointer
with four-headed
arrow

5. Using the same process as in step 4, move the title placeholder immediately above the subtitle, as shown in Figure 4-27.

Figure 4-27

The completed slide
layout master

6. **SAVE** the presentation.

PAUSE. LEAVE the presentation open in Slide Master view to use in the next exercise.

Adding New Elements to a Slide Master

If you add a picture or text to a slide master layout, it will display on all slides that use that layout. You might place the company's logo on each slide, for example, or a copyright notice. In this exercise, you add a copyright notice to the slide master, affecting every layout master that is subordinate to it.

STEP BY STEP   **Add a New Element to a Slide Master**

USE the *Rates Masters* presentation that is still open from the previous exercise.

1. Click the **Slide Master** at the top of the left pane.
2. On the Insert tab, click the **Text Box** button in the Text group.

3. In the bottom left corner of the slide master, click to place a new text box, and type **Copyright 2012 Southridge Video**. See Figure 4-28.

Insert a new text box here.

4. Select all the text in the copyright notice and change its color to **Tan, Background 2, Darker 25%**.

5. Click the **Slide Master** tab, and then click the **Close Master View** button to return to Normal view.

6. View each slide to confirm that the copyright text appears on each one.

PAUSE. LEAVE the presentation open in Slide Master view to use in the next exercise.

Creating a Custom Layout Master

If you need to create a number of slides with a layout different from any of the default layouts, you can create a new custom layout to your own specifications. Or, if you want some slides to use a modified version of one of the default layouts, but you also want to retain that original layout, you may want to create your own slide layout. In this exercise you create a custom layout.

STEP BY STEP **Create a Custom Layout Master**

USE the *Rates Masters* presentation that is still open from the previous exercise.

1. On the View tab, click **Slide Master** to return to Slide Master view.

2. Click the **Slide Master** at the top of the left pane.

3. On the Slide Master tab, click **Insert Layout**. A new blank layout appears at the bottom of the left pane. It is blank except for a title placeholder and the copyright information, as shown in Figure 4-29.

Figure 4-29

A new layout has been created

Click here to create a new layout.

Newly created layout

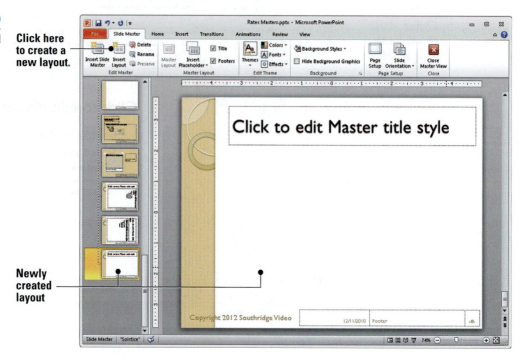

4. On the Slide Master tab, click the **Insert Placeholder button's drop-down arrow**. A menu opens, as in Figure 4-30.

Figure 4-30

Select a type of placeholder

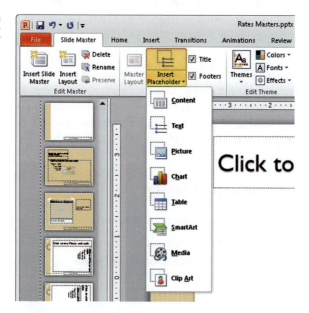

5. In the menu, click **Text**. The mouse pointer turns into a crosshair.

6. Draw a new text placeholder on the slide in the position shown in Figure 4-31.

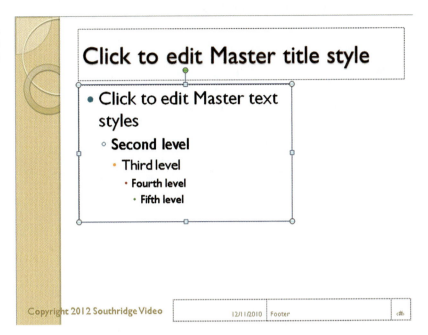

7. Click the **Insert Placeholder drop-down arrow** again, and click **Picture** in the menu that appears. Draw a placeholder box to the right of the text placeholder, as shown in Figure 4-32.

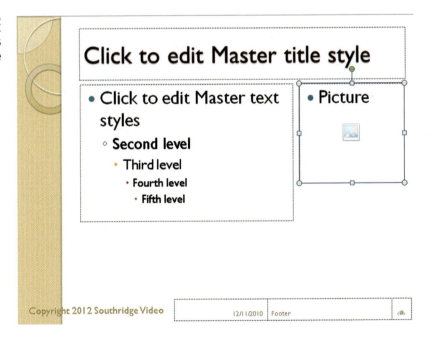

8. Right-click the new layout master in the left pane and click **Rename Layout** in the menu that appears.

9. In the Rename Layout dialog box, type **Text and Picture** and click **OK**.

10. On the Slide Master tab, click **Close Master View**.

11. On the Home tab, click the **New Slide button's drop-down arrow**. On the gallery of layouts that appears, click your new layout, **Text and Picture**, to create a new slide using it. See Figure 4-33.

Figure 4-33

Use the new layout when
creating a new slide

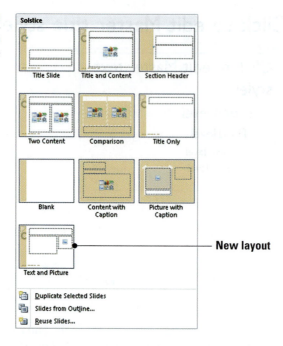

New layout

12. SAVE the presentation.

PAUSE. EXIT PowerPoint.

You can use tools in the Master Layout group to customize placeholders for your new layout. You can decide whether to display a title or the footer placeholders, and you can use the Insert Placeholder button to select from a number of standard placeholders, such as Text, Picture, Clip Art, or Table. If you have inserted a text placeholder, you can format the placeholder text the way you want text to appear on the slides. If you don't specify formatting, the text will be formatted as specified on the slide master.

Take Note   Custom layouts are stored in the presentation in which they are created.

When you have completed the custom layout, use the Rename button on the Slide Master tab to give the custom layout a meaningful name. It will then be available in the slide layout gallery any time you want to add a slide in that presentation.

SKILL SUMMARY

In This Lesson You Learned How To:	Exam Objective	Objective Number
Format presentations with themes.	Modify themes.	2.4.2
Change slide backgrounds.	Apply formatting to a slide.	2.4.4
Work with different layouts.	Switch to a different slide layout.	2.4.3
Insert a date, footer, and slide numbers.	Set up slide footers.	2.4.5
Link to web pages and other programs.	Add hyperlinks to graphical elements.	3.1.7
Work with sections.	Format sections.	2.4.1
Customize slide masters.		

Knowledge Assessment

Fill in the Blank

Fill in each blank with the term or phrase that best completes the statement.

1. A(n) _____ is a file containing color, font, layout, and effect settings that you can apply to a presentation to change its appearance.
2. A slide's _____ determines the positioning and types of placeholders on it.
3. Text that repeats at the bottom of each slide is a(n) _____.
4. Underlined text on a slide usually means that the text is a(n) _____ and opens a web page or another slide when clicked.
5. A(n) _____ button can be placed on a slide to perform a certain activity or jump to a certain slide when clicked.
6. You can organize slides into _____, which group slides together for easier handling.
7. To ensure consistency, make formatting changes to the _____ rather than individual slides.
8. The individual layouts associated with a particular slide master are called _____ masters.
9. To create your own layout, start a new layout and then add one or more _____.
10. Hyperlinks must be tested in _____ view.

Multiple Choice

Circle the correct answer.

1. Which of these does a theme *not* include?
   a. A color palette
   b. Fonts
   c. Graphic effects
   d. Sample content

2. Themes are applied from which tab?
   a. Home
   b. Insert
   c. Design
   d. Transitions

3. How are PowerPoint's built-in font themes named?
   a. They use the same names as the themes from which they come.
   b. They are numbered from 1 to 255.
   c. They are lettered from A to Z.
   d. They are named according to the first font in the font theme.

4. From which tab do you apply a different layout to a slide?
   a. Home
   b. Insert
   c. Design
   d. Transitions

5. Which of these is *not* a type of fill you can use for a slide background?
   a. Solid color
   b. SmartArt
   c. Texture
   d. Gradient

6. To link to a slide in the current presentation, choose _____ in the Insert Hyperlink dialog box.
   a. Existing File or Web Page
   b. Place in This Document
   c. Create New Document
   d. Show Current Slides

7. Where do slide headers appear, if used?
   a. Onscreen during Slide Show view
   b. On printouts of handouts and notes pages
   c. Neither place
   d. Both places

8. After assigning a hyperlink to a graphic, you can test it in _____ view.
   a. Normal
   b. Slide Show
   c. Slide Sorter
   d. Notes Pages

9. Action buttons are selected and inserted from the _____ button's menu on the Insert tab.
   a. Clip Art
   b. SmartArt
   c. Shapes
   d. WordArt

10. What happens when you move a section header?
    a. All the slides in the section move along with it.
    b. The header moves but not the slides in its section.

Competency Assessment

Project 4-1: Service with a Smile

You're the sales manager for a large chain of auto dealerships that prides itself on service and warranty packages that give customers a sense of security. The company, Car King, is rolling out a new line of extended warranties to offer its customers. You have created a presentation that details three levels of warranties. Now you need to improve the look of the slides to make customers take notice.

GET READY. LAUNCH PowerPoint if it is not already running.

The *Warranty Plans* file is available on the book companion website or in WileyPLUS.

1. **OPEN** the *Warranty Plans* presentation and save it as *Warranty Plans Final*.
2. With slide 1 active, click the New Slide button to insert a new Title and Content slide.
3. Click the Layout button, and then click Title Slide.
4. Type the title Car King and the subtitle Extended Warranty Plans.
5. Drag the slide above slide 1 in the Slides tab so the title slide becomes the first slide.
6. Click the Design tab, and then click the More button to display the Themes gallery.
7. Click Foundry to apply this theme to all slides.
8. Click the Fonts button on the Design tab, and then scroll down to locate and click the Metro theme font combination.
9. Click the Colors button on the Design tab, and then click Create New Theme Colors.
10. Click the Accent 1 drop-down arrow, then click the Tan, Text 2, Darker 25% color.
11. Click the Accent 2 drop-down arrow, then click the Tan, Text 2, Darker 50% color.
12. Type CarKing as the color scheme name, and then click Save.
13. Go to slide 1, if necessary.
14. Click the Background Styles button, and then click Style 7.
15. **SAVE** the presentation and **CLOSE** the file.

LEAVE PowerPoint open for use in the next project.

Project 4-2: Special Delivery

As a marketing manager for Consolidated Delivery, you have been asked to prepare and present information on the company's services to a prospective corporate client. You need to add some interactive features to a standard presentation to make your delivery especially interesting.

The *Messenger Service* file is available on the book companion website or in WileyPLUS.

The *Contract Plans* file is available on the book companion website or in WileyPLUS.

1. **OPEN** the *Messenger Service* presentation and save it as *Messenger Service Links*.
2. Go to slide 2 and select the text Contact Consolidated in the text box at the bottom of the slide.
3. Open the Insert Hyperlink dialog box (Ctrl+K is one way), click Place in This Document, and then click 6. Our Numbers in the list of slide titles. Click OK.
4. Go to slide 5 and use the Shapes gallery on the Insert tab to select the Information action button.
5. Draw a button near the bottom of the slide and set the action to Hyperlink to: Other File. Select the file *Contract Plans*.
6. Go to slide 6, select the website address, and use the Insert Hyperlink dialog box to create a link to http://www.consolidatedmessenger.com.
7. Insert an automatically updating date, slide numbers, and the footer Consolidated Messenger on all slides except the title slide. (You may need to adjust the location of your action button on slide 5 after you add slide numbers and the footer.)
8. Press F5 to run the slide show from slide 1. Advance to slide 2 and test the link at the bottom of the slide. Slide 6 displays.
9. Right-click slide 6, point to Go to Slide, and then click 2. Our Services to return to slide 2.
10. Advance to slide 4, and then to slide 5.

11. On slide 5, click the action button to open the *Contract Plans* file. Close Microsoft Word to return to the slide show.

12. Advance to slide 6 and click the website link. Close the browser and end the slide show.

13. **SAVE** the presentation and **CLOSE** the file.

LEAVE PowerPoint open for use in the next project.

Proficiency Assessment

Project 4-3: Travel Tips

You are an assistant at Sunny Day Travel and your boss has created the beginnings of a presentation containing travel tips for various destination types. Because there will eventually be many slides per destination, you will organize the slides into sections for the destination types and make some changes to the slide master that will improve the slides' look.

@ The *Travel Tips* file is available on the book companion website or in WileyPLUS.

1. **OPEN** the *Travel Tips* presentation and save it as *Travel Tips Sections*.

2. Go to slide 2. Notice that the title is obscured by the graphic.

3. Switch to Slide Master view, and select the slide master (the topmost slide in the left pane).

4. Drag the bottom border of the title placeholder upward so its bottom aligns with the 2″ mark on the vertical ruler.

5. Close Slide Master view, and confirm on slide 2 that the title no longer overlaps the graphic.

6. Create a section that starts with slide 3. Name it **Sand and Sun**.

7. Create a section that starts with slide 6. Name it **Adventure**.

8. Create a section that starts with slide 9. Name it **Cruise**.

9. Create a section that starts with slide 12. Name it **City**.

10. Create a section that starts with slide 15. Name it **Summary**.

11. Move the City section before the Cruise section.

12. On slide 2, select the graphic for **Sand and Sun**, and create a hyperlink that jumps to slide 3.

13. Create additional hyperlinks for the other three graphics, jumping to the first slide in their respective sections.

14. **SAVE** the presentation and **CLOSE** the file.

LEAVE PowerPoint open for use in the next project.

Project 4-4: Senior Meals

As the activities director for Senior Meal Services, you are responsible for educating your staff about the dietary recommendations for senior citizens. You have created a presentation, and now you will modify its slide master, theme, and colors to make it more appealing.

@ The *Meals* file is available on the book companion website or in WileyPLUS.

1. **OPEN** the *Meals* presentation and save it as *Senior Meals*.

2. Apply the **Pushpin** theme.

3. Change the font theme to **Newsprint**.

4. Display the slide master, and change the background on the slide master to **Style 2**.

5. Close Slide Master view, and go to slide 1.

6. Select the website address on slide 1, and make it into a live hyperlink.

7. Set the current date to appear at the bottom of each slide, and for it to *not* be automatically updated.

8. **SAVE** the presentation and **CLOSE** the file.

LEAVE PowerPoint open for use in the next project.

Mastery Assessment

Project 4-5: The Art of the Biography

You work for the editorial director of Lucerne Publishing. She has asked you to fine-tune a presentation on new biographies she plans to deliver to the sales force. You want to make some global changes to the presentation by customizing the presentation's slide masters, and you need to create a new layout that you will use to introduce sections of biographies.

@ The *Biographies* file is available on the book companion website or in WileyPLUS.

1. **OPEN** the *Biographies* presentation and save it as *Biographies Masters*.
2. Switch to Slide Master view and apply a new theme of your choice to the slide master.
3. In the left pane, click the Title and Content layout and then click the Insert Layout button in the Edit Master group to insert a new layout.
4. Deselect Title in the Master Layout group to remove the title placeholder from the new layout.
5. Insert a text placeholder in the center of the slide. Delete the sample bulleted text, remove bullet formatting, and change font size to 40 point. Center the text in the placeholder.
6. Apply a new background style to this new layout.
7. Click the Rename button in the Edit Master group and type Introduction as the new layout name.
8. Close Slide Master view.
9. Insert a new slide after slide 1 using the Introduction layout. Type American History in the placeholder.
10. **SAVE** the presentation and **CLOSE** the file.

LEAVE PowerPoint open for use in the next project.

Project 4-6: Adventure Works

You are a coordinator for Adventure Works, a company that manages outdoor adventures for children and teenagers. To introduce your programs, you have created a presentation to show at local schools and recreation centers. Finalize the presentation with design elements and effects that will catch the eye.

@ The *Adventures* file is available on the book companion website or in WileyPLUS.

1. **OPEN** the *Adventures* presentation.
2. Apply a suitable theme to the presentation. Customize theme colors or fonts if desired.
3. Make the email address and website address on slide 5 active hyperlinks.
4. Change the layout to slide 1 to Title Slide.
5. Add a footer that contains the text Adventure Works to all slides, including the title slide.
6. **SAVE** the presentation as *Adventures Final* and **CLOSE** the file.

EXIT PowerPoint.

INTERNET READY

Have you ever wanted to create your own digital movies? Use an Internet search tool to locate information on digital video cameras. Select two that seem to offer quality for a reasonable price and make a list of their features. Create a new presentation with a theme of your choice, insert a title, and add a Comparison slide. List the two cameras you have researched in the subheading placeholders and key features for each camera in the text placeholders. Save the presentation with an appropriate name.

Circling Back 1

You are a sales representative for Contoso Food Services. You are preparing a brief presentation to introduce your company to the Food Services Committee at Trey College, in hopes of receiving a contract to provide food services for the campus dining hall.

Project 1: Create a Presentation

Begin by creating slides from a blank presentation. Then add slides from another presentation, rearrange the slides, and print the presentation.

GET READY. LAUNCH PowerPoint if it is not already running.

@ The *Boilerplate* file is available on the book companion website or in WileyPLUS.

1. Create a new blank presentation and save it as *Trey Proposal*.
2. On the title slide, type **Contoso Food Services** in the title placeholder.
3. Type **Trey College Proposal** in the subtitle placeholder.
4. Reuse slides 2-4 from the *Boilerplate* presentation.
5. Rearrange slides so that slide 2 becomes slide 3.
6. Print the presentation as slides in Grayscale mode.
7. **SAVE** the presentation.

PAUSE. LEAVE PowerPoint and your presentation open for the next project.

Project 2: Format Your Presentation

Now that you have the bare bones of your presentation written, you can concentrate on formatting to improve the presentation's appearance. You will use WordArt, a theme, font styles, and other formatting options to give your slides punch.

USE the presentation that is open from the previous project.

1. Apply the Median theme, and then change colors to the Paper color theme.
2. On slide 1, delete the title text and the title placeholder box.
3. Create a WordArt graphic using the *Fill—Text 2, Outline—Background 2 style* (the first one in the WordArt style gallery). Type the text **CONTOSO FOOD SERVICES**.
4. Make these changes to the WordArt graphic:
    a. Set the font size to **56 pt**. (Hint: Click in the Font Size box on the Ribbon and type 56 directly into it.)
    b. Change the WordArt text fill to a gradient, using the Linear Down option in the Light Variations section of the Gradient gallery. (Hint: use the Text Fill button in the WordArt Styles group on the Drawing Tools Format tab.)
    c. Change the WordArt outline color to **Dark Green, Background 2, Lighter 80%**.
    d. Apply the **Tight Reflection touching** effect to the WordArt graphic.
    e. Reposition the WordArt graphic 0.5" above the slide's subtitle box.

Figure 1

Slide 1 completed

5. Apply italics to the slide 1 subtitle. Figure 1 shows the completed slide 1.
6. Go to slide 2. Make these changes to the text in the right-hand placeholder:
   a. Select all text in the right-hand placeholder and change the font size to **24 pt**.
   b. Right-align the last three paragraphs (the attribution), and adjust line space so there is no extra space above these lines. (Hint: Choose Line Spacing Options at the bottom of the Line Spacing menu.)
   c. Use the Format Painter to copy formats from the quote paragraph and the quote attribution on slide 2 to the quote text and attribution on slide 3.
7. Go to slide 4. Insert a text box below the picture that is as wide as the picture and type the following text:
   Contoso Food Services is proud to serve institutions in fifteen states in this country and three Canadian provinces. Our reputation for quality is second to none.
8. Format the text box as follows:
   a. Center the text in the text box.
   b. Apply a Shape Style of your choice to the text box.
9. **SAVE** the presentation.

PAUSE. LEAVE PowerPoint and your presentation open for the next project.

Project 3: Add Design Touches to Your Presentation

You are ready to do the final formatting and add the finishing touches to the presentation. You will adjust the slide master, add a slide, insert links, and set up transitions and animations.

USE the presentation that is open from the previous project.

1. Insert an automatically updating date and slide numbers that appear on all slides except the title slide. Notice that the date is obscured on slide 4 by the text box you added.
2. In Slide Master view, right-align the date in the date placeholder on the slide master. Close Slide Master view.
3. Insert a new slide at the end of the presentation using the Two Content layout.
4. Type the slide title **Contact Us**.

5. Insert the following contact information in the left-hand text placeholder. Format the information as desired.

   Mailing address:

   17507 Atlantic Blvd

   Boca Raton, FL 33456

   Phone:

   561 555 3663

   561 555 3664

6. Insert the following information in the right-hand text placeholder:

   Email:

   sales@contoso.com

   Website:

   www.contoso.com

7. Create a hyperlink from the website text to the website at http://www.contoso.com if PowerPoint did not make it a hyperlink when you typed it.

8. Apply a different background style to slide 5 only to make it stand out. (Hint: Right-click the desired background style and click Apply to Selected Slides.)

@ The *Pricing* file is available on the book companion website or in WileyPLUS.

9. Go to slide 3. Insert an Information action button above the date in the lower-right corner of the slide that links to the *Pricing* Excel file.

10. Go to slide 2, and apply the Wheat preset gradient shape fill to the text box that contains the quotation.

11. Run the presentation in Slide Show view. Test the action button on slide 3 to make sure it works in Slide Show view.

12. **SAVE** your changes to the presentation.

13. **SAVE** the presentation again as *Trey 2003* in the 97-2003 format, and then **CLOSE** the file.

EXIT PowerPoint.

LESSON SKILL MATRIX

Skill	Exam Objective	Objective Number
Creating Tables	Draw a table.	4.1.1
Inserting a Microsoft Excel Spreadsheet	Insert a Microsoft Excel spreadsheet.	4.1.2
Modifying Table Layout	Adjust columns and rows.	4.1.7
Formatting Tables	Set table style options.	4.1.3
	Add shading.	4.1.4
	Add borders.	4.1.5
	Add effects.	4.1.6
	Adjust columns and rows.	4.1.7

KEY TERMS

- cells
- embedded
- linked
- table
- worksheet

You are an assistant director of ATM operations at Woodgrove Bank. Your job is to help oversee the placement and use of ATMs in your bank's branches and other locations. You often deliver presentations to bank officers to keep them up to date on ATM activities. The best way to organize information that has several related components is to use a table. Distributing information in rows and columns makes the data easy to read and understand. Use the table features of Microsoft Office PowerPoint 2010 to modify the structure and appearance of a table to improve readability and visual interest.

SOFTWARE ORIENTATION

A PowerPoint Table

Tables are designed to organize data in columns and rows, as shown in Figure 5-1.

Figure 5-1

A PowerPoint table and the table tools on the Ribbon

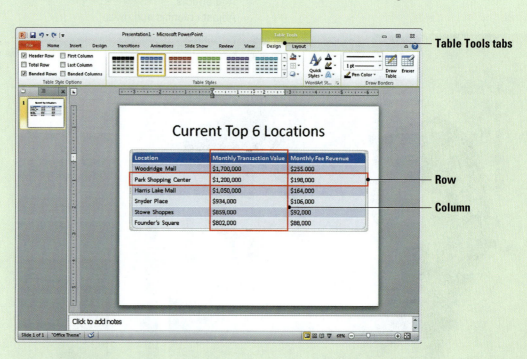

The Table Tools Design tab, shown above, and the Table Tools Layout tab provide tools for modifying and formatting a table. These tabs become active only when a table is selected.

CREATING TABLES

The Bottom Line

When you want to organize complex data on a slide, use a **table**. A table is a grid into which you can type text in the individual **cells** at the intersection of each column and row. A table's column and row structure makes data easy to understand. If you need to organize numerical data that may be used in calculations, you can insert an Excel worksheet right on a slide and use Excel's tools to work with the data.

Inserting a Table

PowerPoint has automated the process of creating a table so that you can simply specify the number of columns and rows and then type data to achieve a professionally formatted result. PowerPoint offers several ways to insert a table. The simplest is to click the Insert Table icon in any content placeholder. You can also insert a table with the Insert Table dialog box. In this exercise, you create tables using both methods.

STEP BY STEP   **Insert a Table**

 The *ATMs* file is available on the book companion website or in WileyPLUS.

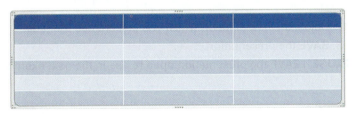

WileyPLUS Extra! features an online tutorial of this task.

GET READY. Before you begin these steps, make sure that your computer is on. Log on, if necessary.

1. **START** PowerPoint, if the program is not already running.
2. Locate and open the *ATMs* presentation and save it as *ATMs Final*.
3. Click below slide 4 in the Slides/Outline pane and press to Insert a new slide with the **Title and Content** layout after slide 4.
4. On the new slide, click in the title placeholder and type the slide title **Proposed ATM Locations**.
5. Click the **Insert Table** icon ▦ in the content placeholder. The Insert Table dialog box opens, as shown in Figure 5-2.

Figure 5-2

The Insert Table dialog box

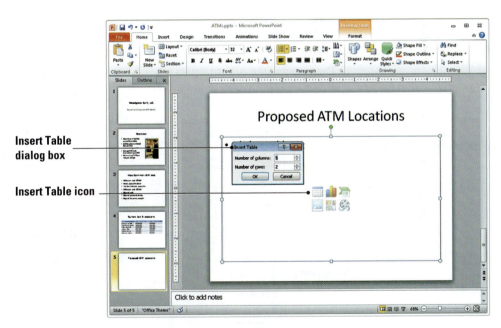

---

6. In the Number of Columns text box, type **3** to specify three columns, press **Tab** to move to the Number of Rows text box, and then type **6** to specify six rows. Click **OK**. PowerPoint creates the table in the content area, as shown in Figure 5-3. Notice that formats specified by the current theme have already been applied to the table.

Figure 5-3

The new table

Proposed ATM Locations

Another Way
You can open the Insert Table dialog box by clicking the Table drop-down arrow on the Insert tab and then clicking Insert Table.

7. Click in the first table cell in the top row and type **Location**. Press **Tab** to move to the next cell and type **Site Study Complete**. Press **Tab** to move to the third cell in the row and type **Nearest Competing ATM**.

8. Type the following information in the table cells, pressing **Tab** to move from cell to cell. Your table should look like Figure 5-4 when you complete it.

1. Springdale Cineplex	Yes	More than 2 miles
2. Glen Avenue BIG Foods	No	Three blocks
3. Findlay Market Square	Yes	One block
4. Center City Arena	Yes	One block
5. Williams State College	No	Half a mile

Figure 5-4

The table with data typed in it

Proposed ATM Locations

Location	Site Study Complete	Nearest Competing ATM
1. Springdale Cineplex	Yes	More than 2 miles
2. Glen Avenue BIG Foods	No	Three blocks
3. Findlay Market Square	Yes	One block
4. Center City Arena	Yes	One block
5. Williams State College	No	Half a mile

9. Insert a new slide with the Title and Content layout at the end of the presentation, and click to display the new slide.

10. On the Insert tab, click **Table** to produce the Table menu and grid.

11. Drag across the grid to select a 5 × 5 block, as in Figure 5-5, and then release the mouse button to create the table.

Figure 5-5

Use the Table button to select a 5×5 block.

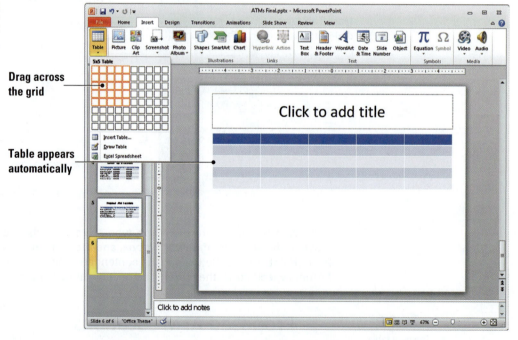

12. Delete the new slide on which you just created the table.

13. **SAVE** the presentation.

PAUSE. LEAVE the presentation open to use in the next exercise.

By default, PowerPoint sizes a new table to fill the width of the content placeholder. If you have only a few columns, you may find the table a little too spacious. You will learn later in this lesson how to adjust column widths and row heights to more closely fit the data you have entered.

If you need to reposition a table on a slide, you can do so by simply dragging its outer frame, as with any other object on a slide. You can resize a table overall by positioning the mouse pointer over one of the corners of its frame, so the mouse pointer becomes a double-headed arrow, and then dragging in or out; this changes the sizes of all rows and columns proportionally.

Drawing a Table

Drawing a table enables you to create a table with different row and column sizes, and with different numbers of rows per column (or columns per row). In this exercise, you will draw a table.

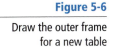

STEP BY STEP   **Draw a Table**

USE the *ATMs Final* presentation that is still open from the previous exercise.

1. Insert a new slide at the end of the presentation with the Title Only layout.

2. On the Insert tab, click **Table** to open the Table menu, and click **Draw Table**. The mouse pointer changes to a pencil.

3. Click and drag the mouse pointer to draw a frame approximately 3" high and the same width as the slide's title placeholder box.

   When you release the mouse button, the new table appears (which has only one big cell), and the Table Tools Design tab is displayed. See Figure 5-6.

Figure 5-6

Draw the outer frame for a new table

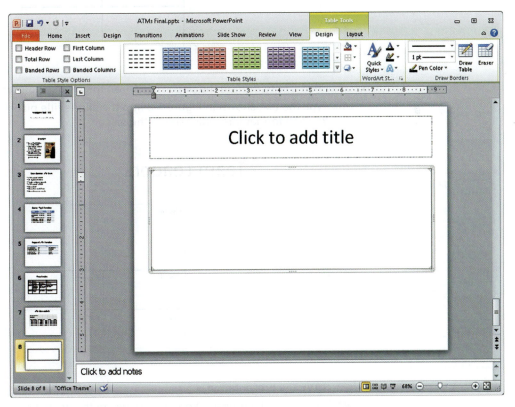

4. On the Table Tools Design tab, click **Draw Table** in the Draw Borders command group. The mouse pointer becomes a pencil again.

5. Click and drag to draw a horizontal line that divides the table in half horizontally. A dotted horizontal line appears. Release the mouse button to accept it.

Take Note   Drag to draw the lines starting slightly inside the border, rather than on the border's edge. If you start dragging too close to the border, PowerPoint creates a new table frame rather than adding to the existing table.

The drawing pencil mouse pointer should stay on; if it turns itself off, click the Draw Table button again to re-enable it.

6. Drag a vertical line through the middle of the table to divide it in half vertically.

7. Drag another vertical line that divides only the lower-right cell of the table vertically.

8. Drag another horizontal line that divides only the lower-right cells of the table horizontally. Figure 5-7 shows the completed table.

Figure 5-7

A drawn table

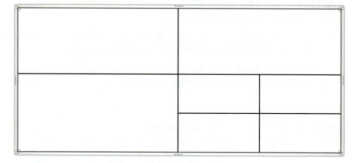

Click to add title

9. Press **Esc** to turn off the pencil cursor on the mouse pointer.

10. Type the text shown in Figure 5-8 into the slide's title placeholder and into the table. You will format this table later in the lesson.

Figure 5-8

The table with text added

Team Leaders

Division	Name	
Eastern	Claude	Simpson
	Mary	Bailey

11. **SAVE** the presentation.

PAUSE. LEAVE the presentation open to use in the next exercise.

CERTIFICATION
READY 4.1.1

How do you draw a table
on a slide?

Drawing a table is useful when you need a table that has different numbers of rows or columns in different spots, as you saw in the preceding exercise. You can also draw a table to create rows and columns of different heights and widths. Later in this lesson you will learn how to resize, merge, and split table rows and columns to create the same kinds of effects after the initial table creation.

INSERTING AN EXCEL WORKSHEET

The Bottom Line

Microsoft Office 2010 allows a great deal of integration among its programs. If you need to show numerical data on a slide, for example, you can insert an Excel worksheet directly on the slide and use it to manipulate data just as you would in Excel.

Using an Excel Worksheet in PowerPoint

If you need to show numerical data on a PowerPoint slide, you can insert an Excel worksheet directly on the slide and use it to manipulate data just as you would in Excel. Inserting an Excel **worksheet** (a spreadsheet from an Excel workbook) gives you access to all of Excel's data manipulation and formatting tools. If you want to show Excel data on a slide and have not yet created the worksheet, it makes sense to create the worksheet directly on the PowerPoint slide. A worksheet you insert in this way is **embedded** on the slide—it is stored within the PowerPoint presentation but can be edited using the tools of its source application, Excel.

When you insert a worksheet using the Excel Spreadsheet command, the worksheet consists of only four visible cells. Drag the bottom or side sizing handle (or the lower-right corner handle) to reveal more cells. When you have finished inserting data, use these handles to adjust the border to hide empty cells that would otherwise show on the PowerPoint slide.

You can also resize a worksheet object by clicking it once to display the heavy, light-blue container border, then dragging a bottom, side, or corner of the container. This action enlarges or reduces the object itself; it does not change font size of the embedded data even though the text may look larger. You can edit an embedded worksheet at any time by double-clicking the worksheet object to open it in Excel. You can remove the object by clicking it once to display the heavy, light-blue container border and then pressing Delete.

In this exercise, you insert an Excel worksheet in a PowerPoint presentation. In some ways the worksheet is like a table; in other ways it differs. You'll see the differences as you work through the exercise.

STEP BY STEP | **Insert an Excel Worksheet**

USE the *ATMs Final* presentation that is still open from the previous exercise.

1. Insert a new slide at the end of the presentation with the Title Only layout.
2. Type the slide title **ATM Cost Analysis**.
3. Click the **Insert** tab, click the **Table drop-down arrow**, and then click **Excel Spreadsheet**. PowerPoint creates a small Excel worksheet on the slide, as shown in Figure 5-9. Note that the PowerPoint Ribbon has been replaced by the Excel Ribbon.

Figure 5-9

A new Excel worksheet on a slide

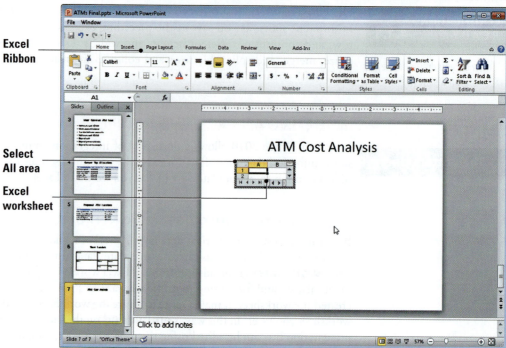

Take Note   When an Excel worksheet is open on the slide, you are actually working in Excel. To return to PowerPoint, click outside the worksheet.

4. Resize the worksheet object by dragging the lower-right corner handle diagonally to the right to display columns A through F and rows 1 through 10.

5. Click the **Select All** area in the upper-left corner of the worksheet object, where the column headers and row headers intersect. The entire worksheet object is selected.

6. Click the **Font Size drop-down arrow** on the Home tab and click **18**.

7. Type data in the worksheet cells as shown in Figure 5-10. To move between cells, use the arrow keys on the keyboard. To adjust column widths, position the pointer on the border between column headings and drag to the right until all data appears.

Figure 5-10

Type the data as shown

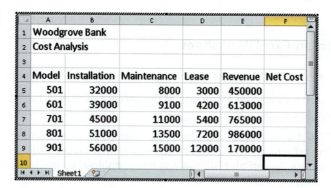

	A	B	C	D	E	F
1	Woodgrove Bank					
2	Cost Analysis					
3						
4	Model	Installation	Maintenance	Lease	Revenue	Net Cost
5	501	32000	8000	3000	450000	
6	601	39000	9100	4200	613000	
7	701	45000	11000	5400	765000	
8	801	51000	13500	7200	986000	
9	901	56000	15000	12000	170000	
10						

8. Click cell **F5** and type the following formula: **=E5–(B5+C5+D5)**. This formula sums the values in B5, C5, and D5, and then subtracts that total from the value in E5.

9. Press **Enter** to complete the formula.

10. Click cell **F5**, click the **Copy** button on the Home tab. Then click and drag over cells F6 through F9 to select them and click the **Paste** button to paste the formula in each of the selected cells.

Don't worry that the font and color of the text are different from the rest of the worksheet at this point.

11. Click then drag over the numbers in columns B through F to select them. Then click the **Accounting Number Format** button in the Number group on the Home tab to apply a currency format to the selected cells.

12. Click cell **B5**, and click the **Format Painter** button on the Home tab. Then click and drag over cell F5 through F9 to paint that formatting onto those cells. (Don't worry if some of the cells fill up with # signs.)

13. Drag over the range B5 to F9 to select it, and then click the **Decrease Decimal** button in the Number group twice to remove the decimal points and trailing zeros for the numbers.

14. Scroll to the right so that the divider between columns F and G is visible, and double-click the divider between the column letters to auto-resize column F to fit its contents.

15. Click cell **A1** and change the font size to **24**.

16. Click outside the worksheet object, and then click again to close the worksheet container. Your slide should look similar to Figure 5-11.

Figure 5-11

The completed Excel worksheet embedded in a slide

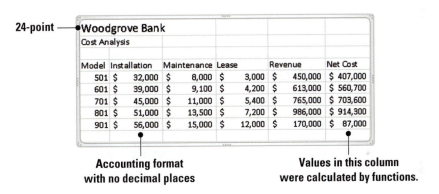

ATM Cost Analysis

24-point

Accounting format with no decimal places

Values in this column were calculated by functions.

17. **SAVE** the presentation.

PAUSE. LEAVE PowerPoint open to use in the next exercise.

Take Note   You know a worksheet is open and ready to edit in Excel when it displays the heavy hatched border.

CERTIFICATION READY   4.1.2

How do you insert an Excel spreadsheet in a slide?

If you have already created an Excel worksheet and want to use the data on a slide, you have several additional options for getting it from Excel to PowerPoint:

• Select the data in Excel, copy it to the Clipboard, and paste it on a PowerPoint slide. This action pastes the Excel data as a PowerPoint table that cannot be edited in Excel but can be modified like any other PowerPoint table.

• Select the data in Excel, copy it to the Clipboard, click the Paste button drop-down arrow in PowerPoint, and select Paste Special. In the Paste Special dialog box, choose to paste the data as an Excel worksheet object. The data is then embedded on the slide just as when you used the Excel Spreadsheet command.

- Select the data in Excel, copy it to the Clipboard, and open the Paste Special dialog box in PowerPoint. Choose to paste link the data as an Excel worksheet object. The data is then **linked** to the Excel worksheet, so that if you make a change to the worksheet in Excel, the data on the slide will show that same change.
- Click the Object button on the Insert tab to open the Insert Object dialog box. Here you can choose to create a new worksheet file or navigate to an existing file and paste or paste link it on the slide.

Take Note   The Insert Object dialog box allows you to create a number of objects other than worksheets. You can create formulas, Word documents in various versions, and even sound files.

You can use the same procedures to copy Excel charts to slides. When simply pasted on a slide, an Excel chart can be formatted using the same tools you use to work with a PowerPoint chart.

 Ref   You will work with PowerPoint charts in Lesson 6.

MODIFYING TABLE LAYOUT

The Bottom Line   It is often necessary to modify layout as you work with a table. For example, you may need to add or delete rows or columns, move data in the table, adjust column widths, or merge or split table cells.

Adding Rows and Columns

One of the most common reasons to change a table's structure is to add data to or remove data from the table. You learn in this exercise that you can easily insert rows and columns in Power-Point tables to keep data accurate and up to date. In the following exercise, you will add a row and a column to a table.

STEP BY STEP   **Add a Row and a Column**

USE the *ATMs Final* presentation that is still open from the previous exercise.

1. Go to slide 6 (the Team Leaders slide).
2. Click at the end of the word Bailey in the last cell, and press Tab. A new row appears.
3. In the new row, type the data shown in Figure 5-12.

Figure 5-12

Adding a row at the bottom of a table

Team Leaders

Division		Name	
Eastern		Claude	Simpson
		Mary	Bailey
Western		Greg	Ballantine

Insert a new row and key this data.

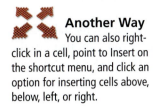

Another Way
You can also right-click in a cell, point to Insert on the shortcut menu, and click an option for inserting cells above, below, left, or right.

4. Click in the cell containing *Eastern* and on the Table Tools Layout tab, click **Insert Above** in the Rows and Columns command group. A new blank row appears above that cell's row.

5. Drag the lower border of the first row upward, decreasing that row's height so the table does not overflow the slide.

6. In the new row, type the data shown in Figure 5-13.

Figure 5-13

Adding a row between two existing rows

Insert Above button

This border was dragged upward to decrease height of first row.

New row inserted

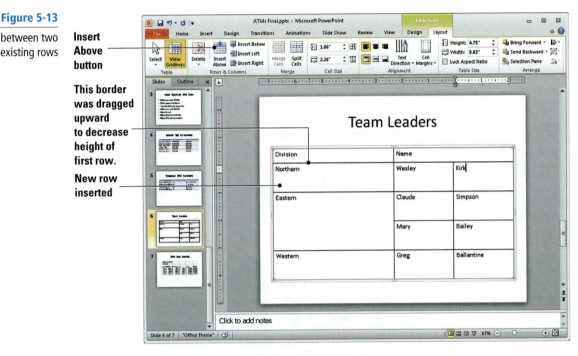

7. Click and drag across all the cells in the Division column to select that column.

8. On the Table Tools Layout tab, click **Insert Right**. A new blank column appears.

9. In the new column, type the data shown in Figure 5-14.

Figure 5-14

Adding a new column

Team Leaders

Division	States	Name		
Northern	Michigan Wisconsin Nebraska North Dakota	Wesley	Kirk	
Eastern	New York Connecticut Rhode Island Vermont Maine New Hampshire New Jersey	Claude	Simpson	
		Mary	Bailey	
Western	California Arizona New Mexico	Greg	Ballantine	

New column added

10. **SAVE** the presentation.

PAUSE. LEAVE the presentation open to use in the next exercise.

To add a new row at the bottom of a table, simply move into the last cell of the table (bottom right) and press Tab. Alternatively, the Tools in the Rows & Columns group on the Table Tools Layout tab make it easy to insert new rows and columns exactly where you want them in the table. Click in a cell near where you want to add the row or column and then click the appropriate button on the tab.

Deleting Rows or Columns

When you delete rows and columns, the table automatically resizes to account for the removal of the data. Note, however, that columns do not automatically resize to fill the area previously occupied by a column. After removing columns, you may need to resize the remaining columns in the table to adjust space. You learn about resizing later in this lesson. In this exercise, you delete a column and a row.

STEP BY STEP **Delete Rows or Columns**

USE the *ATMs Final* presentation that is still open from the previous exercise.

1. On slide 6, click in the upper left cell (Divisions).
2. On the Table Tools Layout tab, click the **Delete** button, and on the menu that appears, click **Delete Columns** (see Figure 5-15). The first column is deleted.

Figure 5-15

Deleting a column

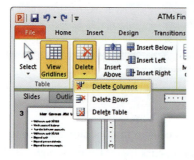

Another Way

You can also press Ctrl+Z to undo.

3. Click the **Undo** button on the Quick Access toolbar to undo the delete operation.
4. Click in the lower-left cell (Western).
5. On the Table Tools Layout tab, click the **Delete** button, and on the menu that appears, click **Delete Rows**. The bottom row is deleted.
6. Click the **Undo** button on the Quick Access toolbar to undo the delete operation.
7. **SAVE** the presentation.

PAUSE. LEAVE the presentation open to use in the next exercise.

Moving Rows and Columns

Move rows and columns when you need to reorder data. You can use drag and drop or the Cut and Paste commands to move row or column data into a new, blank row or column. In this exercise, you will insert a new column and then move content into it.

STEP BY STEP **Move a Column**

USE the *ATMs Final* presentation that is still open from the previous exercise.

1. Go to slide 4, click in the second column, and on the Table Tools Layout tab, click **Insert Left**. A new column is inserted between the first and second columns.
2. Drag across all the cells in the rightmost column to select them.

Another Way
You can also click in the rightmost column and then on the Table Tools Layout tab, click Select and click Column.

3. Drag the selected column and drop it on top of the first cell in the blank column you inserted in step 1. The data from the selected column is moved to the new column, and a blank column remains in the data's previous location, as shown in Figure 5-16.

Figure 5-16

Moving a column

...to here. ———

Data was dragged from here...

Current Top 6 Locations

Location	Monthly Fee Revenue	Monthly Transaction Value	
1. Woodbridge Mall	$225,000	$1,700,000	
2. Park Shopping Center	$198,000	$1,200,000	
3. Harris Lake Mall	$164,000	$1,050,000	
4. Snyder Place	$106,000	$934,000	
5. Stowe Shoppes	$92,000	$859,000	
6. Founder's Square	$88,000	$802,000	

4. With the second column still selected, press **Ctrl+X** to cut the column's data to the clipboard. The column disappears entirely. When you use the **Ctrl+X** command to cut all data from a column, a blank column is not left behind, as with drag and drop.

5. Click in the first row of the empty column on the right side of the table and press **Ctrl+V** to paste the data into that column. The data is placed in the empty column, and the table returns to having only three columns.

6. Drag the table's frame to re-center it on the slide if needed. (It may be slightly skewed to the left.)

7. **SAVE** the presentation.

PAUSE. LEAVE the presentation open to use in the next exercise.

Another Way
You can use the Cut and Paste commands on the Home tab to cut and paste if you prefer, or right-click and choose the Cut or Paste commands.

Moving rows and columns in PowerPoint 2010 is similar to moving rows and columns in a worksheet program such as Excel: you must make sure you have a blank row or column in which to insert the new data. If you simply drag a row or column to a new location, you will overwrite the existing data at that location.

There is one important difference between PowerPoint tables and Excel spreadsheets when moving data. When you move data around in a PowerPoint table, the area to which you paste or drag the content must be empty. Otherwise, the incoming content will overwrite what is already there. Unlike in Excel, the existing content does not move over to accommodate the new content.

Resizing and Distributing Rows and Columns

Row heights and column widths can be easily resized by dragging or double-clicking cell borders.

Adjust column widths or row heights to eliminate unused space or add space to make table text more readable. Dragging allows you to "eyeball" column widths or row heights so that they look attractive on the slide. Double-clicking allows you to immediately set column width to the width of its widest line. Double-clicking does not adjust row height, however. To resize a row that has been enlarged, drag its bottom border. To make all the rows or columns the same width, you can use the Distribute Rows or Distribute Columns buttons.

In this exercise, you will resize rows and columns in two different ways and distribute the column widths evenly.

Resize and Distribute Rows and Columns

USE the *ATMs Final* presentation that is still open from the previous exercise.

1. Go to slide 6, and double-click the vertical border between the first and second columns.

Take Note   Double-clicking a column border adjusts column width to fit the column's widest entry.

2. Drag the horizontal border between the Claude Simpson and Mary Bailey lines in the table upward, so that the Claude Simpson cells are as short as possible without truncating the text. See Figure 5-17.

Figure 5-17

Resize a row by dragging its bottom border

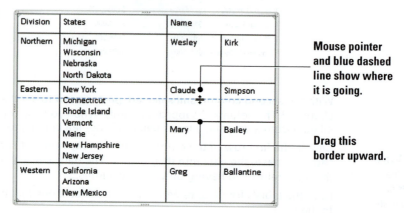

Mouse pointer and blue dashed line show where it is going.

Drag this border upward.

If you need to be more precise in resizing, you can use the tools in the Cell Size group on the Table Tools Layout tab to specify exact widths and heights for table cells.

3. Click in the cell that contains *States*.

4. On the Table Tools Layout tab, in the Cell Size group's Width box, set the value to exactly 4″ by clicking the up increment arrow. See Figure 5-18.

Figure 5-18

Specify an exact width from the Table Tools Layout tab

Set cell width here.

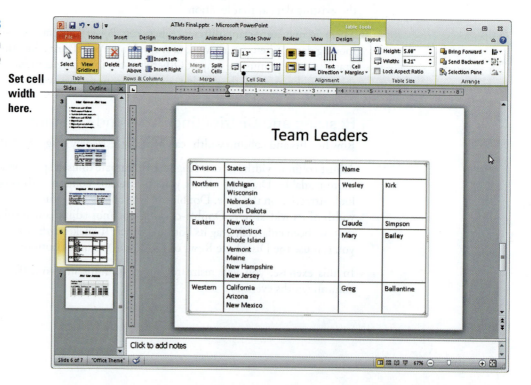

Take Note   The Width setting in the Table Size group controls the width of the entire table.

5. Select the entire table by dragging across it.
6. On the Table Tools Layout tab, click the **Distribute Columns** button. Each column becomes the same width.
7. **SAVE** the presentation.

PAUSE. LEAVE the presentation open to use in the next exercise.

You do not have to select an entire column or row to resize all cells in that column. When you click in any cell and resize a row or column, all cells in that row or column are adjusted at the same time.

If space in a table is extremely tight, you may be able to fit more text in columns and rows by adjusting cell margins. The Cell Margins button in the Alignment group on the Table Tools Layout tab allows you to select from four different cell margin options ranging from None to Wide, or create custom margins.

Merging and Splitting Table Cells

The merge and split features allow you to adjust how content fits in table cells and to modify the internal structure of a table without increasing or reducing its overall width. By merging cells, you can position content so it spans more than one column or row. When two cells merge, all the content is retained; a paragraph break is inserted between their content. Use the split feature when you want to divide a single row or column to accommodate additional entries without modifying the remainder of the table. When you split a cell that contains content, the content goes with the leftmost or upper cell; you may choose to move some or all of the content into the new blank cell(s) after the split. Merging and splitting can modify the internal structure of a table without increasing or reducing its overall width. In this exercise, you practice merging and splitting table cells.

STEP BY STEP   **Merge and Split Table Cells**

USE the *ATMs Final* presentation that is still open from the previous exercise.

1. Go to slide 6 and select the cells containing *Wesley* and *Kirk*.
2. On the Table Tools Layout tab, click **Merge Cells**. The two cells become one, and the text from both cells appears in the merged cell, separated by a paragraph break as shown in Figure 5-19.

Figure 5-19

Merging cells

3. Click at the beginning of the second name and press **Backspace** to delete the paragraph break between the two names, so they appear on the same line.

4. Use the procedures in steps 1-3 to merge each of the other three names (Claude Simpson, Mary Bailey, Greg Ballantine) in the table in the same way.

5. Use the procedures in steps 1-3 to merge the cells containing the names of the representatives for the Eastern region, and leave each name on a separate line as in Figure 5-20.

Figure 5-20

The table after all first and last names have been merged

Division	States	Name
Northern	Michigan Wisconsin Nebraska North Dakota	Wesley Kirk
Eastern	New York Connecticut Rhode Island Vermont Maine New Hampshire New Jersey	Claude Simpson Mary Bailey
Western	California Arizona New Mexico	Greg Ballantine

6. Select all three cells that contain state names, and on the Table Tools Layout tab, click **Split Cells** in the Merge command group. The Split Cells dialog box opens (see Figure 5-21).

Figure 5-21

Splitting a cell into multiple cells

7. In the Number of Columns text box, type **2** to set the number of columns to 2. In the Number of Rows box, type **1** to set the number of rows to 1. Then click **OK**.

8. For each division, move approximately half of the names from the existing cell to the empty cell to its right as shown in Figure 5-22. You can move the text either with drag and drop or cut and paste.

Another Way
To quickly merge or split, right-click in a cell or selected cells and click Merge or Split on the shortcut menu.

Figure 5-22

Move some of the state names into the new cells

Division	States		Name
Northern	Michigan Wisconsin	Nebraska North Dakota	Wesley Kirk
Eastern	New York Connecticut Rhode Island Vermont	Maine New Hampshire New Jersey	Claude Simpson Mary Bailey
Western	California Arizona	New Mexico	Greg Ballantine

Move some of the state names into the new column.

CERTIFICATION READY   4.1.7

How do you merge table cells?

CERTIFICATION READY   4.1.7

How do you split table cells?

9. **SAVE** the presentation file and **CLOSE** it.

PAUSE. LEAVE PowerPoint open to use in the next exercise.

You can also split columns or rows by drawing additional lines with the Draw Table feature, as you did earlier in the lesson. You can use the Eraser tool on the Table Tools Design tab to merge cells by erasing the divider between them.

FORMATTING TABLES

PowerPoint provides default formats to all new tables so that they have an appealing aesthetic. You may want to modify formatting, however, because you do not like the default colors or you want a different look. Use the tools on the Table Tools Design and Table Tools Layout tabs to apply new formatting options.

Changing Table Text Alignment and Orientation

Text can be aligned both vertically and horizontally within a cell. You can also change the text's orientation (rotation) to create visual interest. Use the same tools to align content horizontally in a table cell that you use to align text in a text placeholder. Changing alignment in table cells can improve readability as well as make a table more attractive.

Vertical alignment options control how content appears from top to bottom of a cell. The default option is top alignment, but column heads often look better centered vertically in table cells. When column headings have differing numbers of lines, standard procedure is to align all headings at the bottom.

Use options on the Text Direction menu to change the orientation of text for a special effect. Vertical text or text that reads from bottom to top makes a unique row header, for example. In this exercise, you will change the text direction and alignment in table cells.

STEP BY STEP   **Align and Orient Text in a Table**

GET READY. To align and orient text in a table, do the following:

1. **OPEN** the *Bids* presentation and save it as *Final Bids*.
2. Go to slide 2, and click in the merged cell at the far left of the table.
3. Click the **Table Tools Layout** tab, and then click the **Text Direction** button to display a menu of orientation options.
4. Click **Stacked**. This option will stack text with each letter below the previous one.
5. Type **Vendor** in the merged cell. The text stacks in the merged cell as shown in Figure 5-23.

@ The *Bids* file is available on the book companion website or in WileyPLUS.

Figure 5-23

Stacked text orientation

Overview of Bids

		Model	Price	Price Holds (days)	Warranty (years)
V e n d o r	Datum Corp.	2001	$98,500	30	10
	AT Metrics	1515TG	$101,800	45	15
	Touch-Val	P1004	$99,000	45	12
	Smith & Co.	SC2008	$100,250	30	10
	True-Touch	TT7809	$95,700	30	10

6. Select the text you just typed. Click the **Home** tab, and then click the **Character Spacing** button. Click **Very Tight** (see Figure 5-24).

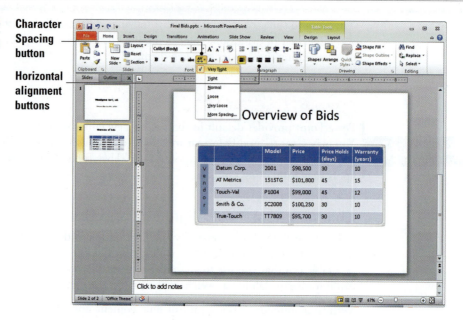

Figure 5-24

Set the character spacing

Character Spacing button

Horizontal alignment buttons

Take Note   When you move the I-beam pointer over rotated or stacked text, its orientation changes to match the text orientation.

7. With text still selected, click the **Bold** button in the Font group on the Home tab.

8. Select the cells with numbers in the Price column. Click the **Align Text Right** button in the **Paragraph** group to align all text in that column along the right side of the cells.

9. Select the cells with numbers in the last two columns. Click the **Center** button to center the contents of those cells.

10. Select the cells in the column header row. Because they are already blue, you won't be able to see that they are selected.

11. Click the **Table Tools Layout** tab, and click the **Align Bottom** button in the Alignment group. All column headings now align at the bottom of the cells, as shown in Figure 5-25.

Figure 5-25

Set vertical alignment

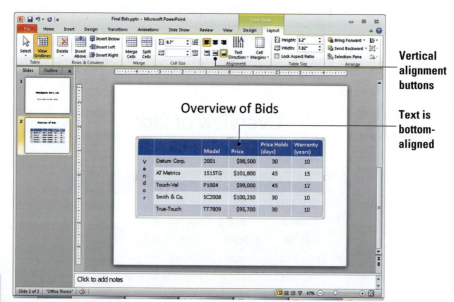

Vertical alignment buttons

Text is bottom-aligned

✂ **Another Way**
Horizontal alignment buttons also appear on the Table Tools Layout tab.

CERTIFICATION READY   4.1.7

How do you change the alignment of table text?

12. **SAVE** the presentation.

PAUSE. LEAVE the presentation open to use in the next exercise.

Applying a Quick Style to a Table

PowerPoint tables are formatted by default with a Quick Style based on the current theme colors. You can choose another Quick Style to change color and shading formats. In this exercise, you will apply a Quick Style to a table.

STEP BY STEP   **Apply a Quick Style to a Table**

USE the *Final Bids* presentation that is still open from the previous exercise.

1. Click anywhere in the table on slide 2, and then click the Table Tools Design tab.

2. Click the More button in the Table Styles group to display the Quick Styles gallery, as shown in Figure 5-26. Note that the table styles are organized into several groups—Best Match for Document, Light, Medium, and Dark.

Figure 5-26

Table Quick Styles gallery

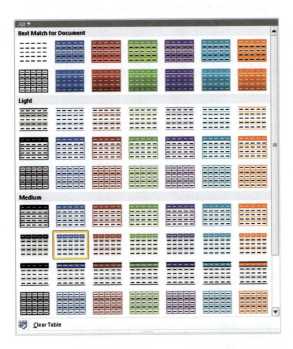

3. Click the Themed Style 2–Accent 6 table style. This is a colorful alternative, but not exactly what you want.

4. Click the More button again, and then click the Medium Style 3 style, a black and gray combination in the first column of the gallery. Your table should look similar to Figure 5-27.

Figure 5-27

New Quick Style applied to entire table

Overview of Bids

		Model	Price	Price Holds (days)	Warranty (years)
V	Datum Corp.	2001	$98,500	30	10
e	AT Metrics	1515TG	$101,800	45	15
n					
d	Touch-Val	P1004	$99,000	45	12
o					
r	Smith & Co.	SC2008	$100,250	30	10
	True-Touch	TT7809	$95,700	30	10

PAUSE. LEAVE the presentation open to use in the next exercise.

Colors available for Quick Style formats are controlled by theme. If you apply a Quick Style and then change the theme, the Quick Style colors will adjust to those of the new theme.

You may on occasion want to remove all table formatting to present data in a simple grid without shading or border colors. You can remove formatting by clicking Clear Table at the bottom of the Quick Styles gallery. Once you have cleared formats, you can reapply them by selecting any table style.

Turning Table Style Options On or Off

The options in the Table Style Options group on the Table Tools Design tab allow you to adjust what part of a table receives special emphasis. If your table has a row that shows totals of calculations, for example, the Total Row option applies color to that row so it stands out. You can use any number of these options in a single table, or you can deselect all of them for a plainer effect. Keep in mind that there is sometimes a fine line between effective emphasis and the visual confusion that can result from too much emphasis. In this exercise, you will modify the formatting applied by a table style by turning certain options on and off.

STEP BY STEP   **Turn Table Style Options On and Off**

USE the *Final Bids* presentation that is still open from the previous exercise.

1. Click anywhere in the table to select it if necessary.
2. Click the **Table Tools Design** tab if it is not already displayed.
3. Click the **Banded Rows** option in the Table Style Options group to deselect the option.
4. Click the **First Column** option. The first column receives special emphasis.
5. Click the **Banded Columns** option. Color bands are applied to the columns. Your table should look similar to Figure 5-28.

Figure 5-28

New table style options have been applied

Overview of Bids

		Model	Price	Price Holds (days)	Warranty (years)
V e n d o r	Datum Corp.	2001	$98,500	30	10
	AT Metrics	1515TG	$101,800	45	15
	Touch-Val	P1004	$99,000	45	12
	Smith & Co.	SC2008	$100,250	30	10
	True-Touch	TT7809	$95,700	30	10

**CERTIFICATION
READY   4.1.3**

How do you set table style options?

6. SAVE and close the presentation.

PAUSE. LEAVE PowerPoint open to use in the next exercise.

Adding Shading to Cells

If you do not like the Quick Style options or want more control over formatting, use the Table Tools Design tab's options for creating shading fills, border styles, and effects. Use the Shading button to display a color palette with the current theme colors. You can also select a color from the Standard color palette or from the Colors dialog box, or choose a picture, gradient, or texture fill. In this exercise, you learn to use the Shading button on the Table Tools Design tab to select your own fill options for table cells. In this exercise, you will add shading to cells.

STEP BY STEP   **Add Shading to Cells**

@ The *Warranties* file is available on the book companion website or in WileyPLUS.

GET READY. To add shading to cells, perform the following steps:

1. **OPEN** the *Warranties* presentation and save it as *Warranties Final*.
2. Go to slide 2, and select the cells in the column header row.
3. Click the **Table Tools Design** tab, and then click the **Shading button drop-down arrow** in the Table Styles group. The **Shading** color palette displays.
4. Click the **Gold, Accent 1** color to fill the column header cells with gold.
5. With the column header cells still selected, click the **Shading drop-down arrow** again, point to **Gradient**, and select the **From Top Right Corner** gradient style in the **Dark Variations** section of the gallery (see Figure 5-29).

Figure 5-29

Select a gradient fill

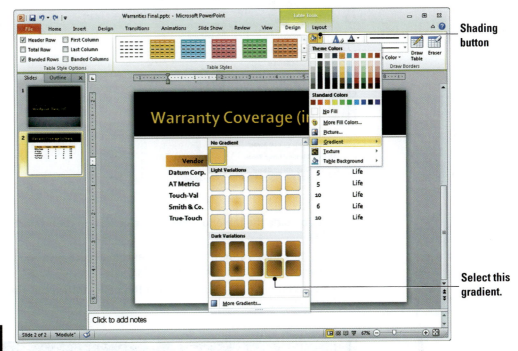

Shading button

Select this gradient.

CERTIFICATION READY   4.1.4

How do you set table cell shading?

6. **SAVE** the presentation.

PAUSE. LEAVE the presentation open to use in the next exercise.

The Shading menu also offers the Table Background option. You can use this command to insert a color or a picture to fill all cells of a table. You will learn more about inserting pictures as background later in this lesson.

Be careful when applying picture or texture fills to an entire table. Your text must remain readable, so choose a light background, adjust transparency if necessary, or be prepared to boldface text.

Adding Borders to Table Cells

The Border menu allows you to quickly apply borders to all sides of selected cells or to any specific side of a cell, giving you considerable flexibility in formatting table cells. You can also remove all borders from a cell or selected cells by selecting No Border. After you have selected a border option, it displays on the button. You can easily reapply that border option by simply clicking the button. In this exercise, you will add borders to table cells.

Add Borders to Table Cells

USE the *Warranties Final* presentation that is still open from the previous exercise.

<table>
<tr><td>CERTIFICATION
READY   4.1.5</td></tr>
<tr><td>How do you add cell
borders?</td></tr>
</table>

1. In the table on slide 2, select all cells *except* those in the first column and the column header cells. (You are selecting the numbers and the Life entries.)
2. On the Table Tools Design tab, click the **Border drop-down arrow** in the Table Styles group. A menu of border options appears.
3. Click **Inside Horizontal Border**, as shown in Figure 5-30.

Figure 5-30

Apply an inside horizontal border to the selected cells

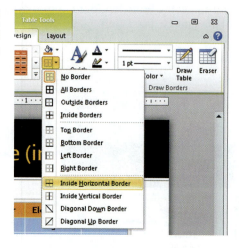

4. Click outside the table to deselect the cells, and then select only the bottom row of the table.
5. Click the **Border drop-down arrow**, and then click **Bottom Border**. A border is applied to the entire bottom row of the table.
6. Click outside the table to deselect the cells. Your table should look like Figure 5-31.

Figure 5-31

Borders applied to the selected cells

Warranty Coverage (in Years)

Vendor	Keypad	Monitor	Electronics	Case
Datum Corp.	5	2	5	Life
AT Metrics	3	1	5	Life
Touch-Val	7	1	10	Life
Smith & Co.	5	3	6	Life
True-Touch	7	3	10	Life

7. **SAVE** the presentation.

PAUSE. LEAVE the presentation open to use in the next exercise.

Take Note   The Shading button also shows the latest shading color you chose, making it easy to apply the same color again.

Note that you can also choose diagonal borders from the Border menu. Use a diagonal border to split a cell so you can insert two values in it, one to the left side of the cell and the other to the right on the other side of the diagonal border.

Take Note   To insert two values in a cell, set left alignment and type the first value, then press **Ctrl+Tab** or use the spacebar to move to the other half of the cell to type the second value.

Adding Special Effects to a Table

The Table Styles group offers an Effects button to let you apply selected special effects. Using the Effects menu, you can apply bevel, shadow, and reflection effects to a table. Bevels can apply to individual cells or selections of cells, but shadows and reflections are applied to the entire table.

STEP BY STEP   **Add Special Effects to a Table**

USE the *Warranties Final* presentation that is still open from the previous exercise.

1. Click anywhere in the table on slide 2.
2. Click the **Effects** button in the Table Styles group, point to Shadow, and click **Offset Diagonal Bottom Right** (see Figure 5-32).

Figure 5-32

Apply a shadow effect to the table

3. Click outside the table to see the effect.
4. **SAVE** the presentation.

PAUSE. **LEAVE** the presentation open to use in the next exercise.

CERTIFICATION READY   **4.1.6**

How do you add effects to a table?

Adding an Image to a Table

An image can serve as the background in one or more table cells. The image is not the cell content, but rather a background fill, just as a color fill would be. The text in the cell appears on top of it. In this exercise, you will learn how to add an image behind the text in some cells in a table.

Add an Image to a Table

USE the *Warranties Final* presentation that is still open from the previous exercise.

1. In the table on slide 2, select the vendor names in the first column of the table. (Do not select the Vendor column heading.)

2. Right-click in one of the selected cells, then click **Format Shape** on the menu that appears. The Format Shape dialog box opens.

 The *ATM.jpg* file is available on the book companion website or in WileyPLUS.

3. In the dialog box, click **Picture or texture fill**.

4. In the Insert From area of the dialog box, click the **File** button and in the Insert Picture dialog box that appears, navigate to the location of your data files. Select *ATM.jpg* and click **Insert**.

5. In the Format Shape dialog box, click to place a checkmark in the **Tile picture as texture** check box.

6. Drag the dialog box's **Transparency** slider until the box to the right of the slider reads 80%. See Figure 5-33.

Figure 5-33

Apply a picture fill

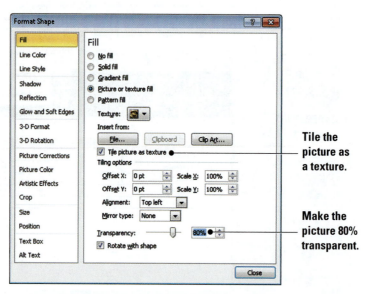

7. Click **Close** to apply your changes and close the dialog box. Click outside the table. The selected cells have a semi-transparent fill using the selected graphic.

8. **SAVE** the presentation.

PAUSE. LEAVE the presentation open to use in the next exercise.

You learned earlier that you can specify a picture as a background using the Table Background command on the Shading menu. Use this option if the picture you want to use is already formatted in such a way that it will not overwhelm the text in the table.

For the most control over an image to be used as a table background, insert it using the Format Shape dialog box, as you did in this exercise. You can insert a picture in a single cell or selected cells by right-clicking a selected cell and choosing Format Shape. Or you can insert the picture in all cells by right-clicking the table's light-blue container frame and then choosing Format Shape. Tiling options in this dialog box allow you to adjust how the tiles display over the table. If you choose not to tile, a separate copy of the picture will appear in every cell of the table. The Transparency slider lets you wash out the picture to make it appropriate for a background.

Images can be used for more than background effects in tables. You can also insert an image as table content. To do so, click in a cell and use the Picture command on the Shading menu. The picture you select is automatically resized to fit into the selected table cell.

Arranging a Table with Other Objects

PowerPoint enables you to stack one object on top of another, and then arrange them to control which one is at the top of the stack. Any transparent areas on the object on top show the underlying object behind them. In this exercise, you arrange a shape with a table so that the shape serves as a decorative frame.

STEP BY STEP   **Arrange a Shape and a Table**

USE the *Warranties Final* presentation that is still open from the previous exercise.

1. Display slide 2 and on the Insert tab, click the **Shape** button to produce the Shape gallery. Then click the rounded rectangle in the first row of shapes.

2. Drag to draw a rounded rectangle that completely covers the table, as in Figure 5-34.

Figure 5-34

Cover the table with a rounded rectangle

Click the Shapes button.

Select the rounded rectangle.

Draw a rectangle that covers the table.

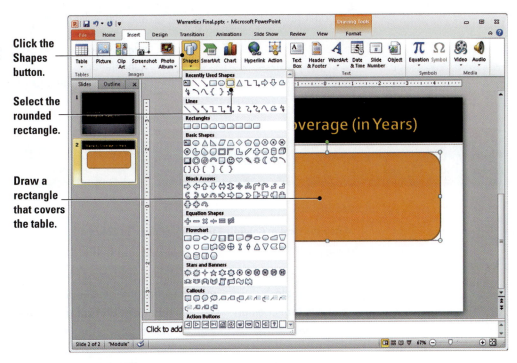

3. On the Drawing Tools Format tab, click **Send Backward** in the Arrange command group. The shape is sent behind the table.

4. With the shape still selected, click the **Shape Fill** button and click **More Fill Colors** from the menu that appears. The Colors dialog box opens.

5. Drag the Transparency slider to 85%, and then click **OK**. The rectangle appears as a lightly shaded background behind the table, as shown in Figure 5-35.

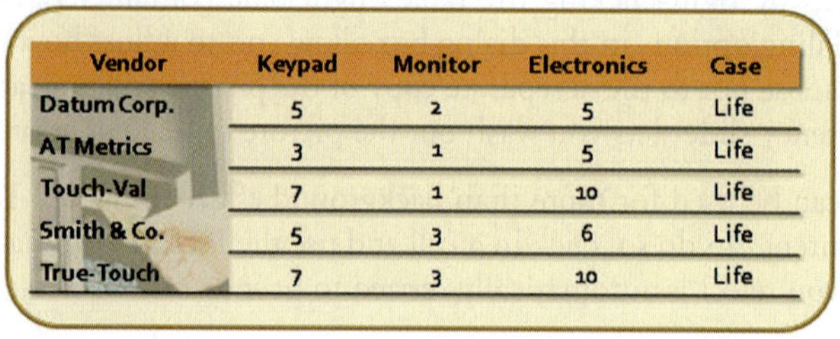

Figure 5-35

The table and the shape stacked together, arranged so that the table is in front

Vendor	Keypad	Monitor	Electronics	Case
Datum Corp.	5	2	5	Life
AT Metrics	3	1	5	Life
Touch-Val	7	1	10	Life
Smith & Co.	5	3	6	Life
True-Touch	7	3	10	Life

CERTIFICATION READY   **4.1.7**

How do you arrange a table with other content?

6. **SAVE** and **CLOSE** the presentation.

EXIT PowerPoint.

SKILL SUMMARY

In This Lesson You Learned How To:	Exam Objective	Objective Number
Create tables.	Draw a table.	**4.1.1**
Insert a Microsoft Excel spreadsheet.	Insert a Microsoft Excel spreadsheet.	**4.1.2**
Modify table layout.	Adjust columns and rows.	**4.1.7**
Format Tables.	Set table style options. Add shading. Add borders. Add effects. Adjust columns and rows.	**4.1.3** **4.1.4** **4.1.5** **4.1.6** **4.1.7**

Knowledge Assessment

Matching

Match the term in Column 1 to its description in Column 2.

Column 1

1. Table source
2. Draw Table
3. Table Tools Design
4. Merge
5. Quick Style
6. Link
7. Shading
8. Embed
9. Table Tools Layout
10. Worksheet

Column 2

a. Insert data so that it maintains a connection to a document
b. A document used to manipulate numerical data
c. A background color for table cells
d. Insert data so that it can be edited using its original application
e. Tab that allows you to insert a new table row
f. An arrangement of columns and rows used to organize data
g. Tab that allows you to apply a Quick Style to a table
h. Option you can use to create a table frame and insert columns and rows where you want them
i. To combine two or more cells to create a larger cell
j. A set of preset formatting that can be applied to a table.

True/False

Circle T if the statement is true or F if the statement is false.

T F 1. To create a new table, click the Insert Object button and then select the type of table to create.

T F 2. By default, a new table is sized to fit the content placeholder in which it was created.

T F 3. To edit a worksheet object, double-click the object to display Excel's tools.

T F 4. You can copy and paste data from Excel to a PowerPoint slide using the Clipboard.

T F 5. You must select an entire row before you can insert a new row above or below it.

T F 6. When moving a column, you do not have to create an empty column first for the moved data to be placed in; the existing content will move over to accommodate it.

T F 7. Use Distribute Columns to quickly resize all columns to the same width.

T F 8. Use the Blank Table option to quickly remove all formatting from a table.

T F 9. Bevel effects automatically apply to an entire table.

T F 10. If you do not specify that a picture should be tiled over selected cells, it will display in each table cell.

Competency Assessment

Project 5-1: Job Fair

You work for Lucerne Executive Recruiters, a company that specializes in finding employees for a variety of clients. You are planning to give a brief presentation at a local job fair and need to prepare a slide that lists some currently available jobs for which you are recruiting candidates. You can use a table to display this information.

GET READY. LAUNCH PowerPoint if it is not already running.

@ The *Jobs* file is available on the book companion website or in WileyPLUS.

1. **OPEN** the *Jobs* presentation and save it as *Jobs Final*.

2. Go to slide 2, and click the **Insert Table** icon in the content placeholder.

3. Create a table with three columns and seven rows.

4. Type the following information in the table:

Title	Company	Salary Range*
Senior Editor	Litware, Inc.	$30K-$42K
Sales Associate	Contoso Pharmaceuticals	$55K-$70K
District Manager	Tailspin Toys	$65K-$80K
Accountant	Fourth Coffee	$53K-$60K
Production Assistant	Fabrikam, Inc.	$38K-$45K

*Starting salary based on experience

5. Click in the **Salary Range** column, and then click the **Insert Right** button on the Table Tools Layout tab to insert a new column.

6. Type the following information in the new column:

Posted
5/01
5/10
4/30
4/27
5/07

7. Click the **Production Assistant** cell, then click the **Insert Below** button on the Table Tools Layout tab to insert a new row.

8. Type the following information in the new row:

   Loan Officer   Woodgrove Bank $42-$54K   5/12

9. Select all the cells in the last row of the table, and then click the **Merge Cells** button on the Table Tools Layout tab.

10. Adjust column widths by dragging or double-clicking cell borders so that all table entries in a given row are on a single line.

11. Format the table as follows:

   a. Select the Salary Range and Posted columns, and then click the **Center** button on the Home tab.

   b. Click in the last row of the table, and then click the **Align Text Right** button.

   c. With the insertion point still in the last row, click the **Shading** button on the Table Tools Design tab, and then click **No Fill**.

   d. Click the **Border** button, and then click **No Border**.

   e. Click the **First Column** table style option to apply emphasis to the first column of the table. Adjust column widths again if necessary to avoid runover lines.

   f. Select all cells in the Loan Officer row of the table, click the **Border** button, and then click **Bottom Border**.

   g. Apply a bevel effect to the column header cells and the first column cells.

12. **SAVE** the presentation and then **CLOSE** the file.

LEAVE PowerPoint open for use in the next project.

Project 5-2: Making the Upgrade

You are a production manager at Tailspin Toys. You have been asked to give a presentation to senior management about anticipated costs of upgrading machinery in the assembly area. Because you want to sum the costs, you will use an Excel worksheet to present the information.

@ The *Upgrades* file is available on the book companion website or in WileyPLUS.

1. **OPEN** the *Upgrades* presentation and save it as *Upgrades Final*.

2. Go to slide 2, click the **Insert** tab, click the **Table drop-down arrow**, and then click **Excel Spreadsheet**.

3. Drag the lower-right corner handle of the worksheet object to reveal columns A through D and rows 1 through 7.

4. Type the following data in the worksheet. (Change the zoom size if desired to make it easier to see the data you are entering.)

Machine	Upgrade	Cost	Time Frame
Conveyor #2	New belt, drive	$28,000	30 days
Conveyor #3	Update software	$5,800	14 days
Drill Press #1	Replace	$32,000	30 days
Vacuum system	New pump, lines	$12,750	30 days
Docks #2–#5	Doors, motors	$14,500	10 days

5. Click the Excel **Page Layout** tab, click the **Themes** button, and then click **Solstice** to apply the same theme to the worksheet that your presentation uses.

6. Adjust column widths by dragging or double-clicking column borders to display all data.

7. Click in cell **B7**, type **Total Costs**, and then press **Tab**.

8. Click the **Sum** button in the Editing group on the Home tab, and then press **Enter** to complete the SUM function.

9. Apply **Quick Styles** to the worksheet as follows:

   a. Select the column headings, and then click the **Cell Styles** button in the Styles group on the Home tab.

   b. Click the **Accent5** style.

   c. Click the **Total Costs** cell, click the **Cell Styles** button, and click the **Accent1** style.

   d. Click the cell that contains the sum of costs, click the **Cell Styles** button, and click the **Total** style.

   e. Apply bold formatting to the column heads and the **Total Costs** cell.

10. Click the **Select All** area at the top left corner of the worksheet, then click the **Font Size drop-down arrow** and click **18**. Adjust column width again if necessary to display all data.

11. Select the entries in the Time Frame column, and click the **Center** button.

12. Click outside the worksheet twice to review your changes.

13. **SAVE** the presentation and **CLOSE** the file.

LEAVE PowerPoint open for use in the next project.

Proficiency Assessment

Project 5-3: Power Up

You are an operations manager for City Power & Light. You have been asked to give a presentation to department heads about scheduled maintenance of power substations around the city. Use a table to present the maintenance schedule.

@ The *Power* file is available on the book companion website or in WileyPLUS.

1. **OPEN** the *Power* presentation and save it as *Power Final*.

2. Go to slide 3. On the Insert tab, click **Table** and drag over the grid to create a table with two columns and seven rows.

3. Type the following information in the table:

Substation	Week of
Eastland	July 13
Morehead	October 1
Huntington	June 6
Parkland	May 21
Midtown	July 28
Elmwood	December 11

4. Apply a **Quick Style** of your choice to the table.

5. Turn on the **First Column** table style, and change any other table style option that improves the look of the table. For example, you might change the font color.

6. Delete the last row of the table.

7. Rearrange the rows so that the dates in the second column are in chronological order.

   Tip: Create a new blank row, and use it as a temporary holding area when moving rows.

8. Click the outside border of the table, hold down the mouse button, and drag straight down to move the table down about half an inch.

9. **SAVE** the presentation and **CLOSE** the file.

LEAVE PowerPoint open for use in the next project.

Project 5-4: Is It on the Agenda?

You are an assistant director of finance at Humongous Insurance Company. You have been tasked with establishing the agenda for a management meeting. You have created the agenda as a table on a slide, which will appear onscreen throughout the day. You think the table could use some additional formatting to make it easier to read and understand.

@ The *Agenda* file is available on the book companion website or in WileyPLUS.

1. **OPEN** the *Agenda* presentation and save it as *Agenda Final*.
2. Center all entries in the second column, and then center the column head only for the third column.
3. Clear all formatting from the table using the Clear Table option on the table Quick Styles gallery.
4. Remove all borders using the No Border option on the Border menu.
5. Format the table's header row as follows:
   a. Increase the height of the column header row to 0.6", and then center the column header text vertically in the row.
   b. Apply bold, 20-point formatting to the column header text.
   c. Select the header row cells and use the Format Shape dialog box to apply the Granite texture. Change the transparency of the texture to 65%.
   d. Apply the **Circle** cell bevel effect to the header row cells.
6. Select the first Break row and apply a shading of **Aqua, Accent 3, Lighter 40%**. Apply the same shading color to the second Break row.
7. Select the Lunch row and apply a shading of **Lavender, Accent 5, Lighter 40%**.
8. Apply the **Inside Diagonal Bottom Right** shadow effect to the entire table.
9. Add a border around the outside of the table and along the bottom of the header row.
10. **SAVE** the presentation as *Agenda Final* and **CLOSE** the file.

LEAVE PowerPoint open for use in the next project.

Mastery Assessment

Project 5-5: Scaling the Summit

You are a district manager for Adventure Works, a travel agency specializing in adventurous destinations. You are preparing a presentation that contains a list of mountain climbing excursions you can use at a travel fair and need to format the table that contains the excursion information.

@ The *Adventures* file is available on the book companion website or in WileyPLUS.

1. **OPEN** the *Adventures* presentation.
2. Go to slide 3 and select all the cells in the table.
3. Use the *Mountain.jpg* picture file as a background fill for the selected cells. Tile the picture, and adjust transparency so that the text can be clearly read against the background.
4. Apply shading formatting of your choice to the column heads, and adjust font color and style as desired to improve appearance.

@ The *Mountain.jpg* file is available on the book companion website or in WileyPLUS.

5. Apply formatting to the header row that makes it stand out from the other text.
6. Apply borders of your choice to the table.
7. Apply an effect of your choice to the table.
8. **SAVE** the presentation as *Adventures Final* and **CLOSE** the file.

LEAVE PowerPoint open for use in the next project.

Project 5-6: Complaint Process

Your employer, Trey Research, has been asked by Center City Hospital to help the hospital conduct an extensive study on patient complaints. You have been asked to tally complaints for the past year and categorize them. You have begun the process of creating a presentation to detail your findings. Your first step is a summary table that lays out the major categories of complaints.

@ The *Complaints* file is available on the book companion website or in WileyPLUS.

1. **OPEN** the *Complaints* presentation.

2. Go to slide 2 and adjust column widths so that all the summary items are on one line.

3. Reorder the rows so that the categories are in alphabetical order.

4. Set the height of each of the rows (except the header row) to exactly 0.4".

5. Split the Complaints column (except the column header cell) into two columns, and move all information from the original Complaints column, including the column header, into the right-hand split.

6. Merge the table cells in the left-hand split. (Do not merge the column header row, only the banded cells.)

7. In the merged cell, rotate the text direction 270 degrees and type **Over 375 complaints received from patients in past 12 months**.

8. Apply different shading colors to each category of complaint, with a border at the bottom of each category section.

9. Adjust column widths again if necessary and adjust alignment as necessary to improve table appearance.

10. **SAVE** the presentation as *Complaints Final* and **CLOSE** the file.

EXIT PowerPoint.

INTERNET READY

You want to take a vacation over the winter holidays next year, but you have not yet decided whether to go skiing, enjoy the sun on a Caribbean island, or venture down under to Australia. Using Internet search tools, find several interesting ski packages in Canada and Europe, resort packages in the Caribbean, and lodgings in Sydney, Australia.

Determine the local price for all these excursions. Create a PowerPoint presentation with a table that lists your possible destinations and dates of travel. Add a new slide and insert a worksheet. Enter the destinations and their costs and the conversion rate to convert local costs to dollars. Create formulas to convert costs so you can compare all package costs in U.S. dollars.

6 Using Charts in a Presentation

LESSON SKILL MATRIX

Skill	Exam Objective	Objective Number
Building Charts	Select a chart type.	4.2.1
	Enter chart data.	4.2.2
	Change the chart type.	4.2.3
	Change the chart layout.	4.2.4
Formatting Charts with Quick Styles	Apply Quick Styles.	4.5.5
Modifying Chart Data and Elements	Select data.	4.2.6
	Edit data.	4.2.7
	Switch row and column.	4.2.5
	Use chart labels.	4.3.1
	Use axes.	4.3.2
	Use gridlines.	4.3.3
Manually Formatting a Chart	Use backgrounds.	4.3.4
	Select chart elements.	4.4.1
	Format selections.	4.4.2
	Arrange chart elements.	4.5.1
	Specify a precise position.	4.5.2
	Apply effects.	4.5.3
	Resize chart elements.	4.5.4
	Apply a border.	4.5.6
	Add hyperlinks.	4.5.7

KEY TERMS

- charts
- chart area
- data marker
- data series
- legend
- plot area

You are the general manager of the Alpine Ski House, a small ski resort. One of your responsibilities is to provide information to the group of investors who share ownership of the resort. You will use PowerPoint presentations to convey that information. PowerPoint's charting capabilities enable you to communicate financial data in a visual way that makes trends and comparisons easy to understand. In this lesson, you learn how to insert different types of charts, as well as how to modify and format a chart so it displays your data in the most attractive and useful way.

SOFTWARE ORIENTATION

A PowerPoint Chart

Charts can help your audience understand relationships among numerical values. Figure 6-1 shows a sample PowerPoint chart with some standard chart features labeled.

Figure 6-1

Components of a chart

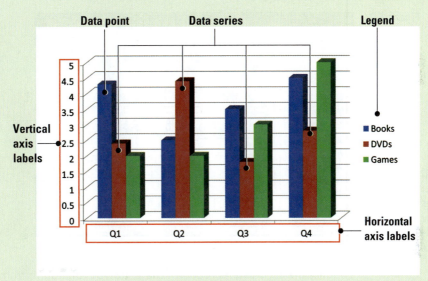

A chart can compare multiple data series, as in Figure 6-1, with each series represented by a different color or pattern. A **legend** explains what each color represents. Category axis labels explain what the groupings of bars represent (on the horizontal axis) and vertical axis labels explain the meaning of the numeric values (on the vertical axis). Optional elements such as gridlines behind the chart help make the chart more readable.

BUILDING CHARTS

The Bottom Line

Charts are visual representations of numerical data. Chart features such as columns, bars, lines, or pie slices make it easy to understand trends or compare values. Once you have created a chart in PowerPoint, you can easily modify the data on which the chart is based, choose a different type of chart to display the data, change the layout of the chart, and modify its formats.

Inserting a Chart from a Content Placeholder

Excel opens when you create a chart in PowerPoint, and you enter the data in Excel that you want to plot on the chart. Then when you return to PowerPoint, the chart appears with the data presented. As with tables and other objects such as diagrams and pictures, the easiest way to insert a chart is to click the Insert Chart icon in any content placeholder. PowerPoint guides you the rest of the way to complete the chart. In the following exercise, you place a chart on a slide using a content placeholder.

STEP BY STEP | **Insert a Chart**

GET READY. Before you begin these steps, make sure that your computer is on. Log on, if necessary.

@ The *Revenues* file is available on the book companion website or in WileyPLUS.

1. **START** PowerPoint, if the program is not already running.
2. Locate and open the **Revenues** presentation and save it as **Revenues Final**.
3. Go to slide 3. Click the **Insert Chart** icon in the center of the content placeholder. The Insert Chart dialog box opens, as shown in Figure 6-2, showing chart types and subtypes.

Figure 6-2

Select a chart type and subtype

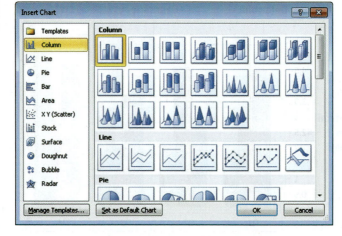

Another Way
To insert a chart on a slide that does not have a content placeholder, click the Chart button on the Insert tab.

4. Click the **3D Clustered Column** chart subtype (the fourth from the left in the top row of the dialog box).
5. Click **OK**. Microsoft Excel opens in a separate window on top of the PowerPoint window. See Figure 6-3. Notice the bright-blue border that surrounds the data range in Excel. This *range border* is used to indicate the data being charted.

Figure 6-3

An Excel sheet opens for entering the data for the chart

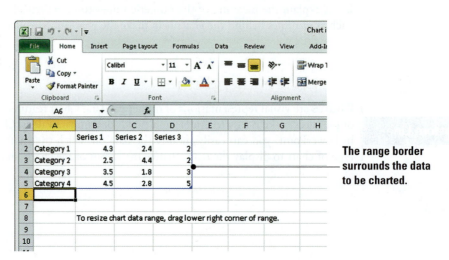

The range border surrounds the data to be charted.

6. Drag the marker in the bottom right corner of the range border so that the range includes only cells A1:C5.

7. Select **Column D**, and then press **Delete** to clear the selected cells.

8. Click cell **B1** and type **2010**, replacing the current entry. Then press **Tab** to move to cell C1. Type **2011**, and press **Enter**.

9. Beginning in cell A2, type the following data in Excel to complete the chart:

Spring	$89,000	$102,000
Summer	$54,000	$62,000
Fall	$102,000	$118,000
Winter	$233,000	$267,000

10. Close Excel and return to PowerPoint. The chart appears with the data you entered, as in Figure 6-4.

Figure 6-4

The completed chart

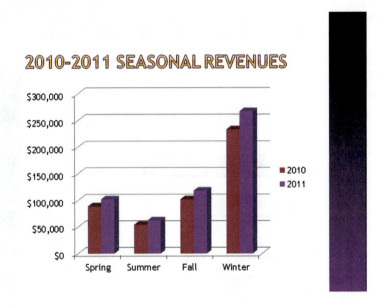

11. **SAVE** the presentation.

PAUSE. LEAVE the presentation open to use in the next exercise.

As you saw in the previous exercise, Excel opens to allow you to insert the data that creates the chart. You must have Excel installed on your PC to take advantage of the full charting capabilities in PowerPoint. If you do not have Excel installed, PowerPoint instead resorts to Microsoft Graph, the charting application used in previous versions of PowerPoint. Microsoft Graph is not covered in this course. After you type the chart data, you can close Excel. You do not have to save your work in Excel because it is saved within the PowerPoint file as part of the chart. You can edit the Excel data any time you want by clicking the Edit Data button on PowerPoint's Chart Tools Design tab (which appears when a chart is selected).

If you want to use data from an existing workbook, open that workbook and Copy and Paste the data into the sheet created for the chart's data. Adjust the range border as needed.

You can also create the chart in Excel, and then copy the completed chart to PowerPoint using the Clipboard.

Choosing a Different Chart Type

After creating a chart, you may choose to change its type and/or its layout. If you decide that the chart type you have chosen does not display the data the way you want, you can choose a different chart type or subtype.

Different chart types display the data series differently. A **data series** consists of all the data points for a particular category, such as all the columns for Quarter 1 values. A data point, sometimes called a **data marker**, is one column or point in a series. The default chart type is a Column chart. In this exercise, you change a chart's type.

Choose a Different Chart Type

USE the *Revenues Final* presentation that is still open from the previous exercise.

Another Way
You also can use a shortcut to change the chart's type. Right-click almost anywhere in the chart and then click Change Chart Type on the shortcut menu.

1. In PowerPoint, click the **Change Chart Type** button on the Chart Tools Design tab. The Change Chart Type dialog box opens, showing the same options that appeared when you first created the chart.

2. On the list of chart types at the left, click **Bar**.

3. Click the **Clustered Horizontal Cylinder** subtype, and then click **OK**. The rectangular columns change to 3-D cylinders, as shown in Figure 6-5. Don't worry if the text is not readable; you will learn to fix that later in this lesson.

Figure 6-5

A new chart type applied

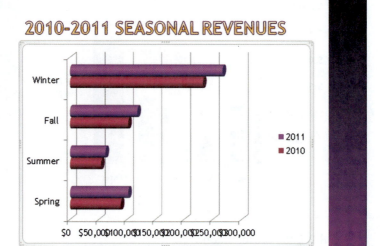

4. **SAVE** the presentation.

PAUSE. LEAVE the presentation open to use in the next exercise.

You can change any chart type to any other type, but the result may not always be what you expect, and you may lose some data. For example, when you change from any multiseries chart (such as a clustered bar or line) to a pie chart, only the first data series appears on the chart. In addition, when you change from a vertical to a horizontal chart, as in the preceding exercise, some of the axis labels may need adjustment, as in Figure 6-5.

If you apply a chart type that does not display your data as you want, use Undo to reverse the change and then try another type.

Troubleshooting   Changing from a 2-D chart type to a 3-D type can yield unexpected results. For some chart types, PowerPoint may display the new chart type in a rotated perspective view that you might not like. It is best to decide when you create the original chart whether you want it to use 2- or 3-D, and then stick with those dimensions when making any change to the chart type.

Applying a Different Chart Layout

PowerPoint supplies several preformatted chart layouts that you can apply quickly to modify the default layout. These layouts may adjust the position of features, such as the legend, or add chart components such as titles and data labels. In this exercise, you choose a different chart layout.

STEP BY STEP   **Apply a Different Chart Layout**

USE the *Revenues Final* presentation that is still open from the previous exercise.

1. With the chart on slide 3 selected, click the **More** button in the Chart Layouts group on the Chart Tools Design tab. The Chart Layout gallery displays, as shown in Figure 6-6.

Figure 6-6

The Chart Layout gallery

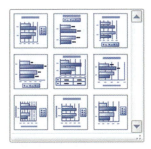

Take Note   The thumbnails in the Chart Layout gallery show in miniature the new layout and elements of the chart.

2. Click **Layout 2** in the gallery. The layout is modified to place the legend above the chart and add data labels to each of the bars. See Figure 6-7.

Figure 6-7

The chart with Layout 2 applied to it

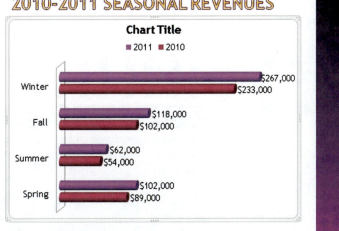

3. Switch to the **Chart Tools Layout** tab.
4. Click the **Chart Title** button to open a menu, and click **None**. The chart title is removed. (It's not necessary because the slide itself provides a title.)
5. **SAVE** the presentation and then **CLOSE** the file.

PAUSE. LEAVE PowerPoint open to use in the next exercise.

CERTIFICATION
READY   4.2.4

How do you change
a chart's layout?

PowerPoint charts can be customized in a very wide variety of ways by adding and removing chart elements such as titles, labels, and gridlines. If you do not want to take the time to add elements, PowerPoint's chart layouts can provide you with some standard appearance options to choose from. You will learn how to add elements yourself later in this lesson.

FORMATTING CHARTS WITH QUICK STYLES

The Bottom Line

Chart Quick Styles provide instant formatting to change the look of a chart. A Quick Style can change colors and borders of data markers, apply effects to the data markers, and apply color to the chart or plot area. (You learn more about these individual chart elements in a later section of this lesson, "Manually Formatting a Chart.")

Applying a Quick Style

You can use a Quick Style to format a chart if you do not have time to adjust formatting of chart elements such as data series or the individual data points in a series. In this exercise, you apply a Quick Style to a chart.

STEP BY STEP   **Apply a Quick Style to a Chart**

@ The *Conditions* file is available on the book companion website or in WileyPLUS.

GET READY. To apply a quick style to a chart, perform the following steps:

1. **OPEN** the *Conditions* presentation and save it as *Conditions Final*.
2. Go to slide 2 and click the chart to select it.
3. On the Chart Tools Design tab, click the **More** button in the Chart Styles group. The Quick Styles gallery appears, as shown in Figure 6-8.

Figure 6-8

The Chart Quick Styles gallery

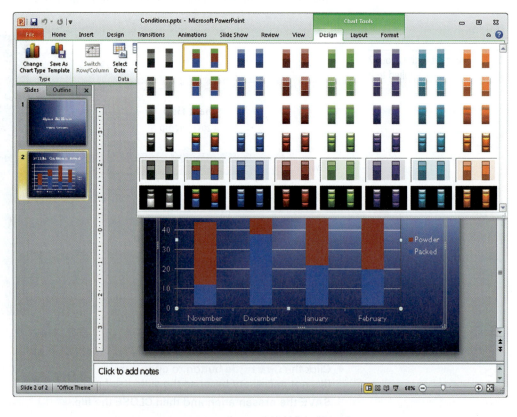

4. Click **Style 7**. The data series' colors change to variations of another theme color. This is not quite dramatic enough for your purpose.

5. Click the **More** button again, and then click **Style 43**. This style applies new theme color, bevel effects, and different chart background colors, as shown in Figure 6-9.

Figure 6-9

The chart is more interesting with the new Quick Style applied

6. **SAVE** the presentation and then **CLOSE** the file.

PAUSE. LEAVE PowerPoint open to use in the next exercise.

MODIFYING CHART DATA AND ELEMENTS

The Bottom Line

It is not uncommon to have to modify a chart after it has been created. You can change the data on which the chart is based at any time or change the way in which the data is plotted. You can also add or remove chart elements as desired to customize your chart.

Editing a Chart's Data

Chart data remains "live" as long as the chart remains on the slide. You can reopen the chart worksheet at any time to adjust the data. Changes you make to the chart data worksheet are immediately reflected on the PowerPoint chart. Use the Edit Data button to reactivate the data worksheet in Excel, and make your changes there. You can also use Switch Rows/Columns to plot the data on different axes.

Before you can edit chart data, you must select it. To select an individual cell in the data sheet, click that cell. To select ranges of cells, drag across them, or click a column or row header to select the entire row or column. In the following exercise, you practice editing chart data, including selecting individual cells and entire columns.

STEP BY STEP   **Edit a Chart's Data**

@ The *Pricing* file is available on the book companion website or in WileyPLUS.

GET READY. To edit a chart's data, do the following:

1. **OPEN** the Pricing presentation and save it as Pricing Final. Examine the information on the slides, and notice that the dates on the title slide do not agree with the dates on the chart.

2. Go to slide 2 and click the **chart** to select it.

3. On the Chart Tools Design tab, click the **Edit Data** button in the Data group. The data worksheet opens in Excel.

4. Click cell **A3** and type **Equipment**, replacing the current entry there.

5. Click column B's column header to select the entire column, and then on the Home tab, click **Delete**. The data in Excel should now resemble Figure 6-10.

Figure 6-10

The edited data for the chart

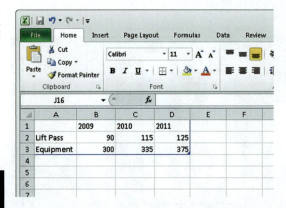

CERTIFICATION READY   4.2.6

How do you select chart data?

6. **CLOSE** Excel, and return to PowerPoint. Notice that the chart on slide 2 has been updated.

7. In PowerPoint, on the Chart Tools Design tab, click the **Switch Row/Column** button. The chart changes to plot the data with the years on the horizontal axis, rather than the categories. See Figure 6-11.

Figure 6-11

The completed chart, with rows and columns switched

Average 3–Day Package Prices

CERTIFICATION READY   4.2.5

How do you switch rows and columns?

CERTIFICATION READY   4.2.7

How do you edit a chart's data?

8. **SAVE** the presentation.

PAUSE. LEAVE the presentation open to use in the next exercise.

The Switch Row/Column feature can be very helpful in adjusting the way data appears in a chart. In essence, the legend entries and the horizontal axis labels switch places. If you find that your chart does not seem to show the data as you wish, try switching rows and columns for a different perspective on the data.

Adding and Deleting Chart Elements

Elements such as axis labels, a chart title, and data labels make your chart more informative. Use the tools on the Chart Tools Layout tab to turn chart elements on or off or adjust settings for a particular element.

The Chart Tools Layout tab has four groups of buttons that control chart elements you can add or remove. When clicked, most of these buttons display a menu of options you can apply by simply clicking. Some include submenus with additional options or a More Options command at the bottom of the menu that takes you to a dialog box where you can find additional formatting options for the element.

You can remove chart elements by turning them off—most of the layout element buttons include a None option—or by simply clicking the item to select it and then pressing Delete.

In this exercise, you will practice adding and deleting chart elements.

STEP BY STEP   **Add and Delete Chart Elements**

USE the *Pricing Final* presentation that is still open from the previous exercise.

1. Click the chart on slide 2 to select it, and click the **Chart Tools Layout** tab.

2. Click the **Gridlines** button, point to **Primary Vertical Gridlines**, and click **Major Gridlines** (see Figure 6-12). Vertical gridlines are added to the chart.

Figure 6-12

Adding vertical gridlines to the chart

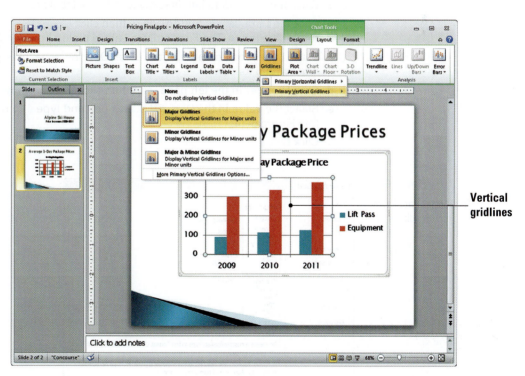

Vertical gridlines

3. Click one of the red bars within the chart to select the Equipment series. All the red bars should be selected.

 **Troubleshooting**   If only one bar is selected, click away from the chart to cancel the selection, and then click a red bar again to retry.

4. Click the **Data Labels** button, and then click **Outside End**. The number for each data point in the selected series appears above the bar, as shown in Figure 6-13.

Figure 6-13

Adding data labels

5. Modify the data labels you just inserted as follows:

   a. Click one of the data labels to select all data labels for the series.

   b. Click the **Data Labels** button again, then click **More Data Label Options** at the bottom of the menu. The Format Data Labels dialog box opens.

   c. In the Label Position area of the Label Options pane, click **Center** to center each label within its bar.

   d. Click **Number** in the left pane, and then click the **Currency** category.

   e. Select the value in the **Decimal places** box and type **0** to reduce decimal places to 0. See Figure 6-14.

   f. Click **Close**.

Figure 6-14

The Format Data Labels dialog box

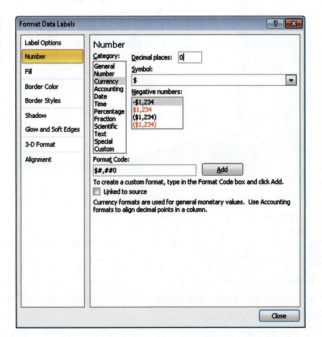

6. Click one of the teal bars, and repeat steps 4 and 5 to add and format currency data labels.

7. Click the **Chart Title** button, and click **None**.

8. Click the **Axis Titles** button, point to Primary Vertical Axis Title, and then click **Rotated Title**. An axis title placeholder appears to the left of the vertical axis.

9. Drag over the placeholder text and type **U.S. Dollars**.

10. Click outside the chart to deselect it. Your chart should look similar to Figure 6-15.

Figure 6-15

Chart elements have been added and removed

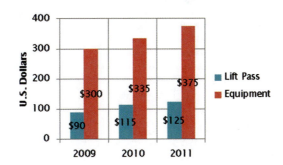

Average 3–Day Package Prices

CERTIFICATION READY **4.3.1**

How do you use chart labels?

CERTIFICATION READY **4.3.3**

How do you use chart gridlines?

11. **SAVE** the presentation.

PAUSE. LEAVE the presentation open to use in the next exercise.

Applying elements such as a chart title or axis titles generally reduces the size of the plot area and the data markers. You can offset this adjustment by resizing the chart or by reducing the font size of axis labels and titles, as you learn later in this lesson.

Adjusting and Formatting Chart Axes

PowerPoint automatically determines the numeric scale to be used for the chart's axes, with the minimum value at zero (usually) and the maximum value slightly higher than the largest value to be plotted. You can adjust the axis scale if you like, however, to create different effects. You can also apply formatting to the axis labels, such as formatting the numbers as currency or changing their font, font size, and font color, or any of the other font-formatting actions you have learned in earlier lessons. In this exercise, you will practice formatting chart axes.

STEP BY STEP   **Adjust a Chart Axis**

USE the *Pricing Final* presentation that is still open from the previous exercise.

1. Click the chart on slide 2 to select it, if necessary.

2. Double-click one of the numbers on the vertical axis (for example, 200). The Format Axis dialog box opens.

3. On the Maximum line, click the **Fixed** button, and change the value to **500** to establish that as the maximum value for the chart's vertical axis, as shown in Figure 6-16.

Figure 6-16

Adjust the maximum value for the vertical axis

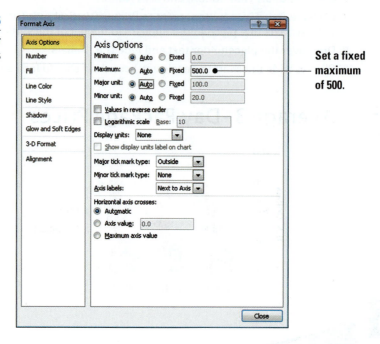

Set a fixed maximum of 500.

4. Click **Number** in the left pane, and then click the **Currency** category.

5. Select the value in the **Decimal** places box and type **0** to reduce decimal places to 0.

6. Click **Close** to close the dialog box and apply your changes.

7. On the Home tab, open the **Font Size drop-down** list and click **14**.

8. Click the **Font Color button's drop-down arrow** to open its palette, and click the **dark blue** square in the Standard Colors section. The chart should resemble Figure 6-17 at this point.

Figure 6-17

The chart's vertical axis has been formatted and its maximum value changed

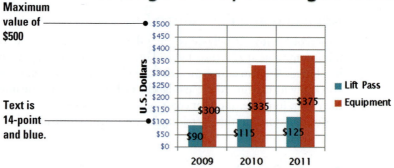

Average 3–Day Package Prices

Maximum value of $500

Text is 14-point and blue.

9. SAVE the presentation and close it.

PAUSE. LEAVE PowerPoint to use in the next exercise.

Adjusting an axis's scale can be useful if you are trying to make the data convey a certain message. If you want to accentuate the differences between values, tighten up the axis scale. For example, if all the data points are between 110 and 120, you might make the minimum value 100 and the maximum value 120. Conversely, if you want to minimize the differences between values, make the axis scale a wider range of values.

By default, a chart's axis and formatting are automatically adjusted as needed when you make changes to the chart. Be aware, however, that if you specify exact values for settings, as you did in the preceding exercise, those settings will remain fixed even if you make changes to the chart.

<table>
<tr><td>CERTIFICATION
R E A D Y</td><td>4.3.2</td></tr>
</table>

How do you use chart axes?

MANUALLY FORMATTING A CHART

The Bottom Line

Once you have final data and have added the elements you want to include in the chart, you can make final adjustments to the size and position of the chart and its elements, and apply final formatting. Use the tools on the Chart Tools Format tab to apply formats to any part of a chart, including the entire chart area, the data series markers, the legend, and the chart's labels and titles.

Positioning Chart Elements

Each chart element has a default position and also several alternate positions you can select instead. You can either use one of the button's menus on the Chart Tools Layout tab to select a precise position, or you can manually drag and drop a chart element into a new position. In this exercise, you practice repositioning chart elements.

STEP BY STEP   **Reposition Chart Elements**

GET READY. To reposition chart elements, perform the following tasks:

@ The *Admissions* file is available on the book companion website or in WileyPLUS.

1. **OPEN** the *Admissions* presentation and save it as *Admissions Final*.
2. Select the chart on slide 2.
3. On the Chart Tools Layout tab, click the **Legend** button, and then click **Show Legend at Bottom**. The legend moves to the bottom of the chart and changes its layout to a single row.
4. Click the **legend** to select it.
5. Point to the border of the legend's frame, so that the mouse becomes a four-headed arrow, and click and drag the legend onto the chart itself, as shown in Figure 6-18.

Figure 6-18

Manually reposition the legend on top of the chart

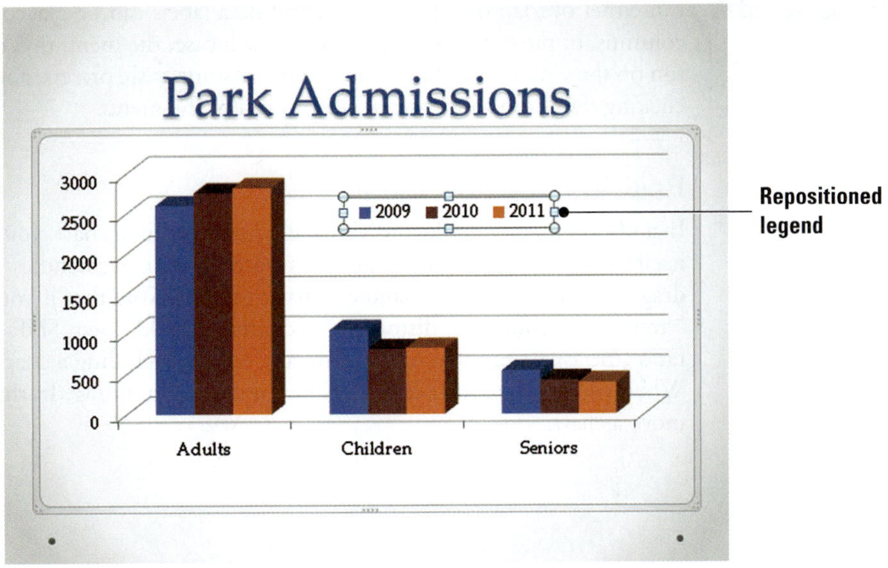

6. Click the **Legend** button again and click **More Legend Options**. The Format Legend dialog box opens.

7. In the Legend Position list, click **Top Right**.

8. Clear the **Show the legend without overlapping the chart** check box. The legend moves to the upper-right corner of the chart, inside the chart frame (see Figure 6-19).

Figure 6-19

Set the legend's position to the upper-right of the chart, within the chart

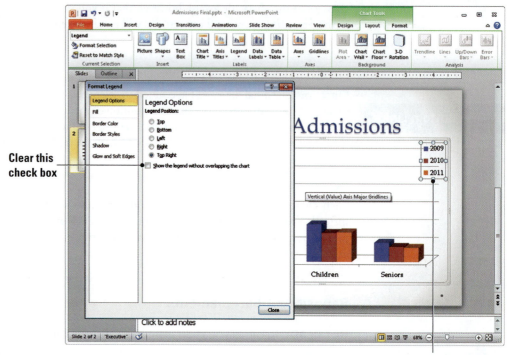

Clear this check box

Repositioned legend

CERTIFICATION READY   4.5.1

How do you arrange chart elements?

9. Click **Close** to close the Format Legend dialog box.

10. **SAVE** the presentation.

PAUSE. LEAVE the presentation open to use in the next exercise.

CERTIFICATION READY   4.5.2

How do you specify a precise position?

Nearly all of the chart elements can be positioned in the same way that you saw in the preceding exercise, but each has its own special options appropriate to it. For example, the chart title can either overlap the chart or not, and data labels can be placed inside or outside of the bars, columns, or pie slices they represent. In each case, the menu that opens when you click the button on the Chart Tools Layout tab contains some basic presets, and you can see more options by clicking the More command at the bottom of the menu.

Resizing and Moving a Chart

In addition to moving the individual elements within a chart, you can move and resize the chart itself. The dotted areas on the chart's border are sizing handles. You can resize any object by dragging a side or corner handle of its container. Note that if you drag a side handle, you may "stretch" the container, distorting its contents. Hold down Shift to maintain the height-width ratio (the aspect ratio). You can move any object, including a chart, by dragging it by its border. When you see the four-headed pointer, just click and drag. In this exercise, you will resize and move a chart.

STEP BY STEP   **Resize and Move a Chart**

USE the *Admissions Final* presentation that is still open from the previous exercise.

1. Select the chart on slide 2 if it is not already selected.

2. Position the pointer on the lower-right corner of the chart's frame, so the mouse pointer becomes a double-headed arrow.

3. Drag inward to decrease the size of the chart by about 1″ in both height and width.

Take Note   Optionally, you can hold down Shift while resizing to maintain the aspect ratio.

4. Position the pointer anywhere on the chart's frame except on one of the sizing handles. The mouse pointer becomes a four-headed arrow.

5. Drag to reposition the chart so that it is centered attractively on the slide, as in Figure 6-20.

Figure 6-20

The chart has been resized and moved

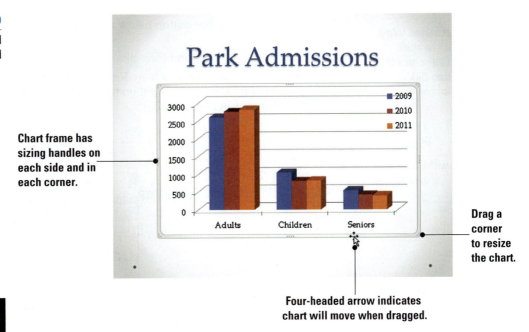

Chart frame has sizing handles on each side and in each corner.

Drag a corner to resize the chart.

Four-headed arrow indicates chart will move when dragged.

CERTIFICATION
READY   4.5.4

How do you resize chart elements?

6. **SAVE** the presentation.

PAUSE. LEAVE the presentation open to use in the next exercise.

Changing the Fill of the Chart Area

To make a chart really "pop" on a slide, you can change its default fill. When you change the **chart area** fill, you format the entire area within the chart's frame. When choosing a fill for the chart area, you have familiar choices: you can select a theme color, picture, gradient, or texture. Take care that colors harmonize with the current theme and that pictures or textures do not overwhelm the other chart elements.

Do not confuse the chart area with the **plot area**. Whereas the chart area includes everything inside the chart's frame, the plot area includes only the area within the chart's frame where the data is plotted. It excludes the extra elements such as the legend, the chart title, and the data table. You can apply different formatting to the plot area than to the chart area. Look back at Figure 6-9, for example; the plot area is gray, and the chart area is black.

You can select a chart element by clicking it, or you can select it from the Chart Elements box on the Chart Tools Layout tab. In this exercise, you will select the chart area and change the chart area's fill.

STEP BY STEP
STEP BY STEP   **Change the Chart Area Fill**

USE the *Admissions Final* presentation that is still open from the previous exercise.

1. Select the chart on slide 2 if it is not already selected.
2. Click the **Chart Tools Format** tab.
3. If Chart Area does not already appear in the Chart Elements box, open the drop-down list in the Current Selection group and select it (see Figure 6-21).

Figure 6-21

Make sure the chart area is selected

Chart Area should appear here.

Format Selection button

Another Way
You can also right-click on a blank area of the chart and then click Format Chart Area on the shortcut menu.

4. Click the **Format Selection** button below the Chart Elements box. The Format Chart Area dialog box opens.
5. Click **Picture or texture fill**, and then click the **Texture** button. The texture gallery opens.
6. Click the **Newsprint** texture, and then drag the Transparency slider to 25%. The chart area has been formatted with a light texture background that makes it stand out from the slide, as shown in Figure 6-22.

Figure 6-22

The chart with background texture applied

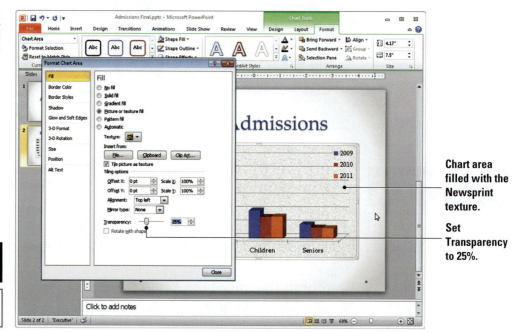

Chart area filled with the Newsprint texture.

Set Transparency to 25%.

CERTIFICATION READY 4.3.4

How do you apply a background to a chart?

CERTIFICATION READY 4.4.1

How do you select chart elements?

7. Click **Close** to close the Chart Area dialog box.
8. **SAVE** the presentation.

PAUSE. LEAVE the presentation open to use in the next exercise.

When formatting parts of a chart, it is sometimes a challenge to make sure you have selected the element you want to change. Use the Chart Elements list in the Current Selection group on either the Chart Tools Layout or Chart Tools Format tab to help you select the element you want. This list clearly identifies all elements of the current chart so that you can easily select the one you want to modify.

CERTIFICATION
READY   4.4.2

How do you format
selections?

You can also select any element on the chart to format by right-clicking it. The shortcut menu displays a Format command at the bottom that corresponds to the element you have clicked. If you right-click one of the columns in the chart, for example, the shortcut menu offers the Format Data Series command.

The dialog box that opens when you select a chart element to format provides options specifically for that element. The Format Axis dialog box, for instance, allows you to change the interval between tick marks on the axis, number style, line color and style, and alignment of axis labels.

Applying a Border to the Chart Area

By default, the chart area does not display a border; this enables the chart to blend in seamlessly with the background of the slide on which you place it. If you prefer, you can apply a border that clearly identifies the chart area. In this exercise, you will add a border to a chart.

STEP BY STEP   **Apply a Border to the Chart Area**

USE the *Admissions Final* presentation that is still open from the previous exercise.

1. Click the outer border of the chart to select the chart area.
2. On the Chart Tools Format tab, click **Format Selection** to open the Format Chart Area dialog box.
3. Click **Border Color**, then click **Solid line**.
4. Click the **Color** button, then click the **Black, Text 1, Lighter 35%** theme color.
5. Click **Border Styles**, then click the **Width up increment arrow** until the width is 3-point.
6. Click **Close** to close the dialog box, then click outside the chart so you can see the chart area border. Your slide should look similar to Figure 6-23.

Figure 6-23

The chart with a border applied

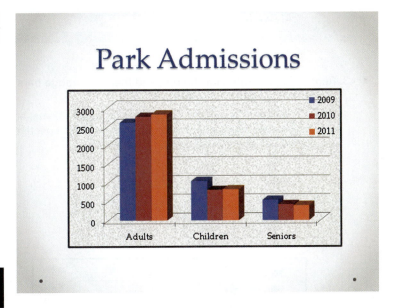

CERTIFICATION
READY   4.5.6

How do you apply a border
to a chart?

7. **SAVE** the presentation.

PAUSE. LEAVE the presentation open to use in the next exercise.

Applying Formatting Effects

You can apply some of the same types of effects to charts that you apply to other objects in PowerPoint. For example, you can add bevels, 3-D effects, and shadows. Some of these effects apply to individual elements in the chart, while others apply to the chart as a whole. In this exercise, you apply formatting effects to a chart.

STEP BY STEP | **Apply Formatting Effects**

USE the *Admissions Final* presentation that is still open from the previous exercise.

1. In the chart on slide 2, click one of the blue bars to select it. All three blue bars become selected.

2. On the Chart Tools Format tab, click the **Shape Effects** button, and on the menu that appears, point to Bevel, and then click the **Circle bevel** (see Figure 6-24).

Figure 6-24

Applying a bevel effect to a data series

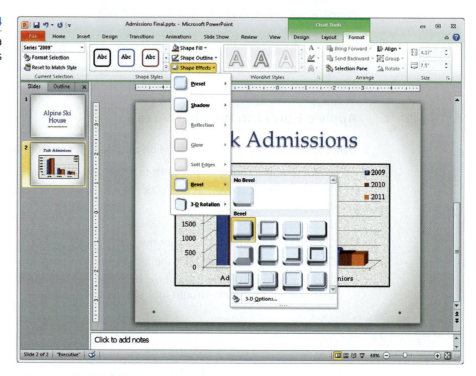

3. Repeat steps 1 and 2 for the red, and then the orange bars, so that all bars are formatted using the same bevel effect.

4. Click the **Shape Effects** button again, point to **3D Effects**, and click the **Perspective Heroic Extreme Right** effect (the last one in the Perspective section). The entire chart receives a 3-D effect, as shown in Figure 6-25.

Figure 6-25

Apply 3-D rotation to the chart

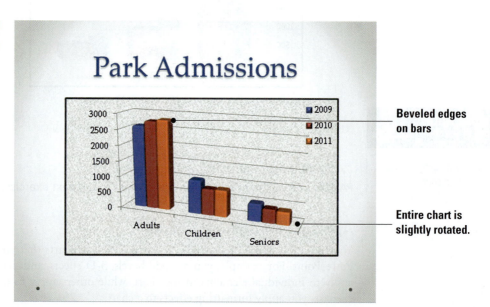

CERTIFICATION READY   4.5.3

How do you apply effects?

5. SAVE the presentation.

PAUSE. LEAVE the presentation open to use in the next exercise.

Formatting a Chart's Data Series

As you learned earlier, a chart's data series is the visual display of the actual data points. Data series can be columns, bars, lines, or pie slices. You can give a chart considerably more visual appeal by customizing data series fill and border options and by applying effects. In this exercise, you will format a data series.

STEP BY STEP   **Format a Chart's Data Series**

USE the *Admissions Final* presentation that is still open from the previous exercise.

1. Click the chart to select it.

2. Click one of the red bars to select the entire data series (all the red bars).

Take Note   If you want to format a single data bar, click on it twice.

3. Click the **Chart Tools Format** tab, and notice that the Chart Elements box in the Current Selection group shows that Series "2010" is selected.

4. Click the **Format Selection** button in the Current Selection group. The Format Data Series dialog box opens.

5. In the **Series Options** pane, drag the Gap Width slider to 300%. The data series are now separated on the slide by a large gap, and the bars are very narrow, as shown in Figure 6-26.

Figure 6-26

Adjusting the gap between bars

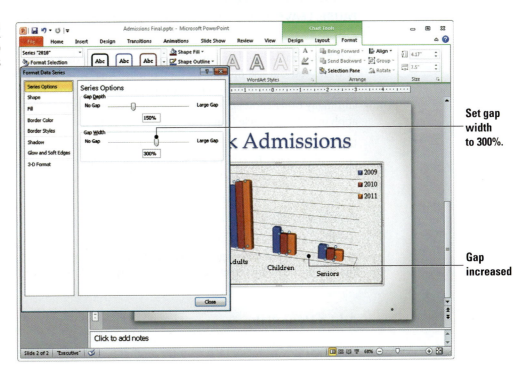

6. With the data series still selected, click **Fill** in the left pane of the dialog box, and click the **Gradient Fill** option button.

7. Open the **Preset Colors drop-down list** and click **Ocean**. See Figure 6-27.

Figure 6-27

Applying a gradient fill to one of the data series

Gradient fill applied

8. Click **Close** to close the dialog box.

9. **SAVE** the presentation.

PAUSE. LEAVE the file open for the next exercise.

You have almost limitless options in formatting the data series for a chart. If you have plenty of time, you can use options in the Format Data Series dialog box and the Shape Fill, Shape Outline, and Shape Effects menus to apply colors, pictures, textures, gradients, shadows, bevels, and many other choices. If your time is limited, you can achieve sophisticated effects by simply applying a Quick Style from the Shape Styles gallery.

In some situations, you may want to apply formats to a specific data marker rather than to the entire data series. To select a single data marker, click it once to select the data series, and then click it again to remove selection handles from the other markers.

Adding a Hyperlink

Just like any other object, a chart (or any part of it) can have a hyperlink attached to it, so clicking on it opens a web page, displays another slide, opens a file, or whatever other action you choose. In the following exercise, you add a hyperlink to a chart.

STEP BY STEP **Add a Hyperlink**

USE the *Admissions Final* presentation that is still open from the previous exercise.

1. Add three new slides at the end of the presentation, all with the Title and Content layout. In the title placeholders, type **2009**, **2010**, and **2011**, respectively.

2. On slide 2, on the chart, click the **2009** entry on the legend to select it. Make sure only the 2009 entry is selected, not the entire legend.

3. Click the **Insert** tab, and click **Hyperlink**. The Insert Hyperlink dialog box opens.

4. Click **Place in This Document**.

5. Click the **2009** slide (see Figure 6-28).

Figure 6-28

Create a hyperlink to the 2009 slide

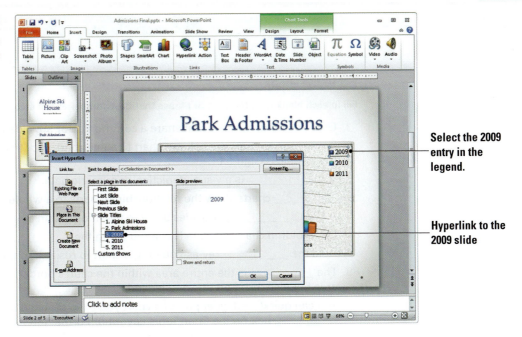

Select the 2009 entry in the legend.

Hyperlink to the 2009 slide

CERTIFICATION
READY 4.5.7

How do you add hyperlinks to a chart?

6. Click **OK**.
7. Repeat steps 2-6 to create hyperlinks for the 2010 and 2011 entries in the legend to their respective slides.
8. Test the hyperlinks in Slide Show view, and then return to **Normal** view
9. **SAVE** the presentation.

PAUSE. EXIT PowerPoint.

SKILL SUMMARY

In This Lesson You Learned How To:	Exam Objective	Objective Number
Build charts.	Select a chart type.	4.2.1
	Enter chart data.	4.2.2
	Change the chart type.	4.2.3
	Change the chart layout.	4.2.4
Format charts with Quick Styles.	Apply Quick Styles.	4.5.5
Modify chart data and elements.	Select data.	4.2.6
	Edit data.	4.2.7
	Switch row and column.	4.2.5
	Use chart labels.	4.3.1
	Use chart axes.	4.3.2
	Use gridlines.	4.3.3
Manually format a chart.	Use backgrounds.	4.3.4
	Select chart elements.	4.4.1
	Format selections.	4.4.2
	Arrange chart elements.	4.5.1
	Specify a precise position.	4.5.2
	Apply effects.	4.5.3
	Resize chart elements.	4.5.4
	Apply a border.	4.5.6
	Add hyperlinks.	4.5.7

Knowledge Assessment

Fill in the Blank

Fill in each blank with the term or phrase that best completes the statement.

1. On a bar chart, the bars that share a common color are a data _____.
2. If you want to change a column chart to a line chart, click the _____ button on the Chart Tools Design tab.
3. A(n) _____ is a visual depiction of numeric data.
4. _____ charts show the relationship of parts to a whole.
5. A chart's _____ provides a key to the information plotted on the chart.
6. On a column chart, the data is charted along the _____ axis.
7. Hold the _____ key as you drag a chart to resize it to maintain its aspect ratio.
8. The _____ is the entire area within the chart's border, including not only the plot area but also the chart title and legend.
9. You can quickly tell what part of a chart you have selected by looking at the _____ box on the Chart Tools Layout or Format tab.
10. The _____ contains the gridlines and elements such as columns or bars.

Multiple Choice

Circle the correct answer.

1. To take full advantage of PowerPoint 2010's charting capabilities, you must also have:
   a. Microsoft Word
   b. Microsoft Excel
   c. Microsoft Equation
   d. Microsoft Chart

2. If you want to select a different range of cells for a chart, use the
   a. Edit Data button on the Chart Tools Design tab
   b. Source Data button on the Chart Tools Design tab
   c. Edit Data button on the Chart Tools Layout tab
   d. Data Source button on the Chart Tools Layout tab

3. The default PowerPoint chart type is a:
   a. column chart
   b. bar chart
   c. line chart
   d. pie chart

4. If you want to show amount of change over time and total value across a trend, use a(n):
   a. column chart
   b. line chart
   c. area chart
   d. pie chart

5. You can move a chart on a slide by:
   a. dragging its border
   b. cutting from one location and pasting elsewhere on the slide
   c. dragging a sizing handle
   d. issuing the Move command

6. _____ enables you to quickly format a chart with different colors, effects, and background.
   a. WordArt
   b. A Quick Style
   c. Chart Themes
   d. SmartArt

7. Select a single data point by:
   a. clicking once on it
   b. clicking once to select the whole series, and then clicking again to select only that data point
   c. right-clicking on it
   d. Shift+clicking on it

8. To change the numbers along the vertical axis on a column chart, adjust the:
   a. legend
   b. data labels
   c. titles
   d. axis scale

9. You can attach a hyperlink to the entire chart, but not to individual elements of the chart.
   a. True
   b. False

10. Text that identifies information about the values on an axis is called a(n):
    a. legend
    b. chart title
    c. plot title
    d. axis label

Competency Assessment

Project 6-1: Voter Turnout

You are a member of the Center City Board of Elections. You have been asked to create a presentation to deliver to the Board showing how turnout has varied in the city over the past four presidential elections. You can create a line chart to display this data clearly.

GET READY. LAUNCH PowerPoint if it is not already running.

@ The *Turnout* file is available on the book companion website or in WileyPLUS.

1. **OPEN** the *Turnout* presentation.

2. Go to slide 2, click the **Insert Chart** icon in the content placeholder, and then click **Line**. Click **OK** to accept the default subtype.

3. Starting in cell A1, type the following data in the Excel worksheet:

Year	Turnout
1996	0.62
2000	0.74
2004	0.49
2008	0.40

4. Adjust the range border to include only the data you typed and then delete all extra data on the sheet.

5. Close the Excel worksheet.

6. Click **Layout 12** in the Chart Layout gallery.

7. Click **Style 36** in the Quick Style gallery.

8. Click the **legend** to select it, then press **Delete**.

9. Select one of the data points, then click **Data Labels** on the Chart Tools Layout tab. Click **Above**.

10. Right-click one of the data labels, then click **Format Data Labels**. Change the number format to **Percentage** with **0** decimal places.

11. **SAVE** the presentation as *Turnout Final* and **CLOSE** the file.

LEAVE PowerPoint open for use in the next project.

Project 6-2: And the Results Are . . .

You are a project manager for Trey Research. You have been asked to create a slide show to present results of a survey you conducted on opinions about violence in the media. You saved your research results as an Excel file that you can use to create a chart in PowerPoint.

1. **OPEN** the *Survey* presentation.

2. Go to slide 2, click the **Insert Chart** icon in the content placeholder, click **3D Clustered Column**, and click **OK** to create the chart.

3. In Excel, open the *Media* workbook. Select the cell range **A3:C6** and click the **Copy** button on the Excel Home tab.

4. In Excel, display the chart worksheet. Click in cell **A1**, and click the **Paste** button on the Home tab.

5. Delete any unnecessary sample data in the worksheet, and make sure the range border surrounds the range A1:C4.

6. Close the Excel worksheet and the *Media* file.

7. On the chart in PowerPoint, right-click the **legend**, click **Format Legend**, and change the legend position to Bottom.

8. Change the fill colors of both series to two different colors of your choice using the Shape Fill palette.

9. Click a vertical axis label to select the axis, click the **Home** tab, click the **Font Size** box, and click **16** to change the font size of all axis labels.

10. Change the horizontal axis labels and the legend labels to 16 points as directed in step 9.

11. **SAVE** the presentation as *Survey Final* and **CLOSE** the file.

LEAVE PowerPoint open for the next project.

The *Survey* file is available on the book companion website or in WileyPLUS.

The *Media* file is available on the book companion website or in WileyPLUS.

Proficiency Assessment

Project 6-3: Visitors Welcome

You work in the Tourist Bureau for the town of Lucerne. As part of your regular duties, you compile a presentation that shows information on visitors. You have created a slide that shows visitors by age. The chart needs some modification and formatting.

The *Tourists* file is available on the book companion website or in WileyPLUS.

1. **OPEN** the *Tourists* presentation.

2. Go to slide 2 and view the chart. The line chart type does not seem appropriate for the data.

3. With the chart selected, click the **Change Chart Type** button and select the **first chart in the Pie category**.

4. Apply **Layout 6** and **Quick Style 10**.

5. Click the outside border of the pie to select the entire pie and apply a bevel effect.

6. Reduce the width of the chart by dragging the right side of its frame about 1 inch to the left, and then center the chart horizontally on the slide by dragging it to the right.

7. Delete the chart title *Percent*.

8. Select the **legend** and apply a light-colored fill. (Change the color of the text if necessary to contrast well with the fill.) Apply a border around the legend.

9. Drag the legend about a quarter of an inch toward the pie, and then apply a bevel effect to the legend.

10. **SAVE** the presentation as *Tourists Final* and **CLOSE** the file.

LEAVE PowerPoint open for use in the next project.

Project 6-4: Free for All

You are a marketing consultant hired by Woodgrove Bank. The bank's managers have asked you to determine which freebies customers would find most attractive when opening a new checking account. One of your assistants has created a chart of the survey results. You need to improve the look of the chart by editing the data and applying formats.

@ The *Freebies* file is available on the book companion website or in WileyPLUS.

1. **OPEN** the *Freebies* presentation.
2. Go to slide 2 and select the chart area.
3. Use the Format Chart Area dialog box to apply a gradient fill of your choice to the chart area.
4. Apply a border color and weight of your choice to the chart area.
5. Change the color of at least one of the data series. (You may change more than one or all colors if desired.)
6. Move the legend to the top of the chart. Then apply a new background fill for the legend and add a border to it.
7. Format the vertical axis to show numbers as percentages rather than decimal values.
8. Set the vertical axis scale to have a maximum value of 1 (100%).
9. Show data labels in percentages.
10. **SAVE** the presentation as *Freebies Final* and **CLOSE** the file.

LEAVE PowerPoint open for use in the next project.

Mastery Assessment

Project 6-5: More Power

You are a financial analyst for City Power & Light. Senior managers have asked you to determine how much power sales increased from 2010 to 2011, based on customer types. You can compare rates of power sales using a bar chart.

1. **OPEN** a new blank presentation and apply a theme of your choice.
2. Change the layout of the first slide to Title and Content, and type the slide title **2010–2011 Sales**.
3. Create a Clustered Bar chart, and type the following chart data:

	Industrial	Commercial	Residential
2010	$3,010	$4,273	$5,777
2011	$2,588	$3,876	$4,578

4. Apply Layout 3 to the chart, and change the chart title to **Sales by Customer Type**.
5. Apply a Quick Style of your choice to the chart.
6. Add a horizontal axis title and type the axis title **In Millions**.
7. Change the size of the horizontal axis labels to 16-point.
8. Insert a border around the legend.
9. **SAVE** the presentation as *Power Sales* and **CLOSE** the file.

LEAVE PowerPoint open for use in the next project.

Project 6-6: Patient Visits

You are a veterinarian hoping to attract investors to your clinic. You have created a chart to be used in a presentation for prospective investors. You want to show investors the reasons for patient visits during a given month, by percentage. You are not satisfied with your chart, however, so you want to improve it before the investor meeting.

@ The *Patients* file is available on the book companion website or in WileyPLUS.

1. **OPEN** the *Patients* presentation.
2. In the chart worksheet, edit the values to become percentages (for example, change 38 to 0.38 and apply the Percent style).
3. Change the chart type from Bar to a 3D Pie Chart.

4. Apply a chart layout to add a legend and data labels. Delete the chart title if your layout added one.

5. Use the 3-D Rotation settings in the Format Chart Area dialog box to set the tilt of the pie to 0.1% so you can see the slices more clearly.

6. Apply a Quick Style, or change the fill of some or all of the pie slices.

7. Select the data labels and increase their size by one point size. Apply bold formatting.

8. With data labels still selected, open the Format Data Labels dialog box and specify a light fill for the labels and a border.

9. Change the fill color of the plot area, and apply a shadow effect to the plot area.

10. Apply the same fill and effect to the legend.

11. **SAVE** the presentation as *Patients Final* and **CLOSE** the file.

EXIT PowerPoint.

INTERNET READY

You have decided you need to improve your fitness level, but you have not yet settled on whether to take up jogging, biking, or rollerblading. Use the Internet to determine relative costs of these three forms of recreation: What kind of apparel do you need? (You may need different apparel at different times of the year.) What kind of equipment (such as running shoes, stopwatch or other monitor, bike, pads, helmet, rollerblades) is required? How much time per week would you need to spend to achieve a good level of fitness? Tabulate your results and create a column chart in PowerPoint that compares apparel costs, equipment costs, and time expenditures for the three fitness ventures.

Workplace *Ready*

CHOOSING THE RIGHT TYPE OF CHART

Each PowerPoint chart type is designed to present a specific type of data. When you create a chart, you should select the chart type that will best display your data. Some of the most commonly used chart types are described below:

- **Column charts:** Column charts are generally used for showing data changes over a period of time or for comparing items. Categories (such as Quarter 1 or 2012) display on the horizontal axis (the X axis), and values display on the vertical axis (the Y axis).

- **Bar charts:** Bar charts are often used to compare individual items. They are especially useful when values are durations. Categories display on the vertical axis and values display on the horizontal axis.

- **Line charts:** Line charts are best used to display values over time or trends in data. Categories are usually evenly spaced items, such as months or years, and display on the horizontal axis.

- **Pie charts:** Pie charts are used to show the relationship of an individual category to the sum of all categories. Data for a pie chart consists of only a single column or row of data in the worksheet.

- **Area charts:** Area charts are used to show the amount of change over time as well as total value across a trend. Like a pie chart, an area chart can show the relationship of an individual category to the sum of all values.

You can learn more about chart types and subtypes and how they are designed to be used by consulting PowerPoint's Help files.

LESSON SKILL MATRIX

Skill	Exam Objective	Objective Number
Adding SmartArt to a Slide	Convert text to SmartArt.	2.5.5
	Convert WordArt to SmartArt.	3.3.4
Modifying SmartArt	Add and remove shapes.	3.4.1
	Change SmartArt styles.	3.4.2
	Change SmartArt layout.	3.4.3
	Reorder shapes.	3.4.4
	Make (SmartArt) shapes larger or smaller.	3.4.7
	Promote bullet levels (in SmartArt).	3.4.8
	Demote bullet levels (in SmartArt).	3.4.9
Converting SmartArt to Other Formats	Convert a SmartArt graphic to text.	3.4.5
	Convert SmartArt to shapes.	3.4.6

KEY TERMS

- assistant
- demote
- organization chart
- promote
- SmartArt diagrams
- SmartArt layout
- subordinates
- text pane
- top-level shape

You are the director of software development for Litware, Inc., which creates computer games that help children learn to read. One of your responsibilities is orienting new software designers who have just joined the company. You can use SmartArt diagrams to explain your company's organization and standard processes to the newcomers. SmartArt diagrams provide an easy way to share complex information in the form of sophisticated graphics that clearly show relationships and processes.

SOFTWARE ORIENTATION

Choosing a SmartArt Graphic

PowerPoint 2010 offers eight different types of SmartArt diagrams, with many layouts for each type. Figure 7-1 shows the dialog box that appears when you choose to insert a SmartArt diagram.

Figure 7-1

Choose a SmartArt Graphic dialog box

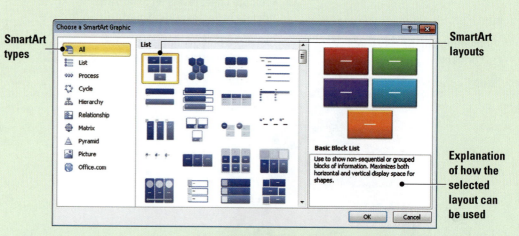

When you click a layout, the right pane of the dialog box shows you a close-up view of the selected layout and provides information on how to use the layout. This description can help you decide whether the layout will be appropriate for your information.

ADDING SMARTART TO A SLIDE

The Bottom Line

Use the Insert SmartArt Graphic icon in any content placeholder to start a new diagram. After you have selected a type and a layout, you can add text to the diagram. PowerPoint also lets you use existing bullet items to create a SmartArt diagram.

Inserting a SmartArt Graphic

SmartArt diagrams (also called SmartArt graphics) are visual representations of information you want to communicate. SmartArt diagrams show items of related information in a graphical way that makes their relationships easy to understand. You can use SmartArt diagrams to present text information in a more visually interesting way than the usual bulleted or numbered formats. An **organization chart** is a type of diagram that shows the relationships among personnel or departments in an organization. Organization charts are included in the Hierarchy type SmartArt layouts. In this exercise, you insert a SmartArt graphic diagram.

Insert an Organization Chart SmartArt Graphic

The *Litware* file is available on the book companion website or in WileyPLUS.

WileyPLUS Extra! features an online tutorial of this task.

Another Way
To insert a SmartArt diagram on a slide that does not have a content placeholder, click the SmartArt button on the Insert tab.

GET READY. Before you begin these steps, make sure that your computer is on. Log on, if necessary.

1. **START** PowerPoint, if the program is not already running.
2. Locate and open the *Litware* presentation and save it as *Litware Final*.
3. Go to slide 3, and click the **Insert SmartArt Graphic** icon in the center of the content placeholder. The Choose a SmartArt Graphic dialog box opens.
4. Click **Hierarchy** in the type list in the left side of the dialog box. The layouts for the Hierarchy type are displayed.
5. Click the first layout in the first row, the Organization Chart. Read the description of the Organization Chart layout in the right pane of the dialog box. See Figure 7-2.

Figure 7-2

The Hierarchy layouts in the Choose a SmartArt Graphic dialog box

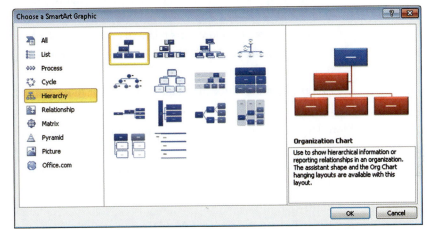

6. Click **OK** to insert the diagram. The diagram appears on the slide, as shown in Figure 7-3.

Figure 7-3

A new, blank organization chart diagram

Text Pane button

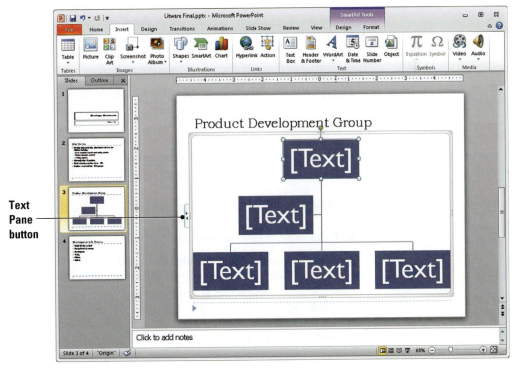

7. **SAVE** the presentation.

PAUSE. LEAVE the presentation open to use in the next exercise.

The Choose a SmartArt Graphic dialog box sorts its many layouts by types such as List, Process, Hierarchy, and so on. A **SmartArt layout** is a particular arrangement of shapes that a diagram can have. The following general descriptions of SmartArt types can help you choose a type and a specific layout within that type:

- **List** layouts display information that does not have to be in a particular order, such as a list of items to purchase.
- **Process** layouts show the steps in a process or timeline, such as the steps in a manufacturing process.
- **Cycle** layouts are useful for showing a repeating process, such as a teaching cycle of preparing for a semester, teaching a class, and submitting grades.
- **Hierarchy** layouts show levels of subordination, such as in an organization chart or a tournament bracket.
- **Relationship** layouts show connections among items, such as the relationship between supply and demand.
- **Matrix** layouts show how parts relate to a whole, similar to a pie chart.
- **Pyramid** layouts display relationships in terms of proportion, from largest at the bottom to smallest at the top.
- **Picture** layouts include placeholders for one or more graphics in addition to the text placeholders.

More layouts can also be found at Office.com. Click the Office.com category to see what's available.

Some layouts appear in more than one type's listing. For example, most of the Picture layouts are also categorized as other types.

Adding Text to a SmartArt Diagram

A new SmartArt diagram appears on the slide with empty shapes to which you add text (and in some cases, pictures) to create the final diagram. The appearance and position of these shapes are guided by the layout you chose, and shape color is controlled by the current theme. As you enter text in the diagram, PowerPoint resizes the shapes to accommodate the longest line of text in the diagram. Font size is also adjusted for the best fit, and PowerPoint keeps the font size the same for all shapes. In this exercise, you learn how to add text to the SmartArt diagram organizational chart you have inserted in your PowerPoint slide.

An organization chart, such as the one you create in this section, has some special terminology and layout requirements. In an organization chart, there can be only one **top-level shape**, which is typically occupied by the name of the person or department at the head of the organization. Persons or departments who report to the top-level entity are **subordinates**. An **assistant** is a person who reports directly to a staff member and usually appears on a separate level.

STEP BY STEP   **Add Text to a SmartArt Diagram**

USE the *Litware Final* presentation that is still open from the previous exercise.

1. If the text pane is not already open, click the **Text Pane arrows** on the left side of the SmartArt object frame (refer to Figure 7-3). This opens the Text pane.
2. Click next to the bullet at the top of the Text pane to place the insertion point there. Type **Ted Hicks** to enter the name in the top-level shape of the diagram. Notice that as you type the text in the Text pane, it appears in the top shape of the diagram, as shown in Figure 7-4, and that the text automatically resizes to fit in the shape.

Figure 7-4

Typing a name in the top-level shape

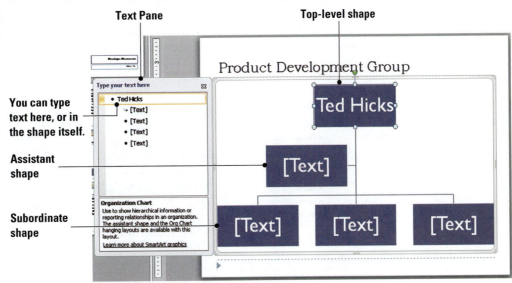

Figure 7-4

Typing a name in the top-level shape

3. Click in the bullet item below Ted Hicks in the Text pane, then type **Rose Lang**. Rose Lang is an assistant to Ted Hicks, and as such, she has an assistant shape on a level between the top-level shape and the subordinate shapes.

4. Click in the next bullet item in the Text pane and type **Marcus Short**. Marcus Short is a subordinate to Ted Hicks.

Troubleshooting Do not press Enter after typing the names because that inserts a new shape. If you accidentally do so, click the Undo button on the Quick Access Toolbar to undo the addition.

5. Click in the next bullet item and type **Ellen Camp**.

6. Click in the last bullet item and type **Pat Cramer**.

7. Click the **Close** button (X) in the Text pane to hide it. You will complete the text entry by typing directly in the diagram's shapes.

8. Click just to the right of the name Hicks in the top-level shape, press **Enter**, and type **Director**. Notice that the text size adjusts in all the shapes to account for the additional entry in the top-level shape.

9. Click after the name Lang in the assistant shape, press **Enter**, and type **Assistant Director**.

10. Use the same process to type the title **Reading Products** for Marcus Short, **Linguistics Products** for Ellen Camp, and **Writing Products** for Pat Cramer.

11. Click away from the SmartArt to deselect it. Your slide should look similar to Figure 7-5.

Figure 7-5

The completed organization chart

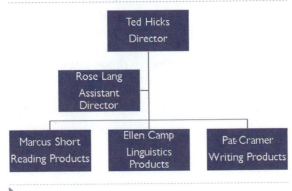

12. **SAVE** the presentation.

PAUSE. LEAVE the presentation open to use in the next exercise.

Text in a diagram appears either within a shape or as a bulleted list, depending on the diagram type and layout option. In the previous exercise, you inserted text only in shapes because an organization chart does not offer the option of bulleted text. Figure 7-6 shows a list type diagram that contains both shape text and bulleted text.

Figure 7-6

Shape text and bulleted text in a diagram

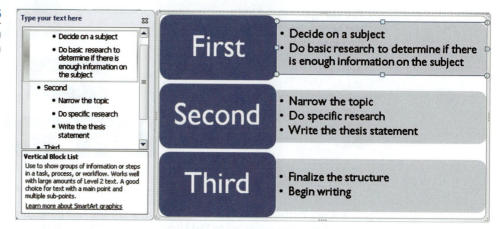

You can display or hide the **Text pane**, which is the panel to the left of a new diagram in which you can type diagram text. In the Text pane, shape text (that is, text that appears in shapes) appears as the top-level bullet items and text that appears on the diagram in bulleted text format is indented below the shape text, similar to the way several levels of bulleted text appear in a content placeholder.

You can use the Text pane to enter text, or you can enter text directly in each shape. Click next to a bullet in the Text pane or click any [Text] placeholder and begin typing text. If you need more bullet items than are supplied in the default layout, press Enter at the end of the current bullet item to add a new one, or click the Add Bullet button in the Create Graphic group on the SmartArt Tools Design tab.

If you don't want to use the Text pane, you can close it to get it out of the way. To redisplay it, click the Text Pane button on the left border of the SmartArt container, or click the Text Pane button in the Create Graphic group on the SmartArt Tools Design tab. You can also right-click anywhere in the diagram and then click Show Text Pane on the shortcut menu.

Take Note   If you need to edit text you have entered in a diagram, you can click the text to activate it and then edit the text as necessary. You can also right-click a shape, click Edit Text on the shortcut menu, and make the necessary changes.

Converting Text or WordArt to a SmartArt Diagram

As you work with slide text, you may realize that the information would work well as a SmartArt diagram. In this situation, you do not have to retype the text in the SmartArt diagram shapes. Simply convert the bulleted list to a diagram. You can create a diagram from any bulleted list on a slide or any WordArt object. You can choose one of the common diagrams in the Convert to SmartArt gallery, or you can access the Choose a SmartArt Diagram dialog box to choose any diagram type or layout. In this exercise, you learn how to convert a list into a SmartArt Cycle diagram, and you convert WordArt text into a single SmartArt object.

Convert Text or WordArt to a SmartArt Diagram

USE the *Litware Final* presentation that is still open from the previous exercise.

1. Go to slide 4 and select the bulleted list.
2. Click the **Home** tab, if necessary, and then click the **Convert to SmartArt** button in the Paragraph group. PowerPoint displays the gallery shown in Figure 7-7.

Figure 7-7

The Convert to SmartArt Gallery

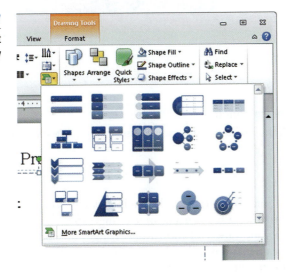

Another Way
Right-click in a bulleted list, and then click Convert to SmartArt on the shortcut menu.

3. Click **More SmartArt Graphics** at the bottom of the gallery. The Choose a SmartArt Graphic dialog box opens.
4. Click **Cycle**, then click the **Block Cycle** layout. Read the description of how best to use the Block Cycle layout.
5. Click **OK**. The bulleted list is converted to a cycle diagram, as shown in Figure 7-8.

Figure 7-8

Bulleted list converted to a SmartArt diagram

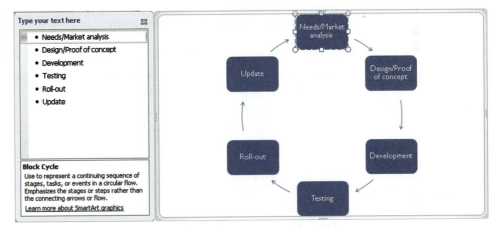

Take Note   The Text pane might appear automatically, as shown in Figure 7-8; if it does not, you can leave it hidden for now, or you can display it by clicking the Show Text Pane arrows on the left side of the SmartArt frame.

Take Note   You may notice that the text in the shapes is quite small. You will learn how to modify shape and text size later in the lesson.

CERTIFICATION
R E A D Y   2.5.5

How do you convert text to SmartArt?

6. Go to slide 1, and triple-click the **Developer Orientation** WordArt object to select it.

7. On the Home tab, click **Convert to SmartArt**, then click **Vertical Bullet List** (the first layout in the first row). The WordArt text is converted to a single-item SmartArt object. See Figure 7-9.

Figure 7-9

WordArt converted to a SmartArt diagram

CERTIFICATION
R E A D Y   3.3.4

How do you convert WordArt to SmartArt?

8. **SAVE** the presentation.

PAUSE. LEAVE the presentation open to use in the next exercise.

MODIFYING SMARTART

The Bottom Line

Although a new SmartArt graphic makes an interesting visual statement on a slide in its default state, you will probably want to make some changes to the graphic to customize it for your use. You can apply a wide variety of formatting changes to modify appearance, and you can also change layout or orientation and add or remove shapes. You can even change the diagram type to another that better fits your data.

Applying a Style to a SmartArt Diagram

Like other graphic objects, SmartArt diagrams can be quickly and easily formatted by applying a SmartArt style. Styles apply fills, borders, and effects to improve the appearance of the diagram's shapes. In this exercise, you will apply a style to a diagram.

STEP BY STEP   **Apply a Style to a SmartArt Diagram**

USE the *Litware Final* presentation that is still open from the previous exercise.

1. Go to slide 3 and click once on the diagram to select it. Take care to select the diagram itself, and not a particular shape within it.

2. Click the **SmartArt Tools Design** tab to activate it.

3. Click the **More** button in the SmartArt Styles group. The SmartArt Style gallery appears, as shown in Figure 7-10.

Figure 7-10

The SmartArt Style gallery

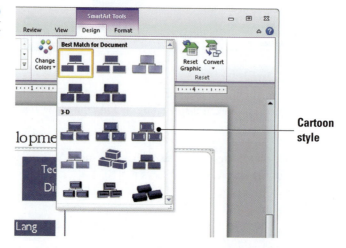

Cartoon style

4. Click the **Cartoon** style. PowerPoint applies the style, as shown in Figure 7-11.

Figure 7-11

A style applied to a diagram

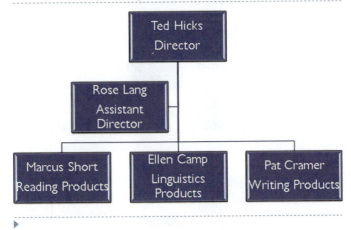

Product Development Group

5. Go to slide 1, click the **SmartArt** object, and repeat steps 2-4 to apply the same style.
6. Go to slide 4, click the **SmartArt** object, and repeat steps 2-4 to apply the same style.
7. **SAVE** the presentation.

PAUSE. LEAVE the presentation open to use in the next exercise.

SmartArt styles can instantly improve a new diagram by applying visual effects to the shapes. Review the results carefully, however, after applying a SmartArt style. If your shapes contain several lines of text, some of the 3-D styles may obscure the text or cause it to run over on the edges—not a very attractive presentation.

If you do not like the formatting you have applied, you can easily revert to the original appearance of the diagram. Click the Reset Graphic button on the SmartArt Tools Design tab to restore the diagram to its default appearance.

CERTIFICATION READY   **3.4.2**

How do you change SmartArt styles?

Selecting a Color Theme for a SmartArt Diagram

By default, diagrams display using variants of a single theme color. Use the Change Colors gallery to apply a different theme color to a diagram. In this exercise, you will apply a different color theme to a SmartArt diagram.

STEP BY STEP   **Apply a Color Theme to a SmartArt Diagram**

USE the *Litware Final* presentation that is still open from the previous exercise.

1. Go to slide 3 and click the diagram to select it. Click the **SmartArt Tools Design** tab.
2. Click the **Change Colors** button in the SmartArt Styles group. The Change Colors gallery opens.
3. Click the fourth style in the Colorful section (**Colorful Range—Accent Colors 4 to 5**). PowerPoint applies theme colors differentiated by level.

Take Note   Differentiating levels or processes by color gives your audience further visual cues that help them understand the diagram.

4. Go to slide 4 and click the diagram to select it.

5. Click the **Change Colors** button in the SmartArt Styles group, opening the Change Colors Gallery, and then click the fourth style in the Colorful section (**Colorful Accent Colors**). PowerPoint uses theme colors to apply different tints to each shape (See Figure 7-12).

Figure 7-12

A different color style applied to the cycle diagram

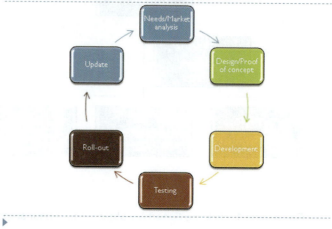

6. **SAVE** the presentation.

PAUSE. LEAVE the presentation open to use in the next exercise.

The Change Colors gallery provides a quick way to apply variations of theme colors to an entire diagram. If the gallery choices don't strike your fancy, you can manually apply theme colors (or any non-theme color) by using tools on the SmartArt Tools Format tab. Click an individual shape or use the Shift or Ctrl keys to select more than one shape, and then choose a shape style from the Shape Styles gallery. You can also use the Shape Fill, Shape Outline, and Shape Effects buttons to choose new colors, outlines, or effects for the selected shapes.

Another Way
You can also format a shape by right-clicking the shape, selecting Format Shape, and using the options in the Format Shape dialog box.

If you do not like the changes you have made to a particular shape, you can reset the shape formats. Right-click the shape, then click Reset Shape on the shortcut menu.

Changing a SmartArt Diagram's Layout

If you decide a particular layout does not present your data as you like, you can easily choose a new layout. A different layout can dramatically change the way the data appears. Different layouts may be more or less suited to your data, so you may want to try several different layouts to find the best match. In this exercise, you will change a SmartArt diagram to a different layout.

STEP BY STEP   **Change the Layout of a SmartArt Diagram**

USE the *Litware Final* presentation that is still open from the previous exercise.

1. Click the diagram on slide 4 to select it, if necessary. Make sure you select the outer frame of the diagram—not an individual shape.

2. Click the **More** button in the Layouts group to display the Layouts gallery.

Take Note   The Layouts gallery displays alternative layouts for the current diagram type.

3. Click **Continuous Cycle** (see Figure 7-13). PowerPoint applies the new cycle layout to the current chart, as shown in Figure 7-14.

Figure 7-13

The Layouts gallery for the Cycle type

Figure 7-14

A new layout has been applied

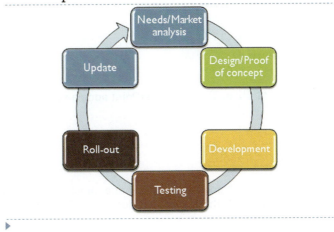

4. SAVE the presentation.

PAUSE. LEAVE the presentation open to use in the next exercise.

When changing a layout, you should generally choose from among the layouts of the current diagram type. In many cases, changing a layout will not result in any additional work for you; PowerPoint simply adjusts the current text into new shapes or configurations, as happened in this exercise.

It is also possible to convert one type of diagram to another type. You will learn more about making this kind of change later in this lesson.

In some cases, however, your information will not convert seamlessly from one layout to another. Some layouts allow only a limited number of shapes, and if your original layout had more than the number allowed in the new layout, information that cannot be displayed in the new layout may disappear.

Take Note

CERTIFICATION READY   3.4.3

How do you change the layout of a diagram?

Adding a New Shape to a Diagram

As you work with diagrams, you may need to add shapes to accommodate your information. Use the Add Shape button to choose what kind of shape to add and where to insert it in the diagram. Adding a new shape to a diagram causes all the existing shapes to resize or reposition in the diagram to make room for the new shape.

Add a Shape to a Diagram

USE the *Litware Final* presentation that is still open from the previous exercise.

1. Go to slide 3 and click the diagram to select it. Make sure you select the diagram's outer frame, and not a specific shape within it.
2. Click the **SmartArt Tools Design** tab.
3. Click the last shape in the last row (**Pat Cramer**) to select it.
4. Click the **Add Shape drop-down arrow** in the Create Graphic group. PowerPoint displays a menu of options for adding a shape relative to the current shape, as shown in Figure 7-15.

Figure 7-15

The Add Shape menu

5. Click **Add Shape Below**. PowerPoint adds a subordinate shape to the Pat Cramer shape.

Take Note   Notice that the new shape, which is on a new level, has a different theme color to differentiate it from the level above.

6. Type **Hannah Wong** in the new shape, press **Enter**, and type **Product Coordinator**. Then click away from the diagram to deselect it. The slide should look similar to Figure 7-16.

Figure 7-16

A new shape has been added to the diagram

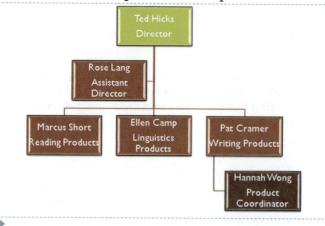

7. Select Hannah Wong's shape. On the SmartArt Tools Design tab, click the **Add Shape drop-down arrow**, then click **Add Shape Below**. PowerPoint adds a subordinate shape.
8. Type **Allan Morgan** into the new shape, press **Enter**, and type **Software Design**.
9. With Allan Morgan's shape still selected, click the **Add Shape drop-down arrow**, then click **Add Shape After**. PowerPoint adds a shape on the same level.

Take Note   In step 9, had you clicked the face of the Add Shape button rather than its arrow, PowerPoint would have added a new shape subordinate to the selected one.

10. Type **Kyle Porter** in the new shape, press **Enter**, and type **Package Design**.
11. Click away from the diagram to deselect it. Your slide should look similar to Figure 7-17.

Figure 7-17

New subordinate shapes have
been added

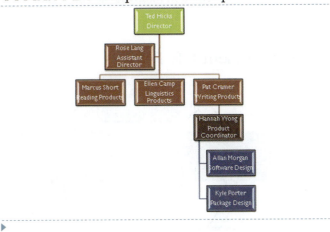

Product Development Group

12. **SAVE** the presentation.
PAUSE. LEAVE the presentation open to use in the next exercise.

The choices available on the Add Shape drop-down menu depend on the type of diagram you are working with. You can choose among some or all of these options:

- **Add Shape After:** Inserts a new shape to the right of the selected shape on the same level. (If the diagram displays shapes vertically, the new shape may appear below the selected shape.)
- **Add Shape Before:** Inserts a new shape to the left of the selected shape on the same level. (If the diagram displays shapes vertically, the new shape may appear above the selected shape.)
- **Add Shape Above:** Inserts a new shape on the level above the selected shape. The new shape is superior to the selected shape.
- **Add Shape Below:** Inserts a new shape in the level below the selected shape. The new shape is subordinate to the selected shape.
- **Add Assistant:** Inserts a new assistant shape subordinate to the selected shape. This option is available only in organization charts.

Take Note   You cannot add a shape above the top-level shape in an organization chart.

Removing a Shape from a Diagram

You can easily delete shapes you don't need. When you remove a shape from a diagram, PowerPoint resizes the other shapes to take advantage of the increased space in the diagram container. Font sizes usually increase accordingly, too. For this reason, you should not do any manual formatting of text and shape size until you have finalized the number of shapes in the diagram. You will learn about manually formatting the text and shapes later in this lesson.

STEP BY STEP **Remove a Shape from a Diagram**

USE the *Litware Final* presentation that is still open from the previous exercise.

1. Go to slide 4, and click the diagram to select it.
2. Click the **Update** shape to select it. Make sure you select the shape, and not the text within it.
3. Press **Delete**. PowerPoint removes the shape and reconfigures the diagram, as shown in Figure 7-18.

Figure 7-18

A shape has been deleted, and the remaining shapes spread out to take up its space

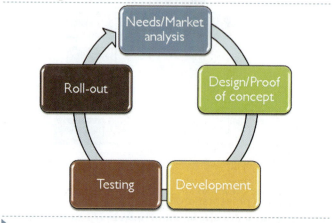

CERTIFICATION READY 3.4.1

How do you add and remove shapes in a diagram?

4. **SAVE** the presentation.

PAUSE. LEAVE the presentation open to use in the next exercise.

Changing a Diagram's Orientation

You can change the look of a diagram by modifying the way shapes are positioned in the diagram. You can use the Right to Left and Layout buttons to adjust diagram orientation. In this exercise, you will reverse a diagram's orientation and change the layout of a section of an organization chart.

STEP BY STEP **Change a Diagram's Orientation**

USE the *Litware Final* presentation that is still open from the previous exercise.

1. Go to slide 3 and click the diagram to select it. Make sure you select the entire diagram.
2. Click the **SmartArt Tools Design** tab, if it is not already displayed.

3. Click the **Right to Left** button in the Create Graphic group. PowerPoint flips the diagram horizontally so that shapes on the right side of the diagram are now on the left side, as shown in Figure 7-19.

Figure 7-19

Use Right to Left to switch the diagram's orientation

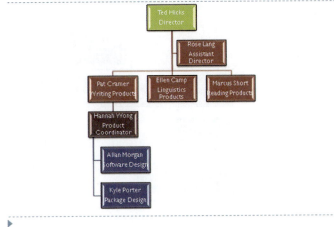

4. Click in the top-level shape (**Ted Hicks**). Make sure you select the shape, and not the text within it.

5. Click the **Layout** button in the Create Graphic group. PowerPoint displays options for positioning the shapes relative to the top-level shape.

6. Click **Left Hanging**. The subordinate shapes are arranged vertically below the top-level shape, rather than horizontally, as shown in Figure 7-20.

Figure 7-20

The subordinate shapes appear vertically

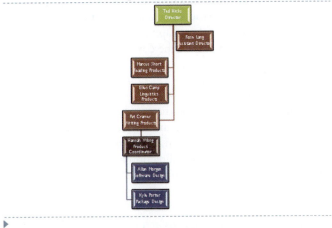

7. Click the **Layout** button, then click **Standard** to restore the original layout.

8. Click the **Hannah Wong** shape, click the **Layout** button, and then click **Both**. The subordinate shapes display horizontally rather than vertically, as shown in Figure 7-21.

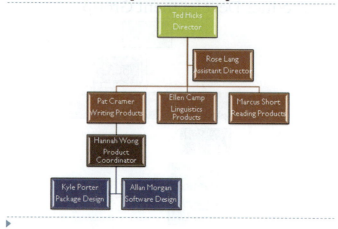

9. **SAVE** the presentation.

PAUSE. LEAVE the presentation open to use in the next exercise.

You can use the Right to Left button with any diagram that distributes shapes and information horizontally across the slide. Right to Left has no impact on diagrams that center information, such as Pyramid diagrams.

The Layout button is available only in organization charts with a shape that is superior to subordinate shapes selected.

You do not have to use the default orientation and positioning of shapes if you would prefer another arrangement. You can click any shape to select it and drag it to a new location. If the shape is connected to other shapes, as in an organization chart, the connector lines shift position or change shape to maintain the connection.

Reordering Shapes

In addition to changing the diagram's entire orientation, you can also reorder the individual shapes by using the Move Up and Move Down buttons. Be aware, however, that the directions "up" and "down" are relative and, depending on the position of the shape in the diagram, may not correspond to the actual direction being moved. In this exercise, you will move a shape to a different location in a diagram.

STEP BY STEP	Move a Shape in a Diagram

USE the *Litware Final* presentation that is still open from the previous exercise.

1. Go to slide 4 and click the diagram to select it.
2. Click the **Testing** shape on the diagram.
3. On the SmartArt Tools Design tab, click **Move Down**. The shape moves one position in a clockwise direction. Note that in this example, Move Down actually moves the shape upward in the diagram.
4. Click **Move Up**. The shape moves one position in a counter-clockwise direction.
5. **SAVE** the presentation.

PAUSE. LEAVE the presentation open to use in the next exercise.

CERTIFICATION READY   **3.4.4**

How do you reorder shapes in a diagram?

Promoting and Demoting Shapes

You can add, remove, or modify shapes by promoting or demoting diagram text. When you **promote** an item, you move it up a level. When you **demote** an item, you make it subordinate to the item above it in the hierarchy. This procedure is similar to changing the indent level of items in a bulleted list. In the following exercise, you learn how to promote a shape.

STEP BY STEP	Promote a Shape

USE the *Litware Final* presentation that is still open from the previous exercise.

1. Click the diagram on slide 3 to select it, if necessary.

2. If the text pane is not already open, click the **Text Pane** button on the SmartArt Tools Design tab.

3. In the Text pane, click the **Hannah Wong** bulleted item. Notice in the Text pane that this item is indented below the Pat Cramer bulleted item.

4. Click the **Promote** button in the Create Graphic group. Hannah Wong's shape jumps up one level, and her two subordinates are also promoted, as shown in Figure 7-22.

CERTIFICATION
READY   **3.4.8**

How do you promote bullet levels in SmartArt?

Figure 7-22

Promoting a shape

Promote button

Hanna Wong has been promoted one level.

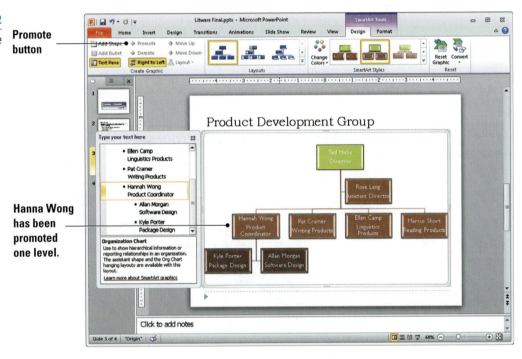

5. Click the **Text Pane** button to hide the text pane again.

6. **SAVE** the presentation.

PAUSE. LEAVE the presentation open to use in the next exercise.

What happens when you promote or demote an item in a diagram depends on whether you are promoting shape text or bulleted text:

- In many diagrams, you cannot promote shape text at all because shapes are already first-level items by default. An exception is hierarchical charts such as organization charts. You can promote any shape except the top-level shape; when you promote a shape, it moves up to the level superior to its original position.

- If you promote a bulleted text item, it becomes a shape containing first-level shape text.

- If you demote shape text, it becomes a bullet item.

- If you demote a bulleted text item, it indents further, just as when you make a bullet item subordinate on a slide.

CERTIFICATION
READY   **3.4.9**

How do you demote bullet levels in SmartArt?

When you promote one bulleted item in a placeholder that contains several bulleted items, the other bulleted items may become subordinate to the new shape text. You may need to move bulleted items back to their original shape in this case. You can use Cut and Paste in the Text pane to move bulleted items from one location to another.

Choosing a Different Type of SmartArt Diagram

Sometimes the hardest part about working with SmartArt is selecting the type and layout that will best display your data. Fortunately, you can easily change the diagram type even after you have created and formatted a diagram. Some diagrams will convert very well to a different type, while others will not fit the shape layout of the new type at all. You may need to retype information to display it properly in a different diagram type. The following exercise shows how to select a different diagram type and layout.

STEP BY STEP **Choose a Different SmartArt Diagram Type and Layout**

USE the *Litware Final* presentation that is still open from the previous exercise.

1. Go to slide 4 and click the diagram to select it.
2. Click the **More** button in the Layouts group, then click **More Layouts** at the bottom of the gallery to open the Choose a SmartArt Graphic dialog box.
3. Click the **Process** type in the left pane, then click the **Upward Arrow** layout in the center pane.
4. Click **OK**. PowerPoint converts the diagram to the process diagram shown in Figure 7-23.

Figure 7-23

The cycle diagram is changed to a process diagram

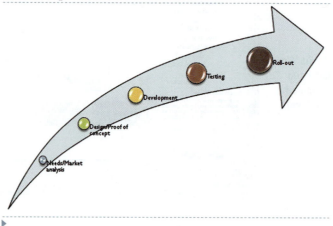

Development Life Process

5. SAVE the presentation.

PAUSE. LEAVE the presentation open to use in the next exercise.

Changing Shape Appearance

Final adjustments to a SmartArt diagram include tweaking the size of shapes and modifying text formatting. PowerPoint formats shapes so that all will fit comfortably in the diagram container. If you have only a few shapes, you might find that this results in a diagram where shapes are much larger than they need to be to hold their text. Conversely, you may want to increase shape size to draw attention to one specific shape. These types of appearance changes can improve the look of a diagram and make it easier to read. In this exercise, you will learn how to change the size of a shape.

STEP BY STEP   **Change Shape Size**

USE the *Litware Final* presentation that is still open from the previous exercise.

1. Close the Text pane if it is open.
2. Select the diagram on slide 4 if it is not already selected, then click the **Needs/Market Analysis** circle (the circle nearest the thin end of the arrow graphic) to select it.
3. Click the **SmartArt Tools Format** tab.
4. Click the **Larger** button in the Shapes group *twice* to increase the size of the smallest circle.
5. Click the **Design/Proof of Concept** circle shape, then click the **Larger** button once to increase the shape's size.
6. Click the **Roll-out** circle shape, then click the **Smaller** button in the Shapes group once to decrease the shape size. Then click away from the diagram to deselect it. Your diagram should look like Figure 7-24.

CERTIFICATION READY   3.4.7

How do you make SmartArt shapes larger or smaller?

Figure 7-24

Several shapes have been resized

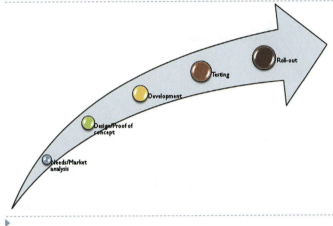

Development Life Process

Roll-out

Testing

Development

Design/Proof of concept

Needs/Market analysis

Troubleshooting   If you select the text box rather than the shape, click outside the text box to deselect it, and then try again by clicking the left edge of the shape with the four-headed pointer.

7. **SAVE** the presentation.

PAUSE. LEAVE the presentation open to use in the next exercise.

Take Note   You can also change shape appearance by selecting a completely new shape: right-click a shape, click Change Shape, and select the desired shape from the Shapes gallery.

Take care when enlarging or reducing shapes. You risk ending up with an inconsistent-looking diagram that is much less attractive than one in which shape sizes are identical or graduated according to an obvious pattern.

Changing Text Formatting

PowerPoint automatically adjusts font sizes to fit in or around shapes. If you do not find the size or color of text in a diagram attractive or easy to read, you can use the Home tab's formatting options to adjust font formats such as size, color, or style. You can also adjust alignment in shapes just as you would in any PowerPoint placeholder.

If you modify text formats with the diagram itself selected, all text within the diagram will display the new format. To apply a new text format to a single shape, select that shape first. Text placeholders in a diagram are selected the same way as other slide placeholders are. In this exercise, you will format the text in a SmartArt diagram.

Change Text Formatting

USE the *Litware Final* presentation that is still open from the previous exercise.

1. On slide 4, select the outer frame of the diagram (not a specific shape within it).
2. On the Home tab, click the **Font Size drop-down arrow**, then click **20**. PowerPoint changes the size of all text in the diagram to 20 point, as shown in Figure 7-25.

Figure 7-25

Enlarging text size for easier reading

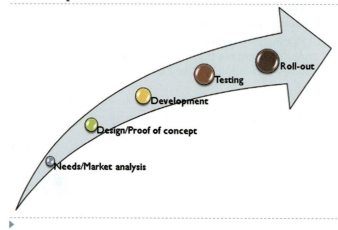

Development Life Process

3. Click the **Needs/Market analysis** text box and drag its border to reduce its width slightly so that the word *Market* moves completely to the second line.
4. Click the **Design/Proof of concept** text box and expand its width so that the word *Proof* displays completely on the first line.
5. Press the right arrow key on the keyboard three times to move the text box slightly to the right so its text does not overlap the circle shape.
6. Widen the *Development* text box so the word fits on a single line, and move the text box to the right slightly, as you did in steps 4 and 5. Your completed diagram should look similar to Figure 7-26.

Figure 7-26

The completed process diagram

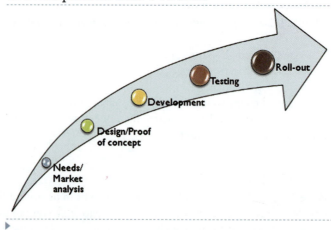

Development Life Process

7. Go to slide 3 and click the diagram to select it.
8. Click the outside edge of the Ted Hicks shape.
9. Click the **Font Color drop-down arrow** on the Home tab, then click **Black, Text 1**. The text in that shape is now easier to read against the light green fill.

10. Click the **Bold** button on the Home tab. All text in the shape is bolded. Your diagram should look like Figure 7-27.

Figure 7-27

The completed organization chart

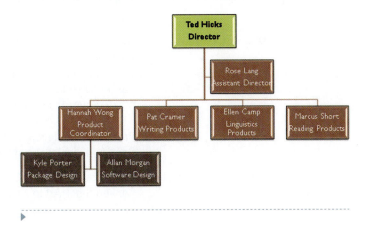

Product Development Group

11. **SAVE** the presentation.

PAUSE. LEAVE the presentation open to use in the next exercise.

CONVERTING SMARTART TO OTHER FORMATS

The Bottom Line

You can change a SmartArt diagram to another content type in PowerPoint without losing your work. If you want to preserve the text you've typed in the diagram, convert it to text. If you want to preserve the look of the SmartArt, but you don't care if it's still editable as a diagram, convert it to shapes.

Converting SmartArt

When you convert SmartArt to text, the text in the SmartArt object changes to a bulleted list. Top-level shape text becomes top-level bullet points, and subordinate shapes become subordinate bullets. When you convert SmartArt to shapes, the diagram changes to a set of drawn shapes and lines, like the ones you might draw yourself using the Shapes button on the Insert tab. In this exercise, you will convert SmartArt diagrams to text and graphics.

STEP BY STEP   **Convert SmartArt**

USE the *Litware Final* presentation that is still open from the previous exercise.

1. Go to slide 4 and select the **SmartArt** object.
2. On the SmartArt Tools Design tab, click the **Convert** button, then click **Convert to Text** from the menu that appears. The SmartArt is converted to a bulleted list.
3. Go to slide 3 and select the **SmartArt** object.
4. On the SmartArt Tools Design tab, click the **Convert** button, then click **Convert to Shapes**. The diagram changes to a set of shapes.
5. Click inside the diagram to confirm that the SmartArt tabs on the Ribbon do not appear.
6. Click one of the diagram's shapes. Notice that the Drawing Tools Format tab becomes available, indicating it is a drawn shape object.
7. **SAVE** the presentation and **CLOSE** it.

EXIT PowerPoint.

CERTIFICATION READY   3.4.5

How do you convert SmartArt to text?

CERTIFICATION READY   3.4.6

How do you convert SmartArt to shapes?

SUMMARY SKILL MATRIX

In This Lesson You Learned How To:	Exam Objective	Objective Number
Add SmartArt to a slide.	Convert text to SmartArt.	2.5.5
	Convert WordArt to SmartArt.	3.3.4
Modify SmartArt.	Add and remove shapes.	3.4.1
	Change SmartArt styles.	3.4.2
	Change SmartArt layout.	3.4.3
	Reorder shapes.	3.4.4
	Make (SmartArt) shapes larger or smaller.	3.4.7
	Promote bullet levels (in SmartArt).	3.4.8
	Demote bullet levels (in SmartArt).	3.4.9
Convert SmartArt to other formats.	Convert a SmartArt graphic to text.	3.4.5
	Convert SmartArt to shapes.	3.4.6

Knowledge Assessment

Matching

Match the term in Column 1 to its description in Column 2.

Column 1	Column 2
1. Promote	**a.** Diagram type that shows relationships among departments or personnel
2. Assistant	**b.** Diagram type that can show steps in a timeline
3. SmartArt	**c.** Holds the name of the person or department at the head of the organization
4. Organization chart	**d.** Person who reports directly to a staff member
5. Process	**e.** Panel in which you can type diagram text
6. Top-level shape	**f.** Change shape text into a bullet item
7. Matrix	**g.** Change a bullet item to shape text
8. Text pane	**h.** Visual representation of information
9. Demote	**i.** Departments that report to the head of the organization
10. Subordinates	**j.** Diagram type that shows how parts relate to a whole

True/False

Circle T if the statement is true or F if the statement is false.

T F   **1.** List type diagrams show information that has to be in a particular order.

T F   **2.** Text in a SmartArt diagram can appear either in a shape or in a bulleted list.

T F   **3.** Use a Cycle type diagram if you want to show a repeating process.

T F   **4.** The Standard Colors gallery allows you to apply variations of theme colors to a diagram.

T F   **5.** You can apply a style to a SmartArt diagram from the SmartArt Tools Layout tab.

T F   **6.** The Add Shape Below option inserts a subordinate shape.

T F   **7.** The Layout button is available for all diagram types.

T F   8. To remove a shape, select it and press the Delete key on the keyboard.

T F   9. You have to retype text if you change from one SmartArt layout to another.

T F   10. SmartArt can be converted to a bulleted list or to shapes.

Competency Assessment

Project 7-1: Corporate Reorganization

You are the director of operations at Fabrikam, Inc., a company that develops fabric treatments for use in the textile industry. Your company is undergoing reorganization, and you need to prepare a presentation that shows how groups will be aligned in the new structure. You can use a SmartArt diagram to show the new organization.

GET READY. LAUNCH PowerPoint if it is not already running.

 The *Reorganization* file is available on the book companion website or in WileyPLUS.

1. **OPEN** the *Reorganization* presentation and save it as *Reorganization Final*.
2. Go to slide 2 and click the **Insert SmartArt Graphic** icon in the content placeholder.
3. Click the **Hierarchy** type, click the **Hierarchy** layout, and then click **OK**.
4. Click in the top-level shape and type **Operations**.
5. Click in the first second-level shape and type **Production**.
6. Click in the second second-level shape and type **R & D**.
7. Click in the first third-level shape and type **Manufacturing**.
8. Delete the other third-level shape under Production.
9. Click in the remaining third-level shape (under R & D) and type **Quality Assurance**.
10. Click the **Manufacturing** shape to select it. Then click the **Add Shape drop-down arrow** and select **Add Shape Below**.
11. Type **Fulfillment** in the new shape.
12. Display the SmartArt Styles gallery and click the **Polished** style (the first style under **3D** Effect).
13. Display the Change Colors gallery and click one of the Colorful gallery choices.
14. Display the Layouts gallery and click the **Horizontal Hierarchy** layout.
15. **SAVE** the presentation and **CLOSE** the file.

LEAVE PowerPoint open for use in the next project.

Project 7-2: Meeting Agenda

You work for the city manager of Center City. She has asked you to create an agenda to display at an upcoming meeting of the city's department heads. She has supplied the bulleted text on an existing slide. You can use this text to make the agenda look more interesting.

 The *Meeting Agenda* file is available on the book companion website or in WileyPLUS.

1. **OPEN** the *Meeting Agenda* presentation.
2. Click in the content placeholder, click the **Convert to SmartArt Graphic** button, and then click **More SmartArt Graphics**.
3. Click the **Vertical Box List** layout, then click **OK**.
4. Click the first shape to select it, click the **Add Shape drop-down arrow**, and then click **Add Shape After**.
5. Type **Budget Cuts** in the new shape.
6. Display the Layout gallery and click the **Vertical Bullet List** layout.
7. Display the Change Colors gallery and click the **Transparent Gradient Range—Accent 5** option.
8. **SAVE** the presentation as *Meeting Agenda Final* and **CLOSE** the file.

LEAVE PowerPoint open for use in the next project.

Proficiency Assessment

Project 7-3: Wine List

You are the general manager of the Coho Winery, and you are about to present some new wines to your staff. You can make the information more visually exciting using a SmartArt diagram.

The *New Wines* file is available on the book companion website or in WileyPLUS.

1. **OPEN** the *New Wines* presentation.
2. Convert the bulleted list to the Vertical Block List diagram.
3. Click the empty shape at the top of the diagram and remove it.
4. Click at the end of the one Premium bulleted item, press **Enter**, and type **Coho Reserve Chardonnay $31.99**.
5. Change the orientation of the diagram so that the shape text is at the right and the bulleted text at the left.
6. Reduce the size of the Whites, Reds, Sparkling, and Premium shapes by selecting each and clicking the **Smaller** button one time.
7. Apply a SmartArt Style of your choice to the diagram.
8. Apply a new color scheme of your choice to the diagram using the Change Colors button on the SmartArt Tools Design tab.
9. Change the text color to black in the shapes at the right side of the diagram.
10. **SAVE** the presentation as *New Wines Final* and **CLOSE** the file.

LEAVE PowerPoint open for use in the next project.

Project 7-4: On Paper

You are the plant manager for Northwind Paper Company. You are scheduled to give a presentation to a class of art students to explain how paper is made. You can use a diagram to make the process more visually interesting.

The *Paper* file is available on the book companion website or in WileyPLUS.

1. **OPEN** the *Paper* presentation.
2. Go to slide 4 and insert a new SmartArt diagram. In the Relationship type, choose the **Funnel** layout.
3. Display the Text pane and replace the placeholder text with the following four items:

    Pulp

    Stock

    Press & Dry

    Paper
4. Apply the Subtle Effect style to the diagram.
5. Change the diagram to the **Staggered Process** layout in the Process type.
6. Change the font size of all shapes in the diagram to 32 pt.
7. **SAVE** the presentation as *Paper Final* and **CLOSE** the file.

LEAVE PowerPoint open for use in the next project.

Mastery Assessment

Project 7-5: Tiger Tales

You are the owner of a karate studio that specializes in teaching youngsters. You are working on a presentation to give at local schools and after-school care centers. You want to add a diagram to your presentation to stress the importance of having the proper attitude when learning karate.

The *Tigers* file is available on the book companion website or in WileyPLUS.

1. **OPEN** the *Tigers* presentation.
2. Go to slide 3 and use the bulleted list to create a new SmartArt diagram using the Titled Matrix layout. Note that only the first bulleted item displays in the diagram.

3. Display the Text pane, if necessary, and click the **Respect** item, which is currently grayed out with a red X over the bullet.

4. Demote this item. It will then display in the upper-left matrix shape. However, you still can't see it because its text is the same color as the background.

5. Change the text color for the demoted text to white.

6. Repeat steps 4 and 5 for each of the other bullet points, so they all become visible.

7. Change the orientation of the diagram to Right-to-Left.

8. Apply a SmartArt style of your choice.

9. Use the Shape Fill menu to apply a fill color to the Core Beliefs shape that is not a theme color but coordinates well with the other shape colors.

10. On the SmartArt Tools Design tab, click Convert, then Convert to Shapes. The diagram is converted to a graphic.

11. **SAVE** the presentation as *Tigers Final* and **CLOSE** the file.

LEAVE PowerPoint open for use in the next project.

Project 7-6: Pie Time

You are the franchising manager for Coho Pie Safe, a chain of bakeries specializing in fresh-baked pies and other bakery treats. You are working on a presentation to help potential franchisees understand the company. Use a diagram to display information about revenue sources.

1. **OPEN** the *Pies* presentation.

2. Go to slide 3 and insert a Basic Pie diagram from the Relationship type.

3. Use the Text pane to insert the following information in the diagram:

> **Birthdays**
>
> **Weddings**
>
> **Reunions**

4. Add two new shapes to the pie with the text Restaurants and Church Socials.

5. Change the diagram type to a Vertical Arrow List layout.

6. Click in the arrow shape to the right of the Birthdays shape and type **All ages**.

7. Add bulleted text as follows for the remaining arrows:

Weddings	**Both formal and informal**
Reunions	**Per item or bulk sales**
Restaurants	**Steady income year round**
Church Socials	**Per item or bulk sales**

8. Adjust shape size and bulleted text size as necessary to make the diagram text smaller so it looks more proportional to the slide title.

9. Apply a SmartArt style and a different color scheme of your choice.

10. Click each of the bulleted list arrow shapes and adjust the vertical text alignment to Middle. (Hint: Use the Align Text button in the Paragraph group on the Home tab.)

11. **SAVE** the presentation as *Pies Final* and **CLOSE** the file.

EXIT PowerPoint.

@ The *Pies* file is available on the book companion website or in WileyPLUS.

INTERNET READY

The U.S. Department of Agriculture has reworked its Food Pyramid a few times over the past decade. Create a presentation to show how food guidelines have evolved from version to version. Use the Internet to find as many previous versions as you can and create pyramid diagrams in your presentation to display the guidelines. Use SmartArt diagrams for each pyramid. Create a final slide that shows the current guidelines. They are displayed as bands that run from the top of the pyramid to the base, but you can convert these bands to typical pyramid slices.

8 Adding Graphics to a Presentation

LESSON SKILL MATRIX

Skill	Exam Objective	Objective Number
Adding a Picture to a Slide		
Formatting Graphical Elements	Resize graphical elements.	3.1.3
	Apply styles to graphical elements.	3.1.5
	Apply color adjustments.	3.2.1
	Apply image corrections.	3.2.2
	Add artistic effects to an image.	3.2.3
	Remove a background.	3.2.4
	Crop a picture.	3.2.5
	Compress selected pictures or all pictures.	3.2.6
	Change a picture.	3.2.7
	Reset a picture.	3.2.8
	Apply effects to graphical elements.	3.1.4
Adding Shapes to Slides	Apply borders to graphical elements.	3.1.6
	Set the formatting of the current shape as the default for future shapes.	3.3.1
	Change the fill color or texture.	3.3.2
Organizing Objects on a Slide	Arrange graphical elements.	3.1.1
	Position graphical elements.	3.1.2
Creating a Photo Album Presentation	Add captions to pictures.	2.1.1
	Insert text.	2.1.2
	Insert images in black and white.	2.1.3
	Reorder pictures in an album.	2.1.4
	Adjust images.	2.1.5

KEY TERMS

- aspect ratio
- clip art
- constrain
- crop
- gridlines
- guides
- keyword
- lassoing
- order
- reset
- rulers
- scaling

You are the director of promotions for the Baldwin Museum of Science. The museum is especially interested in attracting teachers and students to their permanent exhibits, so you have scheduled appearances at a number of high schools in your area, where you plan to present PowerPoint slide shows about the museum and various aspects of science. PowerPoint's graphics capabilities allow you to include and customize pictures, shapes, and movies to enliven your presentations. You can also add sounds to provide the finishing touch to a presentation.

SOFTWARE ORIENTATION

Microsoft PowerPoint's Clip Art Task Pane

The Clip Art task pane, shown in Figure 8-1, allows you to search for graphic and multimedia content you can use to embellish and illustrate your slides. The gallery format of the task pane makes it easy to review content and choose a file to insert.

Figure 8-1

The Clip Art task pane

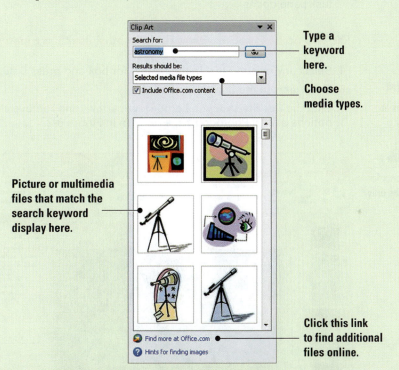

You can use the Clip Art task pane to locate and insert line drawings, photographs, animated graphics, and sound files. If you have a live Internet connection, you have access to thousands of files on the Office Online website.

ADDING A PICTURE TO A SLIDE

The Bottom Line

Pictures can be used to illustrate a slide's content or provide visual interest to help hold the audience's attention. You can insert clip art files that are installed with or accessed through Microsoft Office, or you can insert any picture with a compatible file format.

Inserting a Clip Art Picture

Clip art is predrawn artwork in a wide variety of styles relating to a wide variety of topics. Microsoft Office supplies access to thousands of clip art graphics that you can insert in documents, worksheets, and databases as well as in PowerPoint presentations. Microsoft Office clip art files include not only drawn graphics but photos and other multimedia objects. Use the Clip Art icon in any content placeholder to open the Clip Art task pane and search for clip art pictures. To locate clips, conduct a search through the Clip Art task pane, using a **keyword**—a descriptive word or phrase that relates to the topic you want to illustrate. In this exercise, you learn how to insert a Clip Art picture into a PowerPoint slide.

<table>
<tr><td>**STEP BY STEP**</td><td>**Insert a Clip Art Picture**</td></tr>
</table>

@ The *Exhibits* file for this lesson is available on the book companion website or in WileyPLUS.

GET READY. Before you begin these steps, make sure that your computer is on. Log on, if necessary.

1. **START** PowerPoint, if the program is not already running.
2. Locate and **OPEN** the *Exhibits* presentation and save it as *Exhibits Final*.
3. Go to slide 4 and click the **Clip Art** icon in the empty content placeholder. The Clip Art task pane opens.

Take Note The Clip Art task pane may show the keyword(s) used in the most recent search for clip art.

WileyPLUS Extra! features an online tutorial of this task.

4. Select any existing text in the Search for box and press **Delete** to remove it.
5. Type **gears** in the Search For box.
6. Click the **Results should be drop-down arrow**, and remove check marks from all options *except* Photographs, as shown in Figure 8-2.

Figure 8-2

Choose to search for Photographs only

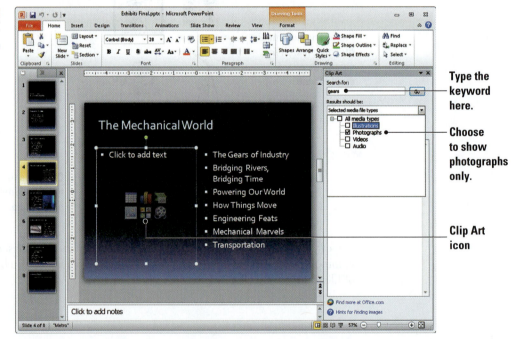

Type the keyword here.

Choose to show photographs only.

Clip Art icon

Another Way
To insert clip art on a slide that does not have a content placeholder, click the Clip Art button on the Insert tab.

7. Click the **Go** button near the top of the task pane. PowerPoint searches for clip art photographs that match the keyword and displays them in the task pane.
8. Click the picture of gears shown in Figure 8-3, or one similar to it. The picture is inserted in the content placeholder. (The picture may not take up the entire placeholder.)

Figure 8-3

Select a photograph of gears

Click Close button to close task pane.

Click the desired clip.

Clip placed on slide

9. Click the **Close** button in the **Clip Art** task pane to close the pane.

10. **SAVE** the presentation.

PAUSE. LEAVE the presentation open to use in the next exercise.

If you have a live Internet connection, PowerPoint will search online graphic files (via Office.com) and display them in the task pane. You can also go directly to the Office Online clip art website by clicking the *Find more at Office.com* link at the bottom of the Clip Art task pane.

Take Note   If you find a clip you like on Office Online, you can download it to your computer by right-clicking it and choosing Make Available Offline. Office will store the clip on your hard disk for future use.

Many clip art graphics are humorous in appearance and may not be suitable for corporate communications or presentations on serious topics. You can use the Clip Art task pane to search for photographs as well as clip art graphics. Photographs provide a more sophisticated and professional look for a presentation. The Clip Art task pane also allows you to search for movies and sound files.

When you insert clip art by using the Clip Art icon in a content placeholder to open the Clip Art task pane, PowerPoint will try to fit the graphic you select into the content placeholder. The graphic may not use up the entire placeholder area, depending on its size and shape. If you insert a graphic on a slide that doesn't have a placeholder, it will generally appear in the center of the slide. You can adjust the graphic's size and position by dragging it, as you will learn later in this lesson.

If you decide you don't like a picture you have inserted, you can easily delete it. Click the picture to select it and then press Delete to remove it from the slide.

Inserting a Picture from a File

You do not have to rely on PowerPoint's clip art files to illustrate your presentation. You can download many pictures for free on the Internet or create your own picture files using a digital camera. In this exercise, you will insert a picture from a file that has already been created.

STEP BY STEP   Insert a Picture from a File

Another Way
Click the Insert
Picture from File icon in any
content placeholder to open
the Insert Picture dialog box.

USE the *Exhibits Final* presentation that is still open from the previous exercise.

1. Go to slide 3 and on the **Insert** tab, click the **Picture** button. The Insert Picture dialog box opens.

2. Navigate to the location of the data files for this lesson, click *Astronomy.jpg*, as shown in Figure 8-4, and then click **Insert**. The dialog box may look different from the one shown in Figure 8-4, depending on your Windows version and the other files in the folder. The picture appears on the slide.

Figure 8-4

Locate a picture file in the Insert Picture dialog box

Select the picture.

You can click here to change the view.

The *Astronomy.jpg* file is available on the book companion website or in WileyPLUS.

3. **SAVE** the presentation.

PAUSE. LEAVE the presentation open to use in the next exercise.

PowerPoint supports a variety of picture file formats, including GIF, JPEG, PNG, TIFF, BMP, and WMF. Be aware that graphic formats differ in how they store graphic information, so some formats create larger files than others.

If you take your own pictures using a digital camera, you do not have to worry about copyright issues, but you should pay attention to copyright permissions for pictures you locate from other sources. It is extremely easy to save any picture from a web page to your system. If you are going to use the picture commercially, you need to contact the copyright holder, if there is one, and ask for specific permission to reuse the picture.

Take Note   U.S. government sites such as NASA, the source of the picture you inserted in the previous exercise, make images available without requiring copyright permission.

FORMATTING GRAPHICAL ELEMENTS

The Bottom Line

PowerPoint provides many options for improving the appearance of pictures. You can reposition and resize them, rotate them, apply special effects such as Quick Styles, adjust brightness and contrast, and even recolor a picture for a special effect. If you do not like formatting changes you have made, you can reset a picture to its original appearance.

Using the Ruler, Gridlines, and Guides

In Normal view and Notes Page view, you can turn on PowerPoint's horizontal and vertical **rulers**, which help you measure the size of an object on the slide, as well as the amount of space between objects. PowerPoint's drawing **guides** line up with measurements on the ruler to provide nonprinting guidelines you can use when positioning objects on a slide. PowerPoint also provides **gridlines**, a set of dotted horizontal and vertical lines that overlay the entire slide. In this exercise, you learn how to use the ruler, guides, and gridlines to position objects so that they align with other objects on a slide and appear consistently throughout a presentation. You can move or copy guides to position them where you need them.

As you move the pointer on a slide, short dotted lines show the pointer position on both the horizontal and vertical rulers. This allows you to be fairly precise when undertaking tasks such as resizing or cropping. You can move guides anywhere on the slide and copy them to create additional guides. To remove a guide, drag it off the slide. Turn on gridlines when you want to arrange a number of objects on the slide or draw shapes to specific sizes.

Take Note   You can adjust the spacing of the dots in the gridlines in the Grid and Guides dialog box.

STEP BY STEP   **Use the Ruler, Gridlines, and Guides**

USE the *Exhibits Final* presentation that is still open from the previous exercise.

1. Go to slide 3. On the View tab, click **Ruler** in the Show/Hide group if this option is not already selected. The vertical and horizontal rulers appear in the Slide pane.

2. Click to mark the **Gridlines** check box. A grid of regularly spaced dots overlays the slide, as shown in Figure 8-5.

Figure 8-5

Rulers and gridlines

Rulers

Gridlines

Another Way
Right-click a slide outside of any placeholder, and then click Ruler.

3. Right-click the current slide near the bottom of the slide (outside any placeholder), and then click **Grid and Guides**. The Grid and Guides dialog box opens, as shown in Figure 8-6.

Figure 8-6

Grid and Guides dialog box

Another Way
Press Alt+F9 to show or hide the guides.

4. In the Guide Settings area of the dialog box, click to mark the **Display drawing guides on screen** check box, then click **OK**. The default vertical and horizontal drawing guides display, intersecting at the center of the slide.

5. The guides will be more useful for positioning pictures in this presentation, so you can turn off the gridlines: click the **View** tab, and click **Gridlines** in the Show/Hide group to remove the check mark and hide the gridlines.

6. Click the **text placeholder** on slide 3 to activate it. You will use the placeholder's selection border to help you position guides.

7. Click the **vertical guide** above the slide title. You should see a ScreenTip that shows the current position of the guide—0.0, indicating the guide is at the 0 inch mark on the horizontal ruler.

8. Click and drag the guide to the left until it aligns on the left border of the text placeholder. The ScreenTip should read 4.50 with a left-pointing arrow. Release the mouse button to drop the guide at that location.

9. Click the **horizontal guide** to the right of the planet picture and drag upward until the ScreenTip reads 1.67 with an upward-pointing arrow. Drop the guide. It should align with the capital letters in the text placeholder.

10. Click the **vertical guide** you positioned near the left edge of the slide, hold down **Ctrl**, and drag a copy of the guide to the right until the ScreenTip reads 4.50 with a right-pointing arrow. Drop the guide by first releasing the mouse button and then releasing the Ctrl key. Your slide should look like Figure 8-7.

Figure 8-7

Drawing guides positioned on the slide

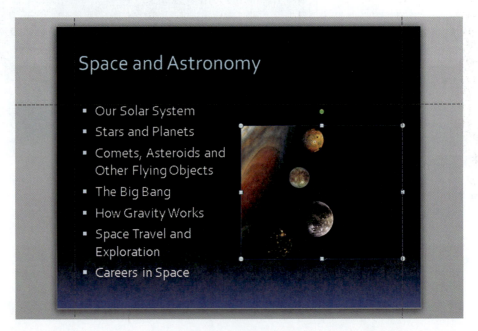

11. Go to slide 4, click the gear picture, and drag it until the upper-left corner of the picture snaps to the intersection of the vertical and horizontal guides. Your slide should look like Figure 8-8.

Figure 8-8

Picture repositioned using the guides

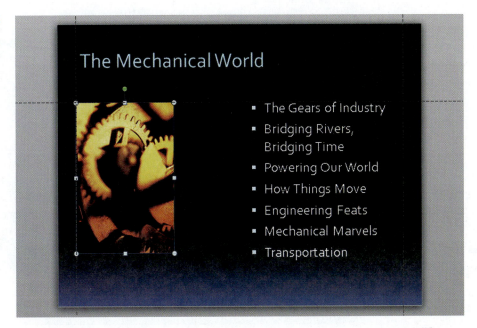

12. Go to slide 5 and drag the picture down and to the left so its upper-right corner snaps to the intersection of the guides.

13. Go to slide 6 and drag the picture up and to the left to snap to the intersection of the two guides.

14. On the View tab, clear the **Guides** check box to turn off the guides.

15. **SAVE** the presentation.

PAUSE. LEAVE the presentation open to use in the next exercise.

By default, objects "snap"—automatically align—to the gridlines even if the gridlines are not currently displayed. This feature can be helpful when you are positioning objects, but you may sometimes find that it hinders precise positioning. You can temporarily override the "snapping" by holding down Alt as you drag an object. Or, you can display the Grid and Guides dialog box and deselect the *Snap objects to grid* check box.

Rotating or Flipping an Object

You can rotate or flip pictures to change their orientation on a slide. Rotating spins the picture around its center; flipping creates a mirror image of it. Rotating and flipping can provide additional visual interest for a graphic or fit it more attractively on a slide.

STEP BY STEP **Rotate an Object**

USE the *Exhibits Final* presentation that is still open from the previous exercise.

1. Go to slide 3, and click the picture to select it.

2. Click the **Picture Tools Format** tab, click **Rotate** in the Arrange group, and then click **Flip Horizontal** in the drop-down menu that appears. The picture reverses its orientation so the planet is on the right and its moons are on the left, as shown in Figure 8-9.

Figure 8-9

The picture has been flipped
horizontally

Another Way
Click the Arrange
button on the Home tab, click
Rotate, and choose a rotation
option.

3. Drag the picture up into the upper-right corner of the slide, so that the top and right
   edges of the picture align with the top and right edges of the slide, as in Figure 8-10.

Figure 8-10

Drag the picture to the upper-
right corner of the slide

4. Go to slide 5 and click the picture to select it.

5. Click the **Picture Tools Format** tab, click **Rotate**, and then click **Rotate Right 90°**. Then
   repeat that command to rotate the picture another 90 degrees.

6. **SAVE** the presentation.

PAUSE. LEAVE the presentation open to use in the next exercise.

PowerPoint offers some set rotation options, such as rotating right or left 90 degrees. For more control over the rotation, you can drag the green rotation handle above the selected object, or click More Rotation Options on the Rotate button's menu to open the Size and Position dialog box, where you can type a specific rotation amount.

Cropping Objects

You have several options for adjusting the size of a picture or other graphic object. You can crop an object to remove part of the object, drag a side or corner, specify exact measurements for an object, or scale it to a percentage of its original size. When you **crop** a picture, you remove a portion of the graphic that you think is unnecessary in order to focus attention on the most important part of a picture. The portion of the picture you cropped is not deleted. You can restore the cropped material by using the crop pointer to drag outward to reveal the material that was previously hidden.

STEP BY STEP   Crop a Picture

USE the *Exhibits Final* presentation that is still open from the previous exercise.

1. Go to slide 4 and click the picture to select it.
2. Click the **Picture Tools Format** tab.
3. Click the **Crop** button in the **Size** group. (Click the upper part of the button, not the arrow below it.) The pointer changes to a crop pointer and crop handles appear around the edges of the picture.
4. Click to position the pointer on the top center crop handle and drag downward until the short dotted line on the vertical ruler is on the 1.5-inch mark, as shown in Figure 8-11.

Figure 8-11

Drag the crop handle down to remove a portion of the picture

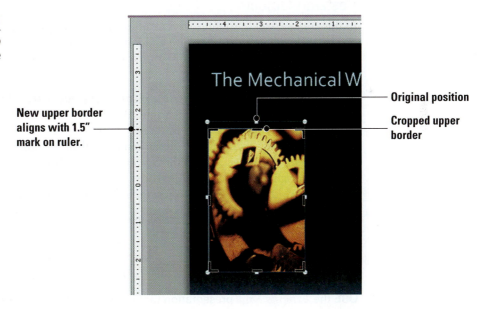

5. Release the mouse button, and then click the **Crop** button again to complete the crop.
6. On the View tab, mark the **Guides** check box to turn the guides back on.

7. Click and drag the cropped picture back up to the intersection of the two guides. Your slide should look similar to Figure 8-12.

Drag the picture up to realign with guides.

8. On the View tab, clear the Guides check box to turn the guides off.
9. **SAVE** the presentation.

PAUSE. LEAVE the presentation open to use in the next exercise.

Resizing Objects

In this exercise, you learn three ways to adjust the size of a picture: by simply dragging a corner, by setting measurements in the Size and Position dialog box, and by setting a measurement in the Size group on the Picture Tools Format tab. You can use these options to resize any object on a slide.

Generally, you will want to maintain a picture's **aspect ratio** when you resize it. The aspect ratio is the relationship of width to height. By default, a change to the width of a picture is also applied to the height to maintain aspect ratio. In some instances, you may want to distort a picture on purpose by changing one dimension more than the other. To do so, you must deselect the *Lock aspect ratio* check box in the Size and Position dialog box. You are then free to change width and height independently. Alternatively, you can drag a side selection handle on the object (not a corner); this allows you to adjust each dimension separately.

In the following exercise, you will resize an object and change its aspect ratio.

STEP BY STEP   Size or Scale an Object

USE the *Exhibits Final* presentation that is still open from the previous exercise.

1. Go to slide 3 and click the picture to select it.
2. Click and drag the lower-left corner of the picture diagonally until the short dotted line on the horizontal ruler is at 0 inches, as shown in Figure 8-13. (Don't worry that the slide title is partially covered; you'll fix this problem in a later exercise.)

Figure 8-13

Resize a picture by dragging a corner

Align left edge of picture with 0 on ruler.

3. Go to slide 4 and click the picture to select it.

4. Right-click the picture, then click **Size and Position** from the shortcut menu. The Format Picture dialog box opens.

5. Click the **Lock aspect ratio** check box to deselect this option. You can now specify the height and width independently.

6. In the Size and Rotate area of the dialog box, click the **Height up arrow** until the height is 4.1 inches. Click the **Width up arrow** until the width is 4.2 inches. See Figure 8-14.

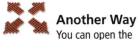

Another Way
You can open the Format Picture dialog box by clicking the dialog box launcher in the Size group on the Picture Tools Format tab.

Figure 8-14

Format Picture dialog box

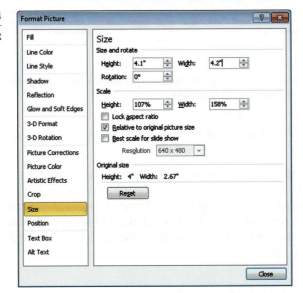

Another Way
You can also specify a percentage of the original dimensions, instead of an exact size. This is called **scaling**.

7. Click **Close** to close the dialog box. Your slide should look similar to Figure 8-15.

Figure 8-15

The picture has been resized

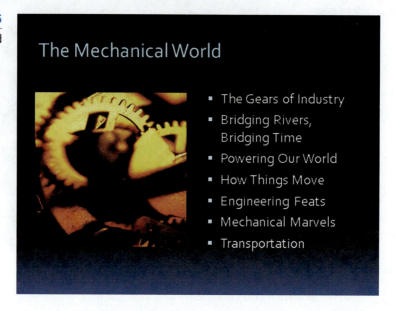

8. Go to slide 5 and click the picture to select it.

9. Click the **Picture Tools Format** tab, then click the **Width down arrow** in the Size group until the picture's width is 4.2 inches. See Figure 8-16.

Figure 8-16

The Width and Height settings on the Ribbon

10. Drag the picture to align its upper-right corner with the intersection of the two guides near the right edge of the slide.

11. **SAVE** the presentation.

PAUSE. LEAVE the presentation open to use in the next exercise.

<table>
<tr><td>**CERTIFICATION**
READY   **3.1.3**</td></tr>
<tr><td>How do you resize graphical elements?</td></tr>
</table>

<table>
<tr><td>**CERTIFICATION**
READY   **3.2.8**</td></tr>
<tr><td>How do you reset a picture?</td></tr>
</table>

You can **reset** a picture to its original appearance to remove any sizing or format changes you have made to it. To do this, open the Format Picture dialog box and click the Reset button on the page containing the setting to reset. For example, to reset the size, click Size at the left side of the dialog box and then click Reset. Refer to Figure 8-14. You can also restore a picture's original appearance by clicking the Reset Picture button in the Adjust group on the Picture Tools Format tab.

Applying a Style to a Picture

PowerPoint provides a number of styles you can use to apply borders and other effects to pictures. You can easily apply styles with heavy borders, shadow and reflection effects, and different shapes such as ovals and rounded corners. Use styles to dress up your pictures or format them consistently throughout a presentation.

Apply a Style to a Picture

USE the *Exhibits Final* presentation that is still open from the previous exercise.

1. Go to slide 5 and click the picture to select it if necessary.
2. On the Picture Tools Format tab, click the **More** button in the Picture Styles group. The Picture Styles gallery appears, as shown in Figure 8-17.

Figure 8-17

The Picture Styles gallery

3. Click the **Soft Edge Oval** style. Your picture should look like the one in Figure 8-18.

Figure 8-18

The style gives the picture a different look

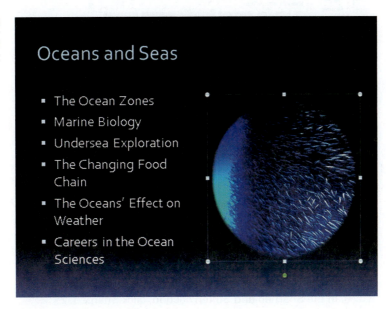

4. **SAVE** the presentation.

PAUSE. LEAVE the presentation open to use in the next exercise.

Take Note   The style's picture borders are black or white by default, but you can apply any color to the border using the Picture Border button.

CERTIFICATION READY 3.1.5

If you have a number of pictures in a presentation, be careful not to apply too many different styles to the pictures. Using just one or two styles throughout a presentation makes it seem more unified and consistent.

How do you apply styles to graphical elements?

Correcting Brightness and Sharpness

You may need to modify a picture's appearance to make it show up well on a slide. This can be particularly important with pictures you insert from files, which may not have been photographed using the optimal settings. In PowerPoint 2010, Brightness, Contrast, and Sharpness/Softness are all controlled from the same menu and the same tab of the Format Picture dialog box. For presets, you can select from the Corrections button's menu. For precise amounts, you can use the dialog box.

STEP BY STEP   **Adjust a Picture's Brightness and Sharpness**

USE the *Exhibits Final* presentation that is still open from the previous exercise.

1. Go to slide 6 and click the picture to select it. This picture is a bit dark.
2. Click the **Picture Tools Format** tab.
3. In the Adjust group, click **Corrections**. A palette of corrections appears, as in Figure 8-19. Notice that there are two sections: Sharpen and Soften and Brightness and Contrast. The center selection in each section is the current setting.

Figure 8-19

Select from the Corrections button's palette

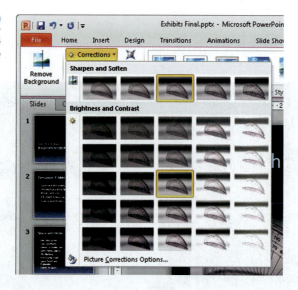

4. In the Brightness and Contrast section, click the **Brightness +20% Contrast; 0% (Normal)** setting.
5. Click the **Corrections** button again, reopening the menu.
6. In the Sharpen and Soften section, click **Sharpen: 25%**.
7. Click the **Corrections** button again, and click **Picture Corrections Options**. The Format Picture dialog box opens.
8. Drag the Soften/Sharpen slider to 30% and drag the Contrast slider to 10%, as shown in Figure 8-20.

Another Way
You can use the increment arrow buttons to set the values instead of dragging if you find that easier.

CERTIFICATION READY   3.2.2

How do you sharpen an image?

Figure 8-20

Correct a picture from the
Format Picture dialog box

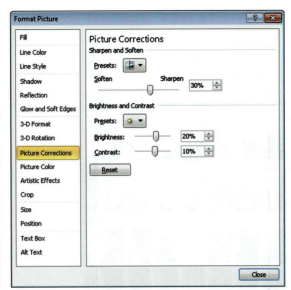

Figure 8-20

Correct a picture from the
Format Picture dialog box

**CERTIFICATION
READY   3.2.2**

How do you soften an image?

**CERTIFICATION
READY   3.2.2**

How do you increase or
decrease the brightness of an
image?

**CERTIFICATION
READY   3.2.2**

How do you increase or
decrease the contrast of an
image?

9. Click **Close** to close the dialog box.

10. **SAVE** the presentation.

PAUSE. LEAVE the presentation open to use in the next exercise.

Applying Color Adjustments

Color adjustments enable you to correct minor exposure or color problems in an image without having to open it in a third-party photo editing program. You can improve the look of a picture by making subtle adjustments, or apply dramatic adjustments that distort the image for a special effect.

Each of the three sections on the Color button's palette controls a different aspect of the color. Color *Saturation* determines the intensity of the color, ranging from 0% (grayscale, no color) to 400% (extremely vivid color). Color *Tone* refers to the subtle tint of the image's color, ranging from warmer shades (more red) to cooler shades (more blue). *Recolor* enables you to select color wash to place over the image or to set it to grayscale, black and white, or washout. In this exercise, you will make some color corrections on a photo.

STEP BY STEP   **Apply Color Adjustments**

USE the *Exhibits Final* presentation that is still open from the previous exercise.

1. Go to slide 5 and click the picture to select it.

2. Click the **Picture Tools Format** tab.

3. In the Adjust group, click **Color**. A palette of color choices appears, as in Figure 8-21.

4. In the Color Saturation section, click **Saturation 66%**.

5. Click **Color** again to reopen the palette, point at **More Variations**, and in the Standard Colors group, click **Light Green**.

6. Click **Color** again to reopen the palette, and click **More Color Options**. The Format Picture dialog box opens.

7. In the Color Tone section, set the **Temperature** slider to **10,000**. See Figure 8-22.

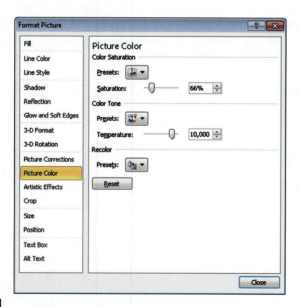

8. Click **Close** to close the dialog box.

9. **SAVE** the presentation.

PAUSE. LEAVE the presentation open to use in the next exercise.

Adding Effects to a Picture

There are two types of effects that you can apply to a picture: picture effects (such as Glow, Shadow, and Bevel), which affect the outer edges of the picture, and artistic effects (such as Chalk Sketch or Line Drawing), which affect the picture itself.

Adding Picture Effects

Picture effects apply to the edges of a picture, and not to the picture itself. For example, you can apply a beveled frame to a picture, or make its edges fuzzy. In the following exercise, you will apply a bevel and a glow effect.

STEP BY STEP   **Add Picture Effects to a Picture**

USE the *Exhibits Final* presentation that is still open from the previous exercise.

1. Go to slide 4 and click the picture to select it.
2. Click the **Picture Tools Format** tab.
3. Click the **Picture Effects** button, point to **Presets** in the drop-down menu that appears, and click **Preset 5**. A preset formatting effect is applied.
4. Click the **Picture Effects** button, point to **Bevel**, and click **Relaxed Inset**. A different bevel is applied.
5. Click the **Picture Effects** button, point to **Glow**, and click **Periwinkle, 8 point glow, Accent color 5**. An 8-point periwinkle blue glow is placed around the picture.
6. Click away from the picture to deselect it so you can see it more clearly. The slide should look like Figure 8-23.

Figure 8-23

The slide after picture effects have been applied to the picture

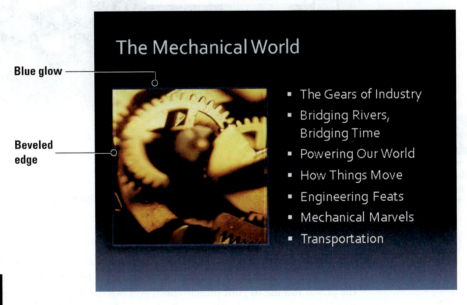

7. **SAVE** the presentation.

PAUSE. LEAVE the presentation open to use in the next exercise.

CERTIFICATION READY   3.1.4

How do you apply effects to graphical elements?

Adding Artistic Effects

Artistic effects are new in PowerPoint 2010. They enable you to transform the picture itself, not just the outer edges. Some of the effects, such as the Pencil Sketch effect you apply in this exercise, can even make the picture look less like a photograph and more like a hand-drawn work of art.

STEP BY STEP   **Add Artistic Effects to a Picture**

USE the *Exhibits Final* presentation that is still open from the previous exercise.

1. Go to slide 7 and click the picture to select it.
2. Click the **Picture Tools Format** tab.
3. Click **Artistic Effects** in the Picture Styles group to open the Artistic Effects gallery, and point to several different settings in the gallery. Observe their effect on the image behind the open palette.
4. Click **Paint Strokes**. Your slide should look similar to Figure 8-24.

Figure 8-24

Apply artistic effects to an image

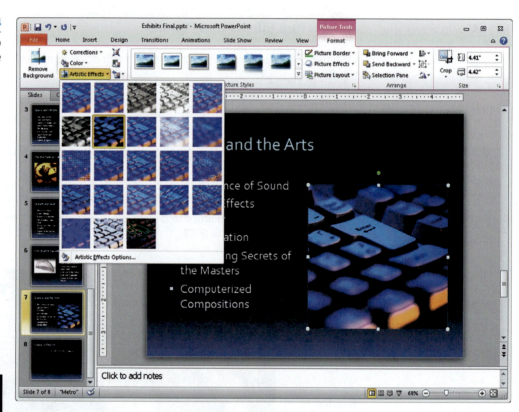

5. **SAVE** the presentation.

PAUSE. LEAVE the presentation open to use in the next exercise.

Removing an Image's Background

Some graphic file formats allow a photo to have a transparent background, but most photos don't use transparency. If you want to make areas of a certain color transparent in the copy of the photo you use in your presentation, you can do so with the Remove Background command. You learn how to use the Remove Background command in this exercise.

STEP BY STEP   **Remove an Image Background**

USE the *Exhibits Final* presentation that is still open from the previous exercise.

1. Go to slide 3 and click the picture to select it.
2. On the Picture Tools Format tab, click **Remove Background**. The Background Removal tab appears on the Ribbon, and the picture turns purple except for one planet, as shown in Figure 8-25. The purple areas are the parts that will be removed.

Figure 8-25

Tools for removing a photo's background

3. Zoom in to **100%** zoom using the Zoom slider in the bottom right corner of the PowerPoint window, and adjust the display so you can see the photo clearly.

4. Notice that inside the picture is a rectangular border with selection handles. Only content within this rectangle will be kept. Drag the corner selection handles of that rectangle so that the entire picture is inside that area.

5. On the Background Removal tab, click **Mark Areas to Keep**.

6. Click one of the planets. If the entire planet does not turn back to its original color with a single click, continue clicking different parts of it until the entire planet appears in its original colors (See Figure 8-26). Zoom in further if needed to see what you are doing.

Figure 8-26

Adjust the areas to keep

Each planet is in full color.

Selection area encompasses entire image.

 **Troubleshooting** If you make a mistake and click too much, and the whole background turns black, press Ctrl+Z to undo your last action and try again.

7. Repeat step 6 until only the background is purple, and all planets appear in their original colors. You may need to click and drag the pencil mouse pointer to remove the purple from some areas of the planets.

8. Click **Keep Changes** in the Close group of the Background Removal tab to finalize the background removal. Now that the background is removed, the slide title is no longer partly obscured. See Figure 8-27.

Figure 8-27

The completed slide with background removed from the photo

9. **SAVE** the presentation.

PAUSE. LEAVE the presentation open to use in the next exercise.

The amount of effort required to remove a photo's background accurately depends on the individual photo and on the amount of contrast between the background and the foreground image. You may need to click several times on different parts of the image to mark them to keep. Other photos may be almost perfectly done with the default setting.

It's easy to make a mistake when marking areas for background removal. The Undo command (Ctrl+Z) easily reverses your last action and can be used when a particular marked area doesn't turn out as you expect. You can also use the Mark Areas to Remove command on the Background Removal tab to mark areas that have erroneously been marked for keeping.

Changing a Picture

After you have made multiple changes to a picture's settings in PowerPoint, such as applying borders, specifying an exact size, and so on, you might not want to lose those settings if you decide to use a different picture instead. By using the Change Picture command, you can swap out the image while retaining the settings.

STEP BY STEP   **Change a Picture**

USE the *Exhibits Final* presentation that is still open from the previous exercise.

The *Gears.jpg* file is available on the book companion website or in WileyPLUS.

1. Go to slide 4.
2. Right-click the picture and click **Change Picture**. The Insert Picture dialog box opens.
3. Navigate to the folder containing the data files for this lesson and click *Gears.jpg*.
4. Click **Insert**. The picture is replaced, but the previously applied formatting (such as the glow effect) remains.
5. If the picture is not aligned attractively, drag it to move it as needed.
6. **SAVE** the presentation.

PAUSE. LEAVE the presentation open to use in the next exercise.

Compressing the Images in a Presentation

When adding pictures to a presentation, you may need to consider the ultimate size of the presentation. Pictures will add considerably to the presentation's file size. This can make a large presentation difficult to store or work with. Compressing images reduces the file size of a presentation by reducing its resolution (dots per inch). This can make the presentation easier to store and to email to others, and it speeds up display if you have to work on a slow projector or computer system.

STEP BY STEP | **Compress the Images in a Presentation**

USE the *Exhibits Final* presentation that is still open from the previous exercise.

1. In Windows, navigate to the folder containing *Exhibits Final.pptx* that you created earlier in this lesson.
2. To check the size of the file, right-click the file and click **Properties** to produce the file's Properties dialog box. The file Size is listed on the General tab of the dialog box.
3. In PowerPoint, click any picture in the presentation to select it, and then click the **Picture Tools Format** tab.
4. Click **Compress Pictures** in the Adjust group. The Compress Pictures dialog box opens.
5. Click the **Email (96 ppi)** option button.
6. Clear the **Apply only to this picture** check box. See Figure 8-28. If you wanted to compress only the selected picture, you would leave this option checked.

Figure 8-28

Compress the pictures in the presentation

7. Click **OK**.
8. **SAVE** the presentation. PowerPoint applies the compression settings you selected.
9. In Windows, repeat step 1 to recheck the presentation's file size.

PAUSE. LEAVE the presentation open to use in the next exercise.

 Ref

You will learn more about sharing a presentation in Lesson 10.

CERTIFICATION READY 3.2.6

How do you compress images in a presentation?

The compression utility allows you to choose several options that can reduce file size. You can choose to delete the hidden portions of cropped pictures, for example. You can also choose a target output setting. If you know your slides will be presented on the web or projected on a monitor, you can choose the lowest dpi (dots per inch) setting. Presentations to be shown on a screen do not have to have the same quality as materials that might be printed because the monitor screen itself is limited in the quality it can display. You can compress pictures individually, or apply the same setting to all pictures in the presentation.

ADDING SHAPES TO SLIDES

PowerPoint offers drawing tools that enable you to create both basic and complex drawings. Use line tools and shapes to construct the drawing. You can easily add text to shapes to identify them and format the drawing using familiar fill, outline, and effects options.

Drawing Lines

PowerPoint supplies a number of different line tools so you can draw horizontal, vertical, diagonal, or free-form lines.

To draw a line, you select the Line tool, click where you want to begin the line, hold down the mouse button, and drag to make the shape the desired size.

You can use the Shift key to **constrain** some shapes to a specific appearance. For example, you can hold down Shift while drawing a line to constrain it to a vertical, horizontal, or 45-degree diagonal orientation.

STEP BY STEP   **Draw Lines**

USE the *Exhibits Final* presentation that is still open from the previous exercise.

1. Go to slide 8. You will create a map on this slide to show potential visitors how to get to the museum. As you work, refer to Figure 8-29 for position of objects.

Figure 8-29

The streets and street names have been added

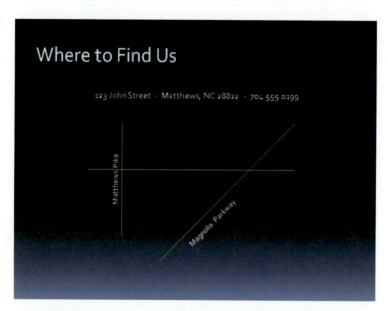

2. Click the **View** tab, and then click **Gridlines** to turn gridlines on.
3. Create the first street for the map as follows:
   a. Click the **Home** tab (or **Insert** tab), then click the **Shapes** button to display the gallery of drawing shapes.
   b. Click **Line** in the Line group. The pointer takes the shape of a crosshair.
   c. Locate the intersection of vertical and horizontal gridlines below the letter *n* in *John*, click at the intersection, and drag downward to create a vertical line three "blocks" long.

Take Note   You can also access the Shapes gallery on the Drawing Tools Format tab.

4. Add the street name as follows:

   a. Click **Text Box** on the Insert tab, click anywhere on the slide, and type the text **Matthews Pike**.

   b. Click the outer border of the text box to select all content within the text box, and change the font size to **16**.

   c. On the Drawing Tools Format tab, click **Rotate**, and click **Rotate Left 90°**.

   d. Move the rotated street name just to the left of the vertical line, as shown in Figure 8-29.

5. Select the **Line** tool again, hold down **Shift**, and draw the diagonal line shown in Figure 8-29.

Take Note   Holding down the Shift key constrains the line to be exactly 45 degrees or exactly vertical or horizontal as you drag.

6. Select the **Line** tool again and draw the horizontal line shown in Figure 8-29.

7. Add the street name for the diagonal street as follows:

   a. Insert a text box anywhere on the slide, and type **Magnolia Parkway**.

   b. Change the font size to **16**.

   c. With the text box still selected, click **Arrange**, point to **Rotate**, and click **More Rotation Options**. The Size and Position dialog box opens.

   d. Type **–45** in the Rotation box, and then click **Close**.

   e. Move the rotated text box to the right of the diagonal line, as shown in Figure 8-29.

8. On the View tab, clear the **Gridlines** check box to turn off gridlines again.

9. **SAVE** the presentation.

PAUSE. LEAVE the presentation open to use in the next exercise.

Selected shapes have selection handles (also called sizing handles) that you can use to adjust the size of the object. Some complex shapes have yellow diamond adjustment handles that allow you to modify the shape. Drag a selected shape anywhere on a slide to reposition it.

Lines and other shapes take their color from the current theme. You can change color, as well as change outline and other effects, at any time while creating a drawing.

Drawing Basic Shapes

PowerPoint's many shape tools allow you to create multisided, elliptical, and even freeform shapes. The Shapes gallery contains well over 100 different shapes. Just select a shape and then drag on the slide to draw it there, or click on the slide to create a shape with a default size and orientation.

When creating shapes, you can simply "eyeball" the size, use the rulers or gridlines to help you size, or use the Height and Width settings in the Size group on the Drawing Tools Format tab to scale the objects. Setting precise measurements can help you maintain the same proportions when creating objects of different shapes, for example, when creating circles and triangles that have to be the same height and width. You can also constrain a shape while drawing it by holding down the Shift key to maintain its aspect ratio. In the following exercise, you will draw some basic shapes.

Draw Basic Shapes

USE the *Exhibits Final* presentation that is still open from the previous exercise. As you work, refer to Figure 8-30 to help you position and size objects.

1. On the Home tab, click **Shapes**, and then click the **Rectangle** tool. Hold down the mouse button, and drag to create the tall shape above the horizontal line shown in Figure 8-30.

Figure 8-30

Basic shapes have been added to the map

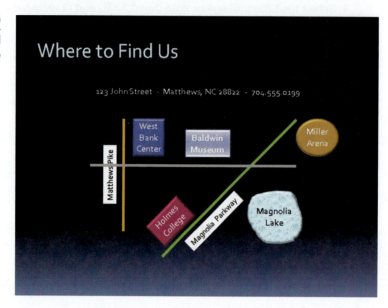

2. With the shape still selected, click the **Drawing Tools Format** tab. Note the measurements in the Size group. If necessary, adjust the size so the shape is 1 inch high by 0.9 inches wide.

3. Select the **Rectangle** tool again and use it to create the wider rectangle shown in Figure 8-30. This shape should be 0.7 inch high by 1.2 inches wide.

4. Select the **Oval** tool, hold down **Shift**, and draw the circle shown in Figure 8-30. This shape should be 1 inch high and wide.

5. Click the **Rectangle** tool and create a rectangle 0.7 inches high by 1 inch wide near the lower end of the diagonal street.

6. Click the shape's green rotation handle and drag to the right to rotate the shape so its right side is parallel to the diagonal road, as shown in Figure 8-30.

7. Click the **Freeform** tool in the Lines group in the Shapes gallery. Near the bottom of the slide (so you can easily see the line you are drawing), draw an irregular oval shape to represent a lake. The shape should be about 1.4 inches high and 1.5 inches wide.

 **Troubleshooting** When using the Freeform tool, if you return to the exact point at which you started drawing, PowerPoint will automatically close and fill the shape with color. If your shape does not fill, double-click to end it, click Undo, and start again.

8. Drag the lake shape to the right of the diagonal line, as shown in Figure 8-30.

9. **SAVE** the presentation.

PAUSE. LEAVE the presentation open to use in the next exercise.

You can save yourself some time when drawing similar or identical shapes by copying shapes. Copy a selected shape, use Paste to paste a copy on the slide, then move or modify the copy as necessary. You can also select a shape, hold down the Ctrl key, and drag a copy of the shape to a new location.

If you are creating a drawing in which you want to show connections between objects, you can use connectors from the Lines group of the Shapes gallery. Connectors automatically snap to points on shape sides, so you can easily draw an arrow, for instance, from one shape to another. As you reposition objects, the connectors remain attached and adjust as necessary to maintain the links between shapes.

Adding Text to Shapes

You can often improve a drawing by labeling the shapes to state what they represent. In Power-Point, you can add text by simply clicking and typing the text. When you add text to a shape, the shape takes the function of a text box. PowerPoint automatically wraps text in the shape as in a text box; if the shape is not large enough to display the text, words will break up or the text will extend above and below the shape. You can solve this problem by resizing the shape or changing the text's size. You can use any text formatting options you like when adding text to shapes, just as when inserting text into a placeholder or text box. To select text in a shape to edit it, drag over it with the I-beam pointer. In the following exercise, you will add some text to shapes.

STEP BY STEP	Add Text to Shapes

USE the *Exhibits Final* presentation that is still open from the previous exercise.

1. Click in the tall rectangle above the horizontal street, and then type **West Bank Center**.
2. Click in the wide rectangle shape, and then type **Baldwin Museum**.
3. Click in the circle shape, and then type **Miller Arena**.
4. Drag the right border of the circle slightly to the right to increase the shape's size so that the text fits.
5. Click in the rotated rectangle, and then type **Holmes College**. Note that the text is rotated as well.
6. Drag the right border of the rotated rectangle slightly up and to the right to increase the shape's size so that the text fits.
7. Click in the freeform lake object, and then type **Magnolia Lake**.
8. Drag over the *Baldwin Museum* text to select it, and then click the **Bold** button to boldface the text. Your map should look similar to Figure 8-31.

Figure 8-31

The map with text added to the shapes

9. **SAVE** the presentation.

PAUSE. LEAVE the presentation open to use in the next exercise.

Take Note

To adjust the way text appears in a shape, right-click the shape, click Format Shape, and access the Text Box settings. For example, you can align the text vertically and horizontally within the shape.

Formatting Shapes

You can apply many of the same formatting effects to drawn lines and shapes that you apply to other objects in PowerPoint. For example, you can change the fill color or texture, add borders, and use effects such as shadows and bevels. You can also save the formatting of a shape as the new default for future shapes you draw. In the following exercise, you will modify a shape by changing its border, fill, and effects.

STEP BY STEP   **Change a Shape's Border, Fill, and Effects**

USE the *Exhibits Final* presentation that is still open from the previous exercise.

1. On the drawing on slide 8, format the *Matthews Pike* line and label as follows:
   a. Click the vertical line that represents Matthews Pike.
   b. On the Drawing Tools Format tab, click the **Shape Outline** button, and then click the **Gold, Accent 3** theme color.

Take Note

You can use the Shape Outline button in the Drawing group on the Home tab or in the Shape Styles group on the Drawing Tools Format tab.

   c. Click the **Shape Outline** button again, point to Weight, and click **6 pt**.
   d. Click the outside border of the Matthews Pike text box to select all content in the text box, and on the Home tab, click **Font Color**, and click **Black, Background 1**.
   e. With the text box still selected, click the **Shape Fill** button, and then click **White, Text 1**.

2. Click the horizontal line and repeat steps 1a-1c to format the line with the **White, Text 1, darker 35%** theme color and **6 pt**. weight. (Don't worry about the street crossing over the *Matthews Pike* text box. You will fix this problem in a later exercise.)

3. Click the diagonal Magnolia Parkway line, click the **Shape Outline** button, point to Weight, and click **6 pt**.

4. Format the *Magnolia Parkway* text box following steps 1d and 1e to change text to black and the fill to white.

5. Format the other shapes as follows:
   a. Click the **West Bank Center shape** above the horizontal street, hold down **Shift**, and click each additional filled shape until all are selected. (Do *not* click any of the lines or the street name text boxes.)
   b. Click **Shape Outline**, and then click **No Outline**. You have removed outlines from the selected shapes.
   c. Click anywhere on the slide to deselect the selected shapes.
   d. Click the **West Bank Center shape**, click **Shape Fill**, and click **Periwinkle, Accent 5, Darker 25%**.
   e. Click the **Miller Arena shape** and fill with **Gold, Accent 3, Darker 25%**.
   f. Click the **Holmes College shape** and fill with **Pink, Accent 2, Darker 25%**.

6. Apply a texture to the Magnolia Lake shape by doing the following:
   a. Click the **Magnolia Lake shape**.
   b. On the Home tab, click **Shape Fill**, point to Texture, and click the **Water Droplets** texture.
   c. Click the **Font Color** button's arrow to open its palette and click **Black, Background 1**.

7. Click the **Baldwin Museum shape**, and on the Drawing Tools Format tab, open the Shapes Styles gallery and click **Periwinkle, Intense Effect, Accent 5**.

8. Select all the filled shapes except the Baldwin Museum shape and the street name text boxes, click **Shape Effects**, point to **Bevel**, and click **Circle**. Your map should look similar to Figure 8-32.

Figure 8-32

The map has been formatted

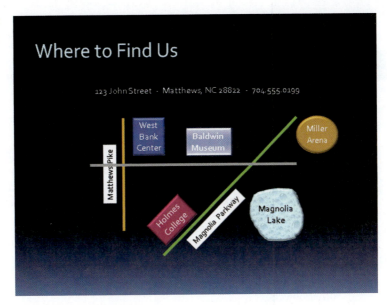

9. **SAVE** the presentation.

PAUSE. LEAVE the presentation open to use in the next exercise.

By now, you should be familiar with applying fills, outlines, and effects. You can format shapes using these options just as you formatted table cells, chart data markers, and SmartArt shapes in previous lessons.

Note that you can access fill, outline, and effect options from either the Home tab or the Drawing Tools Format tab. PowerPoint makes these options available on both tabs to minimize the amount of switching you have to do if you are also formatting text.

Save time when applying the same kinds of formats to a number of objects by selecting all the objects that need the same formatting. You can then apply the format only once to modify all the selected objects. To select several objects, you use the Shift-click method: click the first object you want to select, hold down the Shift key, and then click additional objects. If you select an object for your group by mistake, click it again to exclude it from the selection group.

CERTIFICATION READY   3.3.2

How do you change the fill color or texture?

CERTIFICATION READY   3.1.6

How do you apply borders to graphical elements?

Setting a New Default Format

Changing the default settings for drawn shapes enables you to create drawings more easily, without having to reformat every shape you draw. Define the settings you use most often as the default, and then you need to change only the shapes that are exceptions to your general rule. In this exercise, you will set a shape's formatting to be the default for new shapes.

STEP BY STEP   **Set the Formatting for the Current Shape as the Default**

USE the *Exhibits Final* presentation that is still open from the previous exercise.

1. On the drawing on slide 8, select the **West Bank Center shape**.

2. Right-click the shape and click **Set as Default Shape**.

3. **SAVE** the presentation.

4. Draw another rectangle anywhere on the slide. The new rectangle is formatted the same way as the *West Bank Center* shape.

5. Delete the rectangle you just drew.

6. **SAVE** the presentation.

CERTIFICATION READY   3.3.1

How do you set the formatting for the current shape as the default?

PAUSE. LEAVE the presentation open to use in the next exercise.

ORGANIZING OBJECTS ON A SLIDE

The Bottom Line

It is not uncommon to have to adjust the layout of objects you have added to slides. You may find that objects need to be reordered so they do not obscure other objects, or need to be aligned on the slide to present a neater appearance. You can also group objects together to make it easy to move or resize them all at once.

Setting the Order of Objects

Objects stack up on a slide in the **order** in which you created them, from bottom to top. If you insert a slide title on a slide, it will be the object at the bottom of the stack. The last item you create or add to the slide will be at the top of the stack. You can envision each object as an invisible layer in the stack. You can adjust the order in which objects stack on the slide by using Arrange commands or the Selection and Visibility pane.

Some objects can obscure other objects because of the order in which you add them to the slide. You use the Order options to reposition objects in the stack:

- **Bring to Front:** Moves the selected object to the front or top of the stack, on top of all other objects.
- **Bring Forward:** Moves an object one layer toward the front or top of the stack. Use this option if you need to position an object above some objects but below others.
- **Send to Back:** Moves an object all the way to the back or bottom of the stack, below all other objects.
- **Send Backward:** Moves an object one layer toward the back or bottom of the stack.

In this exercise, you will arrange some objects by changing their stacking order.

STEP BY STEP   **Set the Order of Objects**

USE the *Exhibits Final* presentation that is still open from the previous exercise.

1. Go to slide 3, and click the picture to select it.

2. Cancel the background removal you did earlier by doing the following:

   a. On the Picture Tools Format tab, click the **Remove Background** button. The Background Removal tab appears.

   b. Click **Discard All Changes.** The picture is restored to its default solid background, and the slide title is once again obscured.

3. With the picture still selected, click the **Send Backward** button's down arrow and on the menu that appears, click **Send to Back.** The picture moves behind the slide title placeholder, as shown in Figure 8-33.

Figure 8-33

The picture moves behind the text

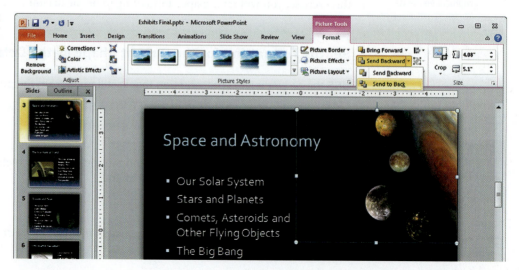

4. Go to slide 8. Click the **Arrange** button, and then click **Selection Pane**. The Selection and Visibility pane opens, as shown in Figure 8-34, showing the current slide content in the order in which it was created, from bottom to top. This order is determined by the order in which the objects were added to the slide.

Figure 8-34

The Selection and Visibility pane shows the current slide content

Another Way
You can also display the Selection and Visibility pane by clicking Select on the Home tab, then clicking Selection Pane.

Take Note   The Arrange tools are available on both the Home tab and the Picture Tools Format tab.

Troubleshooting Don't be concerned if the list in your Selection and Visibility pane doesn't exactly match the one shown in Figure 8-34. The order and numbering of objects in the pane can be affected by many actions.

5. Click the gold **Matthews Pike street line** in the map to see how it is identified in the Selection and Visibility pane—it will have a name such as *Straight Connector 4* and should be near the bottom of the list of objects. Then click the **horizontal street line** to see its name.

6. Click the **Matthew Pike street line** again to select it. Click the **Re-order up arrow** until the selected Straight Connector is above the horizontal Straight Connector in the Selection and Visibility pane. Notice that the gold line is now on top of the light gray line in the map.

7. Click the **Matthews Pike text box** and click the **Re-order up arrow** until the text box is on top of the horizontal gray line in the map.

8. Click the **Magnolia Parkway street line** and click the **Re-order up arrow** until the diagonal street is above the horizontal street in the map.

9. You have one more shape to add to the map: an arrow that labels the horizontal street as John Street and indicates that the street is one way. Click **Shapes** on the Home tab, click **Right Arrow** in the Block Arrows group, and draw a block arrow as shown in Figure 8-35. The arrow should be about 0.7 inches high and 5.2 inches wide.

Take Note   Notice that the shape's formatting matches that of the West Bank Center shape, because of the default you set earlier in the lesson.

Figure 8-35

Draw a block arrow

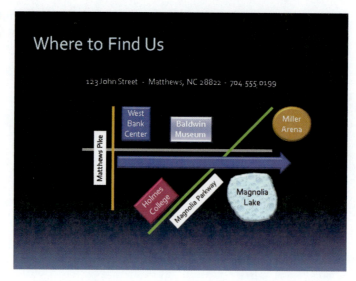

10. In the arrow, key **John Street**, press **Tab** twice, and type **ONE WAY**.

Take Note   Note that the Right Arrow object has been added at the top of the Selection and Visibility pane.

11. Using the Shape Fill button, apply the **Green, Accent 1, Darker 50%** color to the arrow.

12. Right-click a blank area of the block arrow (to the left of the words *John Street*, for example), point to **Send to Back**, and click **Send to Back**. The arrow moves behind all lines and shapes, as shown in Figure 8-36. Note the position of the Right Arrow object in the Selection and Visibility pane.

Figure 8-36

The completed map

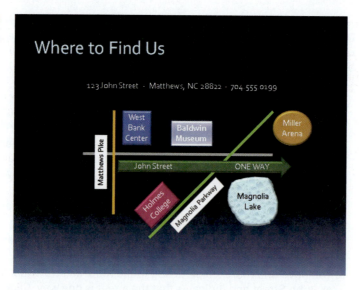

13. Close the **Selection and Visibility** pane.

14. If any of your shapes obscures the text on the block right arrow, adjust their positions as necessary.

15. **SAVE** the presentation.

PAUSE. LEAVE the presentation open to use in the next exercise.

You can clearly see the stacking order of objects on a slide using the Selection and Visibility pane. This pane is similar to the Layers palette in a program such as Illustrator or Photoshop. It allows you to easily move objects up or down in the stacking order. You can click the visibility "eye" to hide objects that might be in your way as you work on another object—a handy feature when creating a complex drawing.

CERTIFICATION
READY   3.1.1

How do you organize
objects on a slide?

If you do not want to use the Selection and Visibility pane, you can use options on the Home tab's Arrange button menu to reorder objects, or you can use buttons in the Drawing Tools Format tab in the Arrange group. You can also access these options readily by right-clicking an object and selecting the appropriate command from the shortcut menu.

Take Note   Arrange options also display on other Format tabs, such as the Picture Tools Format and SmartArt Tools Format tabs.

Aligning Objects with Each Other

Your drawings will present a more pleasing appearance if similar items are aligned with each other or to the slide. Use PowerPoint's alignment options to position objects neatly.

PowerPoint's alignment options allow you to line up objects on a slide both horizontally and vertically:

- Use **Align Left**, **Align Center**, or **Align Right** to align objects horizontally so that their left edges, vertical centers, or right edges are lined up with each other.
- Use **Align Top**, **Align Middle**, or **Align Bottom** to align objects vertically so that their top edges, horizontal centers, or bottom edges are lined up with each other.

You can also use distribute options to space objects evenly, either vertically or horizontally. This feature can be a great time-saver when you have a number of objects that you want to spread out evenly across a slide.

PowerPoint allows you to align (or distribute) objects either to each other or to the slide. If you select Align Selected Objects on the Align menu, PowerPoint will adjust only the selected objects. If you select Align to Slide, PowerPoint will rearrange objects using the entire slide area.

STEP BY STEP   **Align Objects with Each Other**

USE the *Exhibits Final* presentation that is still open from the previous exercise.

1. On slide 8, click the **West Bank Center shape**, hold down **Shift**, and click the **Baldwin Museum** shape and the **Miller Arena** shape. These landmarks are all different distances from the *John Street* horizontal line but can be aligned for a neater appearance.
2. Click the **Drawing Tools Format** tab if necessary, click **Align**, and click **Align Bottom**. The shapes are now aligned at the bottom so they are the same distance from the horizontal line, as shown in Figure 8-37.
3. **SAVE** the presentation.

PAUSE. LEAVE the presentation open to use in the next exercise.

Figure 8-37

Align the selected shapes at their bottoms

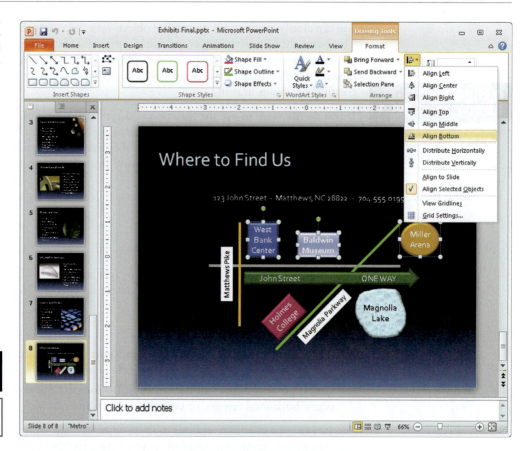

Grouping Objects Together

When a drawing consists of a number of objects, it can be tedious to move each one if you need to reposition the drawing. Grouping objects allows you to work with a number of objects as one unit. In the following exercise, you group objects into a single unit.

STEP BY STEP | **Group Objects Together**

USE the *Exhibits Final* presentation that is still open from the previous exercise.

1. Click above and to the left of the map, and then hold down the left mouse button and drag downward and to the right until you have included the entire map in the selected area. See Figure 8-38. This is called **lassoing** the shapes.

Figure 8-38

To lasso a group of shapes, use the mouse pointer to draw a box around them

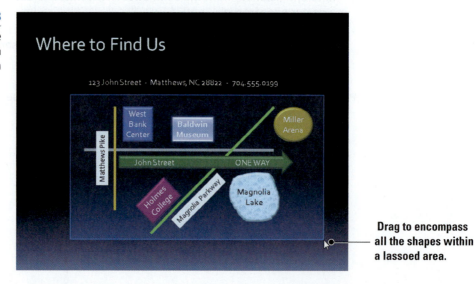

Drag to encompass
all the shapes within
a lassoed area.

2. Release the mouse button. All the shapes within the selection lasso are selected.

3. Click the **Drawing Tools Format** tab, click the **Group** button, and then click **Group**, as in Figure 8-39. All objects are surrounded by a single selection border.

Figure 8-39

Use the Group command to group the selected shapes

4. **SAVE** the presentation and **CLOSE** the file.

PAUSE. LEAVE PowerPoint open to use in the next exercise.

If a drawing contains a number of objects, it makes sense to group the objects when you are finished with the drawing. You can more easily reposition a grouped object, and you can also apply formatting changes to all objects in a group much more quickly than by applying formats to each individual object. To select a group, click any object in the group.

If you find that you need to work further with one object in a group, you can simply click it to activate it. It remains part of the group while you modify it. Most modifications are possible without ungrouping. (Exception: you cannot move the object separately from its group.) If you need to remove objects or make sweeping changes to a group, you can use the Ungroup option to release the group into its component parts. PowerPoint remembers the objects that are in the group so you can use Regroup if desired to restore the group.

If you are creating a very complex drawing, you can group portions of the drawing, then group those groups. This makes it easy to reuse portions of a drawing—simply ungroup the entire drawing, copy the group you need elsewhere, and regroup the whole.

Take Note   It is easy to miss an object when selecting parts of a complex drawing to create a group. To check that you have all objects selected, move the group. You will easily see if one or more objects do not move with the group. Undo the move, click the group, click any other objects that need to belong to the group, and issue the Group command again.

CREATING A PHOTO ALBUM PRESENTATION

The Bottom Line   PowerPoint can create a special type of presentation for situations where the primary purpose is to display photos. Photo album presentations are easy to create and modify using a dialog box interface.

Creating a Photo Album Presentation

A photo album presentation is useful when you want to showcase multiple photographs. This special presentation type enables you to set up consistent formatting that will apply to every photo in the presentation automatically. You can also specify captions for the pictures and display them in color or black and white. In the following exercise, you create a photo album presentation.

STEP BY STEP   Create a Photo Album Presentation

GET READY. Before you begin these steps, start PowerPoint. You do not have to start a new presentation, because you will create one as part of the exercise.

1. On the Insert tab, click **Photo Album**. The Photo Album dialog box opens.

Take Note   Even though you are using the Insert tab, you are not actually inserting the photo album into the existing presentation; instead, you are creating a brand-new presentation file.

@ The *Astronomy.jpg*, *Biology.jpg*, *Chemistry.jpg*, *Circuit.jpg*, *Satellite.jpg*, *Shuttle.jpg*, and *Telescope. jpg* files are available on the book companion website or in WileyPLUS.

2. Click the **File/Disk** button. The Insert New Pictures dialog box opens.

3. Navigate to the location where the data files for this lesson are stored and click *Astronomy.jpg*.

4. Hold down the **Ctrl** key and click the following files: *Biology.jpg, Chemistry.jpg, Circuit .jpg, Satellite.jpg, Shuttle.jpg,* and *Telescope.jpg*. See Figure 8-40.

Figure 8-40

Select multiple graphic files for inclusion

5. Click **Insert**. The Photo Album dialog box reappears, with all the selected pictures listed. See Figure 8-41.

Figure 8-41

The selected photos are now listed in the Photo Album dialog box

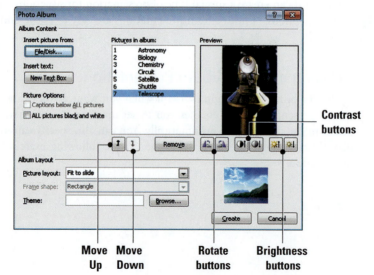

CERTIFICATION
READY 2.1.1

How do you add captions
to a picture?

CERTIFICATION
READY 2.1.2

How do you insert text in a
photo album?

CERTIFICATION
READY 2.1.3

How do you insert images in
black and white?

CERTIFICATION
READY 2.1.4

How do you reorder pictures
in an album?

CERTIFICATION
READY 2.1.5

How do you rotate an
image in a photo album?

CERTIFICATION
READY 2.1.5

How do you adjust an image's
brightness in a photo album?

CERTIFICATION
READY 2.1.5

How do you adjust an image's
contrast in a photo album?

6. Click the **Circuit.jpg** graphic on the list, and then click the **Move Up** arrow three times to move it to the first position in the list.

7. Click **New Text Box**. A text box entry is inserted on the list of graphics between Circuit .jpg and Astronomy.jpg.

8. Click the **Shuttle.jpg** graphic, and then click the **Rotate Right** button to rotate it 90 degrees in a clockwise direction.

9. Click the **Satellite.jpg** graphic, and then click the **Increase Brightness** button twice to brighten the image.

10. Click the **Biology.jpg** graphic, and then click the **Increase Contrast** button to increase the image contrast.

11. Open the **Picture Layout drop-down list** and click **1 Picture**.

12. Open the **Frame Shape drop-down list** and click **Rounded Rectangle**.

13. Click to mark the **Captions Below ALL Pictures** check box.

14. Click **Create**. The presentation is created.

15. Browse through the presentation to see what has been created. Notice that each picture has a caption under it that shows the file name (minus the file extension). Notice that the text box has been placed on its own separate slide, just as if it were a picture.

16. On the Edit tab, click the arrow under the **Photo Album** button, and on the menu that appears, click **Edit Photo Album**. The Edit Photo Album dialog box opens. It is the same as the Photo Album dialog box in Figure 8-41 except for its name.

17. Open the **Picture Layout drop-down list** and click **2 Pictures**.

18. Click the **Browse** button next to Themes. Click the **Metro** theme and click **Select**.

19. Click the **ALL pictures black and white** check box.

20. Click **Update**. The dialog box closes and the changes are reflected in the presentation.

21. Browse through the presentation to see what has been changed.

22. **SAVE** the presentation as *Photo Album Final*.

EXIT PowerPoint.

A photo album presentation is different from a regular presentation file. You could create the same end result using a regular presentation, but it would not be as easy to reformat and manipulate later. Using the Photo Album dialog box, you can easily reorder the pictures, choose whether or not to display captions, add text boxes, and more. You can also apply quick adjustments to photos, such as brightness and contrast changes and rotations.

You must create photo album presentations from scratch; an existing presentation cannot be converted to a photo album.

SKILL SUMMARY

In This Lesson You Learned How To:	Exam Objective	Objective Number
Add a picture to a slide.		
Format graphical elements.	Resize graphical elements.	3.1.3
	Apply styles to graphical elements.	3.1.5
	Apply color adjustments.	3.2.1
	Apply image corrections.	3.2.2
	Add artistic effects to an image.	3.2.3
	Remove a background.	3.2.4
	Crop a picture.	3.2.5
	Compress selected pictures or all pictures.	3.2.6
	Change a picture.	3.2.7
	Reset a picture.	3.2.8
	Apply effects to graphical elements.	3.1.4
Add shapes to slides.	Apply borders to graphical elements.	3.1.6
	Set the formatting of the current shape as the default for future shapes.	3.3.1
	Change the fill color or texture.	3.3.2
Organize objects on a slide.	Arrange graphical elements.	3.1.1
	Position graphical element.	3.1.2
Create a photo album presentation.	Add captions to pictures.	2.1.1
	Insert text.	2.1.2
	Insert images in black and white.	2.1.3
	Reorder pictures in an album.	2.1.4
	Adjust images.	2.1.5

Knowledge Assessment

Matching

Match the term in Column 1 to its description in Column 2.

Column 1	Column 2
1. Order	a. Predrawn graphics you can use to illustrate a slide
2. Clip art	b. The relationship of width to height for a picture
3. Guides	c. A descriptive word or phrase you can use to search for specific types of objects
4. Constrain	d. Sizing to a percentage of the original size
5. Aspect ratio	e. A special type of presentation file designed to display images
6. Scaling	f. To force a drawing tool to create a shape such as a perfect square or circle
7. Keyword	g. A series of vertical and horizontal dotted lines that help you align objects on a slide

8. Crop
9. Photo Album
10. Gridlines

h. To move one object behind or in front of another
i. To remove portions of a picture you don't need
j. Nonprinting lines that you can move or copy to help you position objects on a slide

True/False

Circle T if the statement is true or F if the statement is false.

T F **1.** When adding clip art to a slide, you are limited to the pictures stored on your computer.

T F **2.** PowerPoint allows you to insert pictures that are stored in BMP format.

T F **3.** As you move the pointer, a short dotted line also moves on both rulers.

T F **4.** The Recolor option lets you select colors in a picture and replace them with other colors.

T F **5.** Compressing an image reduces the number of colors used.

T F **6.** The color of a new shape is determined by the default shape formatting.

T F **7.** To add text to a shape, select the shape and begin typing.

T F **8.** If you want an object to be at the bottom of a stack of objects, you would use Send to Back.

T F **9.** You can format a single object in a group without having to ungroup all objects.

T F **10.** Any presentation can be converted to a photo album presentation.

Competency Assessment

Project 8-1: Get the Picture

You are a recruiter for Woodgrove Bank, and you have prepared a presentation to be delivered at a local job fair. You need to locate a picture to illustrate one of the presentation's slides. You can use Microsoft Office clip art files to find a suitable picture.

GET READY. LAUNCH PowerPoint if it is not already running.

@ The *Job Fair* file is available on the book companion website or in WileyPLUS.

1. **OPEN** the *Job Fair* presentation and save it as *Job Fair Final*.

2. Go to slide 5 and click the **Clip Art** icon in the right-hand content placeholder.

3. Type **business** as the keyword, click the **Results should be drop-down arrow**, and select only **Photographs**.

4. Review the results to find a photograph of a professionally dressed business person and then click a picture you like to insert it into the placeholder.

5. Use the Size options on the Picture Tools Format tab to resize the picture to be as wide as the text in the left-hand placeholder, if necessary.

6. Click the **View** tab, and then click **Gridlines**. Use the gridlines to align the top of the picture with the top of the text in the left-hand placeholder.

7. Click the picture to select it, click **Picture Effects** on the Picture Tools Format tab, point to Shadow, and click any shadow effect.

8. Hide the gridlines.

9. **SAVE** the presentation.

LEAVE the presentation open for use in the next project.

Project 8-2: Final Touches

You have decided you need another picture in the Job Fair Final presentation. You have a picture file you think will work.

@ The *Building.jpg* file is available on the book companion website or in WileyPLUS.

1. Go to slide 2 of *Job Fair Final* and click the Insert Picture from File icon in the right-hand content placeholder.

2. Navigate to the data files for this lesson, locate *Building.jpg*, click the file, and click Insert.

3. Right-click the picture and click Size and Position. In the Format Picture dialog box, scale the picture to 90% of its current height and width.

4. Press Alt + F9 to display drawing guides. Click the slide title placeholder to display its border, and then drag the vertical guide to the right to align with the right border of the slide title placeholder.

5. Drag the horizontal placeholder up to align with the top of the capital letter *E* in the first bulleted item in the left-hand placeholder.

6. Reposition the picture so that its upper-right corner snaps to the intersection of the two guides. Press Alt + F9 to hide the guides.

7. Click the More button in the Picture Styles group on the Picture Tools Format tab, and then click the Drop Shadow Rectangle Quick Style.

8. Right-click the picture, click Format Picture, and change Brightness to 5% and Contrast to 10%.

9. Click Compress Pictures in the Adjust group on the Picture Tools Format tab, and then click E-mail (96 ppi) and click OK.

10. SAVE the presentation and then CLOSE the file.

LEAVE PowerPoint open for use in the next project.

Proficiency Assessment

Project 8-3: Go with the Flow

You are a professional trainer teaching a class on basic computer skills. For your class today, you need to explain the systems development life cycle (SDLC) to a group of students. You can use PowerPoint's drawing tools to create a flow chart that shows the process.

1. Create a new, blank presentation, and apply the Median theme. (Remember, the themes are in alphabetical order.)

2. Change the title slide to a Title Only slide, and type the slide title Systems Development Life Cycle (SDLC).

3. Draw five rectangles stacked vertically on the slide (or draw one and then copy it four times). You do not have to worry about alignment or distribution at this point.

4. Type Phase 1: Needs Analysis in the top rectangle.

5. Add text to the remaining rectangles as follows:

> Phase 2: System Design
>
> Phase 3: Development
>
> Phase 4: Implementation
>
> Phase 5: Maintenance

6. Resize the shapes as necessary so that text fits on a single line and all five rectangles fit on the slide with a small amount of space between each shape, as in Figure 8-42.

Figure 8-42

Draw these five rectangles
and add text to them

7. Set the width and height of all five rectangles to be identical if they are not already.

8. With all five rectangles selected, use the Align Left command to align them with one another.

9. Use the Distribute Vertically command to equalize the spacing between the rectangles.

10. Apply a different Shape Styles color to each rectangle. (Use the same effect for all rectangles, but vary the colors for each.)

11. Group all drawing objects.

12. Use the Align Center command to align the object horizontally in the center of the slide.

13. **SAVE** the presentation as *SDLC Final.pptx* and then **CLOSE** the file.

LEAVE PowerPoint open for the next project.

Project 8-4: **Photo Album**

You have been asked by the K-9 Agility Network to create a photo album of some of their dogs competing in a recent show, which they will use as a marketing tool.

1. In PowerPoint, on the Insert tab, click **Photo Album** to begin a new photo album.

The *Dog1.jpg*, *Dog2.jpg*, *Dog3.jpg*, *Dog4.jpg*, *Dog5.jpg*, and *Dog6.jpg* files are available on the book companion website or in WileyPLUS.

2. From the data files for this lesson, add the graphics *Dog1.jpg* through *Dog6.jpg* to the photo album.

3. Reverse the order of the graphics in the photo album so they are listed from Dog6 to Dog1.

4. Set the Picture Layout to **1 picture** and set the Frame shape to **Center Shadow Rectangle**.

5. Select the **Urban** theme.

6. Click **Create**.

7. On the title slide, change the default title (*Photo Album*) to **K-9 Agility Network**.

8. **SAVE** the presentation as *K-9 Final.pptx* and then **CLOSE** the file.

LEAVE PowerPoint open for use in the next project.

Project 8-5: Photo Flair

You are finalizing a presentation to introduce a speaker and want to do some work on the photo of the speaker you have included on a slide. You can use PowerPoint's picture tools to finalize the photo.

@ The *Speaker* file is available on the book companion website or in WileyPLUS.

1. **OPEN** the *Speaker* presentation and save it as *Speaker Final*.
2. Go to slide 2 and select the picture.
3. Crop the picture to remove the coffee cup and newspaper at the right side of the picture.
4. Resize the photo so it is 4 inches high and align it with the top of the vertical line at the center of the slide.
5. Increase the contrast in the picture by 10%.
6. Draw a rectangle that exactly covers the picture. Remove the outline from the rectangle.
7. Click the down arrow key twice and the right arrow key twice to slightly offset the shape from the picture, and then send the shape behind the picture to act as a drop shadow.
8. Choose a new theme color for the rectangle shape that contrasts well with the picture but does not overwhelm it.
9. **SAVE** the presentation and then **CLOSE** the file.

LEAVE PowerPoint open for use in the next project.

Project 8-6: Logo Creation

Your Consolidated Courier presentation needs a new logo. You can create one using the Drawing tools in PowerPoint.

1. Create a new blank presentation.
2. Change the layout of the slide to Blank.
3. Draw the three shapes shown in Figure 8-43.

Figure 8-43

Draw these three shapes

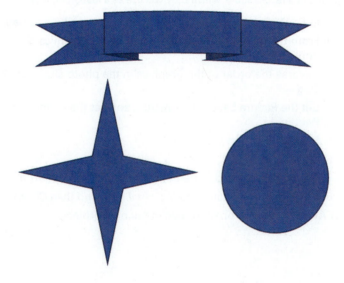

4. Select the banner shape, and fill it with the Dark Red standard color. Change its outline to the Orange standard color and set its Width to 0.25 pt.

5. In the banner shape, type **Consolidated Courier**, pressing **Enter** between the words so each appears on its own line. Set the font to Arial Black.

6. Select the star shape, and fill it with the Dark Red standard color. Remove its outline.

7. Select the circle, and fill it with the Fire preset gradient. Remove its outline.

8. Arrange, align, and size the three shapes into the logo shown in Figure 8-44.

Figure 8-44

Create this logo

9. **SAVE** the presentation as *Logo Final* and then **CLOSE** the file.

EXIT PowerPoint.

INTERNET READY

The local library has asked you to prepare a presentation for their book club, which is about to embark on a Famous Novels series of club meetings. The book club will read novels by Austen, Dickens, Melville, and Steinbeck this year. Using the Internet, research some basic facts about the lives of these four authors and locate and save pictures of each. Create a slide show to present the information you have gathered. On the first slide, use drawing tools to draw a stack or row of books with the names of the authors on the spines. Create a slide for each author and insert life details and the pictures you located. Adjust the pictures as necessary to be about the same size and location on each slide and use any picture formatting tools you like to improve the appearance of the pictures.

9 Using Animation and Multimedia

LESSON SKILL MATRIX

Skill	Exam Objective	Objective Number
Setting Up Slide Transitions	Modify a transition effect.	5.4.1
	Add a sound to a transition.	5.4.2
	Modify transition duration.	5.4.3
	Set up manual or automatically timed advance options.	5.4.4
Animating Your Slides	Use more Entrance Effects.	5.1.1
	Use more Emphasis.	5.1.2
	Use more Exit Effects.	5.1.3
	Use more Motion Paths.	5.1.4
	Set timing.	5.2.1
	Set start option.	5.2.2
	Change the direction of an animation.	5.3.1
	Attach a sound to an animation.	5.3.2
	Use Animation Painter.	5.3.3
	Reorder animation.	5.3.4
	Select text options.	5.3.5
Adding Media Clips to a Presentation	Apply a style to video or audio content.	3.5.1
	Adjust video or audio content.	3.5.2
	Arrange video or audio content.	3.5.3
	Size video or audio content.	3.5.4
	Adjust playback options.	3.5.5
	Show media controls.	8.2.5
	Compress media.	7.2.4

KEY TERMS

- After Previous
- animations
- Animation Painter
- Animation Pane
- audio
- delay
- duration
- emphasis effect
- entrance effects
- exit effect
- motion path
- On Click
- poster frame
- transitions
- video
- With Previous

In your role as director of promotions for the Baldwin Museum of Science, you are responsible for creating a multimedia presentation that will run on the video monitors in the museum's lobby. This self-running presentation should contain plenty of animation and movement to capture people's attention. PowerPoint's animation and multimedia capabilities allow you to include transitions, animations, and audio and video clips to enliven your presentations.

SOFTWARE ORIENTATION

The Animation Pane

The **Animation Pane**, shown in Figure 9-1, enables you to manage all the animation effects on the active slide. Each object can have multiple animation effects, including entrance, exit, emphasis, and motion path effect types.

Figure 9-1

Custom Animation task pane

Clock symbol indicates the effect occurs automatically.

Green icons indicate entrance effects.

Mouse symbol indicates the event occurs on mouse click.

Red icons indicate exit effects.

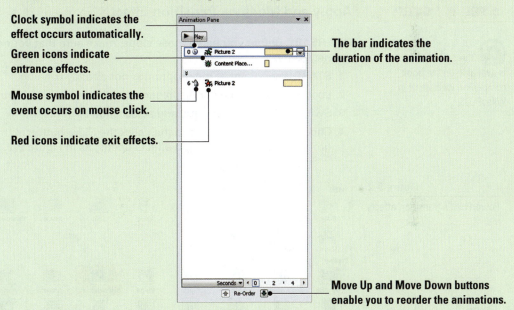

The bar indicates the duration of the animation.

Move Up and Move Down buttons enable you to reorder the animations.

PowerPoint professionals often use complex sequences of animation effects to add movement and interest to an otherwise static presentation. Animation effects applied to static images can be a cost-effective alternative to creating live motion video.

SETTING UP SLIDE TRANSITIONS

The Bottom Line

Transitions are animated effects that occur when you move from one slide to another. They differ from animations in that animations apply to individual items on a slide whereas transitions apply only to entire slides. You can control the effect, its speed, its sound effect (if any), and in some cases other options, such as direction.

Applying and Modifying a Transition Effect

By default, there are no transitions assigned to slides. When you advance to the next slide, it simply appears in place of the previous one. For more impressive-looking transitions, you can choose one of the preset transition effects that PowerPoint provides and then modify it as needed. In this exercise, you will apply and customize a transition effect.

You can apply any of the transition effects from the Transitions tab, and then modify the chosen transition's options. Some transitions have effect options you can choose from the Effect Options button; if you choose a transition that doesn't have any, that button is unavailable.

You can assign a sound to a transition if desired. You can select any of PowerPoint's preset sounds from the Sound menu, or choose Other Sound from the menu to open a dialog box from which you can browse for your own sounds.

The Duration setting for a transition is the number of seconds the effect takes to occur. Each transition has a default duration; increase the duration to slow it down, or decrease the duration to speed it up.

The Apply to All button copies the transition from the active slide to all other slides. To remove the transitions from all slides at once, first set one of the slides to have a transition of None, and then click Apply to All.

STEP BY STEP	Apply and Modify a Transition Effect

The *Lobby* file is available on the book companion website or in WileyPLUS.

GET READY. Before you begin these steps, make sure that your computer is on. Log on, if necessary.

1. **START** PowerPoint, if the program is not already running.
2. Locate and open the *Lobby* presentation and save it as *Lobby Final*.
3. Switch to Slide Sorter view, and select slide 2.
4. Click the **Transitions** tab, and then click the **More** button in the Transition to This Slide group. A palette of transition effects opens, as in Figure 9-2.

Figure 9-2

PowerPoint's transition effects

WileyPLUS Extra! features an online tutorial of this task.

5. Click the **Honeycomb** effect. The effect is previewed immediately on slide 2.

Take Note

Notice that there is a small star below and to the left of slide 2. This indicates that a transition or animation has been applied to it.

6. On the Transitions tab, in the Timing group, set the Duration to **06.00**. This sets the transition to execute in 6 seconds.
7. Open the **Sound drop-down** list and click **Camera**, to add the sound of a camera shutter opening and closing at each transition. See Figure 9-3.

Sound ┐ ┌ Duration

Figure 9-3

Figure 9-3

Set transition options

8. Click the **Preview** button in the Preview group, or click the small star icon below slide 2, to see the effect again at the new speed, including the newly assigned sound. See Figure 9-4.

Figure 9-4

The star indicates there is a transition or animation

Star icon

Permanent Exhibits

- Space and Astronomy
- The Mechanical World
- Oceans and Seas
- Why Math is Necessary
- Science and the Arts

2

 Troubleshooting If you don't hear the sound, try previewing it again. If you still don't hear the sound, make sure your system sound is not muted in Windows, and that the volume is turned up.

9. Click the **More** button again, and in the Subtle section, click **Wipe** to apply the Wipe transition to the selected slide.

Take Note Notice that the Duration setting is reset to the default for the newly chosen transition, but the sound (Camera) previously selected remains selected.

10. Click **Effect Options**. A menu of effect options opens, as shown in Figure 9-5.

Figure 9-5

Select a transition option

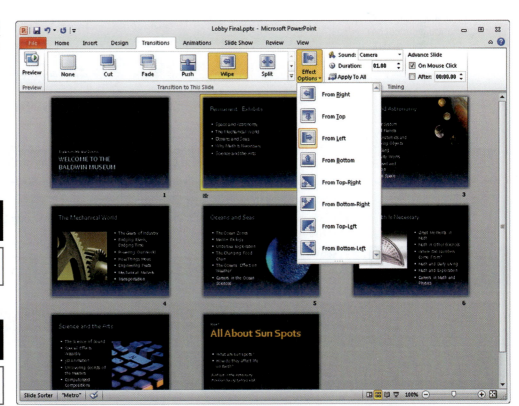

CERTIFICATION
READY   5.4.1

How do you modify a transition?

CERTIFICATION
READY   5.4.2

How do you add sound to a transition?

CERTIFICATION
READY   **5.4.3**

How do you modify a transition duration?

11. Click **From Left**. The new effect option is previewed on the slide automatically.

12. Click **Apply to All**. The transition effect is copied to all the other slides in the presentation. Now all the slides have small star icons beneath them.

13. On the Slide Show tab, click **From Beginning**, and watch the whole presentation from beginning to end, clicking to move to the next slide. When finished, press **Esc** to return to **Slide Sorter** view.

14. **SAVE** the presentation.

PAUSE. LEAVE the presentation open to use in the next exercise.

Determining How Slides Will Advance

By default, the presentation advances from one slide to the next when you click the mouse. Slides can be set to advance automatically after a certain amount of time, manually upon mouse click (or other signal, such as pressing the Enter key), or both. If both are selected, the slide will advance immediately if you click the mouse, otherwise advance will occur when the allotted time elapses. In this exercise, you learn how to set slides to advance automatically after a certain amount of time and to advance manually upon a mouse click.

STEP BY STEP   **Set Slides to Advance Manually or Automatically**

USE the *Lobby Final* presentation that is still open from the previous exercise.

1. Click **slide 1** to select it.

2. On the Transitions tab in the Timing group, mark the **After** check box to indicate that the slide should advance manually after a certain amount of time has passed.

3. Click the **up increment arrow** in the **After** text box until it reads **00:10:00**, to set the amount of time to 10 seconds.

4. Clear the **On Mouse Click** check box, as shown in Figure 9-6.

Does not advance on mouse click

Advances automatically after 10 seconds

5. Click the **Slide Show** tab, then click **From Beginning**, and begin watching the presentation. Try clicking the mouse; notice that it does not advance to the next slide.

6. After viewing three slides, press **Esc** to return to Slide Sorter view.

7. Click to mark the **On Mouse Click** check box again.

8. Click **Apply to All**. Now all slides will advance automatically after 10 seconds, or earlier if the mouse is clicked.

9. **SAVE** the presentation.

PAUSE. LEAVE the presentation open to use in the next exercise.

CERTIFICATION
READY   **5.4.4**

How do you set up manual or automatically timed advance options?

When creating a self-running presentation, such as for a lobby display, it is important that nothing be set to happen only with a mouse click because the audience will have no access to a mouse.

ANIMATING YOUR SLIDES

The Bottom Line

You can animate individual objects on a slide to give the presentation a more active and dynamic feel. Objects can be set to enter or exit the slide in an animated way. For example, a picture could fly onto the slide, stay on the screen for a few seconds, and then fly away again. Text can also be animated; it can be set to appear all at once or one bullet point at a time.

Animations are effects applied to placeholders or other content to move the content in unique ways on the slide. Animations can be roughly divided into four types: entrance, emphasis, exit, and motion paths. **Entrance effects** animate an object's entry onto the slide, separately from the entrance of the slide itself. If an object does not have an entrance effect, it enters at the same time as the slide. An **emphasis effect** modifies an object that is already on the slide, calling attention to it by moving it or changing its colors. An **exit effect** causes the object to leave the slide before the slide itself exits. A **motion path** effect moves the object from point A to point B, following along a path that you create for it.

Applying Animations

The easiest way to take advantage of PowerPoint's animation features is to apply one of the built-in animation presets. Many presets are available for entrance, emphasis, and exit effects, and you can apply them to both graphic objects and text. After applying a preset, you can modify it by changing its options. In this exercise, you will apply an animation effect and then modify it for a custom effect.

STEP BY STEP   **Apply and Modify Animations**

USE the *Lobby Final* presentation that is still open from the previous exercise.

1. Switch to Normal view, and go to slide 2.
2. Click in the bulleted list to move the insertion point there.
3. On the Animations tab, click **Add Animation**. A menu of animation presets appears, as shown in Figure 9-7.

Figure 9-7

Select an entrance animation preset

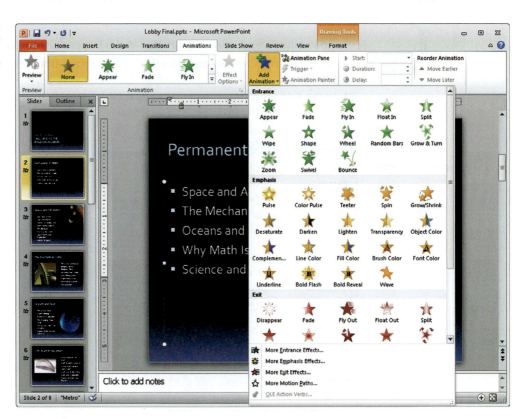

4. Click **Fly In**. The animation is previewed on the slide.

5. Click the **Effect Options** button. A menu of options appears, as shown in Figure 9-8.

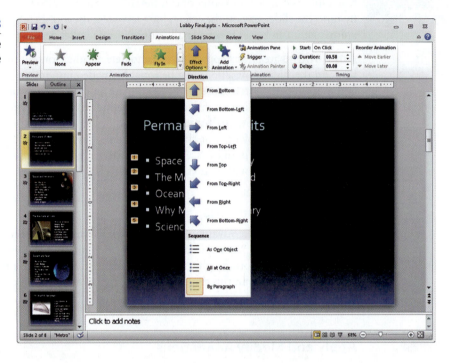

6. Click **From Top-Left**. The effect is previewed. Notice that each bullet point flies in separately.

7. Click the **Effect Options** button again.

8. Click **All at Once**. The effect is previewed. Notice that all the bullets fly in at once.

Take Note   The text options like the one you selected in step 8 are available only when animating text, not graphics.

9. Go to slide 3, and select the graphic in the upper-right corner.

10. On the Animations tab, click the **Add Animation** button, and then click **More Emphasis Effects**.

11. In the Add Emphasis Effect dialog box, click **Pulse**. See Figure 9-9. The effect is previewed on the graphic.

CERTIFICATION READY   5.3.5

How do you select text options?

CERTIFICATION READY   5.3.1

How do you change the direction of an animation?

CERTIFICATION READY   5.1.2

How do you use More Emphasis Effects?

12. Click **OK** to accept the new effect.

13. On the Animations tab, in the Duration box, click the **up increment arrow** until the setting is **04:00**.

14. Click the **Preview** button to preview the animation at its new duration setting.

15. **SAVE** the presentation.

PAUSE. LEAVE the presentation open to use in the next exercise.

The term "preset" may conjure up a simple, rigidly defined choice, but PowerPoint's preset animations are very customizable, as you saw in the preceding exercise. You can adjust their direction, duration, text options, and more. Some animation effects have effect options you can select from the Effect Options button's menu. If the chosen animation has no options, the Effect Options button is unavailable.

When animating text, you have a choice of animating each paragraph individually or animating all the text at once. Keep in mind that each animation will be triggered (by default) by a mouse click, and think about whether you want to introduce each paragraph to the audience individually or not.

Using Motion Path Animation

Motion paths enable you to set a graphic to move from one place to another. You can start with a preset, as you learn to do in this exercise, and then modify the path to fine-tune it. To modify the path, on the Animations tab, click Effect Options, and then click Edit Points. Then you can drag the individual points that comprise the path. The start point is represented by a green arrow. If the start and end point are the same spot, you see only that green arrow; however, if the end point is different, it appears as a red arrow. In this exercise, you will apply a motion path animation to a graphic.

STEP BY STEP   **Use a Motion Path Animation**

USE the *Lobby Final* presentation that is still open from the previous exercise.

1. Go to slide 5 and select the graphic.

2. On the Animations tab, click **Add Animation**, and then click **More Motion Paths**. The Add Motion Path dialog box appears.

3. In the Add Motion Path dialog box, scroll down to the Special section and click **Swoosh**. See Figure 9-10. The animation is previewed on the slide.

Figure 9-10

Select a motion path animation

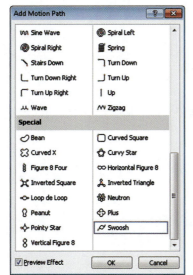

4. Click **OK** to apply the animation. A dotted line appears on the graphic, showing the motion path. This dotted line will not appear in Slide Show view.

5. Click **Effect Options**, and then click **Reverse Path Direction**. The Swoosh effect is previewed again, this time going in the opposite direction.

6. **SAVE** the presentation.

PAUSE. LEAVE the presentation open to use in the next exercise.

Modifying an Animation's Start Options and Timing

Each animation has its own separate start, duration, and delay settings. The animation's **duration** determines how quickly it will execute. Each animation effect has a default duration, which you can adjust up or down. The **delay** is the amount of time to wait between the previous action and this animation. You might, for example, use a delay to give the audience a chance to read some text on the screen. By setting these properties, you can sequence multiple animation effects to produce the exact appearance you want.

Each animation has its own start options and timing settings, separate from the slide itself. The start options available are On Click (the default), With Previous, and After Previous. **On Click** waits for a mouse click to start the animation; the slide show pauses until the click is received. **With Previous** starts the animation simultaneously with the start of the previous action. If it's the first animation on the slide, the previous action is the entrance of the slide itself; otherwise the previous action is the previous animation on that slide. **After Previous** starts the animation after the previous action has completed. If the previous action is very quick, you may not notice any difference between With Previous and After Previous.

In this exercise, you will modify the start options and timing for an animation.

STEP BY STEP   **Modify Animation Start Options and Timing**

USE the *Lobby Final* presentation that is still open from the previous exercise.

1. Go to slide 6, and select the graphic.

2. On the Animations tab, click **Add Animation**, and click **More Entrance Effects**. The Add Entrance Effect dialog box opens.

3. In the Exciting section, click **Pinwheel**. See Figure 9-11.

Figure 9-11

Select an entrance effect

4. Click **OK**.

5. On the Animations tab, open the **Start drop-down list** and click **After Previous**.

6. In the Delay box, click the **up increment arrow** until the setting is 01:00.

7. In the Duration box, click the **up increment arrow** until the setting is 03:00. Figure 9-12 shows the settings on the Animations tab. This animation will start one second after the previous event and will last for three seconds.

Figure 9-12

Animation settings

8. Click the **Preview** button to check the new settings.

9. With the graphic still selected, click **Add Animation**, and click **More Exit Effects**. The Add Exit Effect dialog box opens.

10. Click **Pinwheel**, and click **OK**. Notice that there are 0 and 1 icons in the upper left corner of the graphic on the slide. The 0 represents the first animation effect (the entrance) and the 1 represents the second effect (the exit).

11. Click the **1** icon to make sure that the exit effect animation is selected.

12. On the Animations tab, in the Delay box, click the **up increment arrow** until the setting is 03:00.

13. Click the **Preview** button to watch the entire animation sequence.

14. Click in the bulleted list, and on the Animations tab, click **Add Animation** and then click **Fade**. Notice that each bulleted item has a numbered icon to its left.

15. Click the **1** icon to the left of the graphic, and on the Animations tab, click **Move Later**. The exit effect moves to position 7 (after the bulleted list completes).

16. Click in the bulleted list again, and on the Animations tab, open the **Start drop-down list** and click **With Previous**. Then open the **Effect Options** button's **drop-down list** and click **By Paragraph**. The numbered icons on the slide should appear as in Figure 9-13.

Figure 9-13

The animation effects should be numbered as shown at this point

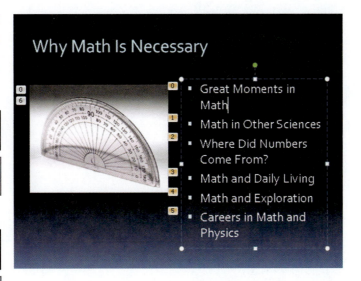

CERTIFICATION
READY **5.1.1**

How do you use more Entrance Effects?

CERTIFICATION
READY **5.1.3**

How do you use more Exit Effects?

17. Click the **Preview** button to check the new settings.

18. SAVE the presentation.

PAUSE. LEAVE the presentation open to use in the next exercise.

Using the Animation Pane

When a slide has multiple animations on it, you might find the Animation pane helpful in viewing and organizing the animations. The Animation Pane lists each of the animations associated with the active slide's content and enables you to make fine-tuning adjustments to them. From the Animation Pane you can reorder animations, adjust their settings, and see how they overlap and interact with one another. Within the Animation Pane, an animated object that consists of multiple paragraphs appears by default as a single item, so you can apply the same settings to all paragraphs. You can optionally expand that entry to a list of each individual paragraph, so you can animate them separately if you prefer. In this exercise, you use the Animation Pane to fine-tune the animation effects on a slide.

In addition to using the controls on the Animations tab on the Ribbon, you can display a dialog box for each animation by opening the animation's menu and choosing Effect Options. The name of the dialog box depends on the animation type. Within this dialog box are settings that, among other things, let you associate a sound with an animation and let you reverse the order in which a list appears. To remove an animation from the slide, select the animation either in the Animation Pane or by clicking the numbered icon to the left of the object on the slide, and then press the Delete key on the keyboard.

STEP BY STEP   **Use the Animation Pane**

USE the *Lobby Final* presentation that is still open from the previous exercise.

1. On the Animations tab, click **Animation Pane**. The Animation Pane appears at the right. It lists three animation items, as shown in Figure 9-14.

2. Click the gray bar that separates the second and third animations. The list expands to show each bulleted list item as a separate animation event. See Figure 9-15.

Figure 9-15

The bulleted list animations are expanded

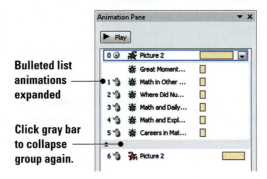

Bulleted list animations expanded

Click gray bar to collapse group again.

Take Note   When the list is expanded, each item is edited separately. If you want to change the settings for the entire list, you should collapse the list again before changing settings.

3. Click the gray bar again to collapse the animations for the bulleted list again.

4. In the Animation Pane, click the **Content Placeholder** animation, and then click the **down arrow** to its right to open its menu. On the menu, click **Effect Options**. The Fade dialog box opens.

5. Click the **Text Animation** tab.

6. Click the **In Reverse Order** check box.

7. Mark the **Automatically after** check box, and click the **up increment arrow** to set the number of seconds to 3. Figure 9-16 shows the dialog box settings.

Figure 9-16

Fine-tune the animation in this dialog box

8. Click **OK**. Notice that the Start setting on the Animations tab has changed to After Previous.

9. Click **Preview** to watch the animation for this slide.

10. Go to slide 8, and select the title placeholder. Then hold down **Shift** and click the bulleted list's text box and the additional text box below it, so all three objects are selected.

11. On the Animations tab, click **Add Animation**, and then in the Entrance section of the presets menu, click **Float In**. The same animation effect is applied to all three objects.

12. Re-select the three objects if needed and then on the Animations tab, open the **Start drop-down list** and click **With Previous**.

13. In the Animation Pane, select the animation for the title (**Title 4**) and press **Delete** to remove the animation for that object.

14. Select only the slide's title text box and then click **Add Animation**, and in the Emphasis section, click **Wave**.

15. In the Animation Pane, confirm that the Title 4 object's animation is already selected, and click the **Move Up arrow** (at the bottom of the task pane) twice to move the animation to the top of the list, so that it executes first.

16. Open the **Start drop-down list** and click **After Previous**, setting the wave animation to occur after the slide appears.

CERTIFICATION
READY   5.3.2

How do you attach a sound to
an animation?

17. On the slide, click the bottom text box (**Find out...**). Its animation becomes selected in the Animation Pane.

18. Click the arrow to the animation's right in the Animation Pane, opening its menu, and click **Effect Options**.

19. Open the **Sound drop-down list**, choose **Arrow**, and click **OK**.

20. Click the **Preview** button to preview the slide's animation.

21. On the Animations tab, click **Animation Pane** to close the pane.

22. **SAVE** the presentation.

PAUSE. LEAVE the presentation open to use in the next exercise.

CERTIFICATION
READY   5.3.4

How do you reorder
animations?

Using Animation Painter

Animation Painter enables you to select an object that already has the animation you want, including the delay, duration, sound effects, and so on, and then copy that animation to another object. Animation Painter is very much like Format Painter, but it works for animation rather than for formatting. When you click Animation Painter, the mouse pointer becomes a paintbrush. You can then navigate to any other slide (or stay on the same slide) and click another object to receive the animation settings. If you double-click Animation Painter rather than single-clicking it, it stays on until you turn it off (by clicking it again, or by pressing Esc), so you can paint the same animation onto multiple objects. In this exercise, you will copy animation from one object to another.

STEP BY STEP   **Use Animation Painter**

USE the *Lobby Final* presentation that is still open from the previous exercise.

1. On slide 8, in the Animation Pane, select the animation **Rectangle 8** (the *Find out...* text box).

2. On the Animations tab, click **Animation Painter**.

3. Go to slide 1 and click **Explore the World of Science**. The animation is copied to that text box, including the associated sound.

4. **SAVE** the presentation.

PAUSE. LEAVE the presentation open to use in the next exercise.

CERTIFICATION
READY   5.3.3

How do you use Animation
Painter?

ADDING MEDIA CLIPS TO A PRESENTATION

The Bottom Line

Audio (sound) and **video** (moving picture) clips can add interest to a presentation by drawing the audience's attention more than a static show. You can include your own audio and video clips that you have recorded or acquired on disk, or select from clips provided by Microsoft via the Clip Art task pane. You can also apply formatting styles to audio and video content, as you do for images.

Adding an Audio File to a Slide

You can add audio from files or from the Clip Organizer. You can specify when the sound will play, how loud it will be (in comparison to the overall sound level), and which user controls will be available onscreen.

You have a number of options for adding audio to a presentation:

• Use **Audio from File** if you have an audio file in a supported format that you want to insert. PowerPoint can handle AIFF, AU, MIDI, MP3, WAV, and WMA files.

• Use **Clip Art Audio** to open the Clip Art task pane and search for an audio file in the same way you searched for clip art. PowerPoint automatically selects Audio in the Results should be list and displays sounds on your system. You can use a keyword search to find specific sounds.

• Use **Record Audio** if you want to record your own audio to play on the slide. You must have a microphone to record audio.

The Audio Tools playback tab provides a number of tools for working with an audio file. You can preview the audio, set its volume for the slide show, hide the sound icon during the slide show (don't use this option if you want to be able to play the audio by clicking on it during the presentation), loop the audio so it repeats until you stop it, adjust whether the audio plays automatically or when you click it, and adjust the maximum audio file size.

In this exercise, you will add audio clips to slides using the Clip Art task pane and using an audio clip from a file.

STEP BY STEP   **Add an Audio Clip to a Slide**

USE the *Lobby Final* presentation that is still open from the previous exercise.

1. Go to slide 1, and on the Insert tab, click the arrow under the Audio button. On the menu that appears, click **Clip Art Audio**. The Clip Art task pane opens, showing audio clips available.

2. Click any of the clips that appear in the results. A sound icon appears in the center of the slide. See Figure 9-17.

Figure 9-17

An audio clip inserted on a slide

Audio clip ——

3. Press **F5** to switch to Slide Show view, and click the sound icon on the slide. The sound plays.

4. Press **Esc** to return to Normal view, and close the Clip Art task pane.

5. Select the sound icon on the slide and press **Delete** on the keyboard to remove it.

6. With slide 1 still displayed, on the Insert tab, click the arrow under the Audio button and click **Audio from File**. The Insert Audio dialog box opens.

7. Navigate to the data files for this lesson, click *Beethoven's Ninth*, and click **Insert**. An icon appears in the center of the slide.

8. Open the **Start drop-down list** and click **Automatically**.

9. Mark the **Hide During Show** check box.

10. On the Audio Tools Playback tab, click the **Volume** button, and then click **Medium**. Figure 9-18 shows the settings on the Audio Tools Playback tab.

@ The *Beethoven's Ninth.wma* file is available on the book companion website or in WileyPLUS.

Figure 9-18

Adjust the sound clip's volume,
start setting, and visibility

Hide the icon in Slide Show view. ⎯⎯⎯   ⎯⎯ **Start automatically**

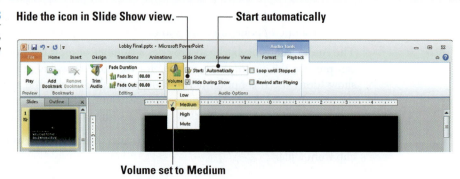

Volume set to Medium

11. View the first two slides in Slide Show view, and notice that the sound quits after the first slide. Press **Esc** to return to Normal view.

12. Select the sound icon on slide 1.

13. On the Audio Tools Playback tab, open the **Start drop-down list** and click **Play Across Slides**.

14. Watch the first several slides in Slide Show view. This time notice that the sound continues as you move from slide 1 to slide 2. Then press **Esc** to return to Normal view.

15. **SAVE** the presentation.

PAUSE. LEAVE the presentation open to use in the next exercise.

Adding a Video to a Slide

You can insert videos from files or from the Clip Art task pane to add visual interest or information to a presentation. PowerPoint 2010 has greatly improved its video support from previous versions, and it now accepts Flash videos as well as many standard formats such as Windows Media, QuickTime, and MP4.

You have three options for inserting a video on a slide:

- Use **Video from File** if you have a video file in a supported format that you want to insert. PowerPoint can handle ASF, AVI, MPEG, or WMV files.
- Use **Video from Web Site** to link to a video clip from a website, such as YouTube.
- Use **Video from Clip Organizer** to open the Clip Art task pane and search for a video file the same way searched for clip art. PowerPoint automatically selects Videos in the Results should be list and displays videos on your system. You can use a keyword search to find specific videos and search Office.com for more files.

In this exercise, you insert a video clip from a file and set it to play automatically.

STEP BY STEP   **Add a Video to a Slide**

USE the *Lobby Final* presentation that is still open from the previous exercise.

1. Go to slide 8 and click the **Insert Media Clip** icon in the empty placeholder box. See Figure 9-19. The Insert Video dialog box opens.

Figure 9-19

Click the Insert Media Clip icon
in the placeholder

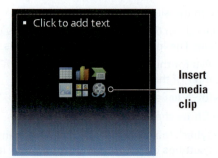

Insert
media
clip

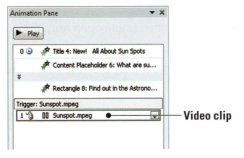 The *Sunspot.mpeg* file is available on the book companion website or in WileyPLUS.

2. Navigate to the folder containing the data files for this lesson and select *Sunspot. mpeg*. Then, click **Insert**. The clip appears in the placeholder, with playback controls beneath it. See Figure 9-20.

Figure 9-20

The video clip appears on the slide

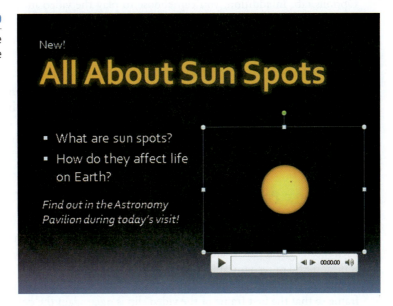

3. On the Animations tab, click **Animation Pane**. The Animation Pane opens. Notice that there is an animation event for the video clip already there, as shown in Figure 9-21.

Figure 9-21

The video clip is part of the slide's animation sequence

4. On the Video Tools Playback tab, open the **Start drop-down list** and click **Automatically**.

Take Note

Notice that a second event is added in the Animation Pane, for pausing the video clip on mouse click.

5. Close the Animation Pane.
6. On the View tab, click **From Current Slide** to watch this slide in Slide Show view.
7. SAVE the presentation.
PAUSE. LEAVE the presentation open to use in the next exercise.

Take Note

Files identified as videos in the Clip Organizer are actually more like animated clip art graphics. They tend to be relatively small and cannot be significantly enlarged without a corresponding loss of quality. But they can still provide multimedia interest on a slide.

The Video Tools Options tab provides some of the same options you find on the Audio Tools Options tab. In addition, you can choose to play the video in the full screen during the slide show and rewind it back to the first frame after it finishes playing.

Formatting Video or Audio Content

Any video clip on a slide and any audio clip that has a visible icon on a slide can be formatted with PowerPoint's built-in styles. This works just like the style-based formatting for graphic objects: You select a style from a gallery. You can then customize it as desired by applying formatting. You can also choose a frame of the video clip that will appear on the slide whenever the video clip is not playing.

Choosing a Poster Frame

A **poster frame** is an image that displays on the slide when the video clip is not actively playing. You can use an outside image, but it is often easier to select a frame from the video clip itself. Poster frames are useful because often the first frame of the video clip is not an image that is meaningful or recognizable. Instead of choosing Current Frame from the menu, as you will do in this exercise, you can choose Image from File to select your own image. To remove any poster frame so that the first frame of the video clip is once again the default image for the clip, choose Reset from the menu. In this exercise, you choose a poster frame to display for a video clip.

| STEP BY STEP | Choose a Poster Frame |

USE the *Lobby Final* presentation that is still open from the previous exercise.

1. On slide 8, click the video clip.
2. Click the **Play** button (the right-pointing triangle) below the video clip to begin its playback. When you see the image onscreen that you want to use as the poster frame, click the clip to pause it.
3. On the Video Tools Format tab, click **Poster Frame** and click **Use Current Frame**. See Figure 9-22.

Figure 9-22

Select a poster frame

4. **SAVE** the presentation.

PAUSE. LEAVE the presentation open to use in the next exercise.

Applying a Video Style and Formatting

Whereas the tools on the Video Tools Playback tab control the clip's motion effects, the tools on the Video Tools Format tab control its static appearance, including its borders, effects, and any color or contrast corrections. The tools here are very similar to those for graphic images, which you learned about in Lesson 8. In this exercise, you will apply a video style and some picture corrections.

STEP BY STEP   **Apply a Video Style and Formatting**

USE the *Lobby Final* presentation that is still open from the previous exercise.

1. On slide 8, click the video clip.

2. On the Video Tools Format tab, click the **More** button in the Video Styles group, opening the Video Styles gallery, as shown in Figure 9-23.

Figure 9-23

The Video Styles gallery

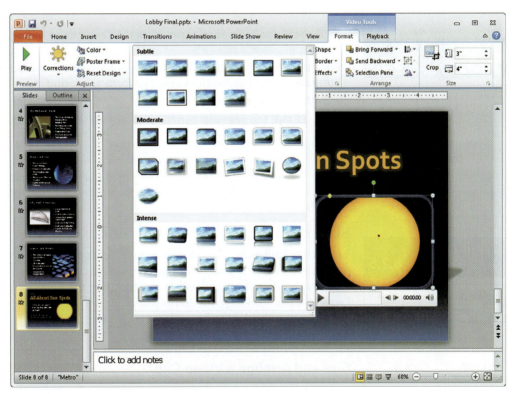

3. In the Subtle section, click the **Simple Frame, White** style. The frame of the video clip changes.

4. Click the **Video Shape** button, and on the Shapes palette that appears, click the **Rounded Rectangle**. The shape of the video clip's frame changes.

5. Click the **Video Border** button, and on the palette of colors that appears, click **Periwinkle, Accent 5, Darker 50%**.

6. Click the **Video Effects** button, point to Glow, and click **Periwinkle, 5 pt glow, Accent Color 5**.

7. Click the **Video Effects** button, point to **Shadow**, and in the Perspective section, click **Perspective Diagonal Upper Right**. Figure 9-24 shows the completed formatting. Yours may look different, depending on the image you chose for the poster frame.

Figure 9-24

The formatted clip

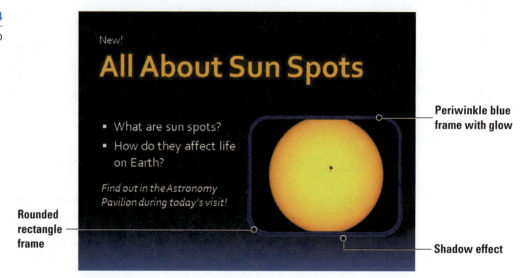

8. On the Video Tools Format tab, click the **Corrections** button, and click **Brightness: 0% (Normal), Contrast +20%**.
9. On the Slide Show tab, clear the **Show Media Controls** check box. This prevents the media controls under the video clip from appearing in Slide Show view.
10. **SAVE** the presentation.

PAUSE. LEAVE the presentation open to use in the next exercise.

CERTIFICATION READY 3.5.1

How do you apply a style to video or audio content?

Take Note
Part of the clip's appearance is the media control bar, or the thick gray bar that appears beneath the clip. If the presentation is self-running, you might prefer to hide that from the audience. To do so, clear the Show Media Controls check box on the Slide Show tab.

Sizing and Arranging Video or Audio Content

CERTIFICATION READY 8.2.5

How do you show or hide media controls?

Video clips (and audio clips that have a visible icon) can be sized and arranged like any other content on a slide. You can drag them to move or resize them or specify exact measurements. You can also align them with other content using the Align tools, which you learned about in Lesson 8 when working with drawn shapes. In this exercise, you change the size of a video clip and align it on the slide using guides.

STEP BY STEP **Size and Arrange a Video Clip**

USE the *Lobby Final* presentation that is still open from the previous exercise.

1. On slide 8, select the video clip.
2. On the Video Tools Format tab, type **3** in the **Height** box and then click away from it. The value in the Width box changes proportionally.
3. Click the video clip again to select it, if necessary.
4. On the View tab, click the **Guides** check box to turn on the guides. Drag the horizontal guide down so it aligns with the 1" mark on the vertical ruler.
5. Move the text box containing the bullets up so its upper-left corner aligns with the intersection of the guides at the left side of the slide.
6. Move the video clip so its upper-right corner aligns with the intersection of the guides at the right side of the slide. See Figure 9-25.

Figure 9-25

Use the guides to arrange the slide content

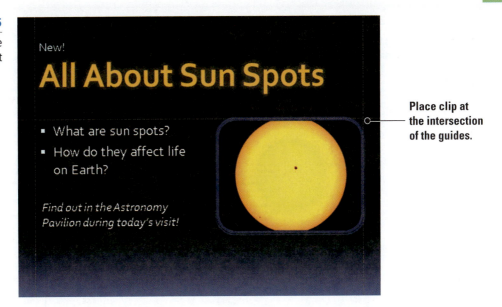

Place clip at the intersection of the guides.

Take Note   Because there is a glow around the clip's border, it may not appear to align precisely with the guides. The glow may hang slightly over the lines.

7. **SAVE** the presentation.

PAUSE. LEAVE the presentation open to use in the next exercise.

There are many ways to size and arrange audio and video clips in PowerPoint. To size a clip, you can drag one of its selection handles, enter precise measurements in the Height and Width boxes on the Video Tools Format tab, or right-click the clip and choose Size and Position to open the size controls in the Format Video dialog box.

CERTIFICATION READY 3.5.3

How do you arrange video or audio content?

To move (arrange) a clip, you can drag it where you want it, with or without the Guides and/or Gridlines to help you. You can also specify a precise position on the Position tab of the Format Video dialog box, or use the Align command on the Video Tools Format tab to align the clip with other clips or with the slide itself.

Take Note   The Align command works only if you are aligning similar objects. In the preceding exercise, you could not have aligned the text box and the video clip with one another using the Align command because when you select both objects, the Video Tools Format tab is no longer available, and that's where the Align command resides.

CERTIFICATION READY 3.5.4

How do you size video or audio content?

Compressing Media

If you plan on sharing a presentation that contains audio and video clips, you may want to compress the media in the presentation to make the overall file size smaller. This is similar to the Compress Pictures command for graphics, but it works with video and audio files. You can choose high, medium, or low quality, depending on how you plan to use the presentation file. In the following exercise, you will compress media in a presentation.

STEP BY STEP   **Compress Media**

USE the *Lobby Final* presentation that is still open from the previous exercise.

1. Click the **File** tab.

2. Under the Media Size and Performance heading, click **Compress Media**. A menu opens showing three choices for media quality. See Figure 9-26.

Figure 9-26

Compress media according to the usage you intend

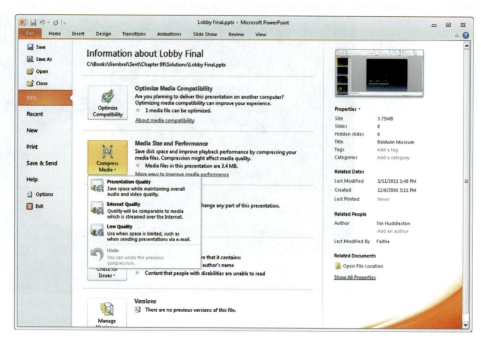

CERTIFICATION
READY   7.2.4

How do you compress media?

3. Click Internet Quality. The Compress Media dialog box opens, showing the progress of compressing each clip.

4. When each clip shows Compressed, click Close.

EXIT PowerPoint.

SKILL SUMMARY

In This Lesson You Learned How To:	Exam Objective	Objective Number
Set up slide transitions.	Modify a transition effect.	5.4.1
	Add a sound to a transition.	5.4.2
	Modify transition duration.	5.4.3
	Set up manual or automatically timed advance options.	5.4.4
Animate your slides.	Use more Entrance Effects.	5.1.1
	Use more Emphasis.	5.1.2
	Use more Exit Effects.	5.1.3
	Use more Motion Paths.	5.1.4
	Set timing.	5.2.1
	Set start option.	5.2.2
	Change the direction of an animation.	5.3.1
	Attach a sound to an animation.	5.3.2
	Use Animation Painter.	5.3.3
	Reorder animation.	5.3.4
	Select text options.	5.3.5
Add media clips to a presentation.	Apply a style to video or audio content.	3.5.1
	Adjust video or audio content.	3.5.2
	Arrange video or audio content.	3.5.3
	Size video or audio content.	3.5.4
	Adjust playback options.	3.5.5
	Show media controls.	8.2.5
	Compress media.	7.2.4

Knowledge Assessment

Matching

Match the term in Column 1 to its description in Column 2.

Column 1	Column 2
1. Exit effect	**a.** Feature that enables you to copy animation effects
2. Emphasis effect	**b.** A sound clip
3. Motion path animation	**c.** The time between the previous and the current event
4. Transition	**d.** The time that an animation event takes to execute
5. Delay	**e.** An animation effect that moves an object along a predefined path that you create for it
6. Duration	**f.** An entrance effect that applies to an entire slide
7. Animations	**g.** The Ribbon tab from which you apply motion effects to individual objects
8. Entrance effect	**h.** An animation effect that determines how an object appears on a slide
9. Animation Painter	**i.** An animation effect that determines how an object leaves a slide
10. Audio	**j.** An animation effect that draws attention to an object on a slide that is neither entering nor exiting the slide

True/False

Circle T if the statement is true or F if the statement is false.

T F 1. A transition can be applied to a specific object on a slide.

T F 2. You can assign your own sound clips to slide transitions.

T F 3. You can set up both transitions and animations from the Animations tab.

T F 4. Not all transition and animation effects have Effect Options you can set.

T F 5. An emphasis effect is a good way to draw audience attention to an object as it enters the slide.

T F 6. To reverse the order of text animation in a text box, click Effect Options and click Reverse Path Direction.

T F 7. An animation set to With Previous begins executing at the same time as the previous animation effect begins.

T F 8. To slow down the speed of an animation effect, increase its Duration setting.

T F 9. If you double-click the Animation Painter button, the feature stays on until you turn it off.

T F 10. You can insert audio and video clips from the Clip Art task pane.

Project 8-1: Make It Self-Running

You have been asked by Woodgrove Bank to modify a presentation that was originally designed to be used with a live speaker to a self-running presentation in which no user interaction is required. To accomplish this, you need to set all the slide transitions to occur automatically. You should also set up a more interesting transition effect than the default.

GET READY. LAUNCH PowerPoint if it is not already running.

@ The *Jobs* file is available on the book companion website or in WileyPLUS.

1. **OPEN** the *Jobs* presentation and save it as *Jobs Final*.
2. On the Transitions tab, mark the **After** check box.
3. Click the **up increment arrow** for the After box until the value is 00:08.00.
4. In the Transition to This Slide group, select the **Push** transition. You might need to click the **More** button to locate it.
5. Click **Effect Options**, and click **From Left**.
6. Click the **down increment arrow** for the Duration box twice to set the duration to 00.50.
7. Click **Apply to All**.
8. On the Slide Show tab, click **From Beginning**, and watch the entire slide show by clicking the mouse to advance through each slide.
9. **SAVE** the presentation.

LEAVE the presentation open for use in the next project.

Project 8-2: Animate It

You have decided to add some object animations to the Woodgrove Bank presentation to make it more eye-catching.

@ The *Jobs 2* file is available on the book companion website or in WileyPLUS.

1. **USE** the *Jobs Final* presentation from the last exercise, or **OPEN** the *Jobs 2* presentation and **SAVE** it as *Jobs Final*.
2. Go to slide 1, and select the subtitle (**Central City Job Fair**).
3. On the Animations tab, click **Add Animation**, and in the Entrance section, click **Swivel**.
4. Go to slide 2, and select the photo.
5. Click **Add Animation**, and in the Emphasis section, click **Pulse**.
6. Open the **Start drop-down list** and click **After Previous**.
7. Click the **up increment arrow** on the Duration box until the duration is 02.00.
8. Select the text box containing the bulleted list.
9. Click **Add Animation**, and click **More Entrance Effects**.
10. In the Subtle section, click **Expand**, and click **OK**.
11. Open the **Start drop-down list** on the Animations tab and click **After Previous**.
12. Click **Move Earlier**.
13. Click **Preview** to preview the slide's animation.
14. **SAVE** the presentation and **CLOSE** it.

LEAVE PowerPoint open for the next project.

Proficiency Assessment

Project 8-3: Adding Sound and Animation

You are teaching a computer basics class and have developed a slide that explains the Systems Development Life Cycle. Now you want to animate it and add some sound effects, to make it more interesting.

The *Life Cycle* file is available on the book companion website or in WileyPLUS.

1. **OPEN** the *Life Cycle* presentation and save it as *Life Cycle Final*.
2. Select all five rectangles.
3. On the Animations tab, click **Add Animation**, and select the **Grow & Turn** entrance effect.
4. Re-select all five rectangles if needed, and then open the **Start drop-down list** and choose **On Click**.
5. Display the Animation Pane.
6. Select all the animations in the Animation Pane, and then right-click any of them and click **Effect Options**.
7. Open the **sound drop-down list** and choose the **Click** sound, and then click **OK**.

The *Soundtrack. wav* file is available on the book companion website or in WileyPLUS.

8. On the Insert tab, click **Audio**. In the Insert Audio dialog box, select *Soundtrack.wav* from the data files for this lesson, and click **Insert**.
9. With the new sound's icon selected, on the Audio Tools Playback tab, mark the **Hide During Show** check box.
10. Open the **Start drop-down list** and choose **Automatically**.
11. Click the **Volume** button, and click **Low**.
12. In the Animation Pane, click the **Move Up** button until the audio clip is at the top of the list.
13. Switch to Slide Show view and click to move through the animations to check them.
14. **SAVE** the presentation and then **CLOSE** the file.

LEAVE PowerPoint open for the next project.

Project 8-4: Enhancing Video

You have been asked by the K-9 Agility Network to add a video clip of a dog agility performance to their marketing presentation. The video provided is not the best quality, but you can do some things in PowerPoint to make it better.

The *Agility* file is available on the book companion website or in WileyPLUS.

1. **OPEN** the *Agility* presentation and save it as *Agility Final*.
2. Go to slide 8, and click the **Insert Media Clip** icon in the placeholder.
3. In the Insert Video dialog box, navigate to the location of the data files for this lesson, select *AgilityRun.wmv*, and click **Insert**.
4. On the Video Tools Format tab, click **Crop**, and then drag the top and bottom selection handles on the clip to crop out the black bars at the top and bottom. Click away from the video to finalize the cropping when finished.
5. Click in the **Height** box on the Video Tools Format tab and set the height to 4.5". Let the Width setting adjust itself automatically.
6. Drag the video clip up or down on the slide to center it vertically between the slide title and the bottom of the slide.
7. Click the **Align** button, and click **Align Center** to center the video clip on the slide.
8. Click the **More** button in the Video Styles group and click **Beveled Rounded Rectangle** in the Moderate section.
9. Click the **Corrections** button, and click **Brightness: +20% Contrast: +40%**.

10. On the Slide Show tab, clear the **Show Media Controls** check box.

11. Click **From Current Slide**, and then click the clip to start it playing. Watch the clip, and then press **Esc** to return to Normal view.

12. **SAVE** the presentation and then **CLOSE** the file.

LEAVE PowerPoint open for the next project.

Mastery Assessment

Project 8-5: Animating a Drawing

You are a professional trainer teaching a class on basic computer skills. You want to make the conceptual drawings and clip art images in your presentation more interesting and fun to view. You can use PowerPoint's animation tools to achieve this.

GET READY. LAUNCH PowerPoint if it is not already running.

1. **OPEN** the *Monitor* presentation and save it as *Monitor Final*.

@ The *Monitor* file is available on the book companion website or in WileyPLUS.

2. Select the spray can graphic, and on the Animations tab, click **Add Animation** and in the Entrance section, click **Fly In**.

3. Click **Effect Options**, and click **From Right**.

4. Open the **Start drop-down list** and choose **After Previous**.

5. Click the spray can graphic again, then click **Add Animation**, and click **More Motion Paths**.

6. Click the **Arc Down** effect and click **OK**.

7. Open the **Start drop-down list** and choose **After Previous**.

8. Click **Effect Options**, and click **Reverse Path Direction**.

9. On the slide, drag the motion path to the left so that the green arrow (the start position) sits where the end position (the red arrow) previously was, where the spray can and the red circle meet. See Figure 9-27.

Figure 9-27

Move the motion path so the start arrow is over the spray can

Don't Use Glass Cleaner on a Monitor

Place starting point (green arrow) here.

Motion path line

10. Click the red circle shape, and click **Add Animation**. In the Entrance section, click **Fade**.

11. Open the **Start drop-down list** and choose **After Previous**.

12. Click the **up increment arrow** on the Delay box to set the delay to 02.00.

13. Click **Preview** to preview the animation.

14. **SAVE** the presentation and then **CLOSE** the file.

LEAVE PowerPoint open for the next project.

Project 8-6: Animating SmartArt

Northwind Paper has a presentation about how paper is made, and the presentation includes a SmartArt diagram. You will apply transitions to each slide, and animate the SmartArt diagram so that each part of the diagram appears on a separate mouse click.

GET READY. LAUNCH PowerPoint if it is not already running.

@ The *Paper Making* file is available on the book companion website or in WileyPLUS.

1. **OPEN** the *Paper Making* presentation and save it as *Paper Making Final*.
2. From the Transitions tab, apply the **Box** transition effect to all slides with a duration of 02.00.
3. Go to slide 4, and from the Animations tab, apply the **Fade** entrance effect to the SmartArt object.
4. Click **Effect Options**, and choose **One by One**.
5. Display the Animation Pane.

Take Note   Notice that there are more animation effects listed than there are boxes on the diagram; that's because the arrows that connect each box are animated along with the box to which they correspond.

6. Add an Object Color emphasis effect to the entire SmartArt diagram, and set its Start setting to **After Previous**.
7. In the Animation Pane, expand the list of the emphasis effects. Select the first two, and then click **Move Up** five times to move the selected effects after the Pulp animation.
8. Select the next two emphasis effects, and then click **Move Up** three times to place the selection after the Stock animation.
9. Select the next two emphasis effects, and then click **Move Up** once to move the selection after the Press & Dry animation.
10. Click **Preview** to preview the slide's animation.
11. Delete the color-changing emphasis effect for the Paper box (the last emphasis effect on the list).
12. Delete the color-changing emphasis effects for each of the three arrows.
13. Watch the slide's animation in Slide Show view to confirm that the mouse clicks trigger each step.
14. **SAVE** the presentation and then **CLOSE** the file.

EXIT PowerPoint.

INTERNET READY

An organization that you belong to (such as a church or club) would like to be able to use PowerPoint to show the lyrics to a song that the group sings, so people who don't know the words can sing along. Use the Internet to find the lyrics to a song that a group sings. (If you don't belong to any group that sings songs, ask a friend to suggest one.) Then create a presentation that shows the lyrics for the first verse of the song. Break up the lyrics into multiple slides, so each slide shows the text large enough for the audience to easily see from a distance.

Find an audio clip of the song being sung and place it on the first slide. Set the audio clip to play across all slides in the presentation. Manually set the timing for each slide's transition to an appropriate amount so that the lyrics appear on-screen as the audio clip is singing them. If you like, instead of manually setting the timings, you can experiment with the Rehearse Timings feature found on the Slide show tab. For an extra challenge, use emphasis animations to dim each line of the song after it has been sung.

Circling Back 2

You are a managing editor at Lucerne Publishing. You are preparing for an important meeting with the senior management team, and you are producing a presentation that should serve two purposes: to show how you intend to grow the publishing plan for the coming year and to convince senior management to let you hire several new editors. You can use PowerPoint tools to focus attention on these two goals.

Project 1: Basic Formatting and Tables

In this project, you will open your draft presentation, apply a theme, and add both a table and an Excel worksheet to present data.

GET READY. LAUNCH PowerPoint if it is not already running.

@ The *Opportunities* file is available on the book companion website or in WileyPLUS.

1. **OPEN** the *Opportunities* presentation and save it as *Opportunities Final*.
2. Apply the Origin theme. Change the theme fonts to those from the Module theme. Change the theme colors to those from the Urban theme.
3. In the header and footer, insert a date that updates automatically, slide numbers, and the footer **Editorial Opportunities**. Apply to all slides except the title slide.
4. Display the Slide Master and make these changes to the slide master (the top master, not one of the individual layout masters):
   a. Change the alignment of the date placeholder to right alignment.
   b. Boldface the slide titles.
   c. Change the color of the first-level bullet character to Indigo, Accent 1, Darker 25%. (Hint: Just change the bullet character, not the text. You can do this from the Bullets and Numbering dialog box.)
   d. Close Slide Master view.
5. Go to slide 4 and create a table that has three columns and six rows. Type the following data in the table:

Division	Current Year	Next Year
History	23	27
Science Fiction	19	23
Literature	12	16
Nonfiction	26	31
Lifestyle	38	43

6. Format the table with the **Light Style 3—Accent 1** Table Style.
7. Turn off banded rows. Select the column heading cells, fill with **Blue-Gray, Accent 6**, and change the font color to **White, Background 1**.
8. Center all entries in the center and right columns. Click the **Table Tools Layout** tab, and in the Table Size group, change the table width to 8".
9. Go to slide 3 and format the existing table to match the one you inserted on slide 4. Be sure to also change column alignment and table size.
10. Go to slide 5 and insert an Excel spreadsheet. Starting in cell A1, type the following data in the worksheet:

Division	Current Year	Next Year
History	4.65	4.89
Science Fiction	3.77	4.01
Literature	8.92	9.15
Nonfiction	4.41	4.79
Lifestyle	3.59	3.95

11. In cell A7 of the worksheet, type **Average**. In cell B7, type the formula **=AVERAGE(B2:B6)**.

12. Copy the formula in cell B7 to cell C7.

13. Format the values in cells B2:C7 as currency with two decimal places.

14. Format the worksheet as follows:

    a. Apply the Urban theme in Excel (you'll find the themes on the Page Layout tab in Excel).

    b. Select the column headers in row 1, click the **Cell Styles** button in the Styles group on the Excel Home tab, and select **Accent6**.

    c. Boldface the column headings.

    d. Center all entries in the center and right columns.

    e. Change the font of the worksheet cells to Corbel to match the text in the presentation. Change the font size to 18 pt.

    f. Adjust columns to a width of 25.

    g. Use the Borders button (in the Font group on the Home tab) to apply a default style border to all sides of all cells in the range A1:C7.

15. Adjust the size of the worksheet's hatched selection border to hide any empty rows or columns. Click outside the worksheet to deselect it.

16. Display the drawing guides and adjust them so the vertical guide aligns with the 4.5" mark on the ruler on the left side of the slide, and the horizontal guide aligns with the 2" marker on the vertical ruler at the top of the slide.

17. On slides 3, 4, and 5, reposition the tables so that their upper-left corners align with the intersection of the guides. Then turn off the guides.

18. **SAVE** the presentation.

PAUSE. LEAVE PowerPoint and your presentation open for the next project.

Project 2: Charting the Data

You are now ready to create a chart that shows the editorial workload for the current year and your projections for the next year. The chart will make it easy for your audience to compare the numbers.

USE the presentation that is open from the previous project.

1. Go to slide 6, and change the layout of the slide to Title and Content.

2. Click the **Insert Chart** icon in the content placeholder to begin a new chart. Select the clustered 3-D bar chart.

3. Insert the following data in the chart worksheet:

Division	Current Year	Next Year
History	5.8	6.8
Science Fiction	6.3	7.6
Literature	4	5.3
Nonfiction	4.3	5.2
Lifestyle	5.4	6.1

4. Delete the unneeded sample data in column D and make sure the range border surrounds only the data you need for your chart. Close the worksheet.

5. Change the chart type to a 3-D clustered column chart.

6. Format the chart as follows:

    a. Apply **Layout 4** and the **Style 18** Chart Style.

    b. Change the font size of the horizontal axis labels to 16 pt.

    c. Display the major primary horizontal axis gridlines.

    d. Turn off the data labels for both data series.

7. Drag the chart frame's bottom selection handle upward about one-half inch, to the 2" mark on the vertical ruler, to free up some room at the bottom of the slide.

8. Draw a text box below the chart and type the text *Books per editor, based on current staffing.

9. If necessary, resize the text box so that all text is on one line, and then apply a Shape Style to the text box that coordinates well with the chart.

10. **SAVE** the presentation.

PAUSE. LEAVE PowerPoint and your presentation open for the next project.

Project 3: Add Diagrams

You are ready to add SmartArt diagrams to display additional information about your organization and your department's work processes.

USE the presentation that is open from the previous project.

1. Go to slide 7 and click the **Insert SmartArt Graphic** icon in the content placeholder to start a new diagram.

2. Choose to create a hierarchy diagram that uses the Organization Chart design, and add text to the chart as follows:

   a. In the top-level box, type the name **Bill Bowen**, press **Enter**, and type the title **Managing Editor**.

   b. In the assistant box, type **Eva Corets**, press **Enter**, and type **Chief Editorial Assistant**.

   c. In the second-level boxes, type the following names, titles, and departments:

Jo Berry	Dan Bacon	Jun Cao
Sr. Editor	Sr. Editor	Sr. Editor
History	Science Fiction	Literature

3. Add a new shape after Jun Cao's shape, type the name **Aaron Con**, the title **Sr. Editor**, and the department **Nonfiction**. Then add a new shape after Aaron Con's shape, type the name **Debra Core**, the title **Sr. Editor**, and the department **Lifestyle**.

4. Apply the Insert SmartArt Style and a one of the color schemes in the Colorful category to the diagram.

5. Delete Debra Core's shape, and then change the division information for Aaron Con's shape to **Nonfiction & Lifestyle**.

6. Boldface the text in the top-level shape.

7. Go to slide 8, and convert the bulleted list to a Vertical Process diagram.

8. Apply the Inset SmartArt style and a color scheme that matches the one you used on slide 7.

9. Change the diagram layout to the Vertical Box List layout.

10. Click in the Notes pane and type **We are rolling the production preparation phase into the copyedit phase to save production time and costs**.

11. **SAVE** the presentation.

PAUSE. LEAVE PowerPoint and your presentation open for the next project.

Project 4: Insert and Format a Picture

Now insert additional visual interest in the form of a picture. You will format the picture to improve its appearance.

USE the presentation that is open from the previous project.

1. Go to slide 2, and click the **Clip Art** icon in the content placeholder to open the Clip Art task pane.

2. Use the keyword **award** to search for a photograph of a trophy. (Look only for photographs, not illustrations.) You should find several if you have a live connection to the Internet. If you do not find a silver trophy on a white background in your results, insert the picture *Award.jpg* in the placeholder.

@ The *Award.jpg* file is available on the book companion website or in WileyPLUS.

3. Adjust the picture's brightness to +10% and contrast to +20%.

4. Apply the **Perspective Shadow, White** Picture Style, and then click **Picture Border** and select a different border color, such as **Teal, Accent 2, Darker 25%**.

5. Move the picture down so that it aligns at the bottom with the last line of text in the text placeholder. (Use a guide to help you. If you can't get the picture to align precisely with the guide, try holding down the Alt key as you drag it.)

6. Compress pictures in the presentation to the Screen setting.

7. **SAVE** the presentation.

PAUSE. LEAVE PowerPoint and your presentation open for the next project.

Project 5: Add a Drawing and Finalize the Presentation

You have been asked to suggest a new office layout to reorganize departments on the production floor. You can create a simple drawing to show the areas where each department, supporting personnel, and production will be placed.

USE the presentation that is open from the previous project.

1. Add a new slide after slide 7 with the Title Only layout. Type the slide title **Revised Office Layout**.

2. Create the drawing objects shown in Figure 1. You can choose your own sizes for objects, but they should be similar in scale to the ones shown.

Figure 1

Create these shapes

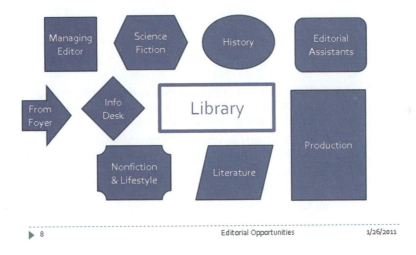

3. Modify your drawing as follows:

   a. Make all the department objects—the shapes for Nonfiction & Lifestyle, Literature, Science Fiction, and History—the same dimensions, even though they are different shapes; that is, they should all be the same height and width. For example, the ones in Figure 1 are 1.25" high and 1.8" wide. Make sure all text displays without breaking after resizing.

   b. Align the *Info Desk* and *Library* shapes to the middle of the block arrow. These three shapes will create a central area for the layout and should all be aligned middle with one another.

   c. Rotate the *Editorial Assistants* shape 90 degrees to the right so it is taller than it is wide. The text is now rotated, too.

   d. Use the Text Direction tool on the Home tab to rotate the text 270 degrees so it is once again running in its normal direction. Widen the shape slightly if needed to make the word Assistants fit on one line.

e. Align the *Managing Editor, Science Fiction, History,* and *Editorial Assistants* shapes by their tops. Align the *Nonfiction Lifestyle, Literature,* and *Production* shapes by their bottoms. Align the *Editorial Assistants* and *Production* shapes by their right sides.

f. Distribute the top four shapes horizontally. Distribute the bottom three shapes horizontally.

g. Make any other adjustments you think necessary to improve the look of the layout.

4. Apply colors and effects or Shape Styles to the shapes as desired to improve its appearance. Give each shape a unique look. Figure 2 shows one possible result.

Figure 2

Format each shape differently

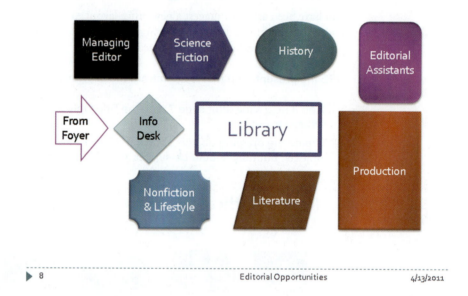

5. Select all objects in the drawing and group them. Right-click any shape in the group and click **Size and Position**. In the Size and Position dialog box, click **Lock aspect ratio** to select it, and scale the group object to 95% of its original size.

6. If the text in any of the shapes runs over after scaling, click the shape in the group to select it and slightly widen the shape size or reduce the font size to fit the text.

7. Center the object horizontally on the slide.

8. Select any slide transition (except None), choose 01.50 as the Duration, and apply it to all slides.

9. Apply animations as follows:

a. On slide 2, apply a built-in fade transition to display the bullet items by first-level paragraphs. Then modify this animation to occur **After Previous**. Set the duration to 01.00 for each bullet point's entrance.

b. Animate the organization chart on slide 7 to fade into view After Previous. Use the Effect Options dialog box to specify that the graphic displays By level one by one.

c. Click the group on slide 8 to select it, and then apply the Diamond entrance animation starting After Previous.

d. Apply a Lighten emphasis effect to the text box at the bottom of slide 6. Set it to occur After Previous, and set the Duration to 02.00.

10. Run the presentation in Slide Show view. Then return to Normal view and make any corrections you think necessary to the animations.

11. **PRINT** the presentation as handouts in grayscale mode.

12. **SAVE** and **CLOSE** the presentation.

EXIT PowerPoint.

Securing and Sharing a Presentation 10

LESSON SKILL MATRIX

Skill	Exam Objective	Objective Number
Working with Comments	Insert and edit comments.	6.1.1
	Show or hide markup.	6.1.2
	Move to the previous or next comment.	6.1.3
	Delete comments.	6.1.4
Merging Changes from Multiple Copies of a Presentation	Compare and combine presentations.	6.2.2
Protecting a Presentation	Set a password.	7.4.1
	Change a password.	7.4.2
	Mark a presentation as final.	7.4.3
Saving a Presentation in Different Formats	Save the presentation as a picture presentation.	7.1.1
	Save the presentation as a PDF.	7.1.2
	Save the presentation as an XPS.	7.1.3
	Save the presentation as an outline.	7.1.4
	Save the presentation as an OpenDocument.	7.1.5
	Save the presentation as a show (.ppsx).	7.1.6
	Save a slide or object as a picture file.	7.1.7
Creating a Video	Create video.	7.2.2

KEY TERMS

- comment
- encrypting
- Mark as Final
- markup
- OpenDocument
- password
- PDF
- picture presentation
- platform-independent
- PowerPoint Show
- Rich Text Format (rtf)
- Windows Movie Video (wmv)
- XPS
- XPS Viewer

You are the Human Resources Director for Contoso, Ltd., a large company that manufactures automotive parts. You must give a 30-minute presentation to senior management and prominent shareholders during the company's annual operations review. You have asked a colleague to give you some feedback, and she has inserted comments that you need to address. You will add some comments of your own before finalizing the presentation and share them with the Vice President for Operations, who has promised to look over the slides before you present them. You can use PowerPoint to handle chores such as viewing and working with comments, password-protecting a file, comparing and combining versions, and saving the presentation in different formats for the various audiences that will be reviewing it, including a video format for people who might not have PowerPoint at all.

SOFTWARE ORIENTATION

Microsoft PowerPoint's Review Tab

Tools on the Review tab make it easy for you to add comments to a slide and apply protection to the presentation. Figure 10-1 shows the Review tab.

Figure 10-1

The Review tab

Besides allowing you to add comments, the Review tab lets you check spelling, access references such as encyclopedias, use a thesaurus, translate a word or phrase, or set the current language.

WORKING WITH COMMENTS

The Bottom Line

A **comment** is a note you insert on a slide. You can insert comments on slides to suggest content changes, add reminders, or solicit feedback. Use comments on your own presentations or on presentations you are reviewing for others. You can also let other people review your presentations and add comments addressed to you. PowerPoint's Review tab makes it easy to view, insert, edit, and delete comments.

Viewing Comments

Use the Show Markup button on the Review tab to show or hide comments. (**Markup** refers to both comments and marked changes in the file, but in this section we deal only with comments.) The Next and Previous buttons make it easy to jump from comment to comment in a presentation. In this exercise, you view the comments in a presentation.

View Comments

The *HR Review* file is available on the book companion website or in WileyPLUS.

GET READY. Before you begin these steps, make sure that your computer is on. Log on, if necessary.

1. **START** PowerPoint, if the program is not already running.
2. Locate and open the *HR Review* presentation and save it as *HR Review Final*.
3. Note the small comment marker in the upper-left corner of the slide, as shown in Figure 10-2.

Figure 10-2

A comment marker indicates a comment on the slide

Comment marker

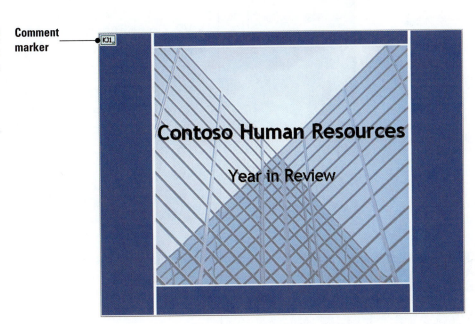

4. Click the **Review** tab, and then click **Show Markup**. The comment marker is hidden.
5. Click **Show Markup** again to redisplay the comment marker.
6. Rest the mouse pointer on the comment marker to display the comment, as shown in Figure 10-3.

Figure 10-3

View the comment by pointing at its marker

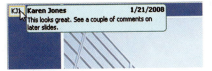

7. Move the mouse pointer away from the comment marker, and on the Review tab, click **Next**. The comment redisplays.
8. Click the **Next** button again to go to the second comment by Karen Jones. Ms. Jones suggests adjusting the diagram.

9. Click the **SmartArt diagram**, click the **SmartArt Tools Design** tab, click the **More** button in the SmartArt Styles group, and click **Intense Effect.** Click **Change Colors**, and click **Gradient Loop-Accent 6**. The diagram now has the "pop" Ms. Jones suggested, as shown in Figure 10-4.

Figure 10-4

The revised diagram

**CERTIFICATION
READY   6.1.2**

How do you show and hide markup?

10. Click the **Review** tab, and then click the **Next** button to go to the next comment by Karen Jones.
11. Click the **Previous** button twice to return to the first comment on slide 1.
12. **SAVE** the presentation.

PAUSE. LEAVE the presentation open to use in the next exercise.

**CERTIFICATION
READY   6.1.3**

How do you move to the previous or next comment?

Comments are identified by the initials of the user who entered them. When you display a comment, the full name of the person who inserted the comment displays, along with the date on which the comment was inserted.

When you open a presentation that has comments inserted, the comment markers are visible by default. If you do not want to see the comment markers as you work, you can click the Show Markup button on the Review tab to hide the markers.

Inserting a Comment

To add a comment to a slide, use the New Comment button on the Review tab. Comment markers are color-coded, so that if more than one reviewer adds comments, it is easy for you to identify the commenter simply by color. Comments are numbered consecutively as they are inserted, regardless of the order of slides. If you insert your first comment on slide 5, it will be numbered 1. If you insert your second comment on slide 1, it will be numbered 2. In this exercise, you will insert a comment in a presentation.

STEP BY STEP   **Insert a Comment**

USE the *HR Review Final* presentation that is still open from the previous exercise. You are now ready to add your own comments to the presentation, which you are going to send to the Vice President for Operations.

1. Click the **File** tab, and click **Options**. The PowerPoint Options dialog box opens.
2. In the PowerPoint Options dialog box, enter your own name and initials in the User Name and Initials boxes (see Figure 10-5). Then click **OK** to accept them.

Figure 10-5

Specify the name and initials to be associated with the comments you will enter

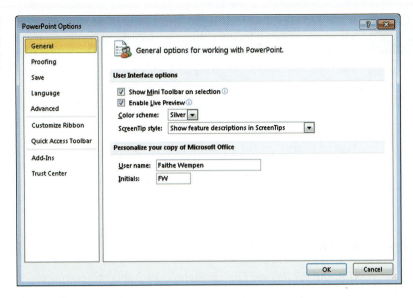

3. With slide 1 displayed, click the **New Comment** button on the Review tab. A new comment box opens, as shown in Figure 10-6.

Figure 10-6

A new comment box ready for you to type a comment

Take Note   Notice that the box color for your comments is different from that used for Karen Jones's comments.

4. Key the following text in the comment box:

   Peter, I have already received feedback from Karen Jones. Please suggest any further changes you think necessary to make this a dynamite presentation.

5. Click outside the comment box to close it. Your comment marker should display on the slide slightly overlapping Karen Jones's comment marker.

6. Go to slide 10, and then click the **New Comment** button.

7. Key the following text in the comment box:

   Peter, please see Karen's comment on this slide. I don't have access to Design Dept. schedules. Can you confirm the lag time is now only 4 to 5 weeks?

8. Click outside the comment box to close it.

9. **SAVE** the presentation.

PAUSE. LEAVE the presentation open to use in the next exercise.

CERTIFICATION
R E A D Y   **6.1.1**

How do you insert a comment
on a slide?

If no object is selected when you insert a comment, the comment marker appears in the upper-left corner of the slide. If an object is selected, the comment marker appears next to the selected object. You can also drag a comment marker anywhere on a slide. Moving a comment marker allows you to associate the comment with a specific area of the slide, such as a picture or a bullet item.

Editing a Comment

Like any other text in a presentation, comment text should be clear and concise. If you find upon review that your comments do not convey the information they should, you can reword, insert, or delete text in the comment box. Use the Edit Comment button to open a comment box so you can modify the text. In this exercise, you edit a comment.

STEP BY STEP   **Edit a Comment**

USE the *HR Review Final* presentation that is still open from the previous exercise.

1. Go to slide 1, click your comment marker, and then click the **Edit Comment** button on the Review tab. The comment box opens for editing, as shown in Figure 10-7.

Figure 10-7

Open the comment box for
editing

2. Select the text *to make this a dynamite presentation* at the end of the second sentence, and press **Delete**. You have removed text from the comment.

Another Way
Right-click the
comment you want to edit,
then select Edit Comment from
the shortcut menu.

3. Click outside the comment box to close it.
4. **SAVE** the presentation.

PAUSE. LEAVE the presentation open to use in the next exercise.

CERTIFICATION
R E A D Y   **6.1.1**

How do you edit comments?

If you rest the pointer on a comment marker or click it, you can read the text but cannot edit it. You must use the Edit Comment button, or double-click the comment, to open the comment box for editing.

Deleting a Comment

You can easily remove comments from slides when they are no longer needed. If you simply click the Delete button on the Review tab, PowerPoint removes the currently selected comment. Click the Delete button's drop-down arrow for other delete options: You can delete the current comment, delete all comments (markup) on the current slide, or delete all comments throughout the presentation. In this exercise, you will delete a comment.

STEP BY STEP **Delete a Comment**

USE the *HR Review Final* presentation that is still open from the previous exercise.

1. With slide 1 displayed, right-click Karen Jones's first comment, then click **Delete Comment** on the shortcut menu. The comment is removed from the slide, leaving only your first comment.

CERTIFICATION
READY **6.1.4**

How do you delete comments?

2. Go to slide 9, click the comment, and then click the **Review** tab if necessary.
3. Click the **Delete** button. The comment is removed from the slide.
4. **SAVE** the presentation.

PAUSE. LEAVE the presentation open to use in the next exercise.

MERGING CHANGES FROM MULTIPLE COPIES OF A PRESENTATION

The Bottom Line

When multiple people make changes on their own copies of a presentation, there is no longer a master copy that incorporates everyone's comments and changes. You can create one integrated copy that contains all changes by comparing and combining presentations.

Comparing and Combining Presentations

Comparing presentations enables you to see the differences between two similar presentation files. You can easily identify the changes that have been made to a copy of a presentation. The Compare feature merges two presentation files. You then can use the Revisions pane and the Compare group on the Review tab to see what differences exist between the merged versions, and either accept or reject each revision. When you mark a revision for acceptance or rejection, the change is not applied immediately; changes occur only when you click End Review. In this exercise, you compare and combine two presentations.

STEP BY STEP **Compare and Combine Presentations**

USE the *HR Review Final* presentation that is still open from the previous exercise.

The *HR Summary* file is available on the book companion website or in WileyPLUS.

1. On the Review tab, click **Compare**. The Choose File to Merge with Current Presentation dialog box opens.
2. Navigate to the folder containing the data files for this lesson and select *HR Summary* (see Figure 10-8).

Figure 10-8

Select the presentation to merge with the current one

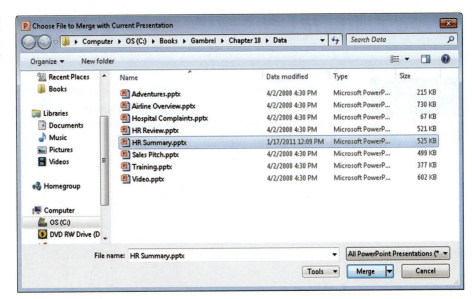

3. Click **Merge**. The Revisions task pane opens, and the first slide appears that contains revisions (slide 3).

4. If the revision details do not appear, click the item in the Slide Changes section of the Revisions task pane. A box appears adjacent to the slide showing the changes that have been made. There were two changes: a deletion and an insertion, as shown in Figure 10-9.

Figure 10-9

Review the changes made to this slide

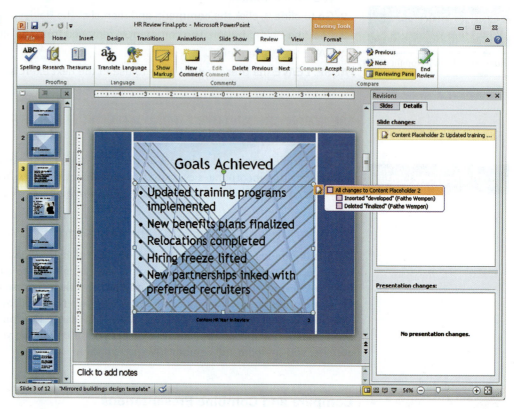

5. On the Review tab, click the **Accept** button.

6. Click the **Next** button in the Compare group. The next revision appears. It is a change from 12% to 10%.

Take Note   Do not confuse the Next button in the Compare group with the Next button in the Comments group.

7. Click the **Accept** button, and then click **Next**. The next revision appears. It is a deletion of a bullet point. Click **Accept**; then click **Reject** to change your mind.

8. Click **Next**. A message appears that you have reached the end of the changes. Click **Cancel**.

9. On the Review tab, click **End Review**. A confirmation box appears; click **Yes**.

10. Browse through the presentation to confirm that the changes were made. The revisions you accepted were finalized, and the revision you rejected was discarded.

11. SAVE the presentation.

PAUSE. LEAVE the presentation open to use in the next exercise.

CERTIFICATION READY   6.2.2

How do you compare and combine presentations?

Take Note   Comments appear as revisions in the Revisions pane, but are not affected by the process of accepting or rejecting revisions.

PROTECTING A PRESENTATION

The Bottom Line

Password-protecting a presentation file ensures that unauthorized users cannot view or make changes to it. You can set, change, and remove passwords from a file. You can also mark a presentation as final, which doesn't provide much security, but can prevent accidental changes.

Setting a Password

A **password** is a word or phrase that you, the user, must enter in order to get access to a file. Adding a password to a presentation prevents anyone from opening the presentation who does not know the password. Passwords are case-sensitive. You will assign a password to a presentation in this exercise.

STEP BY STEP   **Set a Password**

USE the *HR Review Final* presentation that is still open from the previous exercise.

1. Click the **File** tab, and click **Protect Presentation**. A menu appears.
2. Click **Encrypt with Password**. The Encrypt Document dialog box opens.
3. In the Password box, type **ProtectMe**. Black circles appear in place of the actual characters you type. See Figure 10-10.

Figure 10-10

The Encrypt Document dialog box

Take Note   The password used for this exercise is not a very strong password. It would not be that difficult to guess, because it consists only of letters. When creating your own passwords, try to include a combination of uppercase letters, lowercase letters, numbers, symbols, and spaces.

4. Click **OK**. Another dialog box appears asking you to confirm the password; type **ProtectMe** again and click **OK** again.
5. Click the **File** tab, and click **Close**. When prompted to save your changes, click **Save**.
6. Click the **File** tab, and on the Recent list, click the **HR Review Final.pptx** document. A Password dialog box opens.
7. In the Password box, type **ProtectMe** and click **OK**. See Figure 10-11.

Figure 10-11

The Password dialog box

8. **SAVE** the presentation.

PAUSE. LEAVE the presentation open to use in the next exercise.

Password-protecting a file, also called **encrypting**, prevents a presentation from being opened by unauthorized users. Password-protection might be useful on a presentation that contains sensitive data, such as human resources or medical information. If a user does not know the password, he or she cannot open the file.

Another Way

If you want to prevent a file from being changed, but you don't mind it being opened by anyone, you can set the password in a different way. Click the File tab and click Save As, and then at the bottom of the Save As dialog box, click Tools to open a menu, and click General Options. In the dialog box that appears, there are boxes for Password to Open (which is the same as the password you learned to set in the preceding steps) and Password to Modify. If you set a Password to Modify here, anyone will be able to open the file, but only those who know the password will be able to make and save changes.

CERTIFICATION READY   7.4.1

How do you set a password?

When choosing a password, try to think of one that is easy for you to remember but difficult for others to guess. For example, you might use the name of a family pet with a number substituted for one or more of the characters, or a combination of the street name and ZIP code you had as a child.

Changing or Removing a Password

You can change a password in much the same way as you created it. To remove a password entirely, use the same process as for changing it, but change it to a *null string* (blank, no characters, not even spaces). In this exercise, you will remove a password from a presentation.

STEP BY STEP   Change or Remove a Password

USE the *HR Review Final* presentation that is still open from the previous exercise.

1. Click the **File** tab, and click **Protect Presentation**. A menu appears.
2. Click **Encrypt with Password**. The Encrypt Document dialog box opens. The password previously assigned is already filled in.
3. Double-click the current password and press the **Delete** key on the keyboard to clear it.

Take Note   In step 3, you could have entered a different password instead of removing the password entirely.

CERTIFICATION READY   7.4.2

How do you change a password?

---

4. Click **OK**. The password has been removed.
5. Close the presentation and reopen it to confirm that no password prompt appears.

PAUSE. **LEAVE** the presentation open to use in the next exercise.

Marking a Presentation as Final

When you have completed all work on a presentation, you can mark it as final to prevent any further editing. When you use the **Mark as Final** command in a presentation, you can open the presentation and read it, but you can no longer edit it or add comments. You are also restricted in other activities, such as encrypting the document. For this reason, marking a presentation as final should be one of your last tasks when finalizing a presentation. In this exercise, you mark a presentation as final.

STEP BY STEP   Mark a Presentation as Final

USE the *HR Review Final* presentation that is still open from the previous exercise.

1. Click the **File** tab, click **Protect Presentation**, and click **Mark as Final**. A confirmation box appears that it will be marked as final and then saved.
2. Click **OK** to continue. A confirmation box appears that it has been marked as final.
3. Click **OK** to close the confirmation box.
4. Click the **Home** tab. Notice that the Ribbon is missing; instead, an information bar appears with a message that the file is *Marked as Final*, as shown in Figure 10-12.

Figure 10-12

The presentation has been marked as final

Information bar

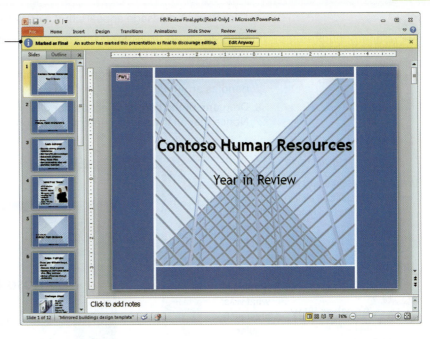

Figure 10-12

The presentation has been marked as final

Information bar

5. Click **Edit Anyway**. The Ribbon and editing capabilities are restored.

PAUSE. LEAVE the presentation open to use in the next exercise.

Marking a presentation as final does not prevent you from ever making additional changes to a presentation. You can reverse the Mark as Final command by clicking Edit Anyway on the information bar. All features are then available to you again.

SAVING AS A PRESENTATION IN DIFFERENT FORMATS

The Bottom Line

You can share your work in PowerPoint with others who do not have PowerPoint 2010 by saving it in different formats. Each format is suited for a different usage; you choose the best one for your situation.

Saving a Picture Presentation

A **picture presentation** looks, on the surface, the same as any other PowerPoint presentation. When you save as a picture presentation, however, PowerPoint saves each slide as a graphic, and then replaces the slide's content with that graphic. This can be useful in cases where you want to copy individual slides into other applications as graphics, for example. In this exercise, you save a presentation as a picture presentation.

STEP BY STEP **Save As a Picture Presentation**

USE the *HR Review Final* presentation that is still open from the previous exercise.

1. Click the **File** tab, click **Save As**.
2. Open the **Save as type drop-down list** and click **PowerPoint Picture Presentation**.
3. In the File name box, type **Pictures**.

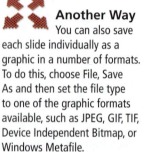 The *Pictures* file is available on the book companion website or in WileyPLUS.

4. Click **Save**. A message appears that a copy has been saved.
5. Click **OK**.
6. Open *Pictures.pptx.*
7. Click the background of slide 1. Notice that the entire slide appears with selection handles around it.
8. Drag one of the corner selection handles inward, decreasing the size of the image. Notice that all the slide's content is a graphic placed on a blank slide (see Figure 10-13).

Figure 10-13

In a picture presentation, each slide is a graphic on a plain slide background

Another Way
You can also save each slide individually as a graphic in a number of formats. To do this, choose File, Save As and then set the file type to one of the graphic formats available, such as JPEG, GIF, TIF, Device Independent Bitmap, or Windows Metafile.

Blank slide behind the graphic

Graphic of what was previously regular slide content

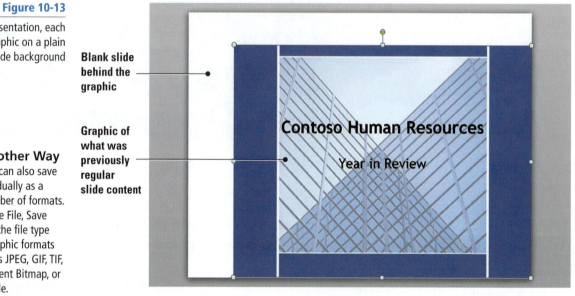

CERTIFICATION READY   7.1.1

How do you save a picture presentation?

9. **CLOSE** *Pictures.pptx* without saving the changes to it.

PAUSE. LEAVE *HR Review Final.pptx* open to use in the next exercise.

Saving a Presentation in PDF or XPS Format

PDF and XPS are page layout formats. They each create **platform-independent** files that can be displayed on any computer system that has a reader for the format, and the files will display and print exactly the same way on any system or any printer. Page layout formats like XPS and PDF are great for situations in which you want the content to be uneditable. People can see the content exactly as you designed it, but cannot modify it. These formats also work well for situations in which you are not sure which applications your audience may have installed, or even what platform (Windows, Macintosh, etc.) they might be using. In this exercise, you save a presentation as an XPS file.

STEP BY STEP   **Save a Presentation as an XPS File**

USE the *HR Review Final* presentation that is still open from the previous exercise.

1. Click the **File** tab, and click **Save & Send**.
2. Click **Create PDF/XPS Document** in the File Types list of the Save & Send pane.
3. Click the **Create PDF/XPS** button on the right side of the pane (see Figure 10-14). The Publish as PDF or XPS dialog box opens.

Figure 10-14

Choose to create a PDF or XPS
document

Figure 10-14

Choose to create a PDF or XPS
document

4. Navigate to the folder where you store files for this lesson.
5. Open the **Save as type drop-down list** and click **XPS Document**.
6. In the File name box, type **HR XPS**.
7. Click **Options**. The Options dialog box opens, as shown in Figure 10-15.

Figure 10-15

The Options dialog box

8. Mark the **Frame slides** check box to add an outline frame around each picture.
9. Clear the **Document properties** check box so that the XPS file does not include the document properties.
10. Click **OK**. You return to the Publish as PDF or XPS dialog box.
11. Click **Publish**. The presentation opens in the **XPS Viewer** utility. This utility comes free with Windows Vista and higher versions.

Troubleshooting If you do not have the XPS Viewer utility, you can download it free from Microsoft.com.

12. Scroll through the presentation in the XPS Viewer, and then **CLOSE** the XPS Viewer window.

PAUSE. LEAVE the *HR Review Final* presentation file open to use in the next exercise.

XPS is a Microsoft page layout format, and XPS documents can only be viewed using the XPS Viewer utility. This utility comes free with Windows Vista and Windows 7, and is available for free download from Microsoft for other operating systems. **PDF** is an Adobe page layout format, and can be viewed using a free utility called Adobe Reader (available for most operating systems) or a full-featured commercial program called Adobe Acrobat. PDF and XPS are roughly equivalent in their functionality; choose which one to use based on what software you think your target audience has.

CERTIFICATION
READY   **7.1.2**

How do you save a presentation in PDF format?

CERTIFICATION
READY   **7.1.3**

How do you save a presentation in XPS format?

Saving a Presentation as an Outline

The text from a presentation can be exported as a text-only outline that you can open in Word, or in any application that supports the **Rich Text Format (rtf)** file type. Rich text format is a generic file format that is compatible with almost all word-processing programs. Exporting text as an outline can be useful if you need to repurpose the text from a presentation for a different situation, say using the headings from a presentation as the basis for a report. In this exercise, you save a presentation as an outline.

STEP BY STEP   **Save a Presentation as an Outline**

USE the *HR Review Final* presentation that is still open from the previous exercise.

1. Click the **File** tab, and click **Save As**.
2. Open the **Save as type drop-down list** and click **Outline/RTF**.
3. In the File name box, type **Outline**.
4. Click **Save**. The file is saved.
5. In Windows, navigate to the location where you saved the Outline.rtf file, and double-click it to open it in the application set as the default for RTF files on your system. (This is probably Microsoft Word.)
6. Switch to **Outline** view in the application. (In Word, the command is View, Outline.) Figure 10-16 shows the file opened in Word and displayed in Outline view.

Figure 10-16

The exported outline opened in Word 2010

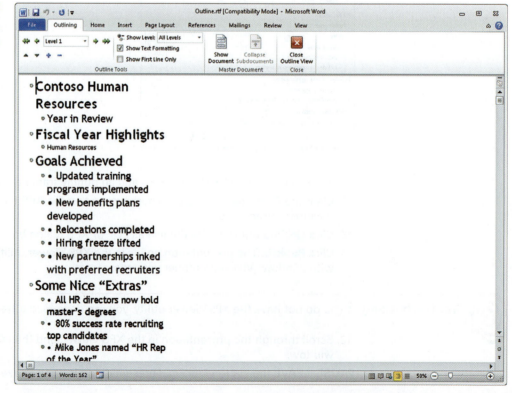

Another Way
Another way to export an outline to Word is to click the File tab, click Save & Send, click Create Handouts, and click the Create Handouts button. Then in the Send to Microsoft Word dialog box shown in Figure 10-17, click Outline Only and click OK.

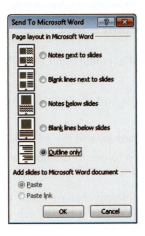

Figure 10-17

Send to Microsoft Word is another way of exporting text as an outline

7. Scroll through the outline to review how it was exported. Then close the application.

PAUSE. LEAVE the presentation file open to use in the next exercise.

Text exported as an outline from PowerPoint does not include text in manually-placed text boxes, or text typed into shapes. Therefore, be careful not to lose essential content when exporting as an outline. You may need to edit the outline afterwards in Word or another word processing program to add important text back in.

Saving a Presentation as an OpenDocument Presentation

OpenDocument is a standard format that many applications, including free Office suites online such as OpenOffice, use to ensure compatibility between programs. If you are going to share PowerPoint files with others who may use one of these applications, you may want to save your work in OpenDocument format. Some of the features of PowerPoint 2010 may not translate to the OpenDocument version, such as certain transitions and object types. In most cases, special object types will be converted to regular graphics when saved in OpenDocument format, such as SmartArt. In this exercise, you save a presentation in OpenDocument format.

STEP BY STEP **Save a Presentation in OpenDocument Format**

USE the *HR Review Final* presentation that is still open from the previous exercise.

1. Click the **File** tab, and click **Save As**.
2. Open the **Save as type drop-down list** and click **OpenDocument Presentation.**
3. In the File name box, type **HR Open**.
4. Click **Save**. A warning appears, stating that the file may contain features that are not compatible with this format.
5. Click **Yes** to confirm. The file is saved.

PAUSE. LEAVE the presentation file open to use in the next exercise.

After completing this exercise, if time permits, you may want to experiment with opening the file in different open-source applications such as Google docs (http://www.google.com/google-d-s/presentations) or Open Office (http://www.openoffice.org).

Saving a Presentation as a PowerPoint Show

A **PowerPoint Show** file is just a regular presentation file except that it opens in Slide Show view by default. You may want to distribute a presentation in this format if you expect your recipients to have PowerPoint installed on their PCs, but to be more interested in viewing the show than in editing it. In this exercise, you save a presentation as a PowerPoint Show.

STEP BY STEP   **Save a Presentation as a PowerPoint Show**

USE the *HR Review Final* presentation that is still open from the previous exercise.

1. Click the **File** tab, and click **Save As**.
2. Open the **Save as type drop-down list** and click **PowerPoint Show**.
3. In the File name box, type **HR Show**.
4. Click **Save**. The file is saved in that format, and the new file is open in PowerPoint.

PAUSE. LEAVE the presentation file open to use in the next exercise.

When you save as a PowerPoint Show, nothing changes about the presentation except its file extension: instead of .pptx, it is .ppsx. This differing extension prompts PowerPoint to open the file in Slide Show view, rather than Normal view.

Saving a Slide or Object as a Picture

You can export individual slides or objects as pictures. In the case of a slide, the entire slide becomes a graphic, which you can then use in any application that accepts graphics. In the case of an object, that individual object is saved as a graphic in any of a variety of formats you choose. In this exercise, you save a slide as a picture.

STEP BY STEP   **Save a Slide or Object as a Picture**

USE the *HR Review Final* presentation that is still open from the previous exercise.

1. Go to slide 3.
2. Click the **File** tab, and click **Save As**.
3. Open the **Save as type drop-down list** and click **JPEG File Interchange Format**.
4. In the File name box, type **Goals Achieved**.
5. Click **Save**. A dialog box prompts you to choose whether to save every slide or only the current slide. See Figure 10-18.

Figure 10-18

Choose to export the current slide or all slides as graphics

6. Click **Current Slide Only**. The current slide is saved as a graphic with the name you specified.
7. Go to slide 4.
8. Right-click the photo and click **Save as Picture**. The Save As Picture dialog box opens.
9. In the File name box, type **Businessman**.
10. Navigate to the folder where you are storing the files for this lesson. (By default your Pictures folder appears.)
11. Click **Save**. That photo is saved as a separate graphic.

PAUSE. LEAVE the presentation file open to use in the next exercise.

Another Way
You can also copy and paste photos from PowerPoint into your favorite graphics program.

Saving objects as graphics enables you to export specific content from PowerPoint for use in other applications. For example, you can use PowerPoint to store photos, and then export them as separate graphics whenever you need one of them.

CREATING A VIDEO

The Bottom Line

You can create a video from a PowerPoint presentation that can then be shared with people who don't have PowerPoint, but who do have some type of application that plays video clips.

Creating a Video

Videos are a great way to distribute self-running presentations to people who don't have PowerPoint. PowerPoint creates videos in **Windows Movie Video (wmv)** format, a common video format that most applications support. You can distribute videos on websites, via email, or on CD-ROM. In this exercise, you will make a video from a presentation.

STEP BY STEP   **Create a Video**

USE the *HR Review Final* presentation that is still open from the previous exercise.

1. Click the File tab, and click Save & Send.
2. Click Create a Video. The Create a Video controls appear in Backstage view. See Figure 10-19.

Figure 10-19

Set the options for creating a video

3. Click the up increment arrow on the Seconds to spend on each slide text box until the setting is 10:00.
4. Click Create Video. The Save As dialog box opens.
5. In the File name box, type HR Video.
6. Navigate to the location where you are storing the files for this lesson.
7. Click Save. The video is created. A progress bar in the status bar shows the creation. Wait until the creation is complete before going on to the next step.
8. CLOSE PowerPoint, saving your changes to the presentation file.
9. In Windows, navigate to the folder containing the video and double-click the video clip to play it in your default application for video clips (probably Windows Media Player).

SKILL SUMMARY

In This Lesson You Learned How To:	Exam Objective	Objective Number
Work with comments.	Insert and edit comments.	6.1.1
	Show or hide markup.	6.1.2
	Move to the previous or next comment.	6.1.3
	Delete comments.	6.1.4
Merge changes from multiple copies of a presentation.	Compare and combine presentations.	6.2.2
Protect a presentation.	Set a password.	7.4.1
	Change a password.	7.4.2
	Mark a presentation as final.	7.4.3
Save a presentation in different formats.	Save the presentation as a picture presentation.	7.1.1
	Save the presentation as a PDF.	7.1.2
	Save the presentation as an XPS.	7.1.3
	Save the presentation as an outline.	7.1.4
	Save the presentation as an OpenDocument.	7.1.5
	Save the presentation as a show (.ppsx).	7.1.6
	Save a slide or object as a picture file.	7.1.7
Create a video.	Create video.	7.2.2

Knowledge Assessment

Fill in the Blank

Fill in each blank with the term or phrase that best completes the statement.

1. A(n) _____ is a note you can insert directly on a slide.

2. When you compare and _____ presentations, you consolidate all changes into a single copy.

3. A(n) _____ encrypts a presentation file so that only authorized users can open it.

4. To make changes to a comment, click the comment marker and then click the _____ button on the Review tab.

5. A(n) _____ presentation converts each slide to a graphic and places the graphics on blank slide backgrounds.

6. PowerPoint saves in page layout formats including XPS and _____.

7. _____ Text Format is a common word processing format to which PowerPoint exports outlines.

8. To exchange files with someone who uses OpenOffice, save your presentation in _____ format.

9. If you save a presentation in PowerPoint Show format, it opens in _____ view by default.

10. When you create a video from a presentation, PowerPoint saves it in _____ format.

Multiple Choice

Circle the correct answer.

1. To hide comments in a presentation, click the _____ button.
   a. Hide Markup
   b. Show Markup
   c. Show/Hide Comments
   d. Change Comment View

2. When you save a PowerPoint 2010 presentation in a file format that doesn't support SmartArt or other PowerPoint-specific graphics, those objects are:
   a. saved as uneditable pictures.
   b. deleted.
   c. preserved just as in the 2010 presentation.
   d. converted to shapes.

3. What color are comment boxes?
   a. Pink
   b. Yellow
   c. Green
   d. Different colors for each user

4. How do you change the user name that will appear on each comment?
   a. Manually type your name into each comment
   b. Click File > Options and type a different User Name and Initials
   c. Click the Change User button on the Home tab
   d. Click the Manage Comments button on the Review tab

5. Passwords you assign to PowerPoint files are case-sensitive.
   a. True
   b. False

6. How do you remove a password from a PowerPoint file?
   a. Change the password to a null string.
   b. Click Encrypt with Password, then click Decrypt.
   c. Click Encrypt with Password, then click Remove.
   d. Click the File tab, then click Unprotect.

7. Marking a presentation as final is:
   a. the same level of security as password protection.
   b. not as strong security as password protection.
   c. stronger security than password protection.

8. What is required in order for a user to read a PDF file?
   a. Adobe Reader or Adobe Acrobat
   b. XPS Viewer
   c. A Macintosh computer
   d. Windows 95 or higher

9. What happens to text that is typed inside shapes or manually created text boxes when you save a presentation as an outline?
   a. It is included in the outline.
   b. It is not included in the outline.
   c. You can specify whether you want it included in the outline.

10. To save as a video, start by clicking the File tab, then click:
    a. Save & Send.
    b. Save As.
    c. Print.
    d. Info.

Project 10-1: Messenger Messages

You are the new Marketing Manager for Consolidated Messenger. The company owner has given you a presentation to review with his comments already inserted and has asked you to add your own comments in response to his and describe any changes you would make.

GET READY. LAUNCH PowerPoint if it is not already running.

@ The *Sales Pitch* file is available on the book companion website or in WileyPLUS.

1. **OPEN** the *Sales Pitch* presentation and save it as *Sales Pitch Final*.
2. Click the **Review** tab, and then click the **Next** button to read the comment on slide 1.
3. Click **Next** and read the comment on slide 3, then click **Next** again to read the comment on slide 5.
4. Click the **Previous** button twice to return to the comment on slide 1.
5. Click the **Delete** button to delete the comment on slide 1.
6. Click the **New Comment** button and insert the following comment:

   I think the template is fine as is.
7. Go to slide 3 and insert the following comment:

   I will try to find a picture with color values more in line with the template.
8. Go to slide 5 and delete the comment.
9. **SAVE** the presentation and then **CLOSE** the file.

LEAVE PowerPoint open for use in the next project.

Project 10-2: Travel Protection

You are a travel agent working for Margie's Travel Agency. Blue Yonder Airlines has asked you to start pitching their services to corporate clients and has sent you a copy of their presentation. Your contact at Blue Yonder has asked you to share the presentation with other agents in your office, but she does not want anyone to change the presentation. You can use PowerPoint features to safeguard the presentation.

@ The *Airline Overview* file is available on the book companion website or in WileyPLUS.

1. **OPEN** the *Airline Overview* presentation and save it as *Airline Overview Final*.
2. Click the comment on slide 1 to open it, and then read the comment.
3. Right-click the comment and then click **Delete Comment**.
4. Click the **File** tab, click **Protect Presentation**, and click **Mark as Final**.
5. Click **OK** twice to save the presentation and mark it as the final version.
6. Close the presentation file.
7. Reopen *Airline Overview*, and save it as *Airline Overview Protected*.
8. Click the **File** tab, click **Protect Presentation**, and click **Encrypt with Password**.
9. In the Password box, type **ProtectMe**, and click **OK**.
10. In the Reenter password box, type **ProtectMe**, and click **OK**.
11. **CLOSE** the file, saving your changes if prompted.

LEAVE PowerPoint open for use in the next project.

Project 10-3: Confidential Feedback

You are the research director at Trey Research. You have just completed a confidential presentation for Center City Hospital regarding recent complaints from patients. You will save the file with a password, and create an XPS version of the presentation to distribute to upper management.

@ The *Hospital Complaints* file is available on the book companion website or in WileyPLUS.

1. **OPEN** the *Hospital Complaints* presentation and save it as *Hospital Complaints Final*.
2. Click the **File** tab and click **Save & Send**.
3. Click **Create PDF/XPS Document**.
4. Click the **Create PDF/XPS** button.

5. In the Publish as PDF or XPS dialog box, change the name in the File name text box to **Hospital Complaints Distribution**.

6. Open the **Save as type drop-down list** and click **XPS Document** if it is not already selected.

7. Click **Publish**.

8. Close the **XPS Viewer**.

9. Click the **File** tab and click **Protect Presentation**, then click **Encrypt** with **Password**.

10. In the Password box, type **ProtectMe** and click **OK**.

11. Type **ProtectMe** again and click **OK**.

12. Click the **Home** tab to exit from Backstage view.

13. **CLOSE** the file, saving changes to it if prompted.

LEAVE PowerPoint open for use in the next project.

Project 10-4: Adventure Review

You are the owner of Adventure Works, a company that offers outdoor adventures for groups of young people. The marketing manager has created a presentation to show to some local civic organizations and wants your feedback on it. You can share your ideas using comments.

@ The *Adventures* file is available on the companion website.

1. **OPEN** the *Adventures* presentation and save it as *Adventures Final*.

2. Read the comment on slide 1.

3. Go to slide 2 and add the following comment:

   Don't forget our new Horseback Trekking adventure.

4. Go to slide 4 and add the following comment:

   Can we replace this picture with a more youth-oriented one?

5. Drag the comment marker closer to the picture.

6. Go to slide 5 and add the following comment:

   Good job, Marie. I like the clean, modern look of this theme.

7. Go to slide 1 and delete Marie's comment.

8. Go back to slide 4 and change your comment to read:

   I like this picture, but can we replace it with a more youth-oriented one?

9. Hide all comments.

10. **SAVE** the presentation and then **CLOSE** the file.

LEAVE PowerPoint open for use in the next project.

Mastery Assessment

Project 10-5: Training Day

You are the Training Manager for Northwind Traders. You have just finished a presentation for your trainers to use in training new cashiers, and a draft has been reviewed by one of your coworkers. You will merge the coworker's changes with your own copy of the presentation. Then you will save the presentation as a Picture presentation, and then save one of the picture presentation's slides as a separate PNG graphic.

@ The *Training* file is available on the book companion website or in WileyPLUS.

1. **OPEN** the *Training* presentation and save it as *Training Final*.

2. Use the Compare feature to merge this presentation with *Training Revisions*.

3. Reject the change on slide 1, and accept the changes on all other slides. End the review.

4. Save the presentation as a Picture presentation. Name the file *Training Pictures*.

5. Close the *Training Final* presentation, and open *Training Pictures*.

6. Right-click slide 5, and choose Save as Picture.

7. Change the Save as type to PNG Portable Network Graphics Format.

8. Save the picture as *Training Common Questions* in the folder where you are storing the files for this lesson.

9. **SAVE** and **CLOSE** the presentation.

LEAVE PowerPoint open for the next project.

Project 10-6: Video Production

You are the owner of Southridge Video. You want to share a presentation you have created with a potential vendor, but he doesn't have PowerPoint. You will make a video of the presentation that you can share with him, and you will export an outline of the text in the presentation.

@ The *Video* file is available on the book companion website or in WileyPLUS.

1. **OPEN** the *Video* presentation.

2. Click the File tab, click Save & Send, and click Create a Video.

3. Set the Seconds to Spend on Each Slide setting to 12 seconds.

4. Save the video as *Southridge.wmv*.

5. Click the File tab, click Save & Send, and click Create Handouts.

6. Create Outline Only handouts in Word.

7. Save the Word document as *Southridge Outline.docx* and close it. Exit Word.

8. **CLOSE** the presentation file. Do not save changes to it if prompted to do so.

EXIT PowerPoint.

INTERNET READY

In this lesson, you learned about several different file formats that PowerPoint can save in. Look in the Save as type drop-down list in the Save as dialog box, and type the names of the file formats into a Word or Notepad document. Use the Internet to find an application that uses each of these file formats, and write a report that explains one possible usage of each of the file formats.

LESSON SKILL MATRIX

Skill	Exam Objective	Objective Number
Adjusting Slide Orientation and Size	Set up a custom size.	2.2.1
	Change the orientation.	2.2.2
Customizing Audience Handouts	Create handouts (send to Microsoft Word).	7.2.3
Choosing Slides to Display	Create a Custom Slide Show.	8.2.7
Rehearsing Your Delivery	Rehearse timings.	8.3.1
	Keep timings.	8.3.2
	Adjust a slide's timing.	8.3.3
Setting Up a Slide Show	Set up a Slide Show.	8.2.1
	Play narrations.	8.2.2
	Set up Presenter view.	8.2.3
	Use timings.	8.2.4
	Show media controls.	8.2.5
Working with Presentation Tools	Add pen and highlighter annotations.	8.1.1
	Change the ink color.	8.1.2
	Erase an annotation.	8.1.3
	Discard annotations upon closing.	8.1.4
	Retain annotations upon closing.	8.1.5
Broadcasting a Presentation	Broadcast presentations.	8.2.6
Recording a Presentation	Start recording from the beginning of a slide show.	8.4.1
	Start recording from the current slide of a slide show.	8.4.2
Packaging a Presentation for CD Delivery	Package a presentation for CD delivery.	7.2.1

KEY TERMS

- annotate
- broadcast
- custom shows
- Handout Master
- ink
- landscape orientation
- orientation
- portrait orientation
- presentation tools
- timings

You are an engineer for A. Datum Corporation, a contractor specializing in pile-driving and heavy concrete construction. Your team has put together a bid on a large bridge construction project for the town of Center City, and you must present the bid package to the client. You will present a slide show for the client before reviewing the bid in detail. Your presentation will introduce your company and provide an overview of the bid itself. PowerPoint provides a number of tools that can help you set up your presentation, rehearse it, and then package it to use in the final presentation.

ADJUSTING SLIDE ORIENTATION AND SIZE

The Bottom Line

Orientation refers to the direction material appears on a page when printed. A page printed in **landscape orientation** is wider than it is tall, like a landscape picture that shows a broad panoramic view. A page printed in **portrait orientation** is taller than it is wide, like a portrait picture that focuses on a single upright figure. Slides are generally displayed at a standard size and orientation. You can adjust orientation and size for special impact or to meet the requirements of a specific projection device or output option.

Selecting Slide Orientation

By default, slides are displayed so they are wider than they are tall (landscape orientation). You may want to change the orientation of a presentation for a special case, such as to accommodate large graphics that have a portrait orientation or to print slides at the same orientation as other materials. You can easily change this orientation by using the Page Setup dialog box or a Ribbon command. In this exercise, you will practice changing slide orientation.

You cannot mix landscape and portrait orientations in a single presentation the way you can in a word processing document. All slides in a presentation must have the same orientation. However, if you need to display one or more slides in a different orientation, you can create a secondary presentation with the different orientation and then provide links between the main presentation and the secondary one. You can easily click the link during the slide show to jump to the secondary presentation and then click another link to return to your main presentation.

Presentation materials such as notes pages and handouts print in portrait orientation by default because this orientation allows the most efficient placement of slide images and text on the page. Adjusting orientation for these materials allows you to fit more information across the longest axis of the page—a plus if you have a great many notes for each slide.

STEP BY STEP   **Select Slide Orientation**

@ The *Bid* file is available on the book companion website or in WileyPLUS.

WILEY PLUS EXTRA

WileyPLUS Extra! features an online tutorial of this task.

GET READY. Before you begin these steps, make sure that your computer is on. Log on, if necessary.

1. **START** PowerPoint, if it is not already running.
2. Locate and open the *Bid* presentation and save it as *Bid Final*.
3. Click the **Design** tab, and then click the **Page Setup** button. The Page Setup dialog box opens, as shown in Figure 11-1. Note the current width and height measurements at the left side of the dialog box.

Figure 11-1

Page Setup dialog box

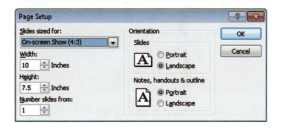

Figure 11-1

Page Setup dialog box

4. Click **Portrait** in the Slides area of the dialog box. Note that the width and height measurements reverse.
5. Click **Landscape** in the Notes, Handouts & Outline area.
6. Click **OK**. The slides are now taller than they are wide, as shown in Figure 11-2.

Figure 11-2

The slides display in portrait orientation

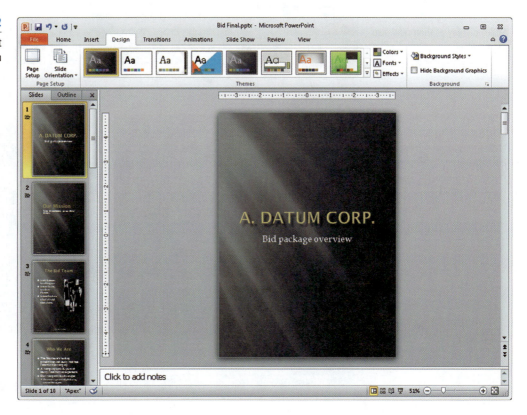

Take Note   You will see the result of this change to handout orientation later in this lesson.

7. Click the **Slide Orientation** button in the Page Setup group, and then click **Landscape**. The slides return to their default landscape orientation.
8. **SAVE** the presentation.

PAUSE. LEAVE the presentation open to use in the next exercise.

CERTIFICATION
READY   2.2.2

How do you change slide orientation?

Setting Slide Size

Slides have a default size that you can change if you need to accommodate a particular kind of projection system or output. Use the Page Setup dialog box to adjust slide size. In this exercise, you try out several different slide sizes.

Slides are sized by default at a 4:3 aspect ratio that allows them to be shown on a standard monitor without distortion. The Slides sized for drop-down list lets you choose from a number of other standard size options, including different screen aspect ratios, standard U.S. and European letter paper sizes, 35 mm slides, overheads, and banners. For a wide-screen monitor, use a 16:9 aspect ratio. Slide sizes apply to all slides in a presentation, not just the currently selected slide.

Set Slide Sizes

USE the *Bid Final* presentation that is still open from the previous exercise.

1. On the Design tab, click the **Page Setup** button. The Page Setup dialog box opens. Note the width and height measurements for the default slide size.
2. Click the **Slides sized for drop-down arrow**, then click **On-screen Show (16:9)**. The width and height measurements change to reflect the new slide size.
3. Click **OK**. The slides are now much wider than they are tall, as shown in Figure 11-3.

Figure 11-3

Slides display at their new size

Take Note   The 16:9 option is an aspect ratio that is used for wide-screen monitors.

4. Click the **Page Setup** button again, click the **Slides sized for drop-down arrow**, then click **35mm Slides**.
5. Click **OK**. The slides are now the proper size to create slides that could be used in an old-style slide projector.
6. Click the **Page Setup** button again, click the **Slides sized for drop-down arrow**, and then click **On-screen Show (4:3)**.
7. Click **OK**. The slides are now the default size again.
8. **SAVE** the presentation.

PAUSE. LEAVE the presentation open to use in the next exercise.

If you do not find a suitable size for a specific need, you can create a custom slide size. Adjust the width and height as desired in the Page Setup dialog box to create the custom slide size.

CERTIFICATION
READY 2.2.2

How do you set up a custom
size for a slide?

The Bottom Line

Besides allowing you to set slide size and orientation, the Page Setup dialog box lets you choose the starting number for slides in a presentation. This is useful if you are combining several separate presentations into one comprehensive slide show.

CUSTOMIZING AUDIENCE HANDOUTS

You can help your audience follow a presentation by giving them handouts, which show small versions of the slides arranged in various ways on a page. Handout layouts are controlled by a **Handout Master**, as slide appearance is controlled by the Slide Master. You can customize the Handout Master to create your own handout layout. You can also export handouts to Microsoft Word, where you can customize them further.

Customizing the Handout Master

You can customize the layout of the Handout Master, which controls how handouts are formatted in PowerPoint. You can add text boxes to it, enable or disable certain placeholders, and format those placeholders. In this exercise, you customize the Handout Master in several ways.

You can create handouts that show one, two, three, four, six, or nine slides on a page. If you make changes to any of these layouts, the changes are reflected on all other layouts.

You cannot adjust the position or size of the slide placeholders in the Handout Master. (You can do that in Word, though, which you'll learn about in the next exercise.) You can, however, adjust both size and position of the Header, Date, Footer, and Page Number placeholders. You can also choose to hide some or all of these placeholders by deselecting their check boxes in the Placeholders group on the Handout Master tab.

The Handout Master tab allows you to change both slide orientation and handout orientation, using buttons in the Page Setup group. To further modify the appearance of handouts, you can change theme colors and fonts (but not the current theme) and apply a different background style. You can format the Header, Date, Footer, and Page Number placeholders like any text box or placeholder using Quick Styles, fills, or outlines.

Note that you can also customize the Notes Master in many of the same ways that you customize the Handout Master. Click the Notes Master button on the View tab to display the Notes Master tab. The Notes Master allows you to adjust the size and position of the slide image as well as other placeholders on the page.

STEP BY STEP   **Customize the Handout Master**

USE the *Bid Final* presentation that is still open from the previous exercise.

1. Click the **Insert** tab, click **Header & Footer**, and click the **Notes and Handouts** tab.
2. Set up headers and footers as follows:
   a. Click to mark the **Date and time** check box, and make sure the *Update automatically* option is selected.
   b. Click to mark the **Header** check box, and type the header **A. Datum Corporation**.
   c. Click to mark the **Footer** check box, and type the footer **No Job Is Too Big for A. Datum**.
   d. Click **Apply to All**.
3. Click the **View** tab, and then click the **Handout Master** button in the Presentation Views group. The Handout Master view opens as shown in Figure 11-4, with the header and footer you supplied in step 2.

Figure 11-4

Handout Master view

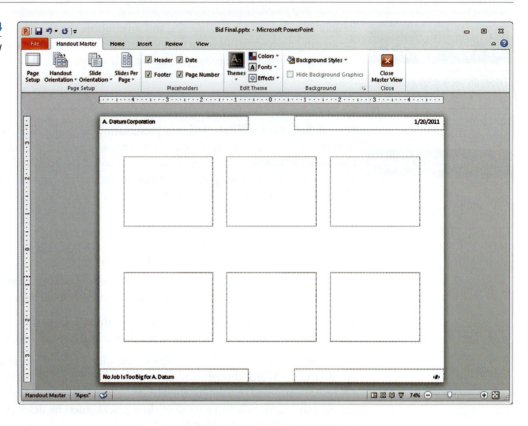

Take Note

The master displays in landscape orientation because you changed the orientation in a previous exercise.

4. Click the **Slides Per Page** button in the Page Setup group, then click **3 Slides**. The Handout Master displays the layout used to show three slides across the width of the page.

5. Click the **Insert** tab, click **Text Box**, and draw a text box above the center slide placeholder of the same width as the placeholder, as shown in Figure 11-5.

Figure 11-5

Add a text box to the Handout Master

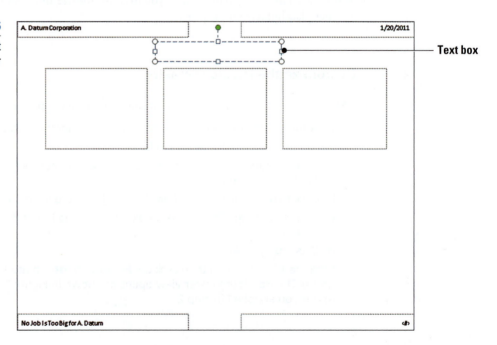

Text box

6. Type **Center City Bridge Project** in the text box.

7. Change the font size of the text box text to **18** if necessary, apply bold formatting, change the color to **Dark Blue, Text 2**, and **center** the text. Adjust the size of the text box as necessary to display the text on one line.

8. Click the outside border of the header placeholder in the upper-left corner of the master, hold down **Shift**, and click the date, footer, and page number placeholders.

9. Change the font size to **14 pt**, apply bold formatting, and change the color to **Dark Blue, Text 2**.

10. Click the **Handout Master** tab, and then click the **Close Master View** button to exit Handout Master view.

11. Click the **File** tab and click **Print**. Open the **Print All Slides** button's list and click **Handouts (3 Slides Per Page)**. Your customized handout master should resemble the one previewed in Figure 11-6.

Figure 11-6

Preview of the customized handout

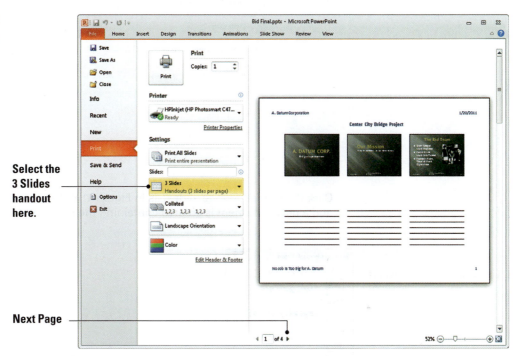

Select the 3 Slides handout here.

Next Page

12. Click the **Next Page** arrow to see that the text box you added displays on each page of the handouts.

13. Click the **Print** button to print the handouts.

14. Click the **Close Print Preview** button to return to Normal view.

15. **SAVE** the presentation.

PAUSE. LEAVE the presentation open to use in the next exercise.

Exporting Handouts to Word

As you saw in the preceding exercise, there's a limit to what you can do with handout layouts in PowerPoint. For maximum control over handouts, including the ability to resize the slide images, you must export handouts to Word. In this exercise, you export handouts to Word.

STEP BY STEP　**Export Handouts to Word**

USE the *Bid Final* presentation that is still open from the previous exercise.

1. Click the **File** tab, click **Save & Send**, click **Create Handouts**, and then click the **Create Handouts** button (see Figure 11-7). The Send to Microsoft Word dialog box opens.

Figure 11-7

Choose to create handouts
from Backstage view

2. Click **Blank lines next to slides**, as in Figure 11-8. Then click **OK**. Microsoft Word opens and a new document is created containing the handouts.

Figure 11-8

Choose which handout format
you want

3. Click the first slide's image, and drag its lower-right corner selection handle to increase the image's size by about 0.25".

4. Drag across the horizontal lines in the first row to select them.

5. On the Home tab, click the **Line and Paragraph Spacing** button, and click **Remove Space After Paragraph**. The spacing between lines tightens up, as in Figure 11-9.

Figure 11-9

Change graphic size and spacing between lines

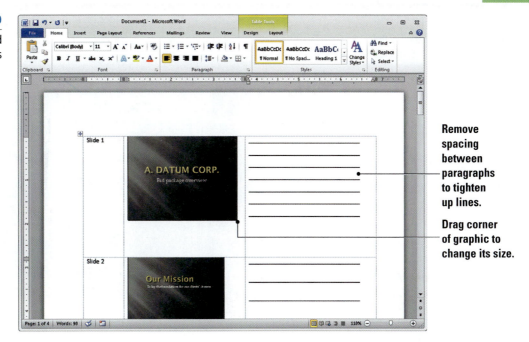

Remove spacing between paragraphs to tighten up lines.

Drag corner of graphic to change its size.

**CERTIFICATION
READY   7.2.3**

How do you create handouts in Microsoft Word?

6. Repeat the changes from steps 3-5 for each slide.
7. **SAVE** the Word document as *Handouts.docx* and **EXIT** Word.
PAUSE. LEAVE the *Bid Final* presentation open to use in the next exercise.

CHOOSING SLIDES TO DISPLAY

The Bottom Line

You may want to present only a portion of the slides you have prepared on a specific subject. You can select the slides to display by hiding slides or by creating a custom slide show.

Omitting Selected Slides from a Presentation

You can omit slides from a presentation by hiding them. Use the Hide Slide button or command to hide a slide so it won't appear during the presentation. In this exercise, you hide a slide.

STEP BY STEP   **Hide a Slide**

USE the presentation that is still open from the previous exercise.

1. Go to slide 2, and then click the **Slide Show** tab.
2. Click the **Hide Slide** button in the Set Up group. The slide is shaded on the Slides tab, as shown in Figure 11-10, and the slide number is surrounded by a box with a diagonal bar across it.

The hidden slide is shaded and its number is crossed out on the Slides/Outline pane.

Another Way
Right-click a slide in the Slides tab or in Slide Sorter view, and click Hide Slide on the shortcut menu.

Another Way
Set a range of slides to show in the Set Up Show dialog box, covered later in this lesson.

3. Press **F5** to start the presentation from slide 1.
4. Click the mouse button and notice that slide 2, *Our Mission*, does not display—you go directly to slide 3, *The Bid Team*.
5. Press **Esc** to stop the slide show.

PAUSE. LEAVE the presentation open to use in the next exercise.

When you hide a slide, you can still see it in Normal view and Slide Sorter view. It is hidden only in Slide Show view, when you present the slides. You can unhide a slide using the same procedure you used to hide it.

If you find that you want to display a hidden slide during the presentation, you can show it using PowerPoint's presentation tools. You will learn more about controlling a presentation with these tools later in this lesson.

Creating a Custom Show

Here we look at how to create **custom shows** to customize presentations for different groups using slides from a single presentation. A comprehensive year-end corporate review presentation, for example, might include information on the company as a whole as well as on the operations of each department. You could show all of the slides to the board of directors and use custom shows to present to each department the general company statistics and the information specific to that department. Custom shows allow you to focus attention on the material most relevant to a specific audience. In this exercise, you will create a custom show that contains a subset of the slides in the main presentation.

You can create any number of custom shows in a presentation. When you set up a presentation for showing, you can specify that only the custom show slides will be presented. You can also choose to run the show while you are in Slide Show view.

You select the slides for a custom show in the Define Custom Show dialog box. Add slide titles from the main presentation to the custom presentation. You can adjust the order in which the slides display in the custom show: Use the up and down arrows to the right of the Slides in custom show list to move a selected title up or down in the list.

Create a Custom Show

USE the *Bid Final* presentation that is still open from the previous exercise.

1. Click the **Slide Show** tab, if necessary, and then click the **Custom Slide Show** button in the Start Slide Show group.
2. Click **Custom Shows**. The Custom Shows dialog box opens.
3. Click the **New** button. The Define Custom Show dialog box opens.
4. In the Slide Show Name box, type **Corporate Information**.
5. Click **slide 2** in the *Slides in presentation* list, then click the **Add** button to place this slide in the *Slides in custom show* list.
6. Add slides 4, 5, and 6 to the custom show list. Your dialog box should look like Figure 11-11.

Another Way
You can quickly select more than one contiguous slide to add by clicking a slide in the list, holding down Shift, and then clicking additional slides. Hold down Ctrl to select non-contiguous slides.

Figure 11-11

Four slides have been added to the custom show

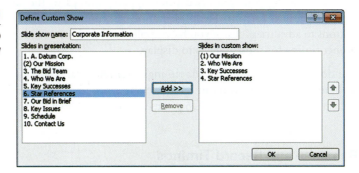

Take Note   The parentheses around slide 2's number indicate it is a hidden slide.

7. Click **OK**, and then click **Show**. The custom show starts with the second slide you added (the first slide, slide 2, is still hidden).
8. Click the mouse button to proceed through the slides of the custom show until the show ends.
9. **SAVE** the presentation.

PAUSE. **LEAVE** the presentation open to use in the next exercise.

CERTIFICATION
R E A D Y   **8.2.7**

How do you create a custom slide show?

Take Note   When you add slides to the Slides in custom show list, they are renumbered in the list, but the slide numbers on the slides do not change.

After you create a custom show, its name appears in the Custom Slide Show drop-down list, as well as in the Custom Shows dialog box. You can run the custom show from either list. You can also select the custom show in the Custom Shows dialog box and choose to edit the show, remove it, or copy it.

REHEARSING YOUR DELIVERY

The Bottom Line

To make sure that your audience will have enough time to read and absorb the content on your slides, you can rehearse your delivery. When you rehearse a presentation, you read it just as if you were a member of the audience viewing the slides for the first time. Look at pictures, charts, and diagrams to read any information they supply. After you rehearse, you have the option of saving your timings to use during your presentation.

Rehearsing Timings

Rehearsing a presentation can help you set the **timings** for it. Slide timings are particularly important if you intend to show the slides as a self-running presentation that viewers cannot control. You should allow plenty of time for viewers to read and understand the content on each slide. (You will learn more about self-running presentations in the next section.) When you rehearse, you read the text on the slide out loud (or silently to yourself) to see how long each slide should appear onscreen. You can then choose to keep those timings after the rehearsal or discard them. In this exercise, you will rehearse timings for a presentation and record the timings for later use.

The Rehearsal toolbar that displays when you rehearse slides shows you how much time you have spent reading the current slide as well as the elapsed time for the entire presentation. You can pause the rehearsal if necessary, then resume it when you are ready to continue. You can also choose to start the time again for a particular slide.

Note that saving your rehearsed times applies timings to the slide that allow PowerPoint to control the slides for you. The presentation can run automatically without your having to click buttons to advance slides. If you have applied animations to slide objects, rehearsing will set the proper timing for those objects to display.

You do not have to save the slide timings after rehearsal if you do not want PowerPoint to control the slides for you. You can tell PowerPoint not to save the timings, or you can deselect Use Rehearsed Timings in the Set Up group on the Slide Show tab to remove slide timings.

STEP BY STEP   **Rehearse and Record Timings**

USE the *Bid Final* presentation that is still open from the previous exercise.

1. On the Slide Show tab, click the **Rehearse Timings** button. The slide show starts from slide 1 and the Rehearsal toolbar appears in the upper-left corner of the screen, as shown in Figure 11-12.

Figure 11-12

The Rehearsal toolbar appears in Slide Show view

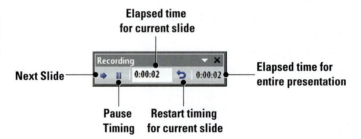

2. Read all the content on each slide, clicking the mouse button to display bullet items and advance slides. As you read, the timer is recording the time you spend. If you get interrupted, you can click the Pause button on the toolbar to pause.

3. When asked if you want to save the slide timings, click **Yes**. The presentation appears in **Slide Sorter** view, with the timing for each slide displayed below it, as shown in Figure 11-13.

Figure 11-13

Slide timings appear beneath each slide

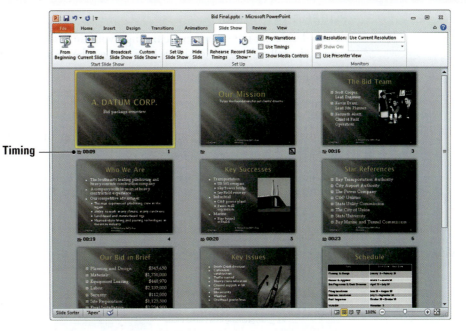

Timing

4. Press **F5** to start the slide show again from slide 1. This time, let PowerPoint control the slides according to the rehearsal times you set.

5. After three or four slides have displayed, press **Esc** to end the slide show. Switch to Normal view.

6. **SAVE** the presentation.

PAUSE. LEAVE the presentation open to use in the next exercise.

Adjusting Timing

After recording the timings for a presentation, you may decide that you need more or less time for a particular slide. You can change the timing on the Transitions tab. In the following exercise, you change the timing for an individual slide.

STEP BY STEP | **Adjust a Slide's Timing**

USE the presentation that is still open from the previous exercise.

1. Click the **Transitions** tab.

2. Select the slide for which you want to change the timing.

3. Click the up or down arrows in the After box in the Timing group, to incrementally adjust the number of seconds up or down (see Figure 11-14).

Figure 11-14

Change the timing for a slide on the Transitions tab

Adjust the timing

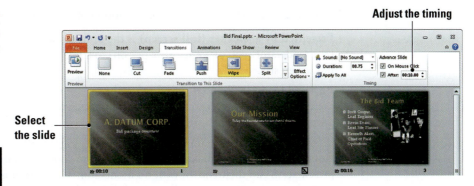

Select the slide

PAUSE. LEAVE the presentation open to use in the next exercise.

Clearing Timings

If you decide not to use automatic timings, you can easily clear all the timings from all slides at once. The following exercise shows how to clear the timings for all slides.

Clear Slide Timings

USE the presentation that is still open from the previous exercise.

1. Click the **Slide Show** tab.
2. Click the arrow below the Record Slide Show button to open a menu, point to **Clear**, and click **Clear Timings on All Slides**. See Figure 11-15.

Figure 11-15

Clear all slide timings from the Slide Show tab

Another Way
You can also turn off all the automatic transitions by clearing the After check box on the Transitions tab and then clicking Apply to All. However, this does not remove the timings; it just disables their ability to execute automatically. You could later re-enable timings for all slides and have your previously set timings back.

3. **SAVE** the presentation.

PAUSE. LEAVE the presentation open to use in the next exercise.

SETTING UP A SLIDE SHOW

The Bottom Line

The Set Up Show dialog box allows you to make a number of decisions about how slides display during a presentation.

Setting Up a Slide Show

The following exercise walks you through the settings in the Set Up Show dialog box. Not all of these settings are applicable to the presentation being used for the example, but all are useful to know about because of the variety of presentations you may create in the future. In this exercise, you configure various settings that govern how a slide show runs in Slide Show view.

When setting up a slide show, you have the option of choosing a Show Type. The choices are:

- **Presented by a speaker (full screen)** is the option to choose if the slides will be presented by a moderator (you or some other person) to a live audience. The slides will display at full screen size.

- **Browsed by an individual (window)** is the option to choose if you are preparing the presentation for a viewer to review on his or her own computer. The slides display within a window that contains a title bar with size/close controls. You can also choose to display a scrollbar to make it easy for the individual to scroll through the slides.

- **Browsed at a kiosk (full screen)** is the option to choose if you intend to have the presentation run unattended, with no moderator. This option is a standard choice for trade shows or other venues where the slides can loop indefinitely for viewers to watch as long as they desire.

STEP BY STEP   Set Up a Slide Show

CERTIFICATION READY 8.2.2

How do you set a slide show to play narrations?

USE the *Bid Final* presentation that is still open from the previous exercise.

1. **SAVE** the presentation as *Bid Kiosk*.
2. On the Slide Show tab, click **Set Up Slide Show**. The Set Up Show dialog box opens.
3. Examine the settings in the Show Type section, but do not make a change yet.
4. In the Show Options section, mark the **Loop continuously until 'Esc'** check box.

Take Note   This setting is turned on automatically if you choose Browsed at a kiosk (full screen) as the show type.

5. Click to mark the **Show without narration** check box.

 Ref   Narrations are recorded when you record a presentation, which is covered later in this lesson.

6. Click to mark the **Show without animation** check box.
7. Click the **Pen Color** button, and click the purple square.

Take Note   The pen color is not important for this presentation because it will be self-running, but it's useful for future reference to know how to change it.

8. In the Show Type section, click **Browsed at a kiosk**.

    Several settings become unavailable when you choose this option, including Loop Continuously Until 'Esc' (which becomes permanently on) and Pen Color. That's why this exercise does not change the show type until after you have tried out those settings.

9. In the Show Slides section, click the **Custom Show** option button.

Take Note   The Corporate Information custom show is automatically selected because it is the only custom show in the presentation.

10. In the Advance Slides section, click the **Use timings, if present** option button. The dialog box should look like Figure 11-16 at this point.

Figure 11-16

The Set Up Show dialog box with custom settings applied

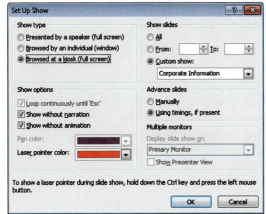

CERTIFICATION READY 8.2.4

How do you set a slide show to use timings?

Take Note   If you have multiple monitors, the controls in the Multiple Monitors section will be available. (They are not available in Figure 11-17.) With multiple monitors, you can mark the Show Presenter View check box, so that one monitor displays presenter controls (including speaker notes) and the other monitor displays the slides in full-screen mode.

CERTIFICATION READY 8.2.3

How do you set up Presenter view?

CERTIFICATION
READY   **8.2.5**

How do you set a slide show to display media controls?

CERTIFICATION
READY   **8.2.1**

How do you set up a slide show?

11. Click **OK**. The dialog box closes.

12. Examine the check boxes in the Set Up group on the Slide Show tab.

Notice that the Play Narrations check box is cleared because of the check box you marked in step 3.

Notice that the Timings check box is marked because of the option button you chose in step 8.

13. Clear the **Show Media Controls** check box.

This setting is not directly applicable to this presentation because it has no video or audio clips in it. However, knowing how to turn on/off the onscreen controls for such clips is useful for future reference. This setting was also covered in Lesson 9.

14. **SAVE** the presentation.

PAUSE. LEAVE the presentation file open to use in the next exercise.

SOFTWARE ORIENTATION

Presentation Tools in Slide Show View

When in Slide Show view, presentation tools appear in the bottom left corner of the screen. They are faint until you point at them; then they become bright icons that you can click to open menus. In Figure 11-17 the Menu button is active and its menu is open.

Figure 11-17

The presentation tools

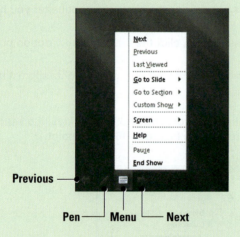

You can also display a navigation menu by right-clicking anywhere on the slide. The right-click menu contains an additional command, Pointer Options, which opens the same menu as the Pen button in the presentation tools.

WORKING WITH PRESENTATION TOOLS

The Bottom Line

PowerPoint offers a number of **presentation tools** you can use during a presentation to control the display of slides and mark directly on the slides if desired. You can use keyboard commands, mouse clicks, presentation tools, or menu commands to control the presentation. You can select from several marking options and colors to annotate your slides during the presentation.

Moving Through a Presentation

There are many ways to move through a presentation's slides. You can simply click to move from start to finish, ignoring any hidden slides. If you want to jump around to other slides that are not in the default sequence, you can use the navigation menu, keyboard shortcuts, or other techniques. In this exercise, you will practice moving through a presentation.

PowerPoint provides many methods so that you can use the tools that are most comfortable for you to go forward, backward, or to a specific slide. Table 11-1 summarizes the most popular navigation options in Slide Show view.

Table 11-1

Navigation Options in Slide Show View

Action	Keyboard	Mouse	Shortcut menu
Show the next slide or animation	N Enter Spacebar Page down Right arrow	Left mouse button	Next
Show the previous slide or animation	P Page up Backspace Left arrow		Previous
Go to the last slide viewed			Last Viewed
Go to a specific slide	Type slide number and press Enter		Go to Slide, then click slide title
End show	Esc		End Show

If you have chosen the *Browsed by an individual (window)* show type in the Set Up Show dialog box (Figure 11-16), the presentation tools at the lower-left corner of the screen do not display and you cannot use the mouse button to go to the next slide. You can use the keyboard options to go to the next or previous slide, or you can use the Next Slide and Previous Slide buttons on the scrollbar if you have chosen to display it. You can also right-click the slide and select Advance to move forward or Reverse to move backward through slides.

STEP BY STEP   **Move through a Presentation**

1. REOPEN the *Bid Final* presentation you worked with earlier in this lesson.

Take Note   An easy way to reopen Bid Final is: click the File tab, click Recent, and click the *Bid Final* file at the top of the list of recent files.

Another Way
You can also start the presentation from the beginning by pressing F5.

2. To confirm that all rehearsed timings are removed, click the **Slide Show** tab, click **Record Slide Show**, and, if it is available, click **Clear**. If the Clear command is unavailable, the timings have already been removed.

3. Click the **From Beginning** button to start the presentation from slide 1.

4. Move the pointer on the slide until you can see the presentation tools in the lower-left corner of the screen, as shown in Figure 11-17.

Another Way
To go to the next slide if it is hidden, you can press H.

5. Click the **Next** button (the right-pointing arrow at the far right of the tools). The next slide displays.

6. Click the **Previous** button (the left-pointing arrow at the far left of the tools). Slide 1 redisplays.

7. Right-click anywhere on the slide to display the presentation shortcut menu, point to **Go to Slide**, and then click the hidden slide, **(2) Our Mission**, as shown in Figure 11-18. The hidden slide displays.

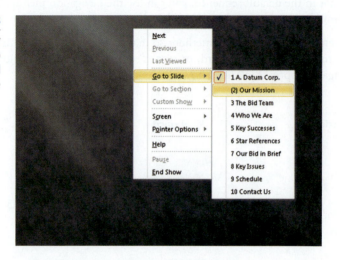

8. Press **Page Down** to display the next slide.

Another Way
You can also end the show by pressing Esc.

9. Click the **Menu** button in the presentation tools (the third button from the left) to display a menu similar to the presentation shortcut menu, and then click **Last Viewed**. The slide you previously viewed (slide 2) displays.

10. Right-click the screen again, then click **End Show** on the presentation shortcut menu to end the presentation.

PAUSE. LEAVE the presentation open to use in the next exercise.

As you work with PowerPoint, you will find that you develop a feel for the navigation tools that you find easiest to use. It is often more efficient, for example, to use keyboard options because they can be quicker than right-clicking and selecting options from shortcut menus.

Annotating Slides with the Pen or Highlighter

As you proceed through a presentation, you may want to pause to emphasize certain points. You can **annotate** (write) directly on a slide with the annotation tools in PowerPoint. You can control these tools, including setting the color and width of the onscreen pen, via the Pen menu in the presentation tools (refer back to Figure 11-16). Various pen types, thicknesses, and colors are available. In the following exercise, you create ink annotations during a slide show.

PowerPoint offers three different annotation pen options: Ball Point Pen, Felt Tip Pen, and Highlighter. These pen options have pointer sizes that roughly correspond to the actual writing instruments. You can change the ink color for any of the pen options.

The Black Screen and White Screen options allow you to replace the current slide with a black or white screen that you can use for annotations or to cover the current material if you want to keep it under wraps while you are discussing some other issue.

STEP BY STEP | **Annotate Slides**

USE the *Bid Final* presentation that is still open from the previous exercise.

Another Way
You can also right-click, point to Go to Slide, and select slide 7.

1. Press **F5** to start the presentation from slide 1, type **7**, and press **Enter**. Slide 7 appears.
2. Click the mouse button until all seven bullet items display on the slide.
3. Right-click the slide, point to **Pointer Options**, and click **Felt Tip Pen**. The pointer changes to a small, round, red pen pointer.
4. Right-click the slide, point to **Pointer Options**, and click **Ink Color**. Then click **Orange** in the Standard Colors palette.
5. Use the pen pointer to circle the value for site preparation, $1,125,500, as shown in Figure 11-19.

Figure 11-19

Make an annotation on a slide

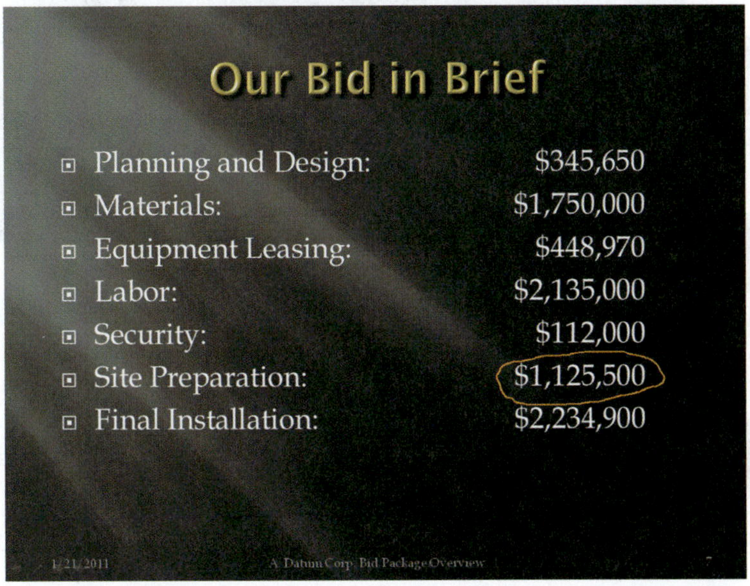

Our Bid in Brief

⊡	Planning and Design:	$345,650
⊡	Materials:	$1,750,000
⊡	Equipment Leasing:	$448,970
⊡	Labor:	$2,135,000
⊡	Security:	$112,000
⊡	Site Preparation:	$1,125,500
⊡	Final Installation:	$2,234,900

1-21-2011   A. Datum Corp. Bid Package Overview

Another Way
You can also use any other method of advancing the presentation to display all bullet points, such as pressing Enter, spacebar, or the right arrow key. This exercise uses a variety of navigation methods for practice.

Troubleshooting If you click too many times and advance to slide 8, press Backspace, Page Up, or the left arrow key to return to slide 7.

6. Press the **B** key on the keyboard. The screen is blacked out so you can annotate without the distraction of the slide material.
7. Use the pen pointer to draw a large U.S. currency symbol ($) in the middle of the slide.

Take Note   While a pen pointer is active, you cannot use the mouse button to advance slides.

8. Right-click the slide, point to **Screen**, and click **Unblack Screen**. The slide background is restored and the annotation disappears.

Another Way
Press Esc to restore the arrow pointer.

9. Click the **Pointer Options** button in the presentation tools (the second tool from the left) and click **Arrow**. The arrow pointer is restored.
10. Click or press **Enter** to go to slide 8.
11. Click or press **Enter** eight times to display all eight bullet items.

12. Click the **Pointer Options** button in the presentation tools, and then click **Highlighter**. Drag the highlighter pointer across the *Weather* bullet item to highlight it, as shown in Figure 11-20.

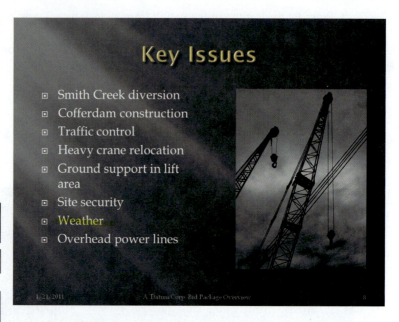

Key Issues

- Smith Creek diversion
- Cofferdam construction
- Traffic control
- Heavy crane relocation
- Ground support in lift area
- Site security
- Weather
- Overhead power lines

1·21·2011   A Datum Corp Bid Package Overview   8

Another Way

Press E to remove all annotations on a slide.

CERTIFICATION READY 8.1.3

How do you erase annotations?

CERTIFICATION READY 8.1.4

How do you discard annotations on closing?

CERTIFICATION READY 8.1.5

How do you save annotations on closing?

CERTIFICATION READY 8.1.1

How do you add pen and highlighter annotations?

13. Click the **Pointer Options** button, and then click **Erase All Ink on Slide**. The highlight you added is removed.

14. End the slide show. When asked if you want to keep your annotations, click **Keep**.

15. **SAVE** the presentation.

PAUSE. LEAVE the presentation open to use in the next exercise.

When you reach the end of the presentation (or end it early), if you have created any annotations, you are prompted to either save or discard them. If you save them, they are saved on the slide as **ink**, which is similar to a drawing you might do with the Shapes tool.

Editing Ink Annotations

You can move and delete individual annotations on slides as you would any other graphics, and you can also manage ink with the Ink Tools Pens tab. In the following exercise, you edit an ink annotation in Normal view and add a new annotation there.

STEP BY STEP   **Edit Ink Annotations**

USE the *Bid Final* presentation that is still open from the previous exercise.

1. In Normal view, display slide 7 and click the orange circle you drew as an annotation. Notice that both the Drawing Tools and Ink Tools contextual tabs appear on the Ribbon.

2. Click the **Ink Tools Pens** tab to examine the options available (see Figure 11-21).

Figure 11-21

Ink Tools Pens tab on the Ribbon

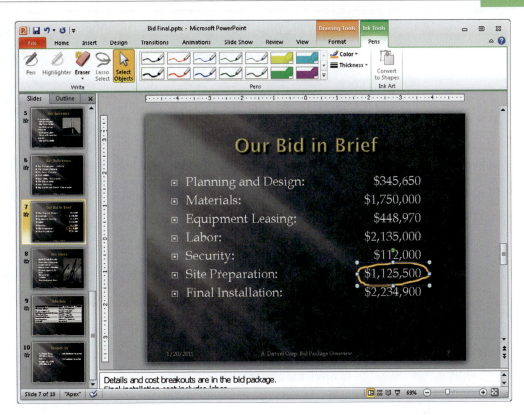

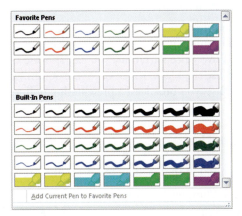

CERTIFICATION
R E A D Y   8.1.2

How do you change the ink color?

3. Click the **Color** button to open its palette, and click **Light Green**. The selected annotation changes color.

4. Click the **Thickness** button to open its menu, and click 3 pt. The selected annotation increases in thickness.

5. Click the **More** button in the Pens group to open a gallery of pen styles. See Figure 11-22.

Figure 11-22

Gallery of pen styles

6. In the Built-In Pens section, click **Red Pen (1.0 mm)**.

Notice that the selected annotation does not change. These pen styles are for creating new annotations, not editing existing ones.

7. Drag to draw an underline beneath Site Preparation. See Figure 11-23.

Figure 11-23

Draw an additional annotation

8. On the Ink Tools Pens tab, click the **Select Objects** button to return to using the arrow pointer again.

9. **SAVE** the presentation.

PAUSE. LEAVE the presentation open to use in the next exercise.

BROADCASTING A PRESENTATION

The Bottom Line

Broadcasting a presentation over the Internet makes it possible for people to see the presentation who may not be able to attend in person. A broadcast is still a live show with a live speaker, but is delivered remotely.

Broadcasting a Presentation

When you **broadcast** a presentation, you make it available for people to watch online. You control the sequence and timing of the slides from your PC, and you can optionally speak into your microphone to add live voice narration. You can also use the ink annotation tools, pause or resume the show, and use the Black Screen or White Screen options or any other Slide Show view feature. In this exercise, you broadcast a presentation online.

STEP BY STEP   **Broadcast a Presentation**

USE the *Bid Final* presentation that is still open from the previous exercise.

1. If you do not have a Windows Live user ID, go to http://www.live.com and get one.

2. In PowerPoint, on the Slide Show tab, click **Broadcast Slide Show**. The Broadcast Slide Show dialog box opens.

Take Note   You must have a Windows Live ID to broadcast a presentation using the PowerPoint Broadcast Service. If you want to use some other service to broadcast your presentation, you can click Change Broadcast Service and specify one. Some large companies may have their own broadcast service.

3. Click **Start Broadcast**. A dialog box appears to log into Windows Live. See Figure 11-24.

Figure 11-24

Log into Windows Live

4. Enter your Windows Live login information and click **OK**. You are logged into the broadcast server. After a short wait, a link appears that you can share with audience members, as shown in Figure 11-25. The link you receive will be different from the one shown.

Figure 11-25

Share the link with audience members

5. (Optional) If you know people who want to see your broadcast, give them the link.

You can do this by clicking Send in Email and emailing them the link, or by distributing the link in some other method, such as manually writing it down on paper. You do not have to have any audience members in order to practice broadcasting, however.

Take Note   To see how a broadcast presentation looks when viewed remotely, team up with a classmate and take turns watching each other's shows.

6. Click **Start Slide Show**. The slide show opens in Slide Show view. You are now broadcasting.

7. Move through the presentation as you normally would. You can optionally use your microphone to comment on the slide content or read it aloud as you go. Figure 11-26 shows how a presentation broadcast looks to someone using Internet Explorer to view the link you provided to them.

Figure 11-26

Figure 11-26

A PowerPoint broadcast viewed
in Internet Explorer

User can click
here to watch
in full-screen
mode.

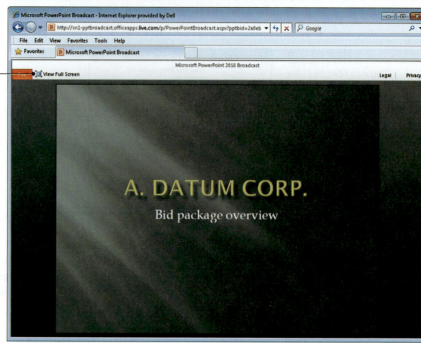

CERTIFICATION
READY   8.2.6

How do you broadcast a
presentation?

8. When you reach the last slide, click one more time to exit, returning to Normal view.

PAUSE. LEAVE the presentation open to use in the next exercise.

RECORDING A PRESENTATION

The Bottom Line

If you can't reach an audience in real time with your presentation, recording the presentation for later playback is an attractive option. You can record a presentation with or without narration (recorded audio commentary), annotations, and other features. You can also record the presentation from start to finish or re-record individual slides.

Recording an Entire Presentation

Recording a presentation, like broadcasting, helps you share your work remotely. The difference is that, with a recording, the audience does not need to be watching it live. They can view your presentation at their convenience. Recording a presentation saves narration, annotations, and timings. It does not create a separate file as a recording; all those settings are saved in the regular PowerPoint file. In the following exercise, you record a presentation from start to finish.

Take Note   If you want to save a separate file for distribution, consider making a video of the presentation, a topic covered in Lesson 10.

Take Note   In order to record narration, you will need a computer that has sound support and a microphone. You should set up and test the microphone ahead of time in Windows. In Windows 7, click Start, type microphone, and then click the Set Up a Microphone link at the top of the Start menu. Follow the prompts to prepare the microphone for recording.

STEP BY STEP   **Record a Presentation from the Beginning**

USE the *Bid Final* presentation that is still open from the previous exercise.

1. On the Slide Show tab, click the **Record Slide Show** button. The Record Slide Show dialog box opens, as shown in Figure 11-27.

Figure 11-27

The Record Slide Show dialog box

Figure 11-27

The Record Slide Show dialog box

2. Make sure your microphone is ready.

3. Click **OK** to begin the recording.

4. Click through the presentation, reading the text of the slides into the microphone at a moderate pace. The Rehearsal toolbar appears as you work through the presentation, the same as when rehearsing timings.

Take Note *If you flub the narration when recording, keep going. You can re-record individual slides after you are finished.*

5. When you reach the end of the presentation, click one more time to return to Normal view.

PAUSE. LEAVE the presentation open to use in the next exercise.

**CERTIFICATION
READY   8.4.1**

How do you start recording from the beginning of a presentation?

Recording the Current Slide

If you make a mistake in recording a certain slide, you can re-record it. In the following exercise, you re-record a single slide.

STEP BY STEP **Record a Presentation from the Current Slide**

USE the *Bid Final* presentation that is still open from the previous exercise.

1. Display slide 8.

2. On the Slide Show tab, click the arrow under the Record Slide Show button and click **Start Recording from Current Slide**. The Record Slide Show dialog box opens.

3. Click **Start Recording**.

4. Click to advance the bullet points on slide 8 at a moderate speed, while reading the text for slide 8 into the microphone.

5. Instead of advancing to the next slide, press **Esc** to quit recording. PowerPoint returns to Normal view.

PAUSE. LEAVE the presentation open to use in the next exercise.

**CERTIFICATION
READY   8.4.2**

How do you start recording from the current slide?

PACKAGING A PRESENTATION FOR CD DELIVERY

The Bottom Line You may need to transport your presentation materials to another computer to run your slide show. The Package for CD feature streamlines the process of packing all the materials you need to show the presentation even if PowerPoint is not installed on the other computer.

Packaging a Presentation for CD

The Package for CD feature makes short work of packing all the files you need to show your slides, no matter what kind of system you have to use to run the show. It also provides a Web page interface that users can employ to watch the show via Web browser if they do not have PowerPoint. In this exercise, you create a version of your presentation on a CD that you can distribute to others.

Take Note Previous versions of PowerPoint packaged presentations to CD along with a PowerPoint Viewer utility. PowerPoint 2010, however, takes a different approach; it packages presentations with a Web page on the CD. On this Web page is a link for downloading the PowerPoint viewer if it is needed. If you plan on showing the presentation somewhere that does not have Internet access, make sure you download the PowerPoint viewer ahead of time on the computer you will be working with if it does not have a full version of PowerPoint on it.

STEP BY STEP   **Package a Presentation for CD**

Take Note You must have a writeable CD drive inserted in your system to complete this exercise. If you do not, or if you do not have a blank writeable CD disc available, skip this exercise.

USE the *Bid Final* presentation that is still open from the previous exercise.

1. Insert a blank writeable CD disc in your writeable CD drive. If an **AutoPlay** box pops up, close it.
2. Click the **File** tab, click **Save & Send**, click **Package Presentation for CD**, and click **Package for CD**. The Package for CD dialog box opens.
3. In the Name the CD box, type **Bid**, replacing the default name. See Figure 11-28.

Figure 11-28

Package for CD dialog box

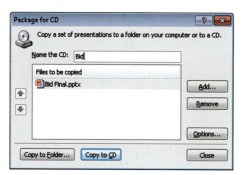

Take Note You can optionally add other presentations onto the same CD to avoid using a separate CD for each presentation. To add other presentations, you would click Add and select the presentations to include. You could then reorder them with the up and down arrow buttons in the dialog box. This exercise packages only one presentation on CD, so it does not include these actions.

4. Click the **Options** button. The Options dialog box opens. Note that linked files are marked to be included, and TrueType fonts will be embedded. Note that you can also optionally specify passwords to control access to the presentation(s). See Figure 11-29.

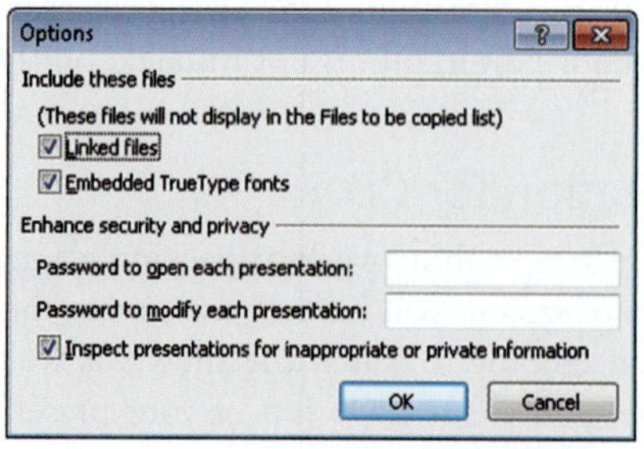

Figure 11-29

The Options dialog box for packaging a presentation

5. Click **OK** to accept the default settings and close the Options dialog box.
6. In the Package for CD dialog box, click **Copy to CD**.
7. A dialog box asks if you want to include linked files in your package. Click **Yes**.

8. A message appears that the presentation contains comments or annotations, stating that these will not be included. Click **Continue**.

9. Wait for the presentation to be written to the CD. It may take several minutes. The CD ejects when finished.

10. In PowerPoint, a message appears stating that the files were successfully copied to CD and offering to copy the same files to another CD. Click **No**.

11. Click **Close** to close the Package for CD dialog box.

12. To test your new CD, reinsert the CD into your computer. If an Auto Play box opens, click **Run PresentationPackage.html**. If no box opens, click the **Start** button, click **Computer**, and double-click the CD drive.

13. A Web page displays, showing a page that lists the presentations on the CD. (There is only one in this case.) A link also appears in the upper-right corner for downloading the PowerPoint Viewer (see Figure 11-30). You do not need it on your PC since you have the full version of PowerPoint.

Figure 11-30

The Web interface for a presentation CD

14. Click the name of the presentation (**Bid Final**). Respond to any security warnings you might see in your Web browser. The presentation opens in PowerPoint, in Protected View.

15. Click the **File** tab and click **Close** to close the copy of the presentation that originated from the CD. (The original *Bid Final* presentation is still open.)

PAUSE. LEAVE the presentation open to use in the next exercise.

CERTIFICATION READY   7.2.1

How do you package presentations for CD delivery?

To make the process of storing files on a CD more efficient, you can choose to copy more than one presentation to the same CD. Click the Add Files button to open additional presentations. This feature can reduce the amount of wasted space that results if you copy a single presentation to a CD.

The Options dialog box that you can access from the Package for CD dialog box gives you additional choices for the packaging process:

- Linked files, such as large movie and sound files, are included automatically, and you will normally want to retain this setting. You can, however, save the package without linked files if desired by deselecting this option.

- Embedding TrueType fonts is a good idea if you are not sure what fonts you might have access to on the system where you will run the presentation. Embedding fonts will add to file size but ensure the quality of your presentation's font appearance.

- You can specify a password to open or modify the presentation, and you can prompt PowerPoint to inspect the presentation for hidden or personal data you do not want to share.

Take Note   Package for CD works only with CD formats. If you want to store a presentation on a DVD, you can save materials in a folder as in step 8 of the previous exercise, and then use your system's DVD burning tools to copy the files to the DVD.

Packaging a Presentation to a Folder

In addition to using Package for CD to create materials to transport a presentation, you can use this feature to archive presentations onto a CD or into folders for storage. The packaging process pulls together all the files you need for a presentation, so your stored presentation provides an excellent long-term backup for your work. In this exercise, you package a presentation to a folder.

STEP BY STEP   **Package a Presentation to a Folder**

USE the *Bid Final* presentation that is still open from the previous exercise.

1. Click the **File** tab, click **Save & Send**, click **Package Presentation for CD**, and click **Package for CD**. The Package for CD dialog box opens.
2. Click **Copy to Folder**. The Copy to Folder dialog box opens.
3. In the Folder name box, change the default name to *Bid Proposal*.
4. In the Location box, change the path to the location where you store files for this lesson (see Figure 11-31).

Figure 11-31

Specify a folder and location for the packaged presentation

5. Click **OK**.
6. A dialog box asks if you want to include linked files in your package. Click **Yes**.
7. A message appears that the presentation contains comments or annotations, and that these will not be included. Click **Continue**.
8. Wait for the presentation to be written to the new folder. It should occur almost instantaneously (unlike when making a CD). The folder opens in Windows when it is finished. See Figure 11-32.

Figure 11-32

The packaged presentation in a folder

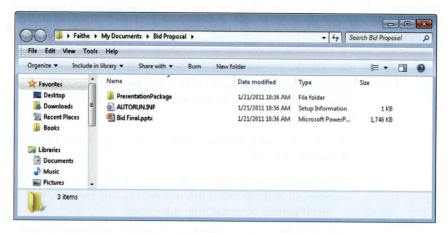

9. In the folder window, double-click the **PresentationPackage** folder to see what's inside it. The folder contains some graphics and support files that are needed to show the Web page (shown in Figure 11-30).
10. Close the folder window and return to PowerPoint. The Package for CD dialog box is still open.
11. Click **Close** to close the dialog box.
12. **SAVE** the presentation and then **CLOSE** the file.

EXIT PowerPoint.

SKILL SUMMARY

In This Lesson You Learned How To:	Exam Objective	Objective Number
Adjust slide orientation and size.	Set up a custom size.	2.2.1
	Change the orientation.	2.2.2
Customize audience handouts.	Create handouts (send to Microsoft Word).	7.2.3
Choose slides to display.	Create a Custom Slide Show.	8.2.7
Rehearse your delivery.	Rehearse timings.	8.3.1
	Keep timings.	8.3.2
	Adjust a slide's timing.	8.3.3
Set up a slide show.	Set up a Slide Show.	8.2.1
	Play narrations.	8.2.2
	Set up Presenter view.	8.2.3
	Use timings.	8.2.4
	Show media controls.	8.2.5
Work with presentation tools.	Add pen and highlighter annotations.	8.1.1
	Change the ink color.	8.1.2
	Erase an annotation.	8.1.3
	Discard annotations upon closing.	8.1.4
	Retain annotations upon closing.	8.1.5
Broadcast a presentation.	Broadcast presentations.	8.2.6
Record a presentation.	Start recording from the beginning of a slide show.	8.4.1
	Start recording from the current slide of the slide show.	8.4.2
Package a presentation for CD delivery.	Package a presentation for CD delivery.	7.2.1

Knowledge Assessment

Fill in the Blank

Fill in each blank with the term or phrase that best completes the statement.

1. Use the _____ dialog box to adjust slide size.
2. You can set up a presentation to loop continuously until you press the _____ key.
3. Use the _____ toolbar to view timings as you rehearse a presentation.
4. For more control over handouts, you can export them to _____ .
5. To display a hidden slide during a presentation, click _____ on the shortcut menu and then click the hidden slide.
6. If the computer on which you will present your slides does not have PowerPoint, you can use the _____ to show the presentation.

7. Customize the _____ to create your own handout layouts.
8. If you want to show your presentation on a projection screen, you can use a(n) _____ that accepts input from your computer.
9. When you _____ slides, you use the pointer to draw or write.
10. _____ a presentation to deliver it in real time over the Internet.

Multiple Choice

Circle the correct answer.

1. A slide that is wider than it is tall is displayed in:
   a. portrait orientation.
   b. column orientation.
   c. picture orientation.
   d. landscape orientation.
2. If you need to show slides on a wide-screen monitor, you might change their size to:
   a. Onscreen Show (16:9).
   b. Onscreen Show (3:4).
   c. 35 mm Slides.
   d. Ledger Paper (11×17 in).
3. Which of these is not one of the standard placeholders on the Handout Master?
   a. Date
   b. Header
   c. Page Number
   d. Author
4. To prevent a slide from displaying during a presentation, select it and then choose:
   a. Delete Slide.
   b. Hide Slide.
   c. Show/Hide Slide.
   d. Conceal Slide.
5. If you want to show only a selected series of slides from a presentation, the most efficient option is to:
   a. hide each slide you do not want to use.
   b. create an entirely new presentation and copy into it the slides you want to use.
   c. create a custom show of the slides you want to show.
   d. copy the presentation and then delete the slides you do not want to use.
6. When you rehearse timings, you should:
   a. skim over the content of each slide.
   b. read the entire content of each slide and look carefully at pictures and diagrams.
   c. allow yourself a set amount of time to view each slide regardless of its content.
   d. look only at the slide titles.
7. If you set up a slide show to be browsed by an individual, the slides display:
   a. using the full screen.
   b. in a virtual kiosk.
   c. in a window with a title bar.
   d. within the PowerPoint window.
8. Which of the following is *not* a way to advance to the next slide during a presentation?
   a. Press Home
   b. Press the spacebar
   c. Click the left mouse button
   d. Press Page Down

9. A quick way to restore the arrow pointer after you have used it for drawing is to:
   a. press End.
   b. double-click the screen.
   c. click the arrow pointer tool in the navigation tools.
   d. press Esc.

10. Package for CD can also package a presentation to
    a. a Web address.
    b. a printer.
    c. a folder on your hard disk.
    d. None of the above

Competency Assessment

Project 11-1: Preparing to Fly

You are nearly ready to present the slide show for Blue Yonder Airlines. Use the tools you have learned about in this lesson to finalize the presentation and create handouts.

GET READY. Launch PowerPoint if it is not already running.

@ The *Airline* file is available on the book companion website or in WileyPLUS.

1. **OPEN** the *Airline* presentation and save it as *Airline Final.*
2. Click the **Design** tab, click the **Slide Orientation** button, and click **Landscape**.
3. Click the **Page Setup** button, click the **Slides sized for drop-down arrow**, and click **On-screen Show (4:3)**. Click **OK** to close the dialog box.
4. Click the **Slide Show** tab, and then click the **Set Up Slide Show** button.
5. Choose the *Presented by a speaker* show type, clear the *Loop continuously until 'Esc'* check box, and choose to have slides advance Manually. Click **OK** to accept the new settings.
6. Click the **Insert** tab, click **Header & Footer**, and for Notes and Handouts, choose to display the date (update automatically), the header *Blue Yonder Airlines*, and page numbers. Click **Apply to All** to apply the setting to all slides.
7. Click the **View** tab, and then click Handout Master to open Handout Master view.
8. Center the header text and date in their placeholders, and right-align the page number in its placeholder. Close Handout Master view.
9. Hide the last slide in the presentation.
10. Click the **File** tab, click **Print**, and set the following print options:
    a. Choose to print handouts with four slides per page, in vertical order.
    b. In the Slides settings, deselect the *Frame* option.
    c. In the Print All Slides settings, deselect the *Print hidden slides* option.
11. Print the handouts.
12. **SAVE** the presentation and **CLOSE** the file.

LEAVE PowerPoint open for use in the next project.

Project 11-2: Twin Cities Crawl

You are ready to finalize the presentation you created to publicize the Twin Cities Gallery Crawl. You need to rehearse and set up the show and then package the presentation for delivery.

@ The *Galleries* file is available on the book companion website or in WileyPLUS.

1. **OPEN** the *Galleries* presentation and save it as *Galleries Final*.
2. Click the **Slide Show** tab, and then click the **Rehearse Timings** button.
3. Read each slide. When the slide show ends, choose to save the rehearsed timings.

4. Click the **Set Up Slide Show** button, and set up the show to be browsed at a kiosk using the timings you saved to advance slides. Click **OK** to close the dialog box.

5. Click the **File** tab, click **Save & Send**, click **Package Presentation for CD**, and click **Package for CD**.

6. Type the package name **Galleries**. If you can copy to a CD, click **Copy to CD** and complete the packaging process. If you cannot copy to a CD, click **Copy to Folder**, select the folder in which you are storing solutions for Lesson 11, and complete the packaging process.

7. Close the Package for CD dialog box.

8. **SAVE** the presentation and then **CLOSE** the file.

LEAVE PowerPoint open for the next project.

Proficiency Assessment

Project 11-3: Final Airline Check

You want to run through the Airline Final presentation before delivering it to make sure you are familiar with content and how to display it during the slide show.

1. **OPEN** the *Airline Final* presentation you created in Project 11-1.

2. Hide slide 7.

3. Press **F5** to view the presentation from slide 1.

4. Use the Next button in the presentation tools to move to slide 3.

5. Use the Previous button in the presentation tools to go backward to slide 1.

6. Right-click the slide to display the shortcut menu, and use Go to Slide to jump to slide 4.

7. Right-click the slide, click **Pointer Options**, and select the **highlighter**.

8. Highlight the bullet items *Caribbean* and *Scuba*.

9. Restore the arrow pointer and press **Esc** to end the show. Choose to save your annotations.

10. Rehearse timings for the presentation. When the presentation ends, save the slide timings.

11. Set up the slide show to use the slide timings you saved.

12. **SAVE** the presentation as *Airline Final Check* and then **CLOSE** the file.

LEAVE PowerPoint open for use in the next project.

Project 11-4: Year-End Review

You are ready to do the final tweaking of the year-end review for Contoso's Human Resources department. You will create a custom show to send to Contoso's president and CEO, customize handouts for the year-end review meeting, and adjust slide size for printing.

@ The *Review* file is available on the book companion website or in WileyPLUS.

1. **OPEN** the *Review* presentation and save it as *Review Custom*.

2. Create a custom show named Review Summary. Include in the custom show slides 1, 3, 4, 6, 7, 9, 10, and 12.

3. Change the slide size to **Letter Paper (8.5×11 in)**.

4. Display a date that updates, the header *Contoso HR Year in Review*, and page numbers for all handouts and notes pages.

5. Display the handout master, and show the 3 Slides layout.

6. Select the Header and Date placeholders, center the text in these placeholders, and adjust the vertical alignment in these placeholders to **Middle**. (Hint: Use Align Text on the Home tab to set Middle alignment.)

7. Reduce the width of each placeholder (both at the top and the bottom of the handout layout) to 2.5 inches wide. (Hint: Use the Width box on the Drawing Tools Format tab.)

8. Move the Header and Date placeholders down about a quarter of an inch from the top of the page.

9. Center the Header placeholder over the slide image column, and center the Date placeholder over the empty column where the lines will appear to the right of the slide images. (You can check placement by displaying the handouts in Print Preview.)

10. Apply the **Colored Outline, Red, Accent 2** shape style (from the Drawing Tools Format tab) to the Header and Date placeholders. Figure 11-33 shows the completed layout.

Figure 11-33

The modified handout layout

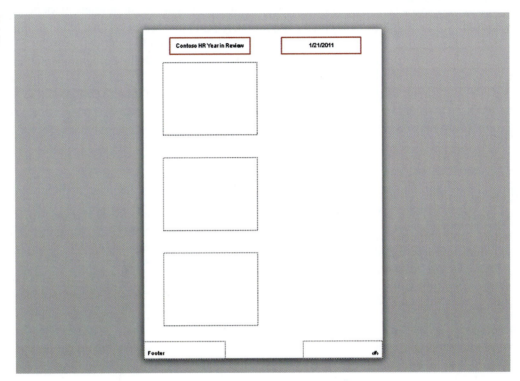

11. Print handouts with three slides per page.

12. **SAVE** the presentation.

LEAVE the presentation open for use the next project.

Mastery Assessment

Project 11-5: Review Final

You need to complete your preparation of the Review Custom presentation and test it before you send it to the HR executive staff.

1. **USE** the file from the previous exercise, and **SAVE** the presentation as *Review Final*.

2. Set the slides for normal screen 4:3 screen display.

3. Set up the slide show to display only the Review Summary custom show for an individual. Turn on the Show Without Animation option, and choose to advance slides manually.

4. Start the slide show from slide 1 and view the slides in the custom show, using keyboard options to advance slides.

5. **SAVE** the presentation and then **CLOSE** the file.

LEAVE PowerPoint open for use in the next project.

Project 11-6: Museum Broadcast

You have been asked to broadcast the Museum presentation over the Internet to some students at a middle school as part of their science and technology class project. You will prepare the presentation for broadcast and then broadcast it.

@ The *Museum* file is available on the book companion website or in WileyPLUS.

1. **OPEN** the *Museum* presentation. **SAVE** the presentation as *Museum Final*.

2. On the Slide Show tab, turn off Use Timings.

3. In the Set Up Show dialog box, set the Show Type to *Presented by a speaker (full screen)* and mark the **Show without animation** check box.

4. Begin a broadcast, logging into Windows Live when prompted. When the link appears to share, send it to your instructor in an email message.

5. Begin the broadcast. Move through the entire presentation, and then end the broadcast.

6. **CLOSE** the PowerPoint Viewer, and then **CLOSE** *Museum Final*.

EXIT PowerPoint.

INTERNET READY

You have been asked to find out what kind of equipment you would need to project presentations in a medium-sized conference room using a computer to control the show. Using the Internet, research what type of digital projector and pull-down screen you would need to purchase. Read reviews if possible to locate several options for good-quality components that are neither the most nor least expensive on the market. Create a presentation with your suggestions in a table or diagram. You may also want to research interactive whiteboards as an alternative to the projector-and-screen combination.

Workplace *Ready*

WAY TO PRESENT SLIDES

You have a number of options for projecting your slides when you are ready to give a presentation. The most popular options include projecting slides on a screen and displaying the slides on a computer monitor. You can also use new technology such as interactive whiteboards.

- **Projection options:** Slide projectors used to be noisy machines that shone bright light through 35-mm slides to project the image on a screen. These projectors are still available, as is the technology to create 35-mm slides from your PowerPoint files, but the most current projectors are digital devices that accept input from a computer. You can control the slide show from your computer monitor. When you use a digital projector, you project slides onto a screen.

- **Displaying slides on a computer monitor:** You do not need a projection device to present slides. You can display your presentation on a computer monitor, just as you do when using Slide Show view in PowerPoint. The computer monitor should be large enough for your audience to see the slide material clearly. Many computers allow you to connect more than one monitor to the video card, allowing you to use PowerPoint's Presenter view to control the slide show: the audience views the presentation on one monitor, while you use the other monitor to control the show.

- **Self-running or individual presentations:** You can also set up a presentation to run by itself on a monitor (see the *Setting Up a Slide Show* section earlier in this lesson), allow individuals to view a presentation on their own computers, or broadcast a presentation to viewers over the Internet.

- **Using an interactive whiteboard:** Interactive whiteboards allow you to project or display a presentation (or any other computer application) on a large white surface. The moderator can control slide display by simply touching the screen.

For best results in presenting slide shows from your computer, you should have a high-quality video card, sound card, and speakers. Quality sound and video components will make the most of multimedia files such as sounds and movies and allow transitions and animations to run smoothly.

If you do not have access to current technology, you can fall back on more traditional methods of presenting slides: you can submit PowerPoint files to photographic sources to prepare 35-mm slides that can be used in standard slide projectors. You can also print slides onto clear film to create transparencies that can be used with overhead projectors.

You are a project manager at Trey Research. You must give a report to your managers on the status of a major project you are running. Use PowerPoint tools and features you have learned about throughout this course to create, format, and finalize a presentation that you can use to report your project status.

Project 1: Create the Presentation

In this project, you will create your presentation and insert a slide from another presentation. You will also create and format a chart and insert headers and footers for slides and handouts.

GET READY. LAUNCH PowerPoint if it is not already running.

1. Create a new blank presentation.
2. **SAVE** the presentation as *Report*.
3. Type the slide title **Trey Research** and the slide subtitle **Woodgrove Bank Customer Survey**.
4. Insert slide 2 from the *Update* data presentation into the current presentation using the Reuse Slides option on the New Slide drop-down list.
5. Apply the **Civic** theme.
6. Go to slide 1 and boldface the slide title. Increase the font size of the subtitle to 18 pt.
7. Add a new slide at the end of the presentation with the Title and Content layout. Type the title **Customer Types**.
8. Insert a 3D pie chart on the slide using the following data:

	Customers
Main office	23
Branches	49
Online	16
Telephone	12

9. Remove the chart title and add data labels at the inside end of the pie slices.
10. Apply the Style 34 chart style to the chart.
11. Select the data labels and click the **Increase Font Size** button on the Home tab to make them one size larger.
12. Insert the date (updating automatically), slide numbers, and the footer **Woodgrove Bank Customer Survey** on all slides except the title slide, and the same footer and page numbers on notes and handouts. Add the header **Trey Research** for notes and handouts.
13. **SAVE** the presentation.

PAUSE. LEAVE PowerPoint and your presentation open for the next project.

@ The *Update* file is available on the book companion website or in WileyPLUS.

Project 2: Add Research Data

You are now ready to add a slide to show the data you have collected in your project. Some of the data is still in an Excel worksheet, so you will add an action button link to the worksheet.

USE the presentation that is open from the previous project.

1. Add a new slide at the end of the *Report* presentation with the Title and Content layout, and type the slide title **Overall Responses**.
2. Insert a new table with four columns and eight rows. Type the following data in the table:

Experience	Positive	Negative	No Response
Customer Service: Overall	91%	8%	1%
Customer Service: Tellers	86%	12.5%	1.5%
Customer Service: Managers	75%	23%	2%
Transaction Handling	80%	20%	0%
Wait Times	41%	58%	1%
Convenience of Facilities	89%	9%	2%
Sense of Security	84%	15%	1%

3. Format the table with the Medium Style 1 – Accent 3 Quick Style. Turn off Banded Rows and turn on Banded Columns.

4. Adjust column widths so that all text in the first column appears on a single line and the other three columns are the same width as one another.

5. Add a shadow effect to the table.

6. Insert a text box at the lower-left of the slide (above the green band that contains the footer and date) and insert the following text:

   For detailed results, visit www.treyresearch.net, log in with your password, and click the Woodgrove Survey link.

7. Check the URL to make sure the hyperlink is to http://www.treyresearch.net.

8. Format the text box to be 7.5" wide, and apply a Shape Style to the text box that coordinates well with the table.

9. Draw an Information action button to the right of the text box, and link the button to the *Woodgrove Results* Excel file.

10. Adjust the button shape's height to be the same as the text box's height, and align the button and text box at the top.

11. Apply the same Shape Style to the action button that you applied to the text box.

12. **SAVE** the presentation.

PAUSE. LEAVE PowerPoint and your presentation open for the next project.

@ The *Woodgrove* Results file is available on the book companion website or in WileyPLUS.

Project 3: Add Graphic Interest

You need to add some graphic interest to the presentation. You will use a clip art picture to illustrate one of the slides. You also need to insert a diagram to show the process required to change customer interaction behavior.

USE the presentation that is open from the previous project.

1. Add a new slide at the end of the *Report* presentation with the Title and Content layout. Type the title **Change Process**.

2. Insert the Staggered Process SmartArt diagram in the content placeholder.

3. Display the Text pane if necessary and insert the following text:

   1. Data collection
   2. Present to management
   3. Revise policies and procedures
   4. Management/HR training
   5. Staff training

4. Apply a new SmartArt style to the diagram such as the Cartoon effect, and change colors to one in the Colorful range.

5. Go to slide 1. Click the **Clip Art** button on the Insert tab to open the Clip Art task pane.

6. Find and insert a photo that could represent a businessperson talking to a customer.

7. Size and format the picture so it looks attractive in the area below the subtitle. If the picture is taller than it is wide, you may want to crop it so it fits better in the space below the subtitle.

8. Center the picture under the subtitle and apply the Beveled Oval Black picture style. Change the picture's border to Ice Blue, Background 2, Lighter 20%.
9. **SAVE** the presentation.

PAUSE. LEAVE PowerPoint and your presentation open for the next project.

Project 4: Prepare for Delivery

You are ready to apply transitions and animations to add interest during the presentation. It is also time to prepare handouts that your audience can use to follow the presentation as you deliver it.

USE the presentation that is open from the previous project.

1. Apply the Wipe transition with the From Top option at a speed of 01.50 all slides.
2. Go to slide 2 and apply the Fade animation effect to the text in the content placeholder.
3. Adjust the animation so it begins After Previous.
4. Insert a comment on slide 2:
   Should we also evaluate the customer service provided by support staff?
5. Export handouts to Microsoft Word, using the blank lines next to slides layout.
6. Save the handouts as a Word document named *Handouts.docx*. Close Word.
7. In PowerPoint, Print the handouts with the Six Slides Horizontal layout.
8. **SAVE** the presentation.

PAUSE. LEAVE PowerPoint and your presentation open for the next project.

Project 5: Final Touches

You are ready to test your presentation. You will review the show, test the annotation options, rehearse timings, and set up the show for its final delivery. Finally, you will package the show so you can transport it easily on the day of the presentation.

USE the presentation that is open from the previous project.

1. Start the slide show from slide 1 and use any combination of keyboard shortcuts, menu commands, or mouse clicks to advance slides until you reach slide 4.
2. On slide 4 (Overall Responses), change the pointer to the Pen and circle the URL in the text box.
3. Restore the arrow pointer and test the action button. Close Excel after you have looked at the data and return to the slide show.
4. Continue with the remaining slide and end the show. Save the annotation.
5. Run the show again to rehearse timings of slides. Save your slide timings.
6. Open the Set Up Show dialog box and make sure the Advance option is set to use slide timings.
7. Package the presentation to a folder named Trey Report. Choose to include linked content in the package.
8. **SAVE** and **CLOSE** the presentation.

EXIT PowerPoint.

Appendix A   Microsoft Office Specialist (MOS) Skills for PowerPoint 2010: Exam 77-883

Matrix Skill	Skill Number	Lesson Number
Managing the PowerPoint Environment	1	
Adjust views.	1.1	
Adjust views by using the Ribbon.	1.1.1	1
Adjust views by status bar commands.	1.1.2	1
Manipulate the PowerPoint window.	1.2	
Work with multiple presentation windows simultaneously.	1.2.1	1
Configure the Quick Access Toolbar.	1.3	
Show the Quick Access Toolbar (QAT) below the Ribbon.	1.3.1	1
Configure PowerPoint file options.	1.4	
Use PowerPoint proofing.	1.4.1	3
Use PowerPoint save options.	1.4.2	2
Creating a Slide Presentation	2	
Construct and edit photo albums.	2.1	
Add captions to pictures.	2.1.1	8
Insert text.	2.1.2	8
Insert images in black and white.	2.1.3	8
Reorder pictures in an album.	2.1.4	8
Adjust images.	2.1.5	8
Apply slide size and orientation settings.	2.2	
Set up a custom size.	2.2.1	11
Change the orientation.	2.2.2	11
Add and remove slides.	2.3	
Insert an outline.	2.3.1	2
Reuse slides from a saved presentation.	2.3.2	2
Reuse slides from a slide library.	2.3.3	2
Duplicate selected slides.	2.3.4	2
Delete multiple slides simultaneously.	2.3.5	2
Include noncontiguous slides in a presentation.	2.3.6	2

Matrix Skill	Skill Number	Lesson Number
Format slides.	2.4	
Format sections.	2.4.1	4
Modify themes.	2.4.2	4
Switch to a different slide layout.	2.4.3	4
Apply formatting to a slide.	2.4.4	4
Set up slide footers.	2.4.5	4
Enter and format text.	2.5	
Use text effects.	2.5.1	3
Change text format.	2.5.2	3
Change the formatting of bulleted and numbered lists.	2.5.3	3
Enter text in a placeholder text box.	2.5.4	1, 2
Convert text to SmartArt.	2.5.5	7
Copy and paste text.	2.5.6	1
Use Paste Special.	2.5.7	2
Use Format Painter.	2.5.8	3
Format text boxes.	2.6	
Apply formatting to a text box.	2.6.1	3
Change the outline of a text box.	2.6.2	3
Change the shape of a text box.	2.6.3	3
Apply effects.	2.6.4	3
Set the alignment.	2.6.5	3
Create columns in a text box.	2.6.6	3
Set internal margins.	2.6.7	3
Set the current text box formatting as the default for new text boxes.	2.6.8	3
Adjust text in a text box.	2.6.9	3
Use AutoFit.	2.6.10	3
Working with Graphical and Multimedia Elements	3	
Manipulate graphical elements.	3.1	
Arrange graphical elements.	3.1.1	8
Position graphical elements.	3.1.2	8
Resize graphical elements.	3.1.3	8
Apply effects to graphical elements.	3.1.4	8

Matrix Skill	Skill Number	Lesson Number
Apply styles to graphical elements.	3.1.5	8
Apply borders to graphical elements.	3.1.6	8
Add hyperlinks to graphical elements.	3.1.7	4
Manipulate images.	3.2	
Apply color adjustments.	3.2.1	8
Apply image corrections.	3.2.2	8
Add artistic effects to an image.	3.2.3	8
Remove a background.	3.2.4	8
Crop a picture.	3.2.5	8
Compress selected pictures or all pictures.	3.2.6	8
Change a picture.	3.2.7	8
Reset a picture.	3.2.8	8
Modify WordArt and shapes.	3.3	
Set the formatting of the current shape as the default for future shapes.	3.3.1	8
Change the fill color or texture.	3.3.2	3, 8
Change WordArt.	3.3.3	3
Convert WordArt to SmartArt.	3.3.4	7
Manipulate SmartArt.	3.4	
Add and remove shapes.	3.4.1	7
Change SmartArt styles.	3.4.2	7
Change the SmartArt layout.	3.4.3	7
Reorder shapes.	3.4.4	7
Convert a SmartArt graphic to text.	3.4.5	7
Convert SmartArt to shapes.	3.4.6	7
Make shapes larger or smaller.	3.4.7	7
Promote bullet levels.	3.4.8	7
Demote bullet levels.	3.4.9	7
Edit video and audio content.	3.5	
Apply a style to video or audio content.	3.5.1	9
Adjust video or audio content.	3.5.2	9
Arrange video or audio content.	3.5.3	9
Size video or audio content.	3.5.4	9

Matrix Skill	Skill Number	Lesson Number
Adjust playback options.	3.5.5	9
Creating Charts and Tables	4	
Construct and modify tables.	4.1	
Draw a table.	4.1.1	5
Insert an spreadsheet.	4.1.2	5
Set table style options.	4.1.3	5
Add shading.	4.1.4	5
Add borders.	4.1.5	5
Add effects.	4.1.6	5
Adjust columns and rows.	4.1.7	5
Insert and modify charts.	4.2	
Select a chart type.	4.2.1	6
Enter chart data.	4.2.2	6
Change the chart type.	4.2.3	6
Change the chart layout.	4.2.4	6
Switch rows and columns.	4.2.5	6
Select data.	4.2.6	6
Edit data.	4.2.7	6
Apply chart elements.	4.3	
Use chart labels.	4.3.1	6
Use axes.	4.3.2	6
Use gridlines.	4.3.3	6
Use backgrounds.	4.3.4	6
Manipulate chart layouts.	4.4	
Select chart elements.	4.4.1	6
Format selections.	4.4.2	6
Manipulate chart elements.	4.5	
Arrange chart elements.	4.5.1	6
Specify a precise position.	4.5.2	6
Apply effects.	4.5.3	6
Resize chart elements.	4.5.4	6
Apply Quick Styles.	4.5.5	6

Matrix Skill	Skill Number	Lesson Number
Apply a border.	4.5.6	6
Apply hyperlinks.	4.5.7	6
Applying Transitions and Animations	5	
Apply built-in and custom animations.	5.1	
Use More Entrance Effects.	5.1.1	9
Use More Emphasis.	5.1.2	9
Use More Exit Effects.	5.1.3	9
Use More Motion Paths.	5.1.4	9
Apply effect and path options.	5.2	
Set timing.	5.2.1	9
Set start options.	5.2.2	9
Manipulate animations.	5.3	
Change the direction of an animation.	5.3.1	9
Attach a sound to an animation.	5.3.2	9
Use Animation Painter.	5.3.3	9
Reorder animation.	5.3.4	9
Select text options.	5.3.5	9
Apply and modify transitions between slides.	5.4	
Modify a transition effect.	5.4.1	9
Add a sound to a transition.	5.4.2	9
Modify transition duration.	5.4.3	9
Set up manual or automatically timed advance options.	5.4.4	9
Collaborating on Presentations	6	
Manage comments in presentations.	6.1	
Insert and edit comments.	6.1.1	10
Show or hide markup.	6.1.2	10
Move to the previous or next comment.	6.1.3	10
Delete comments.	6.1.4	10
Apply proofing tools.	6.2	
Use Spelling and Thesaurus features.	6.2.1	3
Compare and combine presentations.	6.2.2	10

Matrix Skill	Skill Number	Lesson Number
Preparing Presentations for Delivery	**7**	
Save presentations.	**7.1**	
Save the presentation as a picture presentation.	**7.1.1**	**10**
Save the presentation as a PDF.	**7.1.2**	**10**
Save the presentation as an XPS.	**7.1.3**	**10**
Save the presentation as an outline.	**7.1.4**	**10**
Save the presentation as an OpenDocument.	**7.1.5**	**10**
Save the presentation as a show (.ppsx).	**7.1.6**	**10**
Save a slide or object as a picture file.	**7.1.7**	**10**
Share presentations.	**7.2**	
Package a presentation for CD delivery.	**7.2.1**	**11**
Create video.	**7.2.2**	**10**
Create handouts (send to Microsoft Word).	**7.2.3**	**11**
Compress media.	**7.2.4**	**9**
Print presentations.	**7.3**	
Adjust print settings.	**7.3.1**	**2**
Protect presentations.	**7.4**	
Set a password.	**7.4.1**	**10**
Change a password.	**7.4.2**	**10**
Mark a presentation as final.	**7.4.3**	**10**
Delivering Presentations	**8**	
Apply presentation tools.	**8.1**	
Add pen and highlighter annotations.	**8.1.1**	**11**
Change the ink color.	**8.1.2**	**11**
Erase an annotation.	**8.1.3**	**11**
Discard annotations upon closing.	**8.1.4**	**11**
Retain annotations upon closing.	**8.1.5**	**11**

Matrix Skill	Skill Number	Lesson Number
Set up slide shows.	8.2	
Set up a slide show.	8.2.1	11
Play narrations.	8.2.2	11
Set up Presenter view.	8.2.3	11
Use timings.	8.2.4	11
Show media controls.	8.2.5	9, 11
Broadcast presentations.	8.2.6	11
Create a custom slide show.	8.2.7	11
Set presentation timing.	8.3	
Rehearse timings.	8.3.1	11
Keep timings.	8.3.2	11
Adjust a slide's timing.	8.3.3	11
Record presentations.	8.4	
Start recording from the beginning of a slide show.	8.4.1	11
Start recording from the current slide of a slide show.	8.4.2	11

Appendix B Microsoft Office Professional 2010

Component	Requirement
Computer and processor	500 MHz or faster processor.
Memory	256 MB RAM; 512 MB recommended for graphics features, Outlook Instant Search, and certain advanced functionality.[1,2]
Hard disk	3.0 GB available disk space
Display	1024×576 or higher resolution monitor
Operating system	Windows XP (must have SP3) (32-bit), Windows 7, Windows Vista with Service Pack (SP) 1, Windows Server 2003 R2 with MSXML 6.0 (32-bit Office only), Windows Server 2008, or later 32- or 64-bit OS.
Graphics	Graphics hardware acceleration requires a DirectX 9.0c graphics card with 64 MB or more video memory.
Additional requirements	Certain Microsoft® OneNote® features require Windows® Desktop Search 3.0, Windows Media® Player 9.0, Microsoft® ActiveSync® 4.1, microphone, audio output device, video recording device, TWAIN-compatible digital camera, or scanner; sharing notebooks requires users to be on the same network.
	Certain advanced functionality requires connectivity to Microsoft Exchange Server 2003, Microsoft SharePoint Server 2010, and/or Microsoft SharePoint Foundation 2010.
	Certain features require Windows Search 4.0.
	Send to OneNote Print Driver and Integration with Business Connectivity Services require Microsoft .NET Framework 3.5 and/or Windows XPS features.
	Internet Explorer (IE) 6 or later, 32-bit browser only. IE7 or later required to receive broadcast presentations. Internet functionality requires an Internet connection.
	Multi-Touch features require Windows 7 and a touch-enabled device.
	Certain inking features require Windows XP Tablet PC Edition or later.
	Speech recognition functionality requires a close-talk microphone and audio output device.
	Internet Fax not available on Windows Vista Starter, Windows Vista Home Basic, or Windows Vista Home Premium
	Information Rights Management features require access to a Windows 2003 Server with SP1 or later running Windows Rights Management Services.
	Certain online functionality requires a Windows LiveTM ID.
Other	Product functionality and graphics may vary based on your system configuration. Some features may require additional or advanced hardware or server connectivity; **www.office.com/products.**

[1] 512 MB RAM recommended for accessing Outlook data files larger than 1GB.

[2] GHz processor or faster and 1 GB RAM or more recommended for OneNote Audio Search. Close-talking microphone required. Audio Search is not available in all languages.

PowerPoint 2010 Glossary

A

action   A button or text block programmed to perform a specific action, such as jumping to a slide or starting a program.

action button   A graphic that serves as a hyperlink to jump to a location or perform an action.

After Previous   An animation sequencing setting that causes the animation to trigger after the previous event has finished. Compare to *With Previous.*

animation   An effect you apply to placeholders or other content to move the content in unique ways on the slide.

Animation Painter   A feature that copies animation settings from one object to another.

Animation Pane   A pane that enables you to manage all the animation effects on the active slide.

annotate   To write or draw on a slide during a presentation.

aspect ratio   The relationship of width to height in a picture or shape.

assistant   In an organization chart, a person who reports directly to a superior.

audio   A sound or music clip.

B

Backstage view   The view that opens when you click the File tab, containing commands for managing files, setting program options, and printing.

broadcast   To deliver a presentation live in real time via a network or Internet connection.

bulleted list   Groups of items or phrases that present related ideas.

C

cell   In a table or spreadsheet, the text area at the intersection of a row or column.

chart   A visual representation of numerical data.

chart area   The entire area inside the chart container that holds background as well as plotted data.

clip art   Predrawn artwork in a wide variety of styles. Office clip art files can include drawn graphics, photographs, sounds, and animated graphics.

command   A button, list, or other clickable option on the Ribbon.

comment   A note you insert on a slide while reviewing.

constrain   To force a drawing object into a particular shape or alignment.

contiguous   Adjacent to one another. For example, slides 1 and 2 are contiguous.

crop

crop   To remove a portion of a picture or shape that is not needed. The cropped portion is hidden until you compress the picture.

current slide   The slide that is currently being edited.

custom show   A group of slides in a presentation that can be shown separately from the entire presentation.

D

data marker   A single column, pie slice, or point from a data series.

data series   All the data points for a particular category of plotted information.

delay   An animation setting that specifies how long the effect should pause before it begins.

demote   To make an item subordinate to another item.

dialog box   A box that prompts the user for additional information when executing a command.

dialog box launcher   In some command groups on the Ribbon, a small icon that opens a dialog box related to that group.

drop-down arrow   A small, downward-pointing arrow next to some tools on the Ribbon.

drop-down list   A list that appears once a drop-down arrow is clicked, allowing you to choose from available options.

duration   An animation setting that determines how long an animation effect should take to execute.

E

embedded   Data that has been placed in a destination application so that it can be edited with the tools of its original source applications.

emphasis effect   An animation effect that causes an object to move, change color, or otherwise call attention to itself when it is neither entering nor exiting the slide.

encrypting   The process of transforming data into a nonreadable form for security purposes.

entrance effect   An animation effect that occurs when an object is entering the slide.

exit effect   An animation effect that occurs when an object is exiting the slide.

F

File tab   The tab on the Ribbon that opens Backstage view.

font theme   A combination of two fonts to be applied to headings and text as part of a theme.

fonts   Typefaces that are used to display characters, numbers, and symbols in your PowerPoint presentations.

footer   Information such as a date, slide number, or text phrase that appears at the bottom of each slide in a presentation.

Format Painter   A tool to copy character and paragraph formatting.

G

gridlines   A grid of horizontal and vertical lines that can be used as guides when positioning objects on a slide.

group   A set of related tools on the Ribbon.

guides   Nonprinting vertical and horizontal lines that you can move or copy to align objects on a slide.

H

handout   A printed copy of a presentation.

Handout Master   The master that controls the layout and elements of handouts.

header   Information such as a date, slide number, or text phrase that appears at the top of each page of a presentation's handouts or notes.

hyperlink   An address that refers to another location, such as a website, a different slide, or an external file.

I

I-beam pointer   The mouse pointer when over a text box or editable text area, appearing as a curly capital I. If you click when the I-beam pointer is displayed, the insertion point moves to that spot.

indent level   The distance of a paragraph of text from the placeholder's left border.

ink   The annotations created with the pen and highlighter tools during a slide show.

K

KeyTip   A letter or number that appears next to an onscreen tool when the Alt key is pressed; keying that letter or number activates the associated tool.

keyword   A word or phrase that describes a subject or category on which you can search.

L

landscape orientation   A page orientation that is wider than it is tall.

lassoing   To drag an imaginary box around a group of objects to select them.

layout   A predefined arrangement of placeholders for text or objects (such as charts or pictures).

layout master   The slide master for a particular slide layout.

legend   The key to a chart that explains what each data series represents.

line spacing   The amount of vertical space between paragraphs.

linked   Data that has been placed in a destination application so that it maintains a link with its source file; changes to the source file are also made in the linked object.

M

Mark as Final   A setting that prevents changes from being made to a presentation unless the user chooses to acknowledge the warning and edit it anyway; does not provide security.

markup   The changes identified between two versions of a presentation when using Compare.

Mini toolbar   A small toolbar that appears when the mouse pointer is placed on a selected text object; provides commands for working with the text.

motion path   An animation effect that moves an object along a specified path.

N

non-contiguous   Not adjacent to one another. See *contiguous*.

Normal view   PowerPoint's default view, suited for editing individual slides; includes the Slide pane, Notes pane, and Slides/Outline pane.

note   Additional information associated with a slide.

Notes Page view   A view that displays a single slide and its associated notes.

numbered list   A group of steps, procedures, or actions that are listed in numerical order.

O

On Click   A trigger for an animation or transition that occurs when the mouse is clicked.

OpenDocument   A file format that most word processing programs support, including the free OpenOffice suite.

order   The way in which objects stack up on a slide as you create them.

organization chart   A diagram that shows the relationships between personnel or departments in an organization.

orientation   The direction that material appears on a page when printed. See *portrait* and *landscape*.

P

password   A word or phrase that a user must type for access to an encrypted file.

pattern   A repeating pattern of lines in a certain color (the foreground color) on a background of another color (the background color).

PDF   Portable Document Format; one of the page description languages to which PowerPoint can export; requires Adobe Reader or Adobe Acrobat to read.

picture presentation   A presentation that consists of a series of full-screen graphics of slide content, placed on blank slide backgrounds.

placeholder   On a slide, a box that holds a specific type of content, such as text.

platform-independent   Able to be used on a variety of operating systems.

plot area   The area in the chart container that shows the data series compared to the chart's gridlines.

portrait orientation   A page orientation that is taller than it is wide.

PowerPoint show   A presentation that opens by default in Slide Show view.

presentation tools   The tools and commands that are active during Slide Show view.

Presenter view   A viewing mode that allows the presenter to see notes on one screen while the audience views slides on another screen.

promote   To make an item superior to another item.

Q

Quick Access Toolbar   Toolbar at the upper-left corner of the PowerPoint window that provides easy access to tools you use frequently, such as Save and Undo.

Quick Style   Built-in formatting for text, graphics, SmartArt diagrams, charts, WordArt, pictures, tables, and shapes.

R

reset   To restore a picture or other formatted object to its default settings.

Ribbon   A strip of icons that appears across the top of the PowerPoint window; divided into tabs, each of which contains groups of related tools.

Rich Text Format (RTF)   A text file format that most word processing programs can open and save as.

rulers   Horizontal and vertical measures that help you position objects on a slide.

S

scaling   Specifying a percentage of the original dimensions to enlarge or reduce a picture or shape.

ScreenTip   A pop-up box that gives a command's name when you point at its button on the Ribbon.

section   A grouping of contiguous slides.

shortcut menu   A menu that appears when you right-click an area or object.

slide master   A slide that stores information about the formats applied in a presentation, such as theme, fonts, layouts, and colors.

Slide Show view   A view that allows the user to preview a presentation on the screen as it will appear to the audience.

Slide Sorter view   A view that displays all of a presentation's slides in a single window; suited for reorganizing slides.

SmartArt diagram   A visual representation of information.

subordinates   In an organization chart, persons or departments who are subordinate to another person or department.

T

tab   A labeled section of the ribbon; contains a group of related tools.

table   An arrangement of columns and rows used to organize information.

template   A predesigned presentation.

text box   A container that holds text on a slide.

text pane   The fly-out pane that allows you to key information for a SmartArt diagram.

texture   A graphic that repeats to fill an image, creating the appearance that the surface is a certain material, such as marble, wood, or paper.

theme   A scheme of complementing colors.

thumbnail   A small picture of a slide.

timings   The amount of time assigned to each slide before it automatically advances to the next.

top-level shape   In an organization chart, the person or department at the head of the organization.

transition   The movement from one slide to the next.

V

video   A movie, animated graphic, or motion video clip.

views   The ways in which presentation content can be displayed onscreen, such as Normal view, Slide Sorter view, or Slide Show view.

W

Windows Movie Video (WMV)   The format that PowerPoint saves to when creating videos from presentation files.

With Previous   An animation setting that causes the animation to begin executing simultaneously with the previous animation or event.

WordArt   A feature used to turn text into a formatted graphic.

worksheet   An Excel document used to organize numerical data that can then be analyzed or otherwise manipulated.

X

XPS   XML Paper Specification; one of the page description languages to which PowerPoint can export; requires an XPS Viewer utility to view; this utility comes with Windows Vista and higher, and can be downloaded free from Microsoft for other Windows versions.

Z

zoom   The amount of magnification used to show content onscreen; the higher the zoom, the larger the content.

Credits

Index